6 PLAYS *by*

RODGERS *and*

HAMMERSTEIN

OKLAHOMA!

CAROUSEL

ALLEGRO

SOUTH PACIFIC

THE KING AND I

ME AND JULIET

6 PLAYS *by*

RODGERS *and*

HAMMERSTEIN

RICHARD RODGERS
and
OSCAR HAMMERSTEIN II

THE MODERN LIBRARY · NEW YORK

♡ | To Dorothy
with love

Contents

Contents

♡

Oklahoma!

♥

BASED ON *Lynn Riggs'*

GREEN GROW THE LILACS

Oklahoma! *was first produced by The Theatre Guild on April 1, 1943, at the St. James Theatre, New York City, with the following cast:*

IN ORDER OF APPEARANCE

AUNT ELLER	Betty Garde
CURLY	Alfred Drake
LAUREY	Joan Roberts
IKE SKIDMORE	Barry Kelley
FRED	Edwin Clay
SLIM	Herbert Rissman
WILL PARKER	Lee Dixon
JUD FRY	Howard da Silva
ADO ANNIE CARNES	Celeste Holm
ALI HAKIM	Joseph Buloff
GERTIE CUMMINGS	Jane Lawrence
ELLEN	Katharine Sergava
KATE	Ellen Love
SYLVIE	Joan McCracken
ARMINA	Kate Friedlich
AGGIE	Bambi Linn
ANDREW CARNES	Ralph Riggs
CORD ELAM	Owen Martin
JESS	George Church
CHALMERS	David Tihmar
MIKE	Paul Shiers
JOE	George Irving
SAM	Hayes Gordon

DIRECTED BY Rouben Mamoulian
DANCES BY Agnes de Mille
SETTINGS BY Lemuel Ayers
COSTUMES BY Miles White
ORCHESTRA DIRECTED BY Joseph Schwartzdorf
ORCHESTRATIONS BY Russell Bennett
PRODUCTION UNDER THE SUPERVISION OF Theresa Helburn and Lawrence Langner

Scenes

TIME: *Just after the turn of the century*
PLACE: *Indian Territory (Now Oklahoma)*

Musical Numbers

SCENE 2

ACT
ONE

ACT
TWO

ACT ONE | Scene One

SCENE: *The front of* LAUREY'S *farmhouse.*

"It is a radiant summer morning several years ago, the kind of morning which, enveloping the shapes of earth men, cattle in a meadow, blades of the young corn, streams —makes them seem to exist now for the first time, their images giving off a golden emanation that is partly true and partly a trick of the imagination, focusing to keep alive a loveliness that may pass away."

AUNT ELLER MURPHY, *a buxom hearty woman about fifty, is seated behind a wooden, brass-banded churn, looking out over the meadow (which is the audience), a contented look on her face. Like the voice of the morning, a song comes from somewhere, growing louder as the young singer comes nearer.*

CURLY (*Off stage*)
There's a bright, golden haze on the meadow,
There's a bright, golden haze on the meadow.
The corn is as high as a elephant's eye
An' it looks like it's climbin' clear up to the sky.
   (CURLY *saunters on and stands tentatively outside the gate to the front yard*)
Oh, what a beautiful mornin',
Oh, what a beautiful day.
I got a beautiful feelin'
Ev'rythin's goin' my way.
   (CURLY *opens the gate and walks over to the porch, obviously singing for the benefit of someone inside the house.* AUNT ELLER *looks straight ahead, elaborately ignoring* CURLY)
All the cattle are standin' like statues,
All the cattle are standin' like statues.
They don't turn their heads as they see me ride by,
But a little brown mav'rick is winkin' her eye.
   Oh, what a beautiful mornin',

Oh, what a beautiful day.
I got a beautiful feelin'
Ev'rythin's goin' my way.
(CURLY *comes up behind* AUNT ELLER *and shouts in her ear*)
Hi, Aunt Eller!

AUNT ELLER   Skeer me to death! Whut're you doin' around here?

CURLY   Come a-singin' to you. (*Strolling a few steps away*)
All the sounds of the earth are like music—
All the sounds of the earth are like music.
The breeze is so busy it don't miss a tree
And a ol' weepin' willer is laughin' at me!
   Oh, what a beautiful mornin',
   Oh, what a beautiful day.
   I got a beautiful feelin'
   Ev'rythin's goin' my way. . . .
   Oh, what a beautiful day!
(AUNT ELLER *resumes churning.* CURLY *looks wistfully up at the windows of the house, then turns back to* AUNT ELLER)

AUNT ELLER   If I wasn't a ole womern, and if you wasn't so young and smart-alecky––why, I'd marry you and git you to set around at night and sing to me.

CURLY   No, you wouldn't neither. Cuz I wouldn't marry you ner none of yer kinfolks, I could he'p it.

AUNT ELLER (*Wisely*)   Oh, none of my kinfolks, huh?

CURLY (*Raising his voice so that* LAUREY *will hear if she is inside the house*)   And you c'n tell 'em that, *all* of 'm includin' that niece of your'n, Miss Laurey Williams! (AUNT ELLER *continues to churn.* CURLY *comes down to her and speaks deliberately*) Aunt Eller, if you was to tell me whur Laurey was at—whur would you tell me she was at?

AUNT ELLER   I wouldn't tell you a-tall. Fer as fer as I c'n make out, Laurey ain't payin' you no heed.

CURLY   So, she don't take to me much, huh? Whur'd you git sich a uppity niece 'at wouldn't pay no heed to me? Who's the best bronc buster in this yere territory?

AUNT ELLER   You, I bet.

CURLY   And the best bull-dogger in seventeen counties? Me, that's who! And looky here, I'm handsome, ain't I?

AUNT ELLER   Purty as a pitcher.

CURLY   Curly-headed, ain't I? And bow-legged from the saddle fer God knows how long, ain't I?

AUNT ELLER   Couldn't stop a pig in the road.

CURLY   Well, whut else does she want then, the damn she-mule?

AUNT ELLER   I don't know. But I'm shore sartin it ain't you. Who you takin' to the Box Social tonight?

CURLY   Ain't thought much about it.

AUNT ELLER   Bet you come over to ast Laurey.

CURLY   Whut 'f I did?

AUNT ELLER   You astin' me too? I'll wear my fascinator.

CURLY   Yeow, you too.

LAUREY (*Singing off stage*)
Oh, what a beautiful mornin'
    (*She enters*)
Oh, what a beautiful day
    (*Spoken as she gives* CURLY *a brief glance*)
Oh, I thought you was somebody.
    (*She resumes singing, crosses to clothesline and hangs up an apron*)
I got a beautiful feelin'
Ev'rythin's goin' my way.
    (*Spoken as she comes down to* AUNT ELLER)
Is this all that's come a-callin' and it a'ready ten o'clock of a Sattiddy mornin'?

CURLY   You knowed it was me 'fore you opened the door.

LAUREY   No sich of a thing.

CURLY   You did, too! You heard my voice and knowed it was me.

LAUREY   I heared a voice a-talkin' rumbly along with Aunt Eller. And heard someone a-singin' like a bullfrog in a pond.

CURLY   You knowed it was me, so you set in there a-thinkin'
up sump'n mean to say. I'm a good mind not to ast you to the
Box Social.

> (AUNT ELLER *rises, crosses to clothesline, takes down quilt,
> folds it, puts it on porch*)

LAUREY   If you did ast me, I wouldn't go with you. Besides,
how'd you take me? You ain't bought a new buggy with red
wheels onto it, have you?

CURLY   No, I ain't.

LAUREY   And a spankin' team with their bridles all jinglin'?

CURLY   No.

LAUREY   'Spect me to ride on behind ole Dun, I guess. You
better ast that ole Cummin's girl you've tuck sich a shine to,
over acrost the river.

CURLY   If I was to ast you, they'd be a way to take you, Miss
Laurey Smarty.

LAUREY   Oh, they would?

> (CURLY *now proceeds to stagger* LAUREY *with an idea. But
> she doesn't let on at first how she is "tuck up" with it.*
> AUNT ELLER *is the one who falls like a ton of bricks im-
> mediately and helps* CURLY *try to sell it to* LAURY)

CURLY

When I take you out tonight with me,
Honey, here's the way it's goin' to be;
You will set behind a team of snow-white horses
In the slickest gig you ever see!

AUNT ELLER   Lands!

CURLY

Chicks and ducks and geese better scurry
When I take you out in the surrey,
When I take you out in the surrey with the fringe on top!
Watch thet fringe and see how it flutters
When I drive them high-steppin' strutters!
Nosey-pokes'll peek through their shutters and their eyes will
   pop!
The wheels are yeller, the upholstery's brown,
The dashboard's genuine leather,
With isinglass curtains y'c'n roll right down

In case there's a change in the weather—
Two bright side-lights, winkin' and blinkin',
Ain't no finer rig, I'm a-thinkin'!
You c'n keep yer rig if you're thinkin' 'at I'd keer to swap
Fer that shiny little surrey with the fringe on the top!
   (LAUREY *still pretends unconcern, but she is obviously slipping*)

AUNT ELLER   Would y'say the fringe was made of silk?

CURLY   Wouldn't have no other kind but silk.

LAUREY (*She's only human*)   Has it really got a team of snow-white horses?

CURLY   One's like snow—the other's more like milk.

AUNT ELLER   So y'can tell 'em apart!

CURLY
All the world'll fly in a flurry
When I take you out in the surrey,
When I take you out in the surrey with the fringe on top!
When we hit that road, hell fer leather,
Cats and dogs'll dance in the heather,
Birds and frogs'll sing all together and the toads will hop!
The wind'll whistle as we rattle along,
The cows'll moo in the clover,
The river will ripple out a whispered song,
And whisper it over and over:
   (*In a loud whisper*)
Don't you wisht y'd go on ferever?
Don't you wisht y'd go on ferever?
   (AUNT ELLER'S *and* LAUREY'S *lips move involuntarily, shaping the same words*)
Don't you wisht y'd go on ferever and ud never stop
In that shiny little surrey with the fringe on the top?
   (*Music continues under dialogue*)

AUNT ELLER   Y'd shore feel like a queen settin' up in *that* carriage!

CURLY (*Over-confident*)   On'y she talked so mean to me a while back, Aunt Eller, I'm a good mind not to take her.

LAUREY   Ain't said I was goin'!

CURLY (*The fool*)   Ain't ast you!

LAUREY Whur'd you git sich a rig at? (*With explosive laughter, seeing a chance for revenge*) Anh! I bet he's went and h'ard a rig over to Claremore! Thinkin' I'd go with him!

CURLY 'S all you know about it.

LAUREY Spent all his money h'arin' a rig and now ain't got nobody to ride in it!

CURLY Have, too! . . . Did not h'ar it. Made the whole thing up outa my head.

LAUREY What! Made it up?

CURLY Dashboard and all.

LAUREY (*Flying at him*) Oh! Git offa the place, you! Aunt Eller, make him git hisse'f outa here. (*She picks up a fly swatter and chases him*) Tellin' me lies!

CURLY (*Dodging her*) Makin' up a few—look out now! (*He jumps the fence to save himself.* LAUREY *turns her back to him, and sits down. He comes up behind her. The music, which had become more turbulent to match the scene, now softens*) Makin' up a few purties ain't agin' no law 'at I know of. Don't you wisht they *was* sich a rig, though? (*Winking at* AUNT ELLER) Nen y'could go to the play party and do a hoe-down till mornin' if you was a mind to. . . . Nen when you was all wore out, I'd lift you onto the surrey, and jump up alongside of you— And we'd jist point the horses home. . . . I can jist pitcher the whole thing. (AUNT ELLER *beams on them as* CURLY *sings very softly*)

I can see the stars gittin' blurry
When we ride back home in the surrey,
Ridin' slowly home in the surrey with the fringe on top.
I can feel the day gittin' older,
Feel a sleepy head near my shoulder,
Noddin', droopin' close to my shoulder till it falls, kerplop!
The sun is swimmin' on the rim of a hill,
The moon is takin' a header,
And jist as I'm thinkin' all the earth is still,
A lark'll wake up in the medder. . . .
Hush! You bird, my baby's a-sleepin'—
Maybe got a dream worth a-keepin'
  (*Soothing and slower*)
Whoa! You team, and jist keep a-creepin' at a slow clip-clop.
Don't you hurry with the surrey with the fringe on the top.

(*There is silence and contentment, but only for a brief mo-ment.* LAUREY *starts slowly to emerge from the enchantment of his description*)

LAUREY   On'y . . . on'y there ain't no sich rig. You said you made the whole thing up.

CURLY   Well . . .

LAUREY   Why'd you come around here with yer stories and lies, gittin' me all worked up that-a-way? Talkin' 'bout the sun swimmin' on the hill, and all—like it was so. Who'd want to ride 'longside of you anyway?
   (IKE *and* FRED *enter and stand outside the gate, looking on*)

AUNT ELLER   Whyn't you jist grab her and kiss her when she acts that-a-way, Curly? She's jist achin' fer you to, I bet.

LAUREY   Oh, I won't even speak to him, let alone 'low him to kiss me, the braggin', bow-legged, wisht he-had-a-sweetheart bum!
   (*She flounces into the house, slamming the door*)

AUNT ELLER   She likes you—quite a lot.

CURLY   Whew! If she liked me any more she'd sic the dogs onto me.

IKE   Y'git the wagon hitched up?

AUNT ELLER   Whut wagon?

CURLY   They's a crowd of folks comin' down from Bushyhead for the Box Social.

FRED   Curly said mebbe you'd loan us yer big wagon to bring 'em up from the station.

AUNT ELLER   Course I would, if he'd ast me.

CURLY (*Embarrassed*)   Got to talkin' 'bout a lot of other things. I'll go hitch up the horses now 'f you say it's all right.
   (*As he exits, a group of boys run on, leaping the fence, shouting boisterously and pushing* WILL PARKER *in front of them.* WILL *is apparently a favorite with* AUNT ELLER)

SLIM   See whut we brung you, Aunt Eller!

AUNT ELLER   Hi, Will!

WILL   Hi, Aunt Eller!

AUNT ELLER   Whut happened up at the fair? You do any good in the steer ropin'?

WILL   I did purty good. I won it.
  (*The following three speeches overlap*)

IKE   Good boy!

FRED   Always knowed y'would.

AUNT ELLER   Ain't nobody c'n sling a rope like our territory boys.

WILL   Cain't stay but a minnit, Aunt Eller. Got to git over to Ado Annie. Don't you remember, her paw said 'f I ever was worth fifty dollars I could have her?

AUNT ELLER   Fitty dollars! That whut they give you fer prize money?

WILL   That's whut!

AUNT ELLER   Lands, if Ado Annie's paw keeps his promise we'll be dancin' at yer weddin'.

WILL   If he don't keep his promise I'll take her right from under his nose, and I won't give him the present I brung fer him. (*He takes "The Little Wonder" from his pocket. This is a small cylindrical toy with a peep-hole at one end*) Look, fellers, whut I got for Ado Annie's paw! (*The boys crowd around*) 'Scuse us. Aunt Eller. (*Illustrating to the boys, lowering his voice*) You hold it up to yer eyes, like this. Then when you git a good look, you turn it around at th' top and the pitcher changes.

IKE (*Looking into it*)   Well, I'll be side-gaited!
  (*The boys line up, and take turns, making appropriate ejaculations*)

WILL   They call it "The Little Wonder"!

AUNT ELLER   Silly goats! (*But her curiosity gets the better of her. She yanks a little man out of the line, takes his place, gets hold of "The Little Wonder" and takes a look*) The hussy! . . . Ought to be ashamed of herself. (*Glaring at* WILL) You, too! . . . How do you turn the thing to see the other pitcher? (*Looking again, and turning*) Wait, I'm gettin' it. . . . (*When she gets it, she takes it away from her eye quickly and, handing it to* WILL, *walks away in shocked silence. Then she suddenly "busts out laughin' "*) I'm a good mind to tell Ado Annie on yer.

WILL   Please don't, Aunt Eller. She wouldn't understand.

AUNT ELLER   No tellin' what you been up to. Bet you carried on plenty in Kansas City.

WILL   I wouldn't call it carryin' on. But I shore did see some things I never see before. (*Sings*)
I got to Kansas City on a Frid'y.
By Sattidy I l'arned a thing or two.
For up to then I didn't have an idy
Of whut the modern world was comin' to!
I counted twenty gas buggies goin' by theirsel's
Almost ev'ry time I tuck a walk.
Nen I put my ear to a Bell Telephone
And a strange womern started in to talk!

AUNT ELLER   Whut next!

BOYS   Yeah, whut!

WILL   Whut next?
Ev'rythin's up to date in Kansas City.
They've gone about as fur as they c'n go!
They went and built a skyscraper seven stories high—
About as high as a buildin' orta grow.
Ev'rythin's like a dream in Kansas City.
It's better than a magic-lantern show!
Y'c'n turn the radiator on whenever you want some heat.
With ev'ry kind o' comfort ev'ry house is all complete.
You c'n walk to privies in the rain an' never wet yer feet!
They've gone about as fur as they c'n go!

ALL
Yes, sir!
They've gone about as fur as they c'n go!

WILL
Ev'rythin's up to date in Kansas City.
They've gone about as fur as they c'n go!
They got a big theayter they call a burleeque.
Fer fifty cents you c'n see a dandy show.
One of the gals was fat and pink and pretty,

As round above as she was round below.
I could swear that she was padded from her shoulder to her
    heel,
But later in the second act when she begun to peel
She proved that ev'rythin' she had was absolutely real!
She went about as fur as she could go!

ALL
Yes, sir!
She went about as fur as she could go!
    (WILL *starts two-stepping*)

IKE   Whut you doin'?

WILL   This is the two-step. That's all they're dancin' now-
adays. The waltz is through. Ketch on to it? A one and a two
—a one and a two. Course they don't do it alone. C'mon,
Aunt Eller.
    (WILL *dances* AUNT ELLER *around. At the end of the re-
frain she is all tuckered out*)

AUNT ELLER   And that's about as fur as I c'n go!

ALL
Yes, sir!
And that's about as fur as she c'n go!
    (WILL *starts to dance alone*)

FRED   Whut you doin' now, Will?

WILL   That's rag-time. Seen a couple of colored fellers doin'
it.
    (*And* WILL *does his stuff, accompanied by four of the
dancing boys. At end of number* CURLY *enters*)

CURLY   Team's all hitched.

WILL   'Lo, Curly. Cain't stop to talk. Goin' over to Ado
Annie's. I got fifty dollars.

IKE   Time we got goin', boys. Thanks fer the loan of the
wagon, Aunt Eller. (*They all start to leave*) Come on, Curly.

CURLY   I'll ketch up with you. (*He makes sure* IKE *is well
on his way, then turns to* AUNT ELLER) Aunt Eller, I got to
know sumpin'. Listen, who's the low, filthy sneak 'at Laurey's
got her cap set for?

AUNT ELLER   You.

CURLY Never mind 'at. They must be plenty of men a-tryin' to spark her. And she shorely leans to one of 'em. Now don't she?

AUNT ELLER Well, they is that fine farmer, Jace Hutchins, jist this side of Lone Ellum— Nen thet ole widder man at Claremore, makes out he's a doctor or a vet'nary—
  (JUD, *a burly, scowling man enters, carrying firewood*)

CURLY That's whut I thought. Hello, Jud.

JUD Hello, yourself.
  (JUD *exits into house*)

AUNT ELLER (*Significantly, looking in* JUD's *direction*) Nen of course there's someone nearer home that's got her on his mind most of the time, till he don't know a plow from a thrashin' machine.

CURLY (*Jerking his head up toward the house*) Him?

AUNT ELLER Yeah, Jud Fry.

CURLY That bullet-colored, growly man?

AUNT ELLER Now don't you go and say nuthin' agin' him! He's the best hired hand I ever had. Jist about runs the farm by hisself. Well, two women couldn't do it, you orta know that.

CURLY Laurey'd take up 'th a man like that!

AUNT ELLER I ain't said she's tuck up with him.

CURLY Well, he's around all the time, ain't he? Lives here.

AUNT ELLER Out in the smokehouse.
  (JUD *and* LAUREY *enter from the house.* JUD *crosses and speaks to* AUNT ELLER)

JUD Changed my mind about cleanin' the henhouse today. Leavin' it till tomorrow. Got to quit early cuz I'm drivin' Laurey over to the party tonight.
  (*A bombshell!*)

CURLY You're drivin' Laurey?

JUD Ast her.
  (*Pointing to* LAUREY, *who doesn't deny it.* JUD *exits.* CURLY *is completely deflated*)

CURLY Well, wouldn't that just make you bawl! Well, don't fergit, Aunt Eller. You and me's got a date together. And if you make up a nice box of lunch, mebbe I'll bid fer it.

AUNT ELLER How we goin', Curly? In that rig you made up? I'll ride a-straddle of them lights a-winkin' like lightnin' bugs!

CURLY That there ain't no made-up rig, you hear me? I h'ard it over to Claremore.
    (*This stuns* LAUREY)

AUNT ELLER Lands, you did?

CURLY Shore did. (*Refrain of the "Surrey Song" starts in orchestra*) Purty one, too. When I come callin' fer you right after supper, see that you got yer beauty spots fastened onto you proper, so you won't lose 'em off, you hear? 'At's a right smart turnout. (*His voice, a little husky, picks up the refrain:*)
The wheels are yeller, the upholstery's brown,
The dashboard's genuine leather,
With isinglass curtains y'c'n roll right down,
In case there's a change in the weather—
(*He breaks off in the song*) See you before tonight anyways, on the way back from the station— (*Turning, singing to himself as he saunters off*)
Ain't no finer rig, I'm a-thinkin' . . . 'at I'd keer to swap
Fer that shiny little surrey with the fringe on the top—
    (*He is off*)

AUNT ELLER (*Calling off stage to him*) Hey, Curly, tell all the girls in Bushyhead to stop by here and freshen up. It's a long way to Skidmore's. (*Maybe* LAUREY *would like to "bust out" into tears, but she bites her lip, and doesn't.* AUNT ELLER *studies her for a moment after* CURLY *has gone, then starts up toward the house*) That means we'll have a lot of company. Better pack yer lunch hamper.

LAUREY (*A strange, sudden panic in her voice*) Aunt Eller, don't go to Skidmore's with Curly tonight. If you do, I'll have to ride with Jud all alone.

AUNT ELLER That's the way you wanted it, ain't it?

LAUREY No. I did it because Curly was so fresh. But I'm afraid to tell Jud I won't go, Aunt Eller. He'd do sumpin

turrible. He makes me shivver ever' time he gits clost to me.
. . . Ever go down to that ole smokehouse where he's at?

AUNT ELLER Plen'y times. Why?

LAUREY Did you see them pitchers he's got tacked onto the
walls?

AUNT ELLER Oh, yeah, I seed them. But don't you pay them
no mind.

LAUREY Sumpin wrong inside him, Aunt Eller. I hook my
door at night and fasten my winders agin' it. Agin' *it*—and
the sound of feet a-walkin' up and down out there under that
tree outside my room.

AUNT ELLER Laurey!

LAUREY Mornin's he comes to his breakfast and looks at me
out from under his eyebrows like sumpin back in the bresh
som'eres. I know whut I'm talkin' about.
    (*Voices off stage. It's* ADO ANNIE *and the* PEDDLER)

AUNT ELLER You crazy young 'un! Stop actin' like a chicken
with its head cut off! Now who'd you reckon that is drove up?
Why, it's that ole peddler! The one that sold me that egg-
beater!

LAUREY (*Looking off*) He's got Ado Annie with him! Will
Parker's Ado Annie!

AUNT ELLER Ole peddler! You know whut he tol' me? Tol'
me that egg-beater ud beat up eggs, and wring out dishrags,
and turn the ice-cream freezer, and I don't know whut all!

LAUREY (*Calling off stage*) Yoohoo! Ado Annie!

AUNT ELLER (*Shouting off stage*) Hold yer horses, Peddler-
man! I want to talk to you!
    (*She starts off, as* ADO ANNIE *enters with lunch hamper*)

ADO ANNIE Hi, Aunt Eller!

AUNT ELLER Hi, yourself.
    (AUNT ELLER *exits*)

ADO ANNIE Hello, Laurey.

LAUREY Hello. Will Parker's back from Kansas City. He's
lookin' fer yer.

(ADO ANNIE'S *brows knit to meet a sudden problem*)

ADO ANNIE   Will Parker! I didn't count on him bein' back so soon!

LAUREY   I can see that! Been ridin' a piece?

ADO ANNIE   The peddler-man's gonna drive me to the Box Social. I got up sort of a tasty lunch.

LAUREY   Ado Annie! Have you tuck up with that peddler-man?

ADO ANNIE   N-not yit.

LAUREY   But yer promised to Will Parker, ain't yer?

ADO ANNIE   Not what you might say *promised*. I jist told him mebbe.

LAUREY   Don't y' like him no more?

ADO ANNIE   'Course I do. They won't never be nobody like Will.

LAUREY   Then whut about this peddler-man?

ADO ANNIE   (*Looking off wistfully*)   They won't never be nobody like *him,* neither.

LAUREY   Well, which one d'you like the best?

ADO ANNIE   Whutever one I'm with!

LAUREY   Well, you air a silly!

ADO ANNIE   Now, Laurey, you know they didn't nobody pay me no mind up to this year, count of I was scrawny and flat as a beanpole. Nen I kind of rounded up a little and now the boys act diff'rent to me.

LAUREY   Well, whut's wrong with that?

ADO ANNIE   Nuthin' wrong. I like it. I like it so much when a feller talks purty to me I git all shaky from horn to hoof! Don't you?

LAUREY   Can't think whut yer talkin' about.

ADO ANNIE   Don't you feel kind of sorry fer a feller when he looks like he wants to kiss you?

LAUREY Well, you jist can't go around kissin' every man that asts you! Didn't anybody ever tell you that?

ADO ANNIE Yeow, they *told* me. . . . (*Sings*)
It ain't so much a question of not knowin' whut to do,
I knowed whut's right and wrong since I been ten.
I heared a lot of stories—and I reckon they are true—
About how girls're put upon by men.
I know I mustn't fall into the pit,
But when I'm with a feller—I fergit!
I'm jist a girl who cain't say no,
I'm in a turrible fix.
I always say, come on, le's go—
Jist when I orta say nix!
When a person tries to kiss a girl
I know she orta give his face a smack.
But as soon as someone kisses me
I somehow sorta wanta kiss him back!
I'm jist a fool when lights are low.
I cain't be prissy and quaint—
I ain't the type thet c'n faint—
How c'n I be whut I ain't?
I cain't say no!

Whut you goin' to do when a feller gits flirty
And starts to talk purty?
Whut you goin' to do?
S'posin' 'at he says 'at yer lips're like cherries,
Er roses, er berries?
Whut you goin' to do?
S'posin' 'at he says 'at you're sweeter'n cream
And he's gotta have cream er die?
Whut you goin' to do when he talks thet way?
Spit in his eye?

I'm jist a girl who cain't say no,
Cain't seem to say it at all.
I hate to disserpoint a beau
When he is payin' a call.
Fer a while I ack refined and cool,
A-settin' on the velveteen settee—
Nen I think of thet ol' golden rule,
And do fer him whut he would do fer me!

I cain't resist a Romeo
In a sombrero and chaps.
Soon as I sit on their laps
Somethin' inside of me snaps
I cain't say no!
   (*She sits on her hamper, and looks discouraged*)

I'm jist a girl who cain't say no.
Kissin's my favorite food.
With er without the mistletoe
I'm in a holiday mood!
Other girls are coy and hard to catch
But other girls ain't havin' any fun!
Ev'ry time I lose a wrestlin' match
I have a funny feelin' that I won!
Though I c'n feel the undertow,
I never make a complaint
Till it's too late fer restraint,
Then when I want to I cain't.
I cain't say no!
   (*Resuming dialogue, after applause*)
It's like I tole you, I git sorry fer them!

LAUREY   I wouldn't feel sorry fer any man, no matter whut!

ADO ANNIE   I'm shore sorry fer pore Ali Hakim now. Look how Aunt Eller's cussin' him out!

LAUREY   Ali Hakim! That his name?

ADO ANNIE   Yeah, it's Persian.

LAUREY   You shore fer sartin you love him better'n you love Will?

ADO ANNIE   I *was* shore. And now that ole Will has to come home and first thing you know he'll start talkin' purty to me and changin' my mind back!

LAUREY   But Will wants to marry you.

ADO ANNIE   So does Ali Hakim.

LAUREY   Did he ast yer?

ADO ANNIE   Not direckly. But how I know is he said this mornin' that he wanted fer me to drive like that with him to the end of the world. Well, 'f we drove only as fur as Catoosie that'd take to sundown, wouldn't it? Nen we'd have to go som'eres and be all night together, and bein' together all night means he wants a weddin', don't it?

LAUREY   Not to a peddler it don't!
   (*Enter* PEDDLER *and* AUNT ELLER)

PEDDLER   All right! All right! If the egg-beater don't work I give you something just as good!

AUNT ELLER   Jist as good! It's got to be a thousand million times better!
   (*The* PEDDLER *puts down his bulging suitcase, his little beady eyes sparkling professionally. He rushes over and, to* LAUREY'S *alarm, kisses her hand*)

PEDDLER   My, oh, my! Miss Laurey! Jippity crickets, how high you have growed up! Last time I come through here, you was tiny like a shrimp, with freckles. Now look at you— a great big beautiful lady!

LAUREY   Quit it a-bitin' me! If you ain't had no breakfast go and eat yerself a green apple.

PEDDLER   Now, Aunt Eller, just lissen—

AUNT ELLER (*Shouting*)   I ain't yer Aunt Eller! Don't you call me Aunt Eller, you little wart. I'm mad at you.

PEDDLER   Don't you go and be mad at me. Ain't I said I'd give you a present? (*Getting his bag*) Something to wear.

AUNT ELLER   Foot! Got things fer to wear. Wouldn't have it. Whut is it?

PEDDLER (*Holding up garter*)   Real silk. Made in Persia!

AUNT ELLER   Whut'd I want with a ole Persian garter?

ADO ANNIE   They look awful purty, Aunt Eller, with bows onto 'em and all.

AUNT ELLER   I'll try 'em on.

PEDDLER   Hold out your foot.
   (AUNT ELLER *obeys mechanically. But when he gets the garter over her ankle, she kicks him down*)

AUNT ELLER Did you have any idy I was goin' ter let you slide that garter up my limb? (*She stoops over and starts to pull the garter up*) Grab onto my petticoats, Laurey.
(*Noticing the* PEDDLER *looking at her, she turns her back on him pointedly and goes on with the operation. The* PEDDLER *turns to* ADO ANNIE)

PEDDLER Funny woman. Would be much worse if I tried to take your garters off.

ADO ANNIE Yeh, cuz that ud make her stockin's fall down, wouldn't it?

AUNT ELLER Now give me the other one.

PEDDLER Which one? (*Picking it out of his case*) Oh, you want to buy this one to match?

AUNT ELLER Whut do you mean do I want to *buy* it?

PEDDLER I can let you have it for fifty cents—four bits.

AUNT ELLER Do you want me to get that egg-beater and ram it down yer windpipe!
(*She snatches the second one away*)

PEDDLER All right—all right. Don't anybody want to buy something? How about you, Miss Laurey? Must be wanting something—a pretty young girl like you.

LAUREY Me? Course I want sumpin. (*Working up to a kind of abstracted ecstasy*) Want a buckle made outa shiny silver to fasten onto my shoes! Want a dress with lace. Want perfume, wanta be purty, wanta smell like a honeysuckle vine!

AUNT ELLER Give her a cake of soap.

LAUREY Want things I've heard of and never had before—a rubber-t'ard buggy, a cut-glass sugar bowl. Want things I cain't tell you about—not only things to look at and hold in yer hands. Things to happen to you. Things so nice, if they ever did happen to you, yer heart ud quit beatin'. You'd fall down dead!

PEDDLER I've got just the thing for you! (*He fishes into his satchel and pulls out a bottle*) The Elixir of Egypt!
(*He holds the bottle high*)

LAUREY What's 'at?

PEDDLER   It's a secret formula, belonged to Pharaoh's daughter!

AUNT ELLER   (*Leaning over and putting her nose to it*) Smellin' salts!

PEDDLER   (*Snatching it away*)   But a special kind of smelling salts. Read what it says on the label: "Take a deep breath and you see everything clear." That's what Pharaoh's daughter used to do. When she had a hard problem to decide, like what prince she ought to marry, or what dress to wear to a party, or whether she ought to cut off somebody's head— she'd take a whiff of this.

LAUREY   (*Excited*)   I'll take a bottle of that, Mr. Peddler.

PEDDLER   Precious stuff.

LAUREY   How much?

PEDDLER   Two bits.
   (*She pays him and takes the bottle*)

AUNT ELLER   Throwin' away yer money!

LAUREY   (*Holding the bottle close to her, thinking aloud*) Helps you decide what to do!

PEDDLER   Now don't you want me to show you some pretty dewdads? You know, with lace around the bottom, and ribbons running in and out?

AUNT ELLER   You mean fancy drawers?

PEDDLER   (*Taking a pair out of pack*)   All made in Paris.

AUNT ELLER   Well, I never wear that kind myself, but I shore do like to look at 'em.
   (PEDDLER *takes out a pair of red flannel drawers*)

ADO ANNIE   (*Dubiously*)   Y-yeah, they's all right—if you ain't goin' no place.

AUNT ELLER   Bring yer trappin's inside and mebbe I c'n find you sumpin to eat and drink.
   (AUNT ELLER *exits.* PEDDLER *starts to repack. The two girls whisper for a moment*)

LAUREY   Well, ast him, why don't you?
   (*She giggles and exits into house*)

ADO ANNIE   Ali, Laurey and me've been havin' a argument.

PEDDLER   About what, Baby?

ADO ANNIE   About what you meant when you said that about drivin' with me to the end of the world.

PEDDLER (*Cagily*)   Well, I didn't mean really to the end of the world.

ADO ANNIE   Then how fur did you want to go?

PEDDLER   Oh, about as far as—say—Claremore—to the hotel.

ADO ANNIE   Whut's at the hotel?

PEDDLER (*Ready for the kill*)   In front of the hotel is a veranda—inside is a lobby—upstairs—upstairs might be Paradise.

ADO ANNIE   I thought they was jist bedrooms.

PEDDLER   For you and me, Baby—Paradise.

ADO ANNIE   Y'see! I knew I was right and Laurey was wrong! You do want to marry me, don't you?

PEDDLER (*Embracing her impulsively*)   Ah, Ado Annie! (*Pulling away*) What did you say?

ADO ANNIE   I said you do want to marry me, don't you? What did you say?

PEDDLER   I didn't say nothing!

WILL (*Off stage*)   Whoa, Suzanna! Yoohoo, Ado Annie, I'm back!

ADO ANNIE   Oh, foot! Jist when— 'Lo, Will! (WILL *lets out a whoop off stage*) That's Will Parker. Promise me you won't fight him.

PEDDLER   Why fight? I never saw the man before.
   (WILL *enters*)

WILL   Ado Annie! How's my honey-bunch? How's the sweetest little hundred-and-ten pounds of sugar in the territory?

ADO ANNIE (*Confused*)   Er— Will, this is Ali Hakim

WILL   How are yuh, Hak? Don't mind the way I talk. 'S all right. I'm goin' to marry her.

PEDDLER (*Delighted*)   Marry her? On purpose?

WILL   Well, sure.

ADO ANNIE   No sich of a thing!

PEDDLER   It's a wonderful thing to be married.
   (*He starts off*)

ADO ANNIE   Ali!

PEDDLER   I got a brother in Persia, got six wives.

ADO ANNIE   Six wives? All at once?

WILL   Shore. 'At's a way they do in them countries.

PEDDLER   Not always. I got another brother in Persia only got one wife. He's a bachelor.
   (*Exit*)

ADO ANNIE   Look, Will—

WILL   Look, Will, nuthin'. Know whut I got fer first prize at the fair? Fifty dollars!

ADO ANNIE   Well, that was good. . . . (*The significance suddenly dawning on her*) Fifty dollars?

WILL   Ketch on? Yer paw promised I cud marry you 'f I cud git fifty dollars.

ADO ANNIE   'At's right, he did.

WILL   Know whut I done with it? Spent it all on presents fer you!

ADO ANNIE   But if you spent it you ain't got the cash.

WILL   Whut I got is worth more'n the cash. Feller who sold me the stuff told me!

ADO ANNIE   But, Will . . .

WILL   Stop sayin' "But, Will"— When do I git a little kiss? . . . Oh, Ado Annie, honey, y'ain't been off my mind since I left. All the time at the fair grounds even, when I was chasin' steers. I'd rope one under the hoofs and pull him up sharp, and he'd land on his little rump . . . Nen I'd think of you.

ADO ANNIE   Don't start talkin' purty, Will.

WILL   See a lot of beautiful gals in Kansas City. Didn't give one a look.

ADO ANNIE   How could you see 'em if you didn't give 'em a look?

WILL   I mean I didn't look lovin' at 'em—like I look at you. (*He turns her around and looks adoring and pathetic*)

ADO ANNIE (*Backing away*)   Oh, Will, please don't look like that! I cain't bear it.

WILL   Won't stop lookin' like this till you give me a little ole kiss.

ADO ANNIE   Oh, whut's a little ole kiss?

WILL   Nothin'—less'n it comes from you. (*Both stop*)

ADO ANNIE (*Sighing*)   You do talk purty! (WILL *steps up for his kiss. She nearly gives in, but with sudden and unaccounted-for strength of character she turns away*) No, I won't!

WILL (*Singing softly, seductively, "getting" her*)
S'posin' 'at I say 'at yer lips're like cherries,
Er roses er berries?
Whut you gonna do?
   (*Putting her hand on his heart*)
Cain't you feel my heart palpatin' an' bumpin',
A-waitin' fer sumpin,
Sumpin nice from you?
I gotta git a kiss an' it's gotta be quick
Er I'll jump in a crick an' die!

ADO ANNIE (*Overcome*)   Whut's a girl to say when you talk that-a-way?
   (*And he gets his kiss. The boys and girls, and* CURLY *and* GERTIE *enter with lunch hampers, shouting and laughing.* WILL *and* ADO ANNIE *run off.* AUNT ELLER *and* LAUREY *come out of the house.* GERTIE *laughs musically.* LAUREY, *unmindful of the group of girls she has been speaking to, looks across at* CURLY *and* GERTIE *and boils over. All the couples and* CURLY *and* GERTIE *waltz easily, while they sing:*)

ALL   Oh, what a beautiful mornin',

CURLY   Oh, what a beautiful day.

ALL   I got a beautiful feelin'

CURLY   Ev'rythin's goin' my way. . . .

AUNT ELLER (*To the rescue*)   Hey, Curly! Better take the wagon down to the troft and give the team some water.

CURLY   Right away, Aunt Eller.
(*He turns*)

GERTIE   C'n I come, too? Jist love to watch the way you handle horses.

CURLY (*Looking across at* LAUREY)   'At's about all I *can* handle, I guess.

GERTIE   Oh, I cain't believe that, Curly—not from whut I heared about you!
(*She takes his arm and walks him off, turning on more musical laughter. A girl imitates her laugh. Crowd laughs.* LAUREY *takes an involuntary step forward, then stops, frustrated, furious*)

GIRL   Looks like Curly's tuck up with that Cummin's girl.

LAUREY   Whut'd I keer about that?
(*The girls and* LAUREY *chatter and argue, ad lib*)

AUNT ELLER   Come on, boys, better git these hampers out under the trees where it's cool.
(*Exit* AUNT ELLER *and boys. To show "how little she keers,"* LAUREY *sings the following song*)
Why should a womern who is healthy and strong
Blubber like a baby if her man goes away?
A-weepin' and a-wailin' how he's done her wrong—
That's one thing you'll never hear me say!
Never gonna think that the man I lose
Is the only man among men.
I'll snap my fingers to show I don't care.
I'll buy me a brand-new dress to wear.
I'll scrub my neck and I'll bresh my hair,
And start all over again.

Many a new face will please my eye,
Many a new love will find me.

Never've I once looked back to sigh
Over the romance behind me.
Many a new day will dawn before I do!
Many a light lad may kiss and fly,
A kiss gone by is bygone,
Never've I asked an August sky,
"Where has last July gone?"
Never've I wandered through the rye,
Wonderin' where has some guy gone—
Many a new day will dawn before I do!

CHORUS
Many a new face will please my eye,
Many a new love will find me.
Never've I once looked back to sigh
Over the romance behind me.
Many a new day will dawn before I do!

LAUREY
Never've I chased the honey-bee
Who carelessly cajoled me.
Somebody else just as sweet as he
Cheered me and consoled me.
Never've I wept into my tea
Over the deal someone doled me.

CHORUS
Many a new day will dawn,

LAUREY
Many a red sun will set,
Many a blue moon will shine, before I do!
   (*A dance follows.* LAUREY *and girls exit.* PEDDLER *enters
   from house,* ADO ANNIE *from the other side of the stage*)

ADO ANNIE   Ali Hakim—

PEDDLER   Hello, kiddo.

ADO ANNIE   I'm shore sorry to see you so happy, cuz whut
I got to say will make you mis'able. . . . I got to marry
Will.

PEDDLER   That's sad news for me. Well, he is a fine fellow.

ADO ANNIE   Don't hide your feelin's, Ali. I cain't stand it.
I'd ruther have you come right out and say yer heart is busted
in two.

PEDDLER   Are you positive you got to marry Will?

ADO ANNIE   Shore's shootin'.

PEDDLER   And there is no chance for you to change your mind?

ADO ANNIE   No chance.

PEDDLER (*As if granting a small favor*)   All right, then, my heart is busted in two.

ADO ANNIE   Oh, Ali, you do make up purty things to say!

CARNES (*Off stage*)   That you, Annie?

ADO ANNIE   Hello, Paw. (CARNES *enters. He is a scrappy little man, carrying a shotgun*) Whut you been shootin'?

CARNES   Rabbits. That true whut I hear about Will Parker gittin' fifty dollars?

ADO ANNIE   That's right, Paw. And he wants to hold you to yer promise.

CARNES   Too bad. Still and all I cain't go back on my word.

ADO ANNIE   See, Ali Hakim!

CARNES   I advise you to git that money off'n him before he loses it all. Put it in yer stockin' er inside yer corset where he cain't git at it . . . or can he?

ADO ANNIE   But, Paw—he ain't exackly kep' it. He spent it all on presents. . . .
    (*The* PEDDLER *is in a panic*)

CARNES   See! Whut'd I tell you! Now he cain't have you. I said it had to be fifty dollars cash.

PEDDLER   But, Mr. Carnes, is that fair?

CARNES   Who the hell are you?

ADO ANNIE   This is Ali Hakim.

CARNES   Well, shet your face, er I'll fill yer behind so full of buckshot, you'll be walkin' around like a duck the rest of yer life.

ADO ANNIE   Ali, if I don't have to marry Will, mebbe your heart don't have to be busted in two like you said.

PEDDLER   I did not say that.

ADO ANNIE   Oh, yes, you did.

PEDDLER   No, I did not.

CARNES (*Brandishing his gun*)   Are you tryin' to make out my daughter to be a liar?

PEDDLER   No, I'm just making it clear what a liar I am if she's telling the truth.

CARNES   Whut else you been sayin' to my daughter?

ADO ANNIE (*Before the* PEDDLER *can open his mouth*)   Oh, a awful lot.

CARNES (*To* PEDDLER)   When?

ADO ANNIE   Las' night, in the moonlight.

CARNES (*To* PEDDLER)   Where?

ADO ANNIE   'Longside a haystack.

PEDDLER   Listen, Mr. Carnes . . .

CARNES   I'm lissening. Whut else did you say?

ADO ANNIE   He called me his Persian kitten.

CARNES   Why'd you call her that?

PEDDLER   I don't remember.

ADO ANNIE   I do. He said I was like a Persian kitten, cuz they was the cats with the soft round tails.

CARNES (*Cocking his gun*)   That's enough. In this part of the country that better be a proposal of marriage.

ADO ANNIE   That's whut I thought.

CARNES (*To* PEDDLER)   Is that whut you think?

PEDDLER   Look, Mr. Carnes . . .

CARNES (*Taking aim*)   I'm lookin'.

PEDDLER   I'm no good. I'm a peddler. A peddler travels up and down and all around and you'd hardly ever see your daughter no more.

CARNES (*Patting him on back*) 'That'd be all right. Take keer of her, son. Take keer of my little rosebud.

ADO ANNIE   Oh, Paw, that's purty. (CARNES *starts to exit into house*) You shore fer sartin you can bear to let me go, Paw?
   (CARNES *turns*)

PEDDLER   Are you *sure*, Mr. Carnes?

CARNES   Jist try to change my mind and see whut happens to you.
   (*He takes a firmer grip on his gun and exits into the house*)

ADO ANNIE   Oh, Ali Hakim, ain't it wonderful, Paw makin' up our mind fer us? He won't change neither. Onct he gives his word that you c'n have me, why, you *got* me.

PEDDLER   I *know* I got you.

ADO ANNIE (*Starry-eyed*)   Mrs. Ali Hakim . . . the Peddler's bride. Wait till I tell the girls.
   (*She exits.* ALI *leans against the porch post as the music starts. Then he starts to pace up and down, thinking hard, his head bowed, his hands behind his back. The orchestra starts a vamp that continues under the melody. Some men enter and watch him curiously, but he is unmindful of them until they start to sing. Throughout this entire number, the* PEDDLER *must be burning, and he transmits his indignation to the men who sing in a spirit of angry protests, by the time the refrain is reached*)

PEDDLER (*Circling the stage*)
Trapped! . . .
Tricked! . . .
Hoodblinked! . . .
Hambushed! . . .

MEN
Friend,
Whut's on yer mind?
Why do you walk
Around and around,
With yer hands
Folded behind,
And yer chin
Scrapin' the ground?

(*The* PEDDLER *walks away, then comes back to them and starts to pour out his heart*)

PEDDLER

Twenty minutes ago I am free like a breeze,
Free like a bird in the woodland wild,
Free like a gypsy, free like a child,
I'm unattached!
Twenty minutes ago I can do what I please,
Flick my cigar ashes on a rug,
Dunk with a doughnut, drink from a jug—
I'm a happy man!
    (*Crescendo*)
I'm minding my own business like I oughter,
Ain't meaning any harm to anyone.
I'm talking to a certain farmer's daughter—
Then I'm looking in the muzzle of a gun!

MEN

It's gittin' so you cain't have any fun!
Ev'ry daughter has a father with a gun!

It's a scandal, it's a outrage!
How a gal gits a husband today!

PEDDLER

If you make one mistake when the moon is bright,
Then they tie you to a contract, so you'll make it ev'ry night!

MEN

It's a scandal, it's a outrage!
When her fambly surround you and say:
"You gotta take an' make a honest womern outa Nell!"

PEDDLER

To make you make her honest, she will lie like hell!

MEN

It's a scandal, it's a outrage!
On our manhood, it's a blot!
Where is the leader who will save us?
And be the first man to be shot?

PEDDLER (*Spoken*)   Me?

MEN (*Spoken*)   Yes, you!   (*Sing*)
It's a scandal, it's a outrage!

Jist a wink and a kiss and you're through!

PEDDLER
You're a mess, and in less than a year, by heck!
There's a baby on your shoulder making bubbles on your
   neck!

MEN
It's a scandal, it's a outrage!
Any farmer will tell you it's true.

PEDDLER
A rooster in a chickencoop is better off'n men.
He ain't the special property of just one hen!
   (ANNIE *and girls enter at side*)

MEN
It's a scandal, it's a outrage!
It's a problem we must solve!
We gotta start a revolution!

GIRLS   All right, boys! Revolve!
   (*The boys swing around, see the girls and are immediately cowed. The girls pick them off the line and walk off
   with them, to the music. All exit except one girl, who
   stalks around looking for a boy. Suddenly one appears,
   sees the girl and exits fast. She pursues him like mad.
   GERTIE enters through gate with* CURLY. LAUREY *enters on
   the porch and starts packing her lunch hamper*)

GERTIE   Hello, Laurey. Jist packin' yer hamper now?

LAUREY   I been busy.
   (GERTIE *looks in* LAUREY'S *hamper*. AUNT ELLER *enters*)

GERTIE   You got gooseberry tarts, too. Wonder if they is as
light as mine. Mine'd like to float away if you blew on them.

LAUREY   I did blow on one of mine and it broke up into a
million pieces.
   (GERTIE *laughs—that laugh again*)

GERTIE   Ain't she funny!
   (*The girls step toward each other menacingly*)

AUNT ELLER   Gertie! Better come inside, and cool off.

GERTIE   You comin' inside 'th me, Curly?

CURLY　Not jist yet.

GERTIE　Well, don't be too long. And don't fergit when the auction starts tonight, mine's the biggest hamper.
(*The laugh again, and she exits*)

LAUREY (*Going on with her packing*)　So that's the Cummin's girl I heared so much talk of.

CURLY　You seen her before, ain't you?

LAUREY　Yeow. But not since she got so old. Never did see anybody get so peeked-lookin' in sich a short time.

AUNT ELLER (*Amused at* LAUREY)　Yeah, and she says she's only eighteen. I betcha she's nineteen.
(AUNT ELLER *exits*)

CURLY　What yer got in yer hamper?

LAUREY　'At's jist some ole meat pies and apple jelly. Nothin' like whut Gertie Cummin's has in *her* basket.
(*She sits on the arm of a rocking chair*)

CURLY　You really goin' to drive to the Box Social with that Jud feller?
(*Pause*)

LAUREY　Reckon so. Why?

CURLY　Nothin' . . . It's jist that ev'rybody seems to expec' *me* to take you.
(*He sits on the other arm of the rocker*)

LAUREY　Then, mebbe it's jist as well you ain't. We don't want people talkin' 'bout us, do we?

CURLY　You think people *do* talk about us?

LAUREY　Oh, you know how they air—like a swarm of mudwasps. Alw'ys gotta be buzzin' 'bout sumpin.

CURLY (*Rocking the chair gaily*)　Well, whut're they sayin'? That you're stuck on me?

LAUREY　Uh-uh. Most of the talk is that you're stuck on me.

CURLY　Cain't imagine how these ugly rumors start.

LAUREY　Me neither. (*Sings*)
Why do they think up stories that link my name with yours?

CURLY
Why do the neighbors gossip all day behind their doors?

LAUREY
I have a way to prove what they say is quite untrue;
Here is the gist, a practical list of "don'ts" for you:

Don't throw bouquets at me—
Don't please my folks too much,
Don't laugh at my jokes too much—
People will say we're in love!

CURLY (*Leaving her*)　Who laughs at yer jokes?

LAUREY (*Following him*)
Don't sigh and gaze at me,
Your sighs are so like mine,
　　(CURLY *turns to embrace her, she stops him*)
Your eyes mustn't glow like mine—
People will say we're in love!
Don't start collecting things—

CURLY　Like whut?

LAUREY
Give me my rose and my glove.
　　(*He looks away, guiltily*)
Sweetheart, they're suspecting things—
People will say we're in love!

CURLY
Some people claim that you are to blame as much as I—
　　(*She is about to deny this*)
Why do you take the trouble to bake my fav'rit pie?
　　(*Now she looks guilty*)
Grantin' your wish, I carved our initials on that tree . . .
　　(*He points off at the tree*)
Jist keep a slice of all the advice you give, so free!

Don't praise my charm too much,
Don't look so vain with me,
Don't stand in the rain with me,
People will say we're in love!
Don't take my arm too much,
Don't keep your hand in mine,
Your hand looks so grand in mine,
People will say we're in love!

Don't dance all night with me,
Till the stars fade from above.
They'll see it's all right with me,
People will say we're in love!
(*Music continues as* CURLY *speaks*) Don't you reckon y'could tell that Jud you'd ruther go with me tonight?

LAUREY   Curly! I—no, I couldn't.

CURLY   Oh, you couldn't? (*Frowning*) Think I'll go down here to the smokehouse, where Jud's at. See whut's so elegant about him, makes girls wanta go to parties 'th him.
   (*He starts off, angrily*)

LAUREY   Curly!

CURLY (*Turning*)   Whut?

LAUREY   Nothin'. (*She watches* CURLY *as he exits, then sits on rocker crying softly and starts to sing:*)
Don't sigh and gaze at me,
Your sighs are so like mine,
Your eyes mustn't glow like mine—
   (*Music continues. She chokes up, can't go on.* AUNT ELLER *has come out and looks with great understanding*)

AUNT ELLER   Got yer hamper packed?

LAUREY (*Snapping out of it*)   Oh, Aunt Eller. . . . Yes, nearly.

AUNT ELLER   Like a hanky?

LAUREY   Whut'd I want with a ole hanky?

AUNT ELLER (*Handing her hers*)   Y'got a smudge on yer cheek—jist under yer eye.
   (LAUREY *dries her eyes, starts toward the house, thinks about the bottle of "Lixir of Egyp'," picks it up, looks at* AUNT ELLER, *and runs out through the gate and off stage.* AUNT ELLER *sits in the rocker and hums the refrain, happy and contented, as lights dim and the curtain falls*)

ACT ONE | Scene Two

SCENE: *The Smokehouse.*
  Immediately after Scene 1.
  It is a dark, dirty building where the meat was once kept. The rafters are smoky, covered with dust and cobwebs. On a low loft many things are stored—horse collars, plowshares, a binder twine, a keg of nails. Under it, the bed is grimy and never made. On the walls, tobacco advertisements, and pink covers off Police Gazettes. *In a corner there are hoes, rakes and an axe. Two chairs, a table and a spittoon comprise the furniture. There is a mirror for shaving, several farm lanterns and a rope. A small window lets in a little light, but not much.*
  JUD *enters and crosses to table. There is a knock on the door. He rises quickly and tiptoes to the window to peek outside. Then he glides swiftly back to the table. Takes out a pistol and starts to polish it. There is a second knock.*

JUD (*Calling out sullenly*)   Well, open it, cain't you?

CURLY (*Opening the door and strolling in*)   Howdy.

JUD   Whut'd you want?

CURLY   I done got th'ough my business up here at the house. Jist thought I'd pay a call. (*Pause*) You got a gun, I see.

JUD   Good un. Colt forty-five.

CURLY   Whut do you do with it?

JUD   Shoot things.

CURLY   Oh. (*He moseys around the room casually*) That there pink picture—now that's a naked womern, ain't it?

JUD Yer eyes don't lie to you.

CURLY Plumb stark naked as a jaybird. No. No, she ain't. Not quite. Got a couple of thingumbobs tied onto her.

JUD Shucks. That ain't a think to whut I got here. (*He shoves a pack of postcards across the table toward* CURLY) Lookit that top one.

CURLY (*Covering his eyes*) I'll go blind! . . . (*Throwing it back on the table*) That ud give me idys, that would.

JUD (*Picking it up and looking at it*) That's a dinger, that is.

CURLY (*Gravely*) Yeah, that shore is a dinger. . . . (*Taking down a rope*) That's a good-lookin' rope you got there. (*He begins to spin it*) Spins nice. You know Will Parker? He can shore spin a rope. (*He tosses one end of the rope over the rafter and pulls down on both ends, tentatively*) 'S a good strong hook you got there. You could hang yerself on that, Jud.

JUD I could whut?

CURLY (*Cheerfully*) Hang yerself. It ud be as easy as fallin' off a log! Fact is, you could stand on a log—er a cheer if you'd rather—right about here—see? And put this here around yer neck. Tie that good up there first, of course. Then all you'd have to do would be to fall off the log—er the cheer, whichever you'd ruther fall off of. In five minutes, or less, with good luck, you'd be daid as a doornail.

JUD Whut'd you mean by that?

CURLY Nen folks ud come to yer funril and sing sad songs.

JUD (*Disdainfully*) Yamnh!

CURLY They would. You never know how many people like you till you're daid. Y'd prob'ly be laid out in the parlor. Y'd be all diked out in yer best suit with yer hair combed down slick, and a high starched collar.

JUD (*Beginning to get interested*) Would they be any flowers, d'you think?

CURLY Shore would, and palms, too—all around yer cawfin. Nen folks ud stand around you and the men ud bare their

heads and the womern ud sniffle softly. Some'd prob'ly faint
—ones that had tuck a shine to you when you wuz alive.

JUD   Whut womern have tuck a shine to me?

CURLY   Lots of womern. On'y they don't never come right
out and show you how they feel less'n you die first.

JUD (*Thoughtfully*)   I guess that's so.

CURLY   They'd shore sing loud though when the singin'
started—sing like their hearts ud break! (*He starts to sing
very earnestly and solemnly, improvising the sort of thing he
thinks might be sung*)
Pore Jud is daid,
Pore Jud Fry is daid!
All gether 'round his cawfin now and cry.
He had a heart of gold
And he wasn't very old—
Oh, why did sich a feller have to die?
Pore Jud is daid,
Pore Jud Fry is daid!
He's lookin', oh, so peaceful and serene.

JUD (*Touched and suddenly carried away, he sings a soft
response*)   And serene!
   (*Takes off hat*)

CURLY
He's all laid out to rest
With his hands acrost his chest.
His fingernails have never b'en so clean!
   (JUD *turns slowly to question the good taste of this last
   reference, but* CURLY *plunges straight into another item of
   the imagined wake*)
Nen the preacher'd git up and he'd say: "Folks! We are
gethered here to moan and groan over our brother Jud Fry
who hung hisse'f up by a rope in the smokehouse." Nen
there'd be weepin' and wailin' (*Significantly*) from some of
those womern. (JUD *nods his head understandingly*) Nen he'd
say, "Jud was the most misunderstood man in the territory.
People useter think he was a mean, ugly feller. (JUD *looks
up*) And they called him a dirty skunk and a ornery pig-
stealer. (CURLY *switches quickly*) But—the folks 'at really
knowed him, knowed 'at beneath them two dirty shirts he
alw'ys wore, there beat a heart as big as all outdoors.

JUD (*Repeating reverently like a Negro at a revivalist meet·ing*)   As big as all outdoors.

CURLY   Jud Fry loved his fellow man.

JUD   He loved his fellow man.

CURLY (CURLY *is warming up and speaks with the impassioned inflections of an evangelist*)   He loved the birds of the forest and the beasts of the field. He loved the mice and the vermin in the barn, and he treated the rats like equals—which was right. And—he loved little children. He loved ev'body and ev'thin' in the world! . . . On'y he never let on, so nobody ever knowed it! (*Returning to vigorous song*)
Pore Jud is daid,
Pore Jud Fry is daid!
His friends'll weep and wail fer miles around.

JUD (*Now right into it*)   Miles around.

CURLY
The daisies in the dell
Will give out a diff'runt smell
Becuz pore Jud is underneath the ground.
   (JUD *is too emotionally exalted by the spirit of* CURLY'S *singing to be analytical. He now takes up a refrain of his own*)

JUD
Pore Jud is daid,
A candle lights his haid,
He's layin' in a cawfin made of wood.

CURLY   Wood.

JUD
And folks are feelin' sad
Cuz they useter treat him bad,
And now they know their friend has gone fer good.

CURLY (*Softly*)   Good.

JUD AND CURLY
Pore Jud is daid,
A candle lights his haid!

CURLY
He's lookin', oh, so purty and so nice.

He looks like he's asleep.
It's a shame that he won't keep,
But it's summer and we're runnin' out of ice . . .
Pore Jud—Pore Jud!
(JUD *breaks down, weeps, and sits at the table, burying his head in his arms*)
Yes, sir. That's the way it ud be. Shore be a interestin' funril
Wouldn't like to miss it.

JUD (*His eyes narrowing*) Wouldn't like to miss it, eh?
Well, mebbe you will. (*He resumes polishing the gun*) Mebbe
you'll go first.

CURLY (*Sitting down*) Mebbe. . . . Le's see now, whur
did you work at before you come here? Up by Quapaw,
wasn't it?

JUD Yes, and before that over by Tulsa. Lousy they was to
me. Both of 'em. Always makin' out they was better. Treatin'
me like dirt.

CURLY And whut'd you do—git even?

JUD Who said anythin' about gittin' even?

CURLY No one, that I recollect. It jist come into my head.

JUD If it ever come to gittin' even with anybody, I'd know
how to do it.

CURLY That?
(*Looking down at gun and pointing*)

JUD Nanh! They's safer ways than that, if you use yer
brains. . . . 'Member that f'ar on the Bartlett farm over by
Sweetwater?

CURLY Shore do. 'Bout five years ago. Turrible accident.
Burned up the father and mother and daughter.

JUD That warn't no accident. A feller told me—the h'ard
hand was stuck on the Bartlett girl, and he found her in the
hayloft with another feller.

CURLY And it was him that burned the place?

JUD (*Nodding*) It tuck him weeks to git all the kerosene—
buying it at different times—feller who told me made out it

happened in Missouri, but I knowed all the time it was the Bartlett farm. Whut a liar he was!

CURLY   And a kind of a—a kind of a murderer, too. Wasn't he? (CURLY *rises, goes over to the door and opens it*) Git a little air in here.

JUD   You ain't told me yet whut business you had here. We got no cattle to sell ner no cow ponies. The oat crop is done spoke fer.

CURLY   You shore relieved my mind consid'able.

JUD (*Tensely*)   They's on'y one other thing on this farm you could want—and it better not be that!

CURLY (*Closing the door deliberately and turning slowly, to face* JUD)   But that's jist whut it is.

JUD   Better not be! You keep away from her, you hear?

CURLY (*Coolly*)   You know somebody orta tell Laurey whut kind of a man you air. And fer that matter, somebody orta tell *you* onct about yerself.

JUD   You better git outa here, Curly.

CURLY   A feller wouldn't feel very safe in here with you . . . 'f he didn't know you. (*Acidly*) But I know you, Jud. (CURLY *looks him straight in the eye*) In this country, they's two things you c'n do if you're a man. Live out of doors is one. Live in a hole is the other. I've set by my horse in the bresh som'eres and heared a rattlesnake many a time. Rattle, rattle, rattle!—he'd go, skeered to death. Somebody comin' close to his hole! Somebody gonna step on him! Git his old fangs ready, full of pizen! Curl up and wait!—Long's you live in a hole, you're skeered, you got to have pertection. You c'n have muscles, oh, like arn—and still be as weak as a empty bladder—less'n you got things to barb yer hide with. (*Suddenly, harshly, directly to* JUD) How'd you git to be the way you air, anyway—settin' here in this filthy hole—and thinkin' the way you're thinkin'? Why don't you do sumpin healthy onct in a while, 'stid of stayin' shet up here— a-crawlin' and festerin'!

JUD   Anh!
   (*He seizes a gun in a kind of reflex, a kind of desperate*

frenzy, and pulls the trigger. Luckily the gun is pointed toward the ceiling)

CURLY (*Actually in a state of high excitement, but outwardly cool and calm, he draws his own gun*) You orta feel better now. Hard on the roof, though. I wisht you'd let me show you sumpin. (JUD *doesn't move, but stands staring into* CURLY'S *eyes*) They's a knot-hole over there about as big as a dime. See it a-winkin'? I jist want to see if I c'n hit it. (*Unhurriedly, with cat-like tension, he turns and fires at the wall high up*) Bullet right through the knot-hole, 'thout tetchin', slick as a whistle, didn't I? I knowed I could do it. You saw it, too, didn't you? (*Ad lib off stage*) Somebody's a-comin', I 'spect.

(*He listens.* JUD *looks at the floor.* AUNT ELLER, *the* PEDDLER *and several others come running in*)

AUNT ELLER (*Gasping for breath*) Who f'ard off a gun? Was that you, Curly? Don't set there, you lummy, answer when you're spoke to.

CURLY Well, I shot onct.

AUNT ELLER What was you shootin' at?

CURLY (*Rises*) See that knot-hole over there?

AUNT ELLER I see lots of knot-holes.

CURLY Well, it was one of them.

AUNT ELLER (*Exasperated*) Well, ain't you a pair of purty nuthin's, a-pickin' away at knot-holes and skeerin' everybody to death! Orta give you a good Dutch rub and arn some of the craziness out of you! (*Calling off to people in doorway*) 'S all right! Nobody hurt. Jist a pair of fools swappin' noises.
(*She exits*)

PEDDLER Mind if I visit with you, gents? It's good to get away from the women for a while. Now then, we're all by ourselves. I got a few purties, private knickknacks for to show you. Special for the menfolks.
(*Starts to get them out*)

CURLY See you gentlemen later. I gotta git a surrey I h'ard fer tonight.
(*He starts to go*)

PEDDLER (*Shoving cards under* JUD'S *nose*)   Art postcards.

JUD   Who you think yer takin' in that surrey?

CURLY   Aunt Eller—and Laurey, if she'll come with me.

JUD   She won't.

CURLY   Mebbe she will.
(*Exits*)

JUD (*Raising his voice after* CURLY)   She promised to go with me, and she better not change her mind. She better not!

PEDDLER   Now, I want ye to look at these straight from Paris.

JUD   I don't want none o' them things now. Got any frog-stickers?

PEDDLER   You mean one of them long knives? What would you want with a thing like that?

JUD   I dunno. Kill a hog—er a skunk. It's all the same, ain't it? I tell you whut I'd like better'n a frog-sticker, if you got one. Ever hear of one of them things you call "The Little Wonder"? It's a thing you hold up to your eyes to see pitchers, only that ain't all they is to it . . . not quite. Y'see it's got a little jigger onto it, and you tetch it and out springs a sharp blade.

PEDDLER   On a spring, eh?

JUD   Y'say to a feller, "Look through this." Nen when he's lookin' you snap out the blade. It's jist above his chest and, bang! Down you come.
(*Slaps the* PEDDLER *on the chest, knocking the wind from him*)

PEDDLER (*After recovering from blow*)   A good joke to play on a friend . . . I—er—don't handle things like that. Too dangerous. What I'd like to show you is my new stock of postcards.

JUD   Don't want none. Sick of them things. I'm going to get me a real womern.

PEDDLER   What would you want with a woman? Why, I'm having trouble right now, all on account of a woman. They always make trouble. And you say you *want* one. Why? Look

at you? You're a man what is free to come and go as you
please. You got a nice cozy little place. (*Looking place over*)
Private. Nobody to bother you. Artistic pictures. They don't
talk back to you. . . .

JUD   I'm t'ard of all these *pitchers* of women!

PEDDLER   All right. You're tired of them. So throw 'em
away and buy some new ones. (*Showing him cards again*)
You get tired of a woman and what can you do? Nothing!
Just keep getting tireder and tireder!

JUD   I made up my mind.

PEDDLER   (*Packing his bag and starting off*)   So you want a
real woman. . . . Say, do you happen to know a girl named
Ado Annie?

JUD   I don't want her.

PEDDLER   I don't want her either. But I got her!
   (*Exit*)

JUD   Don't want nuthin' from no peddler. Want real things!
Whut am I doin' shet up here—like that feller says—
a-crawlin' and a-festerin'? Whut am I doin' in this lousy
smokehouse? (*He looks about the room, scowling. Then he
starts to sing, half talking at first, then singing in full voice*)
The floor creaks,
The door squeaks,
There's a fieldmouse a-nibblin' on a broom,
And I set by myself
Like a cobweb on a shelf,
By myself in a lonely room.

But when there's a moon in my winder
And it slants down a beam 'crost my bed,
Then the shadder of a tree starts a-dancin' on the wall
And a dream starts a-dancin' in my head.
And all the things that I wish fer
Turn out like I want them to be,
And I'm better'n that Smart Aleck cowhand
Who thinks he is better'n me!
And the girl that I want
Ain't afraid of my arms,
And her own soft arms keep me warm.
And her long, yeller hair

Falls acrost my face
Jist like the rain in a storm!

The floor creaks,
The door squeaks,
And the mouse starts a-nibblin' on the broom.
And the sun flicks my eyes—
It was all a pack o' lies!
I'm awake in a lonely room. . . .

I ain't gonna dream 'bout her arms no more!
I ain't gonna leave her alone!
Goin' outside,
Git myself a bride,
Git me a womern to call my own.

End of Scene II

ACT ONE | Scene Three

AT RISE: *A grove on* LAUREY'S *farm. Singing girls and* GERTIE *seated under tree. A girl,* VIVIAN, *is telling* GERTIE'S *fortune.*

VIVIAN   And to yer house a dark clubman!
   (*Laughter from girls.* LAUREY *enters*)

LAUREY   Girls, could you—could you go som'eres else and tell fortunes? I gotta be here by myself.

GERTIE   (*Pointing to bottle*) Look! She bought 'at ole smellin' salts the peddler tried to sell us!

LAUREY   It ain't smellin' salts. It's goin' to make up my mind fer me. Lookit me take a good whiff now!
   (*She chokes on it*)

GERTIE   That's the camphor.

LAUREY   Please, girls, go away.
  (GERTIE *laughs and exits.* LAUREY *closes her eyes tight*)

ELLEN   Hey, Laurey, is it true you're lettin' Jud take you tonight 'stid of Curly?

LAUREY   Tell you better when I think ever'thin' out clear. Beginnin' to see things clear a'ready.

KATE   I c'n tell you whut you want . . . (*Singing*)
Out of your dreams and into his arms you long to fly.

ELLEN
You don't need Egyptian smellin' salts to tell you why!

KATE
Out of your dreams and into the hush of falling shadows.

VIRGINIA
When the mist is low, and stars are breaking through,

VIVIAN
Then out of your dreams you'll go.

ALL THE GIRLS
Into a dream come true.
Make up your mind, make up your mind, Laurey, Laurey
   dear.
Make up your own, make up your own story, Laurey dear.
Ol' Pharaoh's daughter won't tell you what to do.
Ask your heart—whatever it tells you will be true.
  (*They drift off as* LAUREY *sings*)

LAUREY
Out of my dreams and into your arms I long to fly.
I will come as evening comes to woo a waiting sky.
Out of my dreams and into the hush of falling shadows,
When the mist is low, and stars are breaking through,
Then out of my dreams I'll go,
Into a dream with you.

BALLET
  (*The things* LAUREY *sees in her dream that help her "make up her mind."*)
  (*During the above refrain the lights dim to a spot on* LAUREY. CURLY *enters in another spot, walking slowly and standing perfectly still. Then his ballet counterpart enters and stands behind him.* LAUREY'S *ballet counterpart enters*

and stands behind her. These are figures fading into her dream. The real CURLY *and the real* LAUREY *back off slowly, and leave the stage to their counterparts who move toward the center and into an embrace. The downstage drop is lifted and they are in another scene, full stage.*

These dream figures of LAUREY *and* CURLY *dance ecstatically. A young girl enters, sees them and bounds off to break the news and soon others dance on and off gaily. Two of* CURLY'S *cowboy friends stroll by and wave their greeting. "Curly" kisses "Laurey" again and walks away, happy and smug.*

A little girl runs on, presents "Laurey" with a nosegay and then bursts into tears. More girl friends dance on and embrace her. A bridal veil floats down from the skies and they place it on her head. "Curly" and the boys enter, in the manner of cowboys astride their horses. Following a gay dance, the music slows to wedding-march tempo. "Curly," a serious expression on his face, awaits his bride who walks down an aisle formed by the girls.

Now the ballet counterpart of JUD *walks slowly forward and takes off "Laurey's" veil. Expecting to see her lover,* CURLY, *she looks up and finds "Jud." Horrified, she backs away. Her friends, with stony faces, look straight ahead of them. "Curly," too, is stern and austere and when she appeals to him, he backs away from her. All of them leave her. She is alone with "Jud."*

"Jud" starts to dance with her but he is soon diverted by the entrance of three dance-hall girls who look very much like the Police Gazette *pictures* LAUREY *has seen tacked on his walls in the smokehouse. Some of the cowboys follow the girls on, and whistle at them. But that is as far as they go. The cowboys are timid and inexpert in handling these sophisticated women. The women do an amusing, satirically bawdy dance. Then "Jud" and the boys dance with them. After the girls dance off, "Laurey" and "Jud" are again alone. "Curly" enters, and the long-awaited conflict with "Jud" is now unavoidable. "Curly," his hand holding an imaginary pistol, fires at "Jud" again and again, but "Jud" keeps slowly advancing on him, immune to bullets. He lifts "Curly" in the air and throws him to the ground. A fierce fight ensues. The friends of* LAUREY *and* CURLY *run helplessly from one side to the other. Just when the tables seem*

to have turned in "Curly's" favor, "Jud" gets a death grip on his throat. He is killing "Curly." "Laurey" runs up to him and begs him to release her lover. It is clear by her pantomime that she will give herself to JUD *to save* CURLY. *"Jud" drops "Curly's" limp body, picks up "Laurey" and carries her away. Over "Jud's" shoulder she blows a feeble, heartbroken kiss to "Curly's" prostrate form on the ground. The crowd surround him and carry him off in the dark as a spot comes up revealing the real* LAUREY *being shaken out of her dream by the real* JUD)

JUD   Wake up, Laurey. It's time to start fer the party.
(*As she awakens and starts mechanically to go with* JUD, *the real* CURLY *enters expectantly. She hesitates.* JUD *holds out his arm and scowls. Remembering the disaster of her recent dream, she avoids its reality by taking* JUD'S *arm and going with him, looking wistfully back at* CURLY *with the same sad eyes that her ballet counterpart had on her exit.* CURLY *stands alone, puzzled, dejected and defeated, as the curtain falls*)

ACT TWO | Scene One

SCENE: *The* SKIDMORE *ranch.*
    SKIDMORE'S *guests dancing a "set." Soon after the curtain rises, the melody settles into a "vamp" and* CARNES *holds up his hand as a signal that he wants to sing. The dancing couples retire and listen to him.*

CARNES
The farmer and the cowman should be friends,
Oh, the farmer and the cowman should be friends.
One man likes to push a plow,
The other likes to chase a cow,
But that's no reason why they cain't be friends.

Territory folks should stick together,
Territory folks should all be pals.
Cowboys, dance with the farmers' daughters!
Farmers, dance with the ranchers' gals!
   (*The chorus repeats this last quatrain*)
   (*They dance with gusto—sixteen measures—then the vamp
   is resumed and* CARNES *starts to sing again*)
I'd like to say a word fer the farmer.

AUNT ELLER (*Spoken*)   Well, say it.

CARNES
He come out west and made a lot of changes.

WILL (*Scornfully; singing*)
He come out west and built a lot of fences!

CURLY
And built 'em right acrost our cattle ranges!

CORD ELAM (*A cowman; spoken*)   Whyn't those dirtscratch-
ers stay in Missouri where they belong?

FARMER (*Spoken*)   We got as much right here—

CARNES (*Shouting*)   Gentlemen—shut up! (*Quiet restored,
he resumes singing*)
The farmer is a good and thrifty citizen.

FRED (*Spoken*)   He's thrifty, all right.

CARNES (*Glaring at* FRED, *he continues with song*)
No matter whut the cowman says or thinks,
You seldom see him drinkin' in a barroom—

CURLY   Unless somebody else is buyin' drinks!

CARNES (*Barging in quickly to save the party's respectability*)
The farmer and the cowman should be friends,
Oh, the farmer and the cowman should be friends.
The cowman ropes a cow with ease.
The farmer steals her butter and cheese,
But that's no reason why they cain't be friends!

ALL
Territory folks should stick together,
Territory folks should all be pals.
Cowboys, dance with the farmers' daughters!

Farmers, dance with the ranchers' gals!
  (*Dance, as before. Then back to vamp*)

AUNT ELLER (*Singing*)
I'd like to say a word fer the cowboy . . .

FARMER (*Anxious to get back at the cowmen; spoken*)   **Oh**,
you would!

AUNT ELLER
The road he treads is difficult and stony,
He rides fer days on end
With jist a pony fer a friend. . . .

ADO ANNIE
I shore am feelin' sorry fer the pony.

AUNT ELLER
The farmer should be sociable with the cowboy,
If he rides by and asks fer food and water.
Don't treat him like a louse,
Make him welcome in yer house . . .

CARNES
But be shore that you lock up yer wife and daughter!
  (*Laughs, jibes, protests*)

CORD ELAM (*Spoken from here on*)   Who wants a ole farm
womern anyway?

ADO ANNIE   Notice you married one, so's you c'd git a square
meal!

MAN (*To* CORD ELAM)   You cain't talk that-a-way 'bout our
womern folks!

WILL   He can say whut he wants.
  (WILL *hauls off on him and a free-for-all fight ensues, all
  the men mixing with one another, the women striving
  vainly to keep peace by singing "The farmer and the cowman should be friends!"*)
  (AUNT ELLER *grabs a gun from some man's holster and
  fires it. This freezes the picture. A still, startled crowd stops
  and looks to see who's been shot.* AUNT ELLER *strides forward, separating the fighters, pulling them away from one
  another, and none too gently*)

AUNT ELLER   They ain't nobody goin' to slug out anythin'—
this here's a party! (*Pointing the gun at* CARNES) Sing it,
Andrew! Dum tiddy um tum tum—

CARNES (*Frightened, obeys*)
The farmer and the cowman should be friends . . .
   (AUNT ELLER *points her gun at a group, and conducts
them. They join in quickly*)

RIGHT GROUP
Oh, the farmer and the cowman should be friends.
   (*She turns her gun on the left group and now they all
sing*)

ALL
One man likes to push a plow,
The other likes to chase a cow,
But that's no reason why they cain't be friends!
   (IKE *comes down and joins* AUNT ELLER *and* CARNES)

IKE
And when this territory is a state,
And jines the union jist like all the others,
The farmer and the cowman and the merchant
Must all behave theirsel's and act like brothers.

AUNT ELLER
I'd like to teach you all a little sayin'—
And learn these words by heart the way you should:
"I don't say I'm no better than anybody else,
But I'll be damned if I ain't jist as good!"
   (*They cheer the sentiment, and repeat lustily:*)

ALL
I don't say I'm no better than anybody else,
But I'll be damned if I ain't jist as good!
Territory folks should stick together,
Territory folks should all be pals.
Cowboys, dance with the farmers' daughters!
Farmers, dance with the ranchers' gals!
   (*Now they go into a gay, unrestrained dance*)

IKE (*After number is over*)   C'mon, everybody! Time to
start the Box Social.

CORD ELAM   I'm so hungry I c'd eat a gatepost

DOROTHY Who's goin' to be the auctioneer?

TOM Aunt Eller!
(Shouts of approval from the entire crowd)

AUNT ELLER *(Playing coy)* Let one of the men be the auctioneer.

CROWD "No, Aunt Eller, yore the best." "Ain't any ole men auctioneers as good as you."

AUNT ELLER All right then. Now you know the rules, gentlemen. Y'got to bid blind. Y'ain't s'posed to know whut girl goes with whut hamper. Of course, if yer sweetheart has told you that hers'll be done up in a certain kind of way with a certain color ribbon, that ain't my fault. Now we'll auction all the hampers on t'other side of the house and work around back here. Follow me.
(AUNT ELLER starts off, followed by the crowd. As the crowd exits, the PEDDLER strolls on, meeting WILL ambling along with his bag)

PEDDLER Hello, young fellow.

WILL Oh, it's you!

PEDDLER I was just hoping to meet up with you. It seems like you and me ought to have a little talk.

WILL We only got one thing to talk about. Well, Mr. Hakim, I hear you got yerself engaged to Ado Annie.

PEDDLER Well . . .

WILL Well, nothin'. I don't know what to call you. You ain't purty enough fer a skunk. You ain't skinny enough fer a snake. You're too little to be a man, and too big to be a mouse. I reckon you're a rat.

PEDDLER That's logical.

WILL Answer me one question. Do you really love her?

PEDDLER Well . . .

WILL 'Cuz if I thought you didn't I'd tie you up in this bag and drop you in the river. Are you serious about her?

PEDDLER Yes, I'm serious.

WILL   And do you worship the ground she walks on, like I do? You better say yes!

PEDDLER   Yes—yes—yes.

WILL   The hell you do!

PEDDLER   Yes.

WILL   Would you spend every cent you had fer her? That's whut I did. See that bag? Full of presents. Cost fifty bucks. All I had in the world.

PEDDLER   If you had that fifty dollars cash . . .

WILL   I'd have Ado Annie, and you'd lose her.

PEDDLER   (*Thoughtfully*) Yes. I'd lose her. Let's see what you got in here. Might want to buy something.

WILL   What would you want with them?

PEDDLER   I'm a peddler, ain't I? I buy and sell. Maybe pay you real money. . . . (*Significantly*) Maybe as much as— well, a lot. (WILL *becomes thoughtful. The* PEDDLER *fishes in bag and pulls out an item*) Ah, what a beautiful hot-water bag. It looks French. Must have cost plenty. I'll give you eight dollars for it.

WILL   Eight dollars? That wouldn't be honest. I only paid three-fifty.

PEDDLER   All right. I said I'd give you eight and I will. . . . (*The* PEDDLER *pulls a nightgown out of the bag. It is made of white lawn and is notable for a profusion of ribbons and bows on the neckline*) Say! That's a cracker-jake!

WILL   Take your hands off that! (*Grabbing it and holding it in front of him*) That wuz fer our weddin' night!

PEDDLER   It don't fit you so good. I'll pay you twenty-two dollars.

WILL   But that's—

PEDDLER   All right then—twenty-two-fifty! (*Stuffing it into his coat with the hot-water bag*) Not a cent more.
    (WILL *smiles craftily and starts to count on his fingers. The* PEDDLER *now pulls out a pair of corsets*)

WILL   Them—those—that was fer her to wear.

PEDDLER I didn't hardly think they was for you. (*Looking at them*) Mighty dainty. (*Putting them aside*) Fifteen dollars. Le's see, eight and twenty-two makes thirty and fifteen is forty-five and fifty cents is forty-five-fifty.
(*He looks craftily at* WILL *out of the corner of his eye and watches the idea percolate through* WILL'S *thick head*)

WILL Forty-five-fifty? Say, that's almos'—that's . . . (*Turning anxiously*) Want to buy some more?

PEDDLER Might.

WILL (*Taking "The Little Wonder" out of his pocket*) D'you ever see one of these?

PEDDLER (*Frightened*) What made you buy this? Got it *in* for somebody?

WILL How d'you mean? It's jist funny pitchers.

PEDDLER (*Examining it carefully*) That all you think it is? Well, it's more'n that! It's . . .
(*He breaks off as* LAUREY *runs on, a frightened look on her face*)

LAUREY Whur is ev'ybody? Whur's Aunt Eller?

WILL On t'other side of the house, Laurey.

JUD (*Off stage*) Laurey! Whur'd you run to?
(LAUREY *runs off, around the end of the house, putting hamper on porch*)

WILL How much'll you give me fer that thing?

PEDDLER I don't like to handle things like this. I guess you don't know what it really is.

WILL Shore do. It's jist a girl in pink tights.

JUD (*Entering, carrying* LAUREY'S *basket*) Either of you two see Laurey?

WILL Jist went to th' other side of the house. Auction's goin' on there.
(JUD *grunts and starts upstage*)

PEDDLER (*Calling to him*) Hey, Jud! Here's one of them things you was looking for. "The Little Wonder."
(JUD *comes back and examines it*)

JUD (*To* WILL)   How much?

WILL (*Closing his eyes to struggle with a mathematical problem*)   Three dollars and fifty cents.

JUD (*Digging in his pocket*)   Lotta money but I got an idy it might be worth it.
  (JUD *goes upstage to look it over, then exits*)

WILL   Let's see, three-fifty from him and forty-five-fifty from you. 'At makes fifty dollars, don't it?

PEDDLER   No. One dollar short.

WILL   Darn it. I musta figgered wrong. (*Impulsively*) How much fer all the resta the stuff in this bag?

PEDDLER (*Having the cash all ready*)   One dollar!

WILL   Done! Now I got fifty dollars, ain't I? Know whut that means? Means I'm goin' to take Ado Annie back from you!

PEDDLER   You wouldn't do a thing like that to me!

WILL   Oh, wouldn't I? And when I tell her paw who I got mosta the money offa, mebbe he'll change his mind 'bout who's smart and who's dumb!

PEDDLER   Say, young feller, you certainly bunkoed me!
  (*Off right, there is a hum of voices and the crowd starts to drift on.* AUNT ELLER *enters, followed by the balance of the party.* JUD *eyes* LAUREY *throughout the ensuing dialogue.* CURLY *stands apart and pays little attention to anybody or anything*)

AUNT ELLER   Now, here's the last two hampers. Whose they are I ain't got no idy!

ADO ANNIE (*In a loud voice*)   The little un's mine! And the one next to it is Laurey's!
  (*General laughter*)

AUNT ELLER   Well, that's the end of *that* secret. Now whut am I bid then fer Ado Annie's hamper?

SLIM   Two bits.

CORD ELAM   Four.

AUNT ELLER   Who says six? You, Slim? (SLIM *shakes his head*) Ain't nobody hungry no more?—Whut about you, Peddler-man? Six bits?
(*Pause*)

PEDDLER   Naw!
(CARNES *takes a gun from his pocket and prods the* PEDDLER *in the back*)

CARNES   Come on.

PEDDLER   Six bits!

AUNT ELLER   Six bits ain't enough fer a lunch like Ado Annie c'n make. Le's hear a dollar. How about you, Mike? You won her last year.

MIKE   Yeah. That's right. Hey, Ado Annie, y'got that same sweet-pertater pie like last year?

ADO ANNIE   You bet.

AUNT ELLER   Same old sweet-pertater pie, Mike. Whut d'you say?

MIKE   I say it give me a three-day bellyache!

AUNT ELLER   Never mind about that. Who bids a dollar?

CARNES (*Whispering to* PEDDLER)   Bid!

PEDDLER (*Whispering back*)   Mine's the last bid. I got her fer six bits.

CARNES   Bid a dollar.
(*The* PEDDLER *looks doubtful.* CARNES *prods him with his gun*)

PEDDLER   Ninety cents.

AUNT ELLER   Ninety cents, we're gittin' rich. 'Nother desk fer th' schoolhouse. Do I hear more?

WILL (*Dramatically, his chin thrust forward*)   You hear fifty dollars!

PEDDLER (*Immediately alarmed*)   Hey!

AUNT ELLER   Fifty dollars! Nobody ever bid fifty dollars for a lunch! Nobody ever bid ten.

CARNES He ain't got fifty dollars.

WILL Oh, yes, I have. (*Producing the money*) And 'f yer a man of honor y'gotta say Ado Annie b'longs to me, like y'said she would!

CARNES But where's yer money?

WILL (*Shoving out his hand*) Right here in my hand.

CARNES 'At ain't yours! Y'jist bid it, didn't you? Jist give it to th' schoolhouse. (*To* PEDDLER, *chuckling. Back to* WILL) Got to say the Peddler still gits my daughter's hand.

WILL Now wait a minute. That ain't fair!

AUNT ELLER Goin' fer fifty dollars! Goin' . . .

PEDDLER (*Gulping*) Fifty-one dollars!
  (*A sensation, all turn to* PEDDLER)

CARNES You crazy?

WILL (*Mechanically*) Fif— (*Prompted by frantic signs from the* PEDDLER, *he stops and suddenly realizes the significance of the* PEDDLER'S *bid*) Wait a minute. Wait! 'F I don't bid any more I c'n keep my money, cain't I?

AUNT ELLER (*Grinning*) Shore can.

WILL Nen I still got fifty dollars. (*Waving it in front of* CARNES) This is mine!

CARNES (*To* PEDDLER) You feeble-minded shike-poke!

AUNT ELLER Goin', goin', gone fer fifty-one dollars and 'at means Ado Annie'll git the prize, I guess.

WILL And I git Ado Annie!

CARNES (*To* PEDDLER) And whut're you gittin' fer yer fifty-one dollars?

PEDDLER (*Shrugging his shoulders*) A three-day bellyache!
  (PEDDLER *and* ADO ANNIE *pick up her basket and leave* AUNT ELLER)

AUNT ELLER Now here's my niece's hamper. (*General murmur of excitement runs through the crowd*) I took a peek inside a while ago and I must say it looks mighty tasty. Whut do I hear, gents?

SLIM Two bits!

FRED Four bits!

AUNT ELLER Whut d'you say, Slim? Six?
  (SLIM *shakes his head*)

CARNES I bid one dollar.

AUNT ELLER More like it! Do I hear two?

JUD A dollar and a quarter.
  (LAUREY *gets a start from his voice*)

CORD ELAM Two dollars.

JOE Two-fifty.

CARNES Three dollars!

JUD And two bits.

CORD ELAM Three dollars and four bits!

JOE Four dollars.

JUD (*Doggedly*) And two bits.
  (LAUREY *looks straight ahead of her, grimly.* AUNT ELLER
  catches this look and a deep worry comes into her eyes)

AUNT ELLER Four dollars and a quarter. (*Looking at* CURLY,
an appeal in her voice) Ain't I goin' to hear any more?
(CURLY *turns and walks off, cool and deliberate*) (LAUREY
bites her lip. AUNT ELLER'S *voice has panic in it*) I got a bid
of four and a quarter—from Jud Fry. You goin' to let him
have it?

CARNES Four and a half.

AUNT ELLER (*Shouting, as if she were cheering*) Four and
a half! Goin' fer four and a half! Goin' . . .

JUD Four-seventy-five.

AUNT ELLER (*Deflated*) Four-seventy-five, come on, gentlemen. Schoolhouse ain't built yet. Got to git a nice chimbley.

CORD ELAM Five dollars.

AUNT ELLER Goin' fer five dollars! Goin' . . .

JUD And two bits.

CORD ELAM Too rich for my blood! Cain't afford no more.

AUNT ELLER (*Worried*)   Five and a quarter! Ain't got nearly enough yet. (*Looking at* CARNES) Not fer cold duck with stuffin' and that lemon-meringue pie.

CARNES   Six dollars.

AUNT ELLER   Six dollars! Goin' . . .

JUD   And two bits.

AUNT ELLER   My, you're stubborn, Jud. Mr. Carnes is a richer man'n you. (*Looking at* CARNES) And I know he likes custard with raspberry syrup. (*Pause. No one bids*) Anybody goin' to bid any more?

JUD   No. They all dropped out. Cain't you see?

FRED   You got enough, Aunt Eller.

CARNES   Let's git on.

JUD   Here's the money.

AUNT ELLER (*Looking off*)   Hold on, you! I ain't said "Goin', goin', gone" yet!

JUD   Well, say it!

AUNT ELLER (*Speaking slowly*)   Goin' to Jud fer six dollars and two bits! Goin' . . .
   (CURLY *enters, a saddle over his arm*)

CURLY   Who'd you say was gittin' Laurey?

AUNT ELLER   Jud Fry.

CURLY   And fer how much?

AUNT ELLER   Six and a quarter.

CURLY   I don't figger 'at's quite enough, do you?

JUD   It's more'n *you* got.

CURLY   Got a saddle here cost me thirty dollars.

JUD   Yo' cain't bid saddles. Got to be cash.

CURLY (*Looking around*)   Thirty-dollar saddle must be worth sumpin to somebody.

TOM   I'll give you ten.

SKIDMORE (*To* CURLY)   Don't be a fool, boy. Y'cain't earn a livin' 'thout a saddle.

CURLY (*To* TOM)   Got cash?

TOM   Right in my pocket.
  (CURLY *gives him the saddle*)

CURLY (*Turning to* JUD)   Don't let's waste time. How high you goin'?

JUD   Higher'n you—no matter whut!

CURLY (*To* AUNT ELLER)   Aunt Eller, I'm biddin' all of this ten dollars Tom jist give me.

AUNT ELLER   Ten dollars—goin' . . .
  (*Pause. General murmur of excited comments.* LAUREY'S *eyes are shining now and her shoulders are straighter*)

JUD (*Determinedly*)   Ten dollars *and* two bits.

AUNT ELLER   Curly . . .
  (*Pause.* CURLY *turns to a group of men*)

CURLY   Most of you boys know my horse, Dun. She's a— (*He swallows hard*)—a kinda nice horse—gentle and well broke.

LAUREY   Don't sell Dun, Curly, it ain't worth it.

CORD ELAM   I'll give you twenty-five fer her!

CURLY (*To* CORD ELAM)   I'll sell Dun to you. (*To* AUNT ELLER) That makes the bid thirty-five, Aunt Eller.

AUNT ELLER (*Tickled to death*)   Curly, yer crazy! But it's all fer the schoolhouse, ain't it? All fer educatin' and larnin'. Goin' fer thirty-five. Goin'—

JUD   Hold on! I ain't finished biddin'! (*He grins fiercely at* CURLY) You jist put up everythin' y'got in the world, didn't yer? Cain't bid the clothes off yer back, cuz they ain't worth nuthin'. Cain't bid yer gun cuz you need that. (*Slowly*) Yes, sir. You need that bad. (*Looking at* AUNT ELLER) So, Aunt Eller, I'm jist as reckless as Curly McLain, I guess. Jist as good at gittin' whut I want. Goin' to bid all I got in the world —all I saved fer two years, doin' farm work. All fer Laurey. Here it is! Forty-two dollars and thirty-one cents.

(*He pours the money out of his pocket onto* LAUREY'S *hamper.* CURLY *takes out his gun. The crowd gasps.* JUD *backs away*)

CURLY   Anybody want to buy a gun? You, Joe? Bought it brand new last Thanksgivin'. Worth a lot.

LAUREY   Curly, please don't sell your gun.
   (CURLY *looks at* JOE)

JOE   Give you eighteen dollars fer it.

CURLY   Sold. (*They settle the deal.* CURLY *turns to* AUNT ELLER) That makes my bid fifty-three dollars, Aunt Eller. Anybody going any higher?

AUNT ELLER (*Very quickly*)   Goin'—goin'—gone! Whut's the matter with you folks? Ain't nobody gonna cheer er nuthin'?
   (*Uncertainly they start to sing "The Farmer and the Cow-man."* CURLY *and* LAUREY *carry their basket away.* JUD *moves slowly toward* CURLY. CURLY *sets the basket down and faces him. The singing stops*)

SKIDMORE (*In his deep, booming voice*)   That's the idy! The cowman and the farmer shud be friends. (*His hand on* JUD'S *shoulder*) You lost the bid, but the biddin' was fair. (*To* CURLY) C'mon, cowman—shake the farmer's hand!
   (CURLY *doesn't move a muscle*)

JUD   Shore, I'll shake hands. No hard feelin's, Curly.
   (*He goes to* CURLY, *his hand outstretched. After a pause,* CURLY *takes his hand, but never lets his eyes leave* JUD'S)

SKIDMORE   That's better.
   (*The* PEDDLER *has come downstage and is watching* JUD *narrowly*)

JUD (*With a badly assumed manner of camaraderie*)   Say, Curly, I want to show you sumpin. (*He grins*) 'Scuse us, Laurey. (*Taking* CURLY'S *arm, he leads him aside*) Ever see one of these things?
   (*He takes out "The Little Wonder." The* PEDDLER *is in a panic*)

CURLY   Jist whut *is* that?
   (*The* PEDDLER *rushes to* AUNT ELLER *and starts to whisper in her ear*)

JUD   Something special. You jist put this up to yer eye like this, see?
(CURLY *is about to look when* AUNT ELLER'S *voice rings out, sharp and shrill*)

AUNT ELLER   Curly! Curly, whut you doin'?
(CURLY *turns quickly. So does* JUD, *giving an involuntary grunt of disappointment*)

CURLY   Doin'? Nuthin' much. Whut you want to squeal at a man like 'at fer? Skeer the liver and lights out of a feller.

AUNT ELLER   Well then, stop lookin' at those ole French pitchers and ast me fer a dance. You brung me to the party, didn't you?

CURLY   All right then, you silly ole woman, I'll dance 'th you. Dance you all over the meadow, you want!

AUNT ELLER   Pick 'at banjo to pieces, Sam!
(*And the dance is on. Everyone is dancing now.* WILL *takes* ADO ANNIE *by the waist and swings her around.* JUD *finally snaps the blade of "The Little Wonder" back, slips it into his pocket, then goes up to* LAUREY, *who has started to dance with the* PEDDLER. *He pushes the* PEDDLER *away and dances* LAUREY *off.* WILL *and* ADO ANNIE *dance off. The curtains close. Immediately,* WILL *and* ADO ANNIE *dance on to center stage. He stops dancing. They're alone in a secluded spot now, and he wants to "settle things."*)

WILL   Well, Ado Annie, I got the fifty dollars cash, now you name the day.

ADO ANNIE   August fifteenth.

WILL   Why August fifteenth?

ADO ANNIE   (*Tenderly*)   That was the first day I was kissed.

WILL   (*His face lighting up*)   Was it? I didn't remember that.

ADO ANNIE   You wasn't there.

WILL   Now looka here, we gotta have a serious talk. Now that you're engaged to me, you gotta stop havin' fun! . . . I mean with other fellers. (*Sings*)
You'll have to be a little more stand-offish
When fellers offer you a buggy ride.

ADO ANNIE
I'll give a imitation of a crawfish
And dig myself a hole where I c'n hide.

WILL
I heared how you was kickin' up some capers
When I was off in Kansas City, Mo.
   (*More sternly*)
I heared some things you couldn't print in papers
From fellers who been talkin' like they know!

ADO ANNIE
Foot!
I only did the kind of things I orta—sorta
To you I was as faithful as c'n be—fer me.
Them stories 'bout the way I lost my bloomers—Rumors!
A lot o' tempest in a pot o' tea!

WILL   The whole thing don't sound very good to me—

ADO ANNIE   Well, y'see—

WILL (*Breaking in and spurting out his pent-up resentment at a great injustice*)
I go and sow my last wild oat!
I cut out all shenanigans!
I save my money—don't gamble er drink
In the back room down at Flannigan's!
I give up lotsa other things
A gentleman never mentions—
But before I give up any more,
I wanta know your intentions!

With me it's all er nuthin'!
Is it all er nuthin' with you?
It cain't be "in between"
It cain't be "now and then"
No half-and-half romance will do!
I'm a one-woman man,
Home-lovin' type,
All complete with slippers and pipe.
Take me like I am er leave me be!
If you cain't give me all, give me nuthin'—
And nuthin's whut you'll git from me!
   (*He struts away from her*)

ADO ANNIE   Not even sumpin?

WILL

Nuthin's whut you'll git from me!
  (*Second refrain. He starts to walk away, nonchalantly. She
  follows him*)

ADO ANNIE

It cain't be "in between"?

WILL

Uh-uh.

ADO ANNIE

It cain't be "now and then"?

WILL

No half-and-half romance will do!

ADO ANNIE

Would you build me a house,
All painted white,
Cute and clean and purty and bright?

WILL   Big enough fer two but not fer three!

ADO ANNIE   Supposin' 'at we should have a third one?

WILL (*Barking at her*)   He better look a lot like me!

ADO ANNIE (*Skeered*)   The spit an' image!

WILL   He better look a lot like me!
  (*Two girls come on and do a dance with* WILL *in which
  they lure him away from* ADO ANNIE. ADO ANNIE, *trying to
  get him back, does an oriental dance.* WILL, *accusing her,
  says: "That's Persian!" and returns to the girls. But* ADO
  ANNIE *yanks him back. The girls dance off.* ADO ANNIE
  sings)

ADO ANNIE

With you it's all er nuthin'—
All fer you and nuthin' fer me!
But if a wife is wise
She's gotta realize
That men like you are wild and free.
  (WILL *looks pleased*)
So I ain't gonna fuss,
Ain't gonna frown,
Have your fun, go out on the town,
Stay up late and don't come home till three,

And go right off to sleep if you're sleepy—
There's no use waitin' up fer me!

WILL   Oh, Ado Annie!

ADO ANNIE   There's no use waitin' up fer me!

WILL   Come on and kiss me!
(ADO ANNIE *comes dancing back to* WILL. *They kiss and dance off*)

Blackout

ACT TWO | Scene Two

SCENE: *The kitchen porch of* SKIDMORE'S *ranch house. There are a few benches on the porch and a large coal stove. The music for the dance can still be heard off stage. Immediately after the curtain rises,* JUD *dances on with* LAUREY, *then stops and holds her. She pulls away from him.*

LAUREY   Why we stoppin'? Thought you wanted to dance?

JUD   Want to talk to you. Whut made you slap that whip onto Old Eighty, and nearly make her run away? Whut was yer hurry?

LAUREY   'Fraid we'd be late fer the party.

JUD   You didn't want to be with me by yerself—not a minnit more'n you had to.

LAUREY   Why, I don't know whut you're talking about! I'm with you by myself now, ain't I?

JUD   You wouldn'ta been, you coulda got out of it. Mornin's you stay hid in yer room all the time. Nights you set in the front room, and won't git outa Aunt Eller's sight. . . . Last time I see you alone it was winter 'th the snow six inches deep in drifts when I was sick. You brung me that hot soup out to the smokehouse and give it to me, and me in bed. I hadn't shaved in two days. You ast me 'f I had any fever and you put your hand on my head to see.

LAUREY (*Puzzled and frightened*) I remember . . .

JUD Do you? Bet you don't remember as much as me. I remember eve'ything you ever done—every word you ever said. Cain't think of nuthin' else, . . . See? . . . See how it is? (*He attempts to hold her. She pushes him away*) I ain't good enough, am I? I'm a h'ard hand, got dirt on my hands, pigslop. Ain't fitten to tetch you. You're better, so much better. Yeah, we'll see who's better—Miss Laurey. Nen you'll wisht you wasn't so free 'th yer airs, you're sich a fine lady. . . .

LAUREY (*Suddenly angry and losing her fear*) Air you making threats to me? Air you standing there tryin' to tell me 'f I don't 'low you to slobber over me like a hog, why, you're gonna do sumpin 'bout it? Why, you're nothin' but a mangy dog and somebody orta shoot you. You think so much about being a h'ard hand. Well, I'll jist tell you sumpin that'll rest yer brain, Mr. Jud. You ain't a h'ard hand fer me no more. You c'n jist pack up yer duds and scoot. Oh, and I even got better idys'n that. You ain't to come on the place again, you hear me? I'll send yer stuff any place you say, but don't you's much 's set foot inside the pasture gate or I'll sic the dogs onto you!

JUD (*Standing quite still, absorbed, dark, his voice low*) Said yer say! Brought it on yerself. (*In a voice harsh with an inner frenzy*) Cain't he'p it. Cain't never rest. Told you the way it was. You wouldn't listen—
(*He goes out, passes the corner of the house and disappears.* LAUREY *stands a moment, held by his strangeness, then she starts toward the house, changes her mind and sinks onto a bench, a frightened little girl again*)

LAUREY (*There is a noise off stage.* LAUREY *turns, startled*) Who's 'at?

WILL (*Entering*) It's me, Laurey. Hey, have you seen Ado Annie? She's gone agin.
(LAUREY *shakes her head*)

LAUREY (*Calling to him as he starts away*) Will! . . . Will, could you do sumpin fer me? Go and find Curly and tell him I'm here. (CURLY *enters*) I wanta see Curly awful bad. Got to see him.

CURLY Then whyn't you turn around and look, you crazy womern?

LAUREY (*With great relief*) Curly!

WILL Well, you found yours. Now I gotta look fer mine. (*He exits*)

CURLY Now whut on earth is ailin' the belle of Claremore? By gum, if you ain't cryin'!
(LAUREY *leans against him*)

LAUREY Curly—I'm afraid, 'fraid of my life!

CURLY (*In a flurry of surprise and delight*) Jumpin' toad-stools! (*He puts his arms around* LAUREY, *muttering under his breath*) Great Lord!

LAUREY Don't you leave me. . . .

CURLY Great Godamighty!

LAUREY Don't mind me a-cryin,' I cain't he'p it. . . .

CURLY Cry yer eyes out!

LAUREY Oh, I don't know whut to do!

CURLY Here. I'll show you. (*He lifts her face and kisses her. She puts her arms about his neck*) My goodness! (*He shakes his head as if coming out of a daze, gives a low whistle, and backs away*) Whew! 'Bout all a man c'n stand in public! Go 'way from me, *you!*

LAUREY Oh, you don't like me, Curly—

CURLY Like you? My God! Git away from me, I tell you, plumb away from me!
(*He backs away and sits on the stove*)

LAUREY Curly! You're settin' on the stove!

CURLY (*Leaping up*) Godamighty! (*He turns around, puts his hand down gingerly on the lid*) Aw! 'S cold's a hunk of ice!

LAUREY Wisht it ud burnt a hole in yer pants.

CURLY (*Grinning at her, understandingly*) You do, do you?

LAUREY (*Turning away to hide her smile*) *You* heared me.

CURLY Laurey, now looky here, you stand over there right whur you air, and I'll set over here—and you tell me whut you wanted with me.

LAUREY (*Grave again*) Well—Jud was here. (*She shudders*) He skeered me . . . he's crazy. I never saw nobody like him. He talked wild and he threatened me. So I—I f'ard him! I wisht I hadn'ta! They ain't no tellin' whut he'll do now!

CURLY You f'ard him? Well then! That's all they is to it! Tomorrow, I'll get you a new h'ard hand. I'll stay on the place myself tonight, 'f you're nervous about that hound-dog. Now quit yer worryin' about it, er I'll spank you. (*His manner changes. He becomes shy. He turns away unable to meet her eyes as he asks the question*) Hey, while I think of it— how—how 'bout marryin' me?
  (LAUREY, *confused, turns too. They are back to back*)

LAUREY Gracious, whut'd I wanta marry you fer?

CURLY Well, couldn't you mebbe think of some reason why you might?

LAUREY I cain't think of none right now, hardly.

CURLY (*Following her*) Laurey, please, ma'am—marry me. I—don't know whut I'm gonna do if you—if you don't.

LAUREY (*Touched*) Curly—why, I'll marry you—'f you want me to. . . .
  (*They kiss*)

CURLY I'll be the happiest man alive soon as we're married. Oh, I got to learn to be a farmer, I see that! Quit a-thinkin' about th'owin' the rope, and start in to git my hands blistered a new way! Oh, things is changin' right and left! Buy up mowin' machines, cut down the prairies! Shoe yer horses, drag them plows under the sod! They gonna make a state outa this, they gonna put it in the Union! Country a-changin', got to change with it! Bring up a pair of boys, new stock, to keep up 'th the way things is goin' in this here crazy country! Now I got you to he'p me—I'll 'mount to sumpin yit! Oh, I 'member the first time I ever seen you. It was at the fair. You was a-ridin' that gray filly of Blue Starr's, and I says to someone—"Who's that skinny little thing with a bang down on her forehead?"

LAUREY   Yeow, I 'member. You was riding broncs that day.

CURLY   That's right.

LAUREY   And one of 'em th'owed you.

CURLY   That's— Did not th'ow me!

LAUREY   Guess you jumped off, then.

CURLY   Shore I jumped off.

LAUREY   Yeow, you shore did.
  (*He kisses her*)

CURLY (*Shouting over music*)   Hey! 'F there's anybody out around this yard 'at c'n hear my voice, I'd like fer you to know that Laurey Williams is my girl.

LAUREY   Curly!

CURLY   And she's went and got me to ast her to marry me!

LAUREY   They'll hear you all the way to Catoosie!

CURLY   Let 'em! (*Singing*) Let people say we're in love! (*Making a gesture with his arm*) Who keers whut happens now!

LAUREY (*Reaching out, grabbing his hand and putting it back in hers*)
Jist keep your hand in mine.
Your hand feels so grand in mine—

BOTH
Let people say we're in love!
Starlight looks well on us,
Let the stars beam from above,
Who cares if they tell on us?
Let people say we're in love!
  (*The curtains close. In front of curtain, the* PEDDLER *walks on, with* ADO ANNIE)

PEDDLER   I'll say good-bye here, Baby.

ADO ANNIE   Cain't y'even stay to drink to Curly and Laurey?

PEDDLER (*Shaking his head*)   Time for the lonely gypsy to go back to the open road.

ADO ANNIE   Wisht I was goin'—nen you wouldn't be so lonely.

PEDDLER   Look, Ado Annie, there is a man I know who loves you like nothing ever loved nobody.

ADO ANNIE   Yes, Ali Hakim.

PEDDLER   A man who will stick to you all your life and be a regular Darby and Jones. And that's the man for you—Will Parker.

ADO ANNIE   (*Recovering from surprise*)   Oh . . . yeh . . . well, I like Will a lot.

PEDDLER   He is a fine fellow. Strong like an ox. Young and handsome.

ADO ANNIE   I love him, all right, I guess.

PEDDLER   Of course you do! And you love those clear blue eyes of his, and the way his mouth wrinkles up when he smiles—

ADO ANNIE   Do you love him too?

PEDDLER   I love him because he will make my Ado Annie happy. (*Taking her in his arms*) Good-bye, my baby. I will show you how we say good-bye in Persia.
    (*He draws her tenderly to him and plants a long kiss on her lips*)

ADO ANNIE   (*Wistfully as he releases her*)   That was good-bye?

PEDDLER   (*His arms still around her*)   We have an old song in Persia. It says: (*Singing*) One good-bye—(*Speaking*)—is never enough. (*He kisses her again.* WILL *enters and stands still and stunned. He slowly awakes to action and starts moving toward them, but then the* PEDDLER *starts to talk and* WILL *stops again, surprised even more by what he hears than by what he saw*) I am glad you will marry such a wonderful man as this Will Parker. You deserve a fine man and you got one.
    (WILL *is almost ashamed of his resentment*)

ADO ANNIE   (*Seeing* WILL *for the first time*)   Hello, Will. Ali Hakim is sayin' good-bye.

PEDDLER   Ah, Will! I want to say good-bye to you, too.
   (*Starting to embrace him*)

WILL   No, you don't. I just saw the last one.

PEDDLER (*Patting* WILL *on the cheek*)   Ah, you were made
for each other! (*He pulls* ADO ANNIE *close to him with one
arm, and puts the other hand affectionately on* WILL'S *shoulder*) Be good to her, Will. (*Giving* ADO ANNIE *a squeeze*)
And you be good to him! (*Smiling disarmingly at* WILL) You
don't mind? I am a friend of the family now?
   (*He gives* ADO ANNIE *a little kiss*)

WILL   Did you say you was goin'?

PEDDLER   Yes. I must. Back to the open road. A poor gypsy.
Good-bye, my baby—(*Smiling back at* WILL *before he kisses*
ADO ANNIE, *pointing to himself*) Friend of the family. I show
you how we say good-bye in my country. (ADO ANNIE *gets set
for that old Persian good-bye again. The* PEDDLER *finally
releases her and turns back to* WILL) Persian good-bye. Lucky
fellow! I wish it was me she was marrying instead of you.

WILL   It don't seem to make no difference hardly.

PEDDLER   Well, back to the open road, the lonely gypsy.
   (*He sings a snatch of the Persian song as he exits*)

WILL   You ain't goin' to think of that ole peddler any more,
air you?

ADO ANNIE   'Course not. Never think of no one less'n he's
with me.

WILL   Then I'm never goin' to leave yer side.

ADO ANNIE   Even if you don't, even if you never go away on
a trip er nuthin', cain't you—onct in a while—give me one of
them Persian good-byes?

WILL   Persian good-bye? Why, that ain't nuthin' compared to
a Oklahoma hello!
   (*He wraps her up in his arms and gives her a long kiss.
When he lets her go, she looks up, supreme contentment
in her voice*)

ADO ANNIE   Hello, Will!
                                    Blackout

ACT TWO | Scene Three

SCENE: *Back of* LAUREY'S *house. Shouts, cheers and laughter are heard behind the curtain, continuing as it rises.*
  CARNES *and* IKE *walk down toward house.* CARNES *carries a lantern.*

IKE   Well, Andrew, why ain't you back of the barn gettin' drunk with us? Never see you stay so sober at a weddin' party.

CARNES   Been skeered all night. Skeered 'at Jud Fry ud come up and start for Curly.

IKE   Why, Jud Fry's been out of the territory for three weeks.

CARNES   He's back. See him at Claremore last night, drunk as a lord!
  (*Crowd starts to pour in.* IKE *and* CARNES, *continuing their conversation, are drowned out by the shouts and laughter of the crowd as they fill the stage.* LAUREY *wears her moth-er's wedding dress. The following lines are sung*)

AUNT ELLER
They couldn't pick a better time to start in life!

IKE
It ain't too early and it ain't too late.

CURLY
Startin' as a farmer with a brand-new wife—

LAUREY
Soon be livin' in a brand-new state!

ALL
Brand-new state

Gonna treat you great!

FRED
Gonna give you barley,
Carrots and pertaters—

CORD ELAM
Pasture for the cattle—

CARNES
Spinach and termayters!

AUNT ELLER
Flowers on the prairie where the June bugs zoom—

IKE
Plen'y of air and plen'y of room—

FRED
Plen'y of room to swing a rope!

AUNT ELLER
Plen'y of heart and plen'y of hope. . . .

CURLY
Oklahoma,
Where the wind comes sweepin' down the plain,
And the wavin' wheat
Can sure smell sweet
When the wind comes right behind the rain.
Oklahoma,
Every night my honey lamb and I
Sit alone and talk
And watch a hawk
Makin' lazy circles in the sky.
We know we belong to the land,
And the land we belong to is grand!
And when we say:
Ee-ee-ow! A-yip-i-o-ee-ay!
We're only sayin',
"You're doin' fine, Oklahoma!
Oklahoma, O.K.!"

> (*The full company now joins in a refrain immediately following this one, singing with infectious enthusiasm. A special and stirring vocal arrangement*)

CURLY (*After number*)   Hey! Y'better hurry into that other dress! Gotta git goin' in a minnit!

AUNT ELLER   You hurry and pack yer own duds! They're layin' all over my room.

CURLY   Hey, Will! Would you hitch the team to the surrey fer me?

WILL   Shore will! Have it up in a jiffy!
(WILL *runs off.* CURLY *exits into house.* CORD ELAM *runs over to door. The manner of the group of men that surrounds the door becomes mysterious. Their voices are low and their talk is punctuated with winks and nudges*)

IKE (*To* CORD ELAM)   He's gone upstairs.

CORD ELAM   Yeah.
(*The girls cross to men, but are shooed away. The men whisper and slip quietly off, except for* CARNES)

ADO ANNIE   Whut you goin' to do, Paw? Give Laurey and Curly a shivoree? I wisht you wouldn't.

CARNES   Aw, it's a good old custom. Never hurt anybody. You women jist keep outa the way. Vamoose!

ADO ANNIE   It ain't goin' to be rough, is it?

CARNES   Sh! Stop gabbin' about it!
(CARNES *exits, leaving only women on the stage*)

ADO ANNIE   Seems like they's times when men ain't got no need for womern.

SECOND GIRL   Well, they's times when womern ain't got no need fer men.

ADO ANNIE   Yeow, but who wants to be dead?
(GERTIE'S *well-known laugh is heard off stage*)

ELLEN   Gertie!
(GERTIE *enters*)

ADO ANNIE   Thought you was in Bushyhead.

GERTIE (*Obviously having swallowed a canary*)   Jist come from there.

ELLEN   Too bad you missed Laurey's wedding.

GERTIE   Been havin' one of my own.

ELLEN   Lands! Who'd you marry? Where is he?

ADO ANNIE (*Looking off stage*)   Is that him?

GERTIE (*Triumphantly*)   That's him!
(*All look off right. The* PEDDLER *enters, dejected, sheepish, dispirited, a ghost of the man he was*)

ADO ANNIE   Ali Hakim!

PEDDLER (*In a weak voice*)   Hello. Hello, Ado Annie.

GERTIE   Did you see my ring, girls?
(*The girls surround* GERTIE *to admire and exclaim. The* PEDDLER *and* ADO ANNIE *are left apart from the group*)

ADO ANNIE   How long you been married?

PEDDLER   Four days. (GERTIE'S *laugh is heard from group. He winces*) Four days with that laugh should count like a golden wedding.

ADO ANNIE   But if you married her, you musta wanted to.

PEDDLER   Sure I wanted to. I wanted to marry her when I saw the moonlight shining on the barrel of her father's shotgun! I thought it would be better to be alive. Now I ain't so sure.

GERTIE (*Coming out of group*)   Ali ain't goin' to travel around the country no more. I decided he orta settle down in Bushyhead and run Papa's store.
(WILL *enters*)

ADO ANNIE   Hey, Will! D'you hear the news? Gertie married the peddler.

WILL (*To* PEDDLER)   Mighty glad to hear that, peddler man. (*Turning to* GERTIE, *and getting an idea*) I think I orta kiss the bride. (*He goes toward* GERTIE, *then looks back at* PEDDLER) Friend of the fambly . . . remember? (*He gives* GERTIE *a big kiss, not realizing that it is* ADO ANNIE *and not the* PEDDLER *he is burning*) Hey, Gertie, have you ever had a Oklahoma hello?
(*He plants a long one on* GERTIE. ADO ANNIE *pulls her away and stands in her place.* ADO ANNIE *socks* WILL, *then* GERTIE. GERTIE *strikes back.* WILL *comes between them but is beaten off by both of them. Kicking and slugging, the women resume the fight until* GERTIE *retreats, with* ADO ANNIE *close on her heels. The other girls follow.* WILL, *too,*

is about to go after them when he is called back by the PEDDLER)

PEDDLER   Hey! Where you goin'?

WILL   I'm goin' to stop Ado Annie from killin' yer wife.

PEDDLER (*Grabbing* WILL'S *arm*)   Mind yer own business! (*He leads* WILL *off. The stage is empty and quiet. A man sneaks on, then another, then more. Cautiously they advance on the house. One of the more agile climbs up a trellis and looks in the window of the second floor. He suppresses a laugh, leans down and reports to the others. There are suppressed giggles and snorts. He takes another peek, then comes down and whispers to them. The joke is passed from one to the other; they are doubled up with laughter. At a signal from one, they all start to pound on tinpans with spoons and set up a terrific din*)

AUNT ELLER (*Coming to the window with a lamp in her hand*)   Whut you doin' down there, makin' all thet racket, you bunch o' pig-stealers?

FRED (*Shouting up*)   Come on down peaceable, Laurcy sugar!

IKE   And you, too, you curly-headed cowboy.

CORD ELAM   With the dimple on yer chin!

IKE   Come on, fellers, let's git 'em down! (*Three of the men run into the house. Those outside toss up rag dolls*)

MEN
Hey, Laurey! Here's a girl baby fer you!
And here's a baby boy!
Here's twins!
(CURLY *is pulled from the house and hoisted on the shoulders of his friends.* LAUREY *and* AUNT ELLER *come out of the house. All are in high spirits. It is a good-natured hazing. Now* JUD *enters. Everyone becomes quiet and still, sensing trouble*)

JUD   Weddin' party still goin' on? Glad I ain't too late. Got a present fer the groom. But first I wanta kiss the bride. (*He grabs* LAUREY. CURLY *pulls him off*) An' here's my present fer you!

(*He socks* CURLY. *The fight starts, with the crowd moving around the two men.* JUD *pulls out a knife and goes for* CURLY. CURLY *grabs his arm and succeeds in throwing him.* JUD *falls on his knife, groans and lies still. The crowd surges toward his motionless body*)

CURLY   Look— Look at him! Fell on his own knife.
   (*He backs away, shaken, limp. Some of the men bend over the prostrate form*)

MEN
Whut's the matter?
Don't you tetch it!
Turn him over—
He's breathin', ain't he?
Feel his heart.
How'd it happen?

FRED   Whut'll we do? Ain't he all right?

SLIM   'S he jist stunned?

CORD ELAM   Git away, some of you. Let me look at him.
   (*He bends down, the men crowding around. The women, huddled together, look on, struck with horror.* CURLY *has slumped back away from the crowd like a sick man.* LAUREY *looks at* CURLY, *dazed, a question in her eye*)

LAUREY   Curly—is he—?

CURLY   Don't say anythin'.

LAUREY   It cain't be that-a-way.

CURLY   I didn't *go* to.

LAUREY   *Cain't be!* Like that—to happen to us.

CORD ELAM (*Getting up*)   Cain't do a thing now. Try to get him to a doctor, but I don't know—

MAN   Here, some of you, carry him over to my rig. I'll drive him over to Doctor Tyler's.

CORD ELAM   Quick! I'm 'fraid it's too late.
   (*The men lift* JUD *up*)

MEN
Handle him easy!

Don't shake him!
Hold on to him, careful there!
(*A woman points to* JUD, *being carried off.* IKE *and his companions run up and exit with the other men*)

CURLY (*To* LAUREY *and* AUNT ELLER)   I got to go see if there's anythin' c'n be done fer him. (*He kisses* LAUREY) Take keer of her, Aunt Eller.
(*He exits*)

AUNT ELLER   Mebbe it's better fer you and Curly not to go 'way tonight.
(*She breaks off, realizing how feeble this must sound*)

LAUREY (*As if she hadn't heard* AUNT ELLER)   I don't see why this had to happen, when everythin' was so fine.

AUNT ELLER   Don't let yer mind run on it.

LAUREY   Cain't fergit, I tell you. Never will!

AUNT ELLER   'At's all right, Laurey baby. If you cain't fergit, jist don't try to, honey. Oh, lots of things happens to folks. Sickness, er bein' pore and hungry even—bein' old and afeared to die. That's the way it is—cradle to grave. And you can stand it. They's one way. You gotta be hearty, you got to be. You cain't deserve the sweet and tender things in life less'n you're tough.

LAUREY   I—I wisht I was the way you are.

AUNT ELLER   Fiddlesticks! Scrawny and old? You couldn't h'ar me to be the way I am!
(LAUREY *laughs through her tears*)

LAUREY   Oh, whut ud I do 'thout you, you're sich a crazy!

AUNT ELLER (*Hugging* LAUREY)   Shore's you're borned!
(*She breaks off as* CURLY *enters with* CORD ELAM, CARNES *and a few others. Their manner is sober. Some of the women come out of the house to hear what the men have to say*)

CORD ELAM   They're takin' Jud over to Dave Tyler's till the mornin'.

AUNT ELLER   Is he—alive?
(CORD ELAM *shakes his head*)

CURLY   Laurey honey, Cord Elam here, he's a Fed'ral Marshal, y'know. And he thinks I orta give myself up— Tonight, he thinks.

LAUREY   Tonight!

AUNT ELLER   Why, yer train leaves Claremore in twenty minutes.

CORD ELAM   Best thing is fer Curly to go of his own accord and tell the Judge.

AUNT ELLER (*To* CARNES)   Why, you're the Judge, ain't you, Andrew?

CARNES   Yes, but—

LAUREY (*Urging* CURLY *forward*)   Well, tell him now and git it over with.

CORD ELAM   'T wouldn't be proper. You have to do it in court.

AUNT ELLER   Oh, fiddlesticks. Le's do it here and say we did it in court.

CORD ELAM   We can't do that. That's breaking the law.

AUNT ELLER   Well, le's not break the law. Le's just bend it a little. C'mon, Andrew, and start the trial. We ain't got but a few minnits.

CORD ELAM   Andrew—I got to protest.

CARNES   Oh, shet yer trap. We can give the boy a fair trial without lockin' him up on his weddin' night! Here's the long and short of it. First I got to ask you: Whut's your plea? (CURLY *doesn't answer.* CARNES *prompts him*) 'At means why did you do it?

CURLY   Why'd I do it? Cuz he'd been pesterin' Laurey and I always said some day I'd—

CARNES   Jist a minnit! Jist a minnit! Don't let yer tongue wobble around in yer mouth like 'at. Listen to my question. Whut happened tonight 'at made you kill him?

CURLY   Why, he come at me with a knife and—and—

CARNES   And you had to defend yerself, didn't you?

CURLY   Why, yes—and furthermore . . .

CARNES Never mind the furthermores—the plea is self-defense— (*The women start to chatter*) Quiet! . . . Now is there a witness who saw this happen?

MEN (*All at once*)
I seen it.
Shore did.
Self-defense all right.
Tried to stab him 'th a frog-sticker.

CORD ELAM (*Shaking his head*) Feel funny about it. Feel funny.

AUNT ELLER And you'll feel funny when I tell yer wife you're carryin' on 'th another womern, won't you?

CORD ELAM I ain't carryin' on 'th no one.

AUNT ELLER Mebbe not, but you'll shore feel funny when I tell yer *wife* you air.
    (*Boisterous laughter*)

CORD ELAM Laugh all you like, but as a Fed'ral Marshal—

SKIDMORE Oh, shet up about bein' a marshal! We ain't goin' to let you send the boy to jail on his weddin' night. We just ain't goin' to *let* you. So shet up!
    (*This firm and conclusive statement is cheered and applauded*)

SLIM C'mon, fellers! Let's pull them to their train in Curly's surrey! We'll be the horses.

CARNES Hey, wait! I ain't even told the verdick yet!
    (*Everything stops still at this unpleasant reminder*)

CURLY Well—the verdick's not guilty, ain't it?

CARNES 'Course, but . . .

LAUREY Well, then *say* it!
    (CARNES *starts, but the crowd drowns him out*)

ALL Not guilty!
    (CURLY *and* LAUREY *run into the house. The rest run out toward the stable.* CARNES *is left downstage without a court*)

CARNES Court's adjourned!
    (CARNES *joins* AUNT ELLER, *who has sat down to rest, after*

all this excitement. ADO ANNIE *and* WILL *enter, holding hands soulfully.* ADO ANNIE'S *hair is mussed, and a contented look graces her face)*

AUNT ELLER   Why, Ado Annie, where on earth you been?

ADO ANNIE   Will and me had a misunderstandin'. But he explained it fine.
(ADO ANNIE *and* WILL *go upstage and now tell-tale wisps of straw are seen clinging to* ADO ANNIE'S *back. Amid shouts and laughter, the surrey is pulled on)*

IKE   Hey, there, bride and groom, y'ready?

CURLY   (*Running out of the house with* LAUREY)   Here we come!
(*The crowd starts to sing lustily, "Oh, What a Beautiful Mornin'." * LAUREY *runs over and kisses* AUNT ELLER. *Then she is lifted up alongside* CURLY. AUNT ELLER *and three girls start to cry. Everyone else sings gaily and loudly)*

ALL   Oh, what a beautiful day!
(*The men start to pull off the surrey. Everybody waves and shouts.* CURLY *and* LAUREY *wave back)*

Curtain

♡

Carousel

♥

BASED ON *Ferenc Molnár's*

LILIOM

AS ADAPTED BY BENJAMIN GLAZER

Cast

CARRIE PIPPERIDGE	Jean Darling
JULIE JORDAN	Jan Clayton
MRS. MULLIN	Jean Casto
BILLY BIGELOW	John Raitt
BESSIE	Mimi Strongin
JESSIE	Jimsie Somers
JUGGLER	Lew Foldes
1ST POLICEMAN	Robert Byrn
DAVID BASCOMBE	Franklyn Fox
NETTIE FOWLER	Christine Johnson
JUNE GIRL	Pearl Lang
ENOCH SNOW	Eric Mattson
JIGGER CRAIGIN	Murvyn Vye
HANNAH	Annabelle Lyon
BOATSWAIN	Peter Birch
ARMINY	Connie Baxter
PENNY	Marilyn Merkt
JENNIE	Joan Keenan
VIRGINIA	Ginna Moise
SUSAN	Suzanne Tafel
JONATHAN	Richard H. Gordon
2ND POLICEMAN	Larry Evers
CAPTAIN	Blake Ritter
1ST HEAVENLY FRIEND (BROTHER JOSHUA)	Jay Velie
2ND HEAVENLY FRIEND	Tom McDuffie
STARKEEPER	Russell Collins
LOUISE	Bambi Linn
CARNIVAL BOY	Robert Pagent
ENOCH SNOW, JR.	Ralph Linn
PRINCIPAL	Lester Freedman

PRODUCTION DIRECTED BY Rouben Mamoulian
DANCES BY Agnes De Mille
SETTINGS BY Jo Mielziner
COSTUMES BY Miles White
PRODUCTION SUPERVISED BY Lawrence Langner and Theresa
Helburn

WITH

John Raitt	Jan Clayton
Jean Darling	Eric Mattson
Christine Johnson	Jean Casto
Murvyn Vye	Bambi Linn
Peter Birch	Annabelle Lyon

Robert Pagent

MUSICAL DIRECTOR, Joseph Littau
ORCHESTRATIONS BY Don Walker

Synopsis of Scenes

TIME: 1873-1888

ACT ONE | Scene One

WALTZ PRELUDE: Carousel.

SCENE: *An Amusement Park on the New England Coast.*

TIME: *Late afternoon.*

    Extending from stage right to the center is a merry-go-round labeled "Mullin's Carousel." Below the merry-go-round, right center, is the stand of BILLY BIGELOW, *the barker for the carousel. Left center is the ticket-seller's stand where* MRS. MULLIN *herself presides. Up on the extreme left is a platform backed by an ornate show tent occupied by "The Beauties of Europe." Below this platform, down left, is another stand occupied by the barker for the "Beauties." The two barker stands are elevated so that these two characters can be easily seen above the heads of the crowd.* MRS. MULLIN *is seated on a high stool behind her stand so that she is also visible at all times. Downstage extreme right is a Hoky Poky Ice Cream wagon; a* MAN *standing upstage from it is selling ice-cream cornucopias.*

NOTE: *This scene is set to the music of a waltz suite. The only sound comes from the orchestra pit. The pantomimic action is synchronized to the music, but it is in no sense a ballet treatment.*

AT RISE: FISHERMEN, SAILORS, *their* WIVES, CHILDREN, GIRLS *from the local mill, and other types of a coastal town are seen moving about the park, patronizing the various concessions and in general "seeing the sights." The carousel is in full motion as the curtain rises, the "Three Beauties of Europe" are dancing on the platform, a juggler is busy juggling downstage left.* BILLY *is standing downstage of his stand and leaning against the stand just watching the proceedings. The whole stage seems to be alive and everyone is having a good time.*

    Almost immediately we see the JUGGLER *cross to the*

center of the stage to juggle a hat on one stick and a plate on another. As he does this the carousel comes to a stop. The RIDERS descend from their animals and leave the platform in all directions to mill around with the crowd. The "Three Beauties of Europe" stop dancing. They slip into robes for their rest period. One KID on the carousel during all this movement has stubbornly clung to his horse, and neither his MOTHER nor his big SISTER can get him off. The SISTER, a tattle-tale type, skips happily across to her father, who is talking to another gentleman. She pulls at his sleeve and points to her rebellious brother DAVID. MR. BASCOMBE, a formidable fellow with sideburns on his cheeks and a heavy gold watch-chain across his belly, starts out with his daughter to aid his wife against his recalcitrant son. When he gets there he stands in back of DAVID, JR., with that stern look he reserves for such occasions. That's all there is to it. DAVID knows the jig is up. He gets off the horse, and the family now walk across the stage with the pomp that befits the richest clan in the locality. They own the Bascombe Cotton Mills, "a little ways up the river." Several people greet them with respectful awe, and they return a gracious but dignified bow to all.

The JUGGLER, center stage, has by this time stopped juggling and one of the dancers on the platform has come down and is passing a hat among the crowd for a little collection. As the JUGGLER goes back to his corner down left, we see a GIRL and a SAILOR enter from right. They cross down in front of BILLY, and as they pass him the GIRL turns to look at BILLY. She decides she wants to talk to him, so she crosses to her sailor friend and asks him to buy her some ice cream. The SAILOR crosses to the ice-cream wagon to buy the cones, and as he does, the GIRL crosses to BILLY and talks to him. The SAILOR, having bought the cones, crosses back to the spot where he was, but sees no girl. He turns upstage, sees her flirting with BILLY. Crossing up between the two, he looks angrily at BILLY, turns to his girl, and tells her to hold the cones. She does. The SAILOR turns to BILLY and is just about to take a good sock at him when he notices that BILLY towers over him. BILLY smiles and the SAILOR'S look is now one of "I'd better leave this guy alone." He saunters off to the left with his girl. BILLY then crosses up to MRS. MULLIN, a small group of adoring young females following his every movement with worshipful eyes. MRS. MULLIN *is completely mollified by the little attention and gives him a nice big hug.*

CARRIE *and* JULIE *enter from down left.* CARRIE *is a naïve, direct, and normal young woman of the period.* JULIE *is more complex, quieter, deeper. They look around at the gay sights, two mill girls on an afternoon off.* JULIE *crosses to right center.* CARRIE *is mixing in with the crowd left center when* BILLY *crosses to go back to his stand down right. On the way he nearly bumps into* JULIE. *Their eyes meet for a moment. Then he goes on.*

About this time the BARKER *of "The Beauties of Europe" comes out and gets on his stand and tries to attract the crowd by pointing to his weary dancers. But now* BILLY *starts his spiel and the entire stageful turns toward him and the carousel while* MRS. MULLIN, *the proprietress, beams above them. Everyone on the stage starts to sway unconsciously with the rhythm of* BILLY'S *words (unheard by the audience)—all but* JULIE. JULIE *just stands, looking at him over the heads of the others, her gaze steady, her body motionless.* BILLY *becomes conscious of her. He looks curiously at her. She takes his mind off his work. He mechanically repeats his spiel. The heads turned up at him now follow his eyes and turn slowly toward* JULIE. *This is also the direction of "The Beauties of Europe," and the enterprising* BARKER *of that attraction immediately takes advantage of this and starts his dancers dancing feverishly, doing bumps that they probably learned at Coney Island. The crowd is now completely "Beauty"-conscious.* BILLY *is* JULIE-*conscious and gets down off his stand.* MRS. MULLIN, *realizing the situation, runs over to* BILLY *and seems to shout up at him.*

BILLY *comes to. His barker's pride reawakened, he mounts his stand and proceeds to win back his public. He starts his regular spiel. The girls all turn back to* BILLY *and sway with his rhythm again. Some of the men go along with the "Beauties"—all except the ones whose wives pull them away.*

When BILLY *finishes, there is a stampede of girls to buy tickets for the carousel.* JULIE *tries too, but she gets crowded out.* BILLY *notices this; pretty soon there will be no more places left. He smiles and with exaggerated gal-*

*lantry walks over to her and offers his arm. With a fright-
ened little grin she accepts it and he leads her grandly toward the carousel.* MRS. MULLIN, *her nose out of joint, yells
at* JULIE, *motioning to her that she wants her five-cent fare.*

JULIE *fumbles in her purse. After some delay, occa-
sioned by her excitement, she finally produces a nickel.
Then* MRS. MULLIN *takes her time about giving her a ticket.
In fact, she stalls until the carousel actually gets started.
When she has her ticket,* JULIE *dashes back to the carousel.
It is going slowly and she is afraid to get on.* BILLY *laughs
and suddenly lifts her up and puts her on the only remain-
ing horse on the carousel.*

(*It must be understood that* BILLY'S *attitude to* JULIE
*throughout this scene is one of only casual and laconic
interest. He can get all the girls he wants. One is like another. This one is a cute little thing. Like hundreds of
others.*)

*Once he has got her on the carousel, he dismisses her
from his mind. He turns back to* MRS. MULLIN, *but for
some reason that lady gives him an icy glare. He shrugs his
shoulders, looks again to the carousel, and collects the
tickets from the people seated on the various animals.*
JULIE *comes around again. He waves at her patronizingly.
It means nothing to him. She waves back. It means so
much to her that she nearly falls off! He laughs. The
carousel is revolving faster now, but he hops on and leans
against the horse on which* JULIE *is seated.* MRS. MULLIN,
*seeing this, is so furious that she gets down from her stand
and starts to pace the stage angrily. Great excitement is
stirring down right. A group of* KIDS *herald the approach of
a* BEAR *being led on stage by a* BALLERINA *in a short ruffly
skirt.* (*The* BEAR *is a small man in a well-made bearskin.*)

*Arriving stage center, the girl in the ruffly skirt executes
a few dance steps. Then, to the great delight of all, the*
BEAR *does exactly the same steps. A* CLOWN *now enters
from down right, goes on stage next to the* BEAR, *and does
some acrobatic tricks. The* JUGGLER *starts juggling again,
the dancers dance. The entire stage is in a bedlam of excitement, the carousel keeps turning at full speed,* BILLY *is
leaning closer to* JULIE, *the music rises in an ecstatic
crescendo, but the lights, as if they sensed that we have
accomplished all we wanted to in this scene, black out and
the curtains close.*

ACT ONE | Scene Two

SCENE: *A tree-lined path along the shore. A few minutes later. Near sundown. Through the trees the lights of the amusement park can be seen on the curves of the bay.*

The music of the merry-go-round is heard faintly in the distance.

AT RISE: *There is a park bench just right of center. Soon after the curtain opens,* CARRIE *backs on to the stage from down right, followed by* JULIE.

CARRIE   C'mon, Julie, it's gettin' late. . . . Julie! That's right! Don't you pay her no mind. (*Looking off stage*) Look! She's comin' at you again. Let's run!

JULIE (*Holding her ground*)   I ain't skeered o' her. (*But she is a little*)

MRS. MULLIN (*Entering, in no mood to be trifled with*)   I got one more thing to tell you, young woman. If y'ever so much as poke your nose in my carousel again, you'll be thrown out. Right on your little pink behind!

CARRIE   You got no call t'talk t'her like that! She ain't doin' you no harm.

MRS. MULLIN   Oh, ain't she? Think I wanta get in trouble with the police and lose my license?

JULIE (*To* CARRIE)   What *is* the woman talkin' about?

MRS. MULLIN (*Scornfully*)   Lettin' my barker fool with you! Ain't you ashamed?

JULIE   I don't let no man . . .

MRS. MULLIN (*To* CARRIE) He leaned against her all through the ride.

JULIE (*To* CARRIE) He leaned against the horse. (*To* MRS. MULLIN) But he didn't lay a hand on me!

MRS. MULLIN Oh no, Miss Innercence! And he didn't put his arm around yer waist neither.

CARRIE And suppose he did. Is that a reason to hev a capuluptic fit?

MRS. MULLIN You keep out o' this, you rip! (*To* JULIE) You've had my warnin'. If you come back you'll be thrown out!

JULIE Who'll throw me out?

MRS. MULLIN Billy Bigelow—the barker. Same feller you let get so free with you.

JULIE I—I bet he wouldn't. He wouldn't throw me out!

CARRIE I bet the same thing.
(BILLY BIGELOW *enters, followed by* TWO GIRLS. *He hears and sees the argument; he turns and tells the girls to leave. They exit*)

MRS. MULLIN (*To* CARRIE) You mind yer business, hussy!

CARRIE Go back to yer carousel and leave us alone!

JULIE Yes. Leave us alone, y'old—y'old—

MRS. MULLIN I don't run my business for a lot o' chippies.

CARRIE Chippy, yerself!

JULIE Yes, Chippy yerself!

BILLY (*Shouting*) *Shut up!* Jabber jabber jabber! . . . (*They stand before him like three guilty schoolgirls. He makes his voice shrill to imitate them*) Jabber jabber jabber jabber jabber. . . . What's goin' on anyway? Spittin' and sputt'rin'—like three lumps of corn poppin' on a shovel!

JULIE Mr. Bigelow, please—

BILLY Don't yell!

JULIE (*Backing away a step*) I didn't yell.

BILLY Well—don't. (*To* MRS. MULLIN) What's the matter?

MRS. MULLIN Take a look at that girl, Billy. She ain't ever to be allowed on my carousel again. Next time she tries to get in—if she ever dares—I want you to throw her out! Understand? Throw her out!

BILLY (*Turning to* JULIE) All right. You heard what the lady said. Run home now.

CARRIE C'mon, Julie.

JULIE (*Looking at* BILLY, *amazed*) No, I won't.

MRS. MULLIN (*To* BILLY) Like a drink?

BILLY Sure.

JULIE (*Speaking very earnestly, as if it meant a great deal to her*) Mr. Bigelow, tell me please—honest and truly—if I came to the carousel, would you throw me out?
  (*He looks at* MRS. MULLIN, *then at* JULIE, *then back at* MRS. MULLIN)

BILLY What did she do, anyway?

JULIE She says you put your arm around my waist.

BILLY (*The light dawning on him*) So that's it! (*Turning to* MRS. MULLIN) Here's something new! Can't put my arm around a girl without I ask your permission! That how it is?

MRS. MULLIN (*For the first time on the defensive*) I just don't want *that* one around no more.

BILLY (*Turning to* JULIE) You come round all you want, see? And if y'ain't got the price Billy Bigelow'll treat you to a ride.

MRS. MULLIN Big talker, ain't you, Mr. Bigelow? I suppose you think I can't throw *you* out too, if I wanta! (BILLY, *ignoring her, looks straight ahead of him, complacently*) You're such a good barker I can't get along without you. That it? Well, just for that you're discharged. Your services are no longer required. You're bounced! See?

BILLY Very well, Mrs. Mullin.

MRS. MULLIN (*In retreat*) You know I *could* bounce you if I felt like it!

BILLY And you felt like it just now. So I'm bounced.

MRS. MULLIN   Do you have to pick up every word I say? I only said—

BILLY   That my services were no longer required. Very good. We'll let it go at that, Mrs. Mullin.

MRS. MULLIN   All right, you devil! (*Shouting*) We'll *let* it go at that!

JULIE   Mr. Bigelow, if she's willin' to say she'll change her mind—

BILLY   You keep out of it.

JULIE   I don't want this to happen 'count of me.

BILLY (*Suddenly, to* MRS. MULLIN, *pointing at* JULIE)   Apologize to her!

CARRIE   A—ha!

MRS. MULLIN   Me apologize to *her!* Fer what? Fer spoilin' the good name of my carousel—the business that was left to me by my dear, saintly, departed husband, Mr. Mullin? (*Led toward tears by her own eloquence*) I only wish my poor husband was alive this minute.

BILLY   I bet *he* don't.

MRS. MULLIN   He'd give you such a smack on the jaw—!

BILLY   That's just what *I'm* goin' to give you if you don't dry up! (*He advances threateningly*)

MRS. MULLIN (*Backing away*)   You upstart! After all I done for you! Now I'm through with you for good! Y'hear?

BILLY (*Making as if to take a swipe at her with the back of his hand*)   Get!

MRS. MULLIN (*As she goes off*)   Through fer good! I won't take you back like before!
   (BILLY *watches her go, then crosses back to* JULIE. *There is a moment of awkward silence*)

CARRIE   Mr. Bigelow—

BILLY   Don't get sorry for me or I'll give *you* a slap on the jaw! (*More silence. He looks at* JULIE. *She lowers her eyes*) And don't *you* feel sorry for me either!

JULIE (*Frightened*)   I don't feel sorry for you, Mr. Bigelow.

BILLY   You're a liar, you *are* feelin' sorry for me. I can see it in your face. (*Faces front, throws out chest, proud*) You think, now that she fired me, I won't be able to get another job. . . .

JULIE   What *will* you do now, Mr. Bigelow?

BILLY   First of all, I'll go get myself—a glass of beer. Whenever anything bothers me I always drink a glass of beer.

JULIE   Then you *are* bothered about losing your job!

BILLY   No. Only about how I'm goin' t'pay fer the beer. (*To* CARRIE, *gesturing with right hand*) Will *you* pay for it? (CARRIE *looks doubtful. He speaks to* JULIE) Will you? (JULIE *doesn't answer*) How much money have you got?

JULIE   Forty-three cents.

BILLY (*To* CARRIE)   And you? (CARRIE *lowers her eyes and turns left*) I asked you how much you've got? (CARRIE *begins to weep softly*) Uh, I understand. Well, you needn't cry about it. . . . I'm goin' to the carousel to get my things. Stay here till I come back. Then we'll go have a drink. (JULIE *is fumbling for change. She holds it up to* BILLY) It's all right. (*He pushes her hand gently away*) Keep your money. I'll pay.
   (*He exits whistling down right.* JULIE *continues to look silently off at the departing figure of* BILLY. CARRIE *studies her for a moment, then timidly opens the subject of her interest by calling* JULIE'S *name. She crosses to bench left of* JULIE *and sits*)

CARRIE   Julie— (*No answer. From here the lines are synchronized to music*) Julie— Do you like him?

JULIE (*Dreaming*)   I dunno.
   (*She sits on bench*)

CARRIE
Did you like it when he talked to you today?
When he put you on the carousel, that way?
Did you like that?

JULIE
'D ruther not say.

CARRIE (*Shakes her head and chides her*)
You're a queer one, Julie Jordan!

You are quieter and deeper than a well,
And you never tell me nothin'—

CARRIE

JULIE

There's nothin' that I keer t'choose t'tell!

CARRIE

You been actin' most peculiar!
Ev'ry mornin' you're awake ahead of me,
Alw'ys settin' by the winder—

JULIE

I like to watch the river meet the sea.

CARRIE

When we work in the mill, weavin' at the loom,
Y'gaze absent-minded at the roof,
And half the time yer shuttle gets twisted in the threads
Till y'can't tell the warp from the woof!

JULIE (*Looking away and smiling. She knows it's true*)
'T ain't so!

CARRIE

You're a queer one, Julie Jordan!
You won't ever tell a body what you think.
You're as tight-lipped as an oyster,
And as silent as an old Sahaira Spink!

JULIE   Spinx.
   (*These lines are spoken over music*)

CARRIE   Huh?

JULIE   Spinx.

CARRIE   Uh-uh. Spink.

JULIE   Y'spell it with an "x."

CARRIE   That's only when there's more than one.

JULIE (*Outbluffed*)   Oh.

CARRIE (*Looking sly*)   Julie, I been bustin' t'tell *you* somethin' lately.

JULIE   Y'hev?

CARRIE   Reason I didn't keer t'tell you before was 'cause

you didn't hev a feller of yer own. Now y'got one, I ken tell y'about mine.

JULIE (*Quietly and thoughtfully*) I'm glad you got a feller, Carrie. What's his name?

CARRIE (*Now she sings, almost reverently*)
His name is Mister Snow,
And an upstandin' man is he.
He comes home ev'ry night in his round-bottomed boat
With a net full of herring from the sea.

An almost perfect beau,
As refined as a girl could wish,
But he spends so much time in his round-bottomed boat
That he can't seem to lose the smell of fish!

The fust time he kissed me, the whiff of his clo'es
Knocked me flat on the floor of the room;
But now that I love him, my heart's in my nose,
And fish is my fav'rit perfume!
Last night he spoke quite low,
And a fair-spoken man is he,
  (*Memorizing exactly what he said*)
And he said, "Miss Pipperidge, I'd like it fine
If I could be wed with a wife.
And, indeed, Miss Pipperidge, if you'll be mine,
I'll be yours fer the rest of my life."

Next moment we were promised!
And now my mind's in a maze,
Fer all I ken do is look forward to
That wonderful day of days. . . .

When I marry Mister Snow,
The flowers'll be buzzin' with the hum of bees,
The birds'll make a racket in the churchyard trees,
When I marry Mister Snow.

Then it's off to home we'll go,
And both of us'll look a little dreamy-eyed,
A-drivin' to a cottage by the oceanside
Where the salty breezes blow.
He'll carry me 'cross the threshold,
And I'll be as meek as a lamb.

Then he'll set me on my feet
And I'll say, kinda sweet:
"Well, Mister Snow, here I am!"

Then I'll kiss him so he'll know
That ev'rythin'll be as right as right ken be
A-livin' in a cottage by the sea with me,
For I love that Mister Snow—
That young, seafarin', bold and darin'
Big, bewhiskered, overbearin' darlin', *Mister Snow!*
> (*She looks soulfully ahead of her, and sits down, in a trance of her own making*)

JULIE   Carrie! I'm so happy fer you!

CARRIE   So y'see I ken understand now how *you* feel about Billy Bigelow.
> (BILLY *enters down right, carrying a suitcase and with a coat on his arm. He puts the suitcase down and the coat on top of it*)

BILLY   You still here?
> (*They both rise, looking at* BILLY)

CARRIE   You *told* us to wait fer you.

BILLY   What you think I want with two of you? I meant that *one* of you was to wait. The other can go home.

CARRIE   All right.

JULIE (*Almost simultaneously*)   All right.
> (*They look at each other, then at* BILLY, *smiling inanely*)

BILLY   One of you goes home. (*To* CARRIE) Where do you work?

CARRIE   Bascombe's Cotton Mill, a little ways up the river.

BILLY   And you?

JULIE   I work there, too.

BILLY   Well, one of you goes home. Which of you *wants* to stay? (*No answer*) Come on, speak up! Which of you stays?

CARRIE   Whoever stays loses her job.

BILLY   How do you mean?

CARRIE   All Bascombe's girls hev to be respectable. We all hev to live in the mill boarding-house, and if we're late they lock us out and we can't go back to work there any more.

BILLY   Is that true? Will they bounce you if you're not home on time?
   (*Both girls nod*)

JULIE   That's right.

CARRIE   Julie, should I go?

JULIE   I—can't tell you what to do.

CARRIE   All right—you stay, if y'like.

BILLY   That right, you'll be discharged if you stay?
   (JULIE *nods*)

CARRIE   Julie, should I go?

JULIE (*Embarrassed*)   Why do you keep askin' me that?

CARRIE   You know what's best to do.

JULIE (*Profoundly moved, slowly*)   All right, Carrie, you can go home.
   (*Pause. Then reluctantly* CARRIE *starts off. As she gets left center, she turns and says, uncertainly:*)

CARRIE   Well, good night.
   (*She waits a moment to see if* JULIE *will follow her.* JULIE *doesn't move.* CARRIE *exits*)

BILLY (*Speaking as he crosses to left center*)   Now we're both out of a job. (*No answer. He whistles softly*) Have you had your supper?

JULIE   No.

BILLY   Want to eat out on the pier?

JULIE   No.

BILLY   Anywhere's else?

JULIE   No.
   (*He whistles a few more bars. He sits on the bench, looking her over, up and down*)

BILLY   You don't come to the carousel much. Only see you three times before today.

JULIE (*Breathless, she crosses to bench and sits beside him*)
I been there much more than that.

BILLY   That right? Did you see me?

JULIE   Yes.

BILLY   Did you know I was Billy Bigelow?

JULIE   They told me.
(*He whistles again, then turns to her*)

BILLY   Have you got a sweetheart?

JULIE   No.

BILLY   Ah, don't lie to me.

JULIE   I heven't anybody.

BILLY   You stayed here with me first time I asked you. You
know your way around all right, all right!

JULIE   No, I don't, Mr. Bigelow.

BILLY   And I suppose you don't know why you're sittin'
here—like this—alone with me. You wouldn' of stayed so
quick if you hadna done it before. . . . What did you stay
for, anyway?

JULIE   So you wouldn't be left alone.

BILLY   Alone! God, you're dumb! I don't need to be alone.
I can have all the girls I want. Don't you know that?

JULIE   I know, Mr. Bigelow.

BILLY   What do you know?

JULIE   That all the girls are crazy fer you. But that's not
why *I* stayed. I stayed because you been so good to me.

BILLY   Well, then you can go home.

JULIE   I don't want to go home now.

BILLY   And suppose I go away and leave you sittin' here?

JULIE   Even then I wouldn't go home.

BILLY   Do you know what you remind me of? A girl I knew
in Coney Island. Tell you how I met her. One night at

closin' time—we had put out the lights in the carousel, and just as I was—

(*He breaks off suddenly as, during the above speech, a* POLICEMAN *has entered from down left and comes across stage.* BILLY *instinctively takes on an attitude of guilty silence. The* POLICEMAN *frowns down at them as he walks by.* BILLY *follows him with his eyes. At the same time that the* POLICEMAN *entered from left,* MR. BASCOMBE *has come in from right. He flourishes his cane and breathes in the night air as if he enjoyed it*)

POLICEMAN   Evenin', Mr. Bascombe.

BASCOMBE   Good evening, Timony. Nice night.

POLICEMAN   'Deed it is. (*Whispers into* BASCOMBE'S *left ear*) Er—Mr. Bascombe. That girl is one of your girls.

BASCOMBE (*In a low voice*)   One of my girls? (*The* POLICE-MAN *nods.* BASCOMBE *crosses in front of the* POLICEMAN *to the right of* JULIE *and peers at her in the darkness*) Is that *you,* Miss Jordan?

JULIE   Yes, Mr. Bascombe.

BASCOMBE   What ever are you doing out at this hour?

JULIE   I—I—

BASCOMBE   You know what time we close our doors at the mill boarding-house. You couldn't be home on time now if you ran all the way.

JULIE   No, sir.

BILLY (*To* JULIE)   Who's old sideburns?

POLICEMAN   Here, now! Don't you go t'callin' Mr. Bascombe names—'Less you're fixin' t'git yerself into trouble. (BILLY *shuts up. Policemen have this effect on him. The* POLICEMAN *turns to* BASCOMBE) We got a report on this feller from the police chief at Bangor. He's a pretty fly gazaybo. Come up from Coney Island.

BASCOMBE   New York, eh?

POLICEMAN   He works on carousels, makes a specialty of young things like this'n. Gets 'em all moony-eyed. Promises to marry 'em, then takes their money.

JULIE (*Promptly and brightly*)   I ain't got any money.

POLICEMAN   Speak when you're spoken to, miss!

BASCOMBE   Julie, you've heard what kind of blackguard this man is. You're an inexperienced girl and he's imposed on you and deluded you. That's why I'm inclined to give you one more chance.

POLICEMAN (*To* JULIE)   Y'hear that?

BASCOMBE   I'm meeting Mrs. Bascombe at the church. We'll drive you home and I'll explain everything to the house matron. (*He holds out his hand*) Come, my child.
    (*But she doesn't move*)

POLICEMAN   Well, girl! Don't be settin' there like you didn't hev good sense!

JULIE   Do I *hev* to go with you?

BASCOMBE   No. You don't have to.

JULIE   Then I'll stay.

POLICEMAN   After I warned you!

BASCOMBE   You see, Timony! There are some of them you just can't help. Good night!
    (*He exits*)

POLICEMAN   Good night, Mr. Bascombe. (*He looks down at* BILLY, *starts to go, then turns to* BILLY *and speaks*) You! You low-down scalawag! I oughta throw you in jail.

BILLY   What for?

POLICEMAN (*After a pause*)   Dunno. Wish I did. (*He exits.* BILLY *looks after him*)

JULIE   Well, and *then* what?

BILLY   Huh?

JULIE   You were startin' to tell me a story.

BILLY   Me?

JULIE   About that girl in Coney Island. You said you just put out the lights in the carousel—that's as far as you got.

BILLY   Oh, yes. Yes, well, just as the lights went out, some-one came along. A little girl with a shawl—you know, she—

(*Puzzled*) Say, tell me somethin'—ain't you scared of me?
(*Music starts here*) I mean, after what the cop said about
me takin' money from girls.

JULIE I ain't skeered

BILLY That your name? Julie? Julie somethin'?

JULIE Julie Jordan.
  (BILLY *whistles reflectively*)

BILLY (*Singing softly, shaking head*)
You're a queer one, Julie Jordan.
Ain't you sorry that you didn't run away?
You can still go, if you wanta—

JULIE (*Singing, looking away so as not to meet his eye*)
I reckon that I keer t'choose t'stay.
You couldn't take my money
If I didn't *hev* any,
And I don't hev a penny, that's true!
And if I *did* hev money
You couldn't take any
'Cause you'd ask, and I'd give it to you!

BILLY (*Singing*)
You're a queer one, Julie Jordan. . . .
Ain't y'ever had a feller you give money to?

JULIE No.

BILLY Ain't y'ever had a feller at all?

JULIE No.

BILLY Well y'musta had a feller you went walkin' with—

JULIE Yes.

BILLY Where'd you walk?

JULIE Nowhere special I recall.

BILLY In the woods?

JULIE No.

BILLY On the beach?

JULIE No.

BILLY Did you love him?

JULIE   No! Never loved no one—I *told* you that!

BILLY   Say, you're a funny kid. Want to go into town and dance maybe? Or—

JULIE   No. I have to be keerful.

BILLY   Of what?

JULIE   My character. Y'see, I'm never goin' to marry. (*Singing*)
I'm never goin' to marry.
If I was goin' to marry,
I wouldn't hev t'be sech a stickler.
But I'm never goin' to marry,
And a girl who don't marry
Hes got to be much more pertickler!
   (*Following lines spoken*)

BILLY   Suppose I was to say to you that I'd marry you?

JULIE   You?

BILLY   That scares you, don't it? You're thinkin' what that cop said.

JULIE   No, I ain't. I never paid no mind to what he said.

BILLY   But you wouldn't marry anyone like me, would you?

JULIE   Yes, I would, if I loved you. It wouldn't make any difference what you—even if I died fer it.

BILLY   How do you know what you'd do if you loved me? Or how you'd feel—or anythin'?

JULIE   I dunno how I know.

BILLY   Ah—

JULIE   Jest the same, I know how I—how it'd be—if I loved you. (*Singing*)
When I worked in the mill, weavin' at the loom,
I'd gaze absent-minded at the roof,
And half the time the shuttle'd tangle in the threads,
And the warp'd get mixed with the woof . . .
If I loved you—

BILLY (*Spoken*)   But you don't.

JULIE (*Spoken*) No I don't. . . . (*Smiles and sings*)
But somehow I ken see
Jest exackly how I'd be . . .

If I loved you,
Time and again I would try to say
All I'd want you to know.
If I loved you,
Words wouldn't come in an easy way—
Round in circles I'd go!
Longin' to tell you, but afraid and shy,
I'd let my golden chances pass me by.
Soon you'd leave me,
Off you would go in the mist of day,
Never, never to know
How I loved you—
If I loved you.
   (*Pause*)

BILLY   Well, anyway— You don't love me. That's what you
said.

JULIE   Yes. . . . I can smell them, can you? The blossoms.
(BILLY *picks some blossoms up and drops them*) The wind
brings them down.

BILLY   Ain't *much* wind tonight. Hardly any. (*Singing*)
You can't hear a sound—not the turn of a leaf,
Nor the fall of a wave, hittin' the sand.
The tide's creepin' up on the beach like a thief,
Afraid to be caught stealin' the land.
On a night like this I start to wonder what life is all about.

JULIE   And I always say two heads are better than one, to
figger it out.

BILLY (*Spoken over short musical interlude*)   I don't need
you or anyone to help me. I got it figgered out for myself.
We ain't important. What are we? A couple of specks of
nothin'. Look up there. (*He points up. They both look up*)
(*He sings*)
There's a helluva lot o' stars in the sky,
And the sky's so big the sea looks small,
And two little people—
You and I—
We don't count at all.

JULIE

There's a feathery little cloud floatin' by
Like a lonely leaf on a big blue stream.

BILLY

And two little people—you and I—
Who cares what we dream?
   (*They are silent for a while, the music continuing.* BILLY
   looks down at her and speaks)
You're a funny kid. Don't remember ever meetin' a girl like
you. (*A thought strikes him suddenly. He looks suspicious. He
lets her hand go and backs away*) You—are you tryin' t'get
me to marry you?

JULIE   No.

BILLY   Then what's puttin' it into my head? (*He thinks it
out. She smiles. He looks down at her*) You're different all
right. Don't know what it is. (*Holds her chin in his right
hand*) You look up at me with that little kid face like—like
you trusted me. (*She looks at him steadily, smiling sadly, as if
she were sorry for him and wanted to help him. He looks
thoughtful, then talks to himself, but audibly*) I wonder what
it'd be like.

JULIE   What?

BILLY   Nothin'. (*To himself again*) I know what it'd be
like. It'd be awful. I can just see myself— (*He sings*)
Kinda scrawny and pale, pickin' at my food,
And lovesick like any other guy—
I'd throw away my sweater and dress up like a dude
In a dickey and a collar and a tie . . .
If I loved you—-

JULIE (*Speaking*)   But you don't.

BILLY (*Speaking*)   No I don't. (*Singing*)
But somehow I can see
Just exactly how I'd be.

If I loved you,
Time and again I would try to say
All I'd want you to know.
If I loved you,
Words wouldn't come in an easy way—
Round in circles I'd go!

Longing to tell you, but afraid and shy,
I'd let my golden chances pass me by.
Soon you'd leave me,
Off you would go in the mist of day,
Never, never to know
How I loved you—
If I loved you.
(*He thinks it over for a few silent moments. Then he
shakes his head ruefully. He turns to* JULIE *and frowns at
her. The rest of the scene is spoken over music*)
I'm not a feller to marry anybody. Even if a girl was foolish
enough to want me to, I wouldn't.

JULIE (*Looking right up at him*)   Don't worry about it—
Billy.

BILLY   Who's worried!
(*She smiles and looks up at the trees*)

JULIE   You're right about there bein' no wind. The blossoms
are jest comin' down by theirselves. Jest their time to, I
reckon.
(BILLY *looks straight ahead of him, a troubled expression
in his eyes.* JULIE *looks up at him, smiling, patient. The
music rises ecstatically. He crosses nearer to her and looks
down at her. She doesn't move her eyes from his. He takes
her face in his hands, leans down, and kisses her gently.
The curtains close as the lights dim*)

ACT ONE | Scene Three

SCENE: *Nettie Fowler's Spa on the ocean front. June. Up
right is Nettie's establishment (and residence combined)
of gray, weathered clapboard and shingled roof. Just left
of the door, on the porch, there is a good-sized arbor,
overhung with wistaria. Under the arbor are a table and*

three chairs. From the house to off-stage left platforms are built up and appear to be docks. The backdrop, painted blue, depicts the bay. On the drop is painted a moored ketch and other sailing craft.

AT RISE: *Men carrying bushel baskets of clams and piling them on the dock, preparatory to loading the boats. During the scene more men come on.*

 A group stand outside the spa to heckle NETTIE *and the women who are inside, cooking. Other men enter and join the hecklers.*

 Music continues, but the first lines are not sung or metrically synchronized.

1ST MAN Nettie!

2ND MAN (*Cupping his hands and calling off*) Oh, Nettie Fowler!

NETTIE (*In the house*) Hold yer horses!

1ST MAN Got any of them doughnuts fried yet?

3RD MAN How 'bout some apple turnovers?

NETTIE (*Still inside, getting irritated*) Hold yer horses!
 (*The* MEN *laugh, now that they're getting a rise out of her*)

2ND MAN (*Crossing up to porch*) Hey, what're you and them women doin' in there?

WOMEN (*Off*) *Hold yer horses!*
 (*The* MEN *slap their thighs, and one another's backs. This is rich!*)

1ST MAN Are y'cookin' the ice cream?
 (*This convulses them. Throws his arm on* 3RD MAN'S *shoulders*)

3RD MAN Roastin' the lemonade?

ALL MEN
Nettie Fowler!
Yoo-hoo!
Nettie Fow-w-w-w-ler!
 (*Some* WOMEN *come out of the house.* CARRIE *follows.*

pushing her way through the crowd and coming up front. The GIRLS *carry rolling-pins and spoons—a formidable crowd of angry females interrupted at their work in the kitchen. Their stern looks soon reduce the male laughter to faint snickers and sheepish grins*)

SEVERAL GIRLS Will you stop that racket!

CARRIE Git away you passel o' demons!

1ST MAN Where's Nettie?

CARRIE In the kitchen busier'n a bee in a bucket o' tar— and y'oughter be ashamed, makin' yersel's a plague and a nuisance with yer yellin' and screamin' and carryin' on.
(*From here on, the dialogue is sung, unless otherwise indicated*)

GIRLS
Give it to 'em good, Carrie,
Give it to 'em good!

CARRIE
Get away, you no-account nothin's
With yer silly jokes and prattle!
If y'packed all yer brains in a butterfly's head
They'd still hev room to rattle.

GIRLS
Give it to 'em good, Carrie,
Give it to 'em good!
Tell 'em somethin' that'll l'arn 'em!

CARRIE
Get away you roustabout riff-raff,
With yer bellies full of grog.
If y'packed all yer brains in a pollywog's head,
He'd never even grow to be a frog!

GIRLS
The pollywog'd never be a frog!
That'll l'arn 'em, darn 'em!

ALL MEN
Now jest a minute, ladies,
You got no call to fret.
We only asked perlitely
If you was ready yet.

We'd kinda like this clambake
To get an early start,
And wanted fer to tell you
We went and done our part.

BASSES (*Pointing to pile of baskets*)
Look at them clams!

BARITONES
Been diggin' 'em since sunup!

BASSES
Look at them clams!

TENORS
All ready fer the boats.

ALL MEN
Diggin' them clams,

TENORS
We're all wore out and done up—

ALL
And what's more we're as hungry as goats!

ALL GIRLS
You'll get no drinks er vittles
Till we get across the bay,
So pull in yer belts
And load them boats
And let's get under way.

The sooner we sail,
The sooner we start
The clambake across the bay!
(*They snap their fingers and turn. But the boys' attention
has been caught by the entrance of* NETTIE, *coming out of
the house carrying a tray piled high with doughnuts. Shc
is followed by a* LITTLE GIRL, *carrying a large tray of
coffee cups*)
(*The following lines are spoken*)

NETTIE   Here, boys: Here's some doughnuts and coffee. Fall
to! (*Crosses to center*)

MEN (*As they fall to, speeches overlapping*)
Doughnuts, hooray!

That's our Nettie!
Yer heart's in the right place, Nettie!
Lemme in there!
Quit yer shovin'!

NETTIE   Here now, don't jump at it like you was a lotta animals in a menag'ry!
(*She laughs as she crosses over to the* GIRLS)

GIRLS   Nettie! After us jest tellin' 'em! Whatcher doin' that fer?

NETTIE   They been diggin' clams since five this mornin'—I see 'em myself, down on the beach.

GIRLS   After the way they been pesterin' and annoyin' you!

CARRIE   Nettie, yer a soft-hearted ninny!

NETTIE   Oh, y'can't blame 'em. First clambake o' the year they're always like this. It's like unlockin' a door, and all the crazy notions they kep' shet up fer the winter come whoopin' out into the sunshine. This year's jest like ev'ry other. (*The following lines are sung*)
March went out like a lion,
A-whippin' up the water in the bay.
Then April cried
And stepped aside,
And along come pretty little May!

May was full of promises
But she didn't keep 'em quick enough fer some,
And a crowd of doubtin' Thomases
Was predictin' that the summer'd never come!

MEN SINGERS
But it's comin', by gum!
Y'ken feel it come!
Y'ken feel it in yer heart,
Y'ken see it in the ground!

GIRLS
Y'ken hear it in the trees,
Y'ken smell it in the breeze—

ALL
Look around, look around, look around!

NETTIE
June is bustin' out all over,
All over the meadow and the hill!
Buds're bustin' outa bushes,
And the rompin' river pushes
Ev'ry little wheel that wheels beside a mill.

ALL
June is bustin' out all over.

NETTIE
The feelin' is gettin' so intense,
That the young Virginia creepers
Hev been huggin' the bejeepers
Outa all the mornin'-glories on the fence.
Because it's June!

MEN
June, June, June—

ALL
Jest because it's June—
June—Ju-u-une!

NETTIE
Fresh and alive and gay and young,
June is a love song, sweetly sung.

ALL (*Softly*)
June is bustin' out all over!

MAN
The saplin's are bustin' out with sap!

GIRL
Love hes found my brother, junior—

2ND MAN
And my sister's even lunier!

2ND GIRL
And my ma is gettin' kittenish with Pap!

ALL
June is bustin' out all over!

NETTIE
To ladies the men are payin' court.
Lotsa ships are kept at anchor

Jest because the captains hanker
Fer a comfort they ken only get in port!

ALL
Because it's June!
June—June—June—
Jest because it's June—June—Ju-u-ne!

NETTIE
June makes the bay look bright and new,
Sails gleaming white on sunlit blue—

CARRIE
June is bustin' out all over,
The ocean is full of Jacks and Jills.
With her little tail a-swishin'
Ev'ry lady fish is wishin'
That a male would come and grab her by the gills!

ALL
June is bustin' out all over!

NETTIE
The sheep aren't sleepin' any more.
All the rams that chase the ewe sheep
Are determined there'll be new sheep
And the ewe sheep aren't even keepin' score!

ALL
On accounta it's June!
June—June—June—
Jest because it's June—
June—
June!

NETTIE
June is bustin' out all over,
All over the beaches ev'ry night.
From Pennobscot to Augusty
All the boys are feelin' lusty,
And the girls ain't even puttin' up a fight.

ALL
Because it's June,
June, June, June,
Jest because it's June! June! June!

(Dance. After the dance all exit except NETTIE, CARRIE, *and a small group of* GIRLS. JULIE *enters)*

CARRIE   Hello, Julie.

NETTIE   Did you find him?

JULIE   No. *(Explaining to* CARRIE*)* He went out with Jigger Craigin last night and he didn't come home.

CARRIE   Jigger Craigin?

JULIE   His new friend—he's a sailor on that big whaler, the *Nancy B.* She's sailing tomorrow. I'll be glad.

NETTIE   Why don't you two visit for a while. *(Necks are craned, ears cocked.* NETTIE *notices this)* Look, girls, we got work to do. C'mon. You sweep those steps up there. *(Herding the* GIRLS *upstage)* You set up there and keep outa the way and don't poke yer noses in other people's business.

JULIE   You need me, Cousin Nettie?

NETTIE   No. You stay out here and visit with Carrie. You haven't seen each other fer a long time. Do you good.
   (She exits into the house. JULIE *and* CARRIE *sit on the bait box,* JULIE *right of* CARRIE. *All ears are open upstage)*

CARRIE   Is he workin' yet?

JULIE   No. Nettie's been awful kind to us, lettin' us stay here with her.

CARRIE   Mr. Snow says a man that can't find work these days is jest bone lazy.

JULIE   Billy don't know any trade. He's only good at what he used to do. So now he jest don't do anythin'.

CARRIE   Wouldn't the carousel woman take him back?

JULIE   I think she would, but he won't go. I ask him **why** and he won't tell me. . . . Last Monday he hit me.

CARRIE   Did you hit him back?

JULIE   No.

CARRIE   Whyn't you leave him?

JULIE   I don't want to.

CARRIE   I would. I'd leave him. Thinks he ken do whatever he likes jest because he's Billy Bigelow. Don't support you! Beats you! . . . He's a bad'n.

JULIE   He ain't willin'ly er meanin'ly bad.

CARRIE   (*Afraid she's hurting* JULIE)   Mebbe he ain't. That night you set on the bench together—he was gentle then, you told me.

JULIE   Yes, he was.

CARRIE   But now he's alw'ys actin' up—

JULIE   Not alw'ys. Sometimes he's gentle—even now. After supper, when he stands out here and listens to the music from the carousel—somethin' comes over him—and he's gentle.

CARRIE   What's he say?

JULIE   Nothin'. He jest sets and gets thoughtful. Y'see he's unhappy 'cause he ain't workin'. That's really why he hit me on Monday.

CARRIE   Fine reason fer hittin' you. Beats his wife 'cause he ain't workin'.
   (*She turns her head up left.* GIRLS, *caught eavesdropping, start to sweep vigorously*)

JULIE   It preys on his mind.

CARRIE   Did he hurt you?

JULIE   (*Very eagerly*)   Oh, no—no.

CARRIE   Julie, I got some good news to tell you about me—about Mr. Snow and me. We're goin' to be cried in church nex' Sunday!
   (*The* GIRLS *who have been upstage turn quickly, come down and cluster around* CARRIE, *proving they haven't missed a thing.* CARRIE *rises*)

ALL GIRLS   What's thet you say, Carrie? (*Ad libs of excitement*)
Carrie!
Honest and truly?
You fixin' t'get hitched?

Well, I never!
Do tell!

CARRIE   Jest a minute! Stop yer racket! Don't all come at me together! (*But she is really pleased*)

GIRL   Well, tell us! How long hev you been bespoke?

CARRIE   Near on t'two months. Julie was the fust t'know.

GIRL   What's he like, Julie?

CARRIE   Julie hes never seen him. But you all will soon. He's comin' here. I asked him to the clambake.

GIRL   Can't hardly wait'll I see him.

2ND GIRL   I can't hardly wait fer the weddin'.
   (*All look at each other and giggle*)

CARRIE (*Giggling*)   Me neither.

JULIE   What a day that'll be fer you!

GIRLS (*Singing*)
When you walk down the aisle
All the heads will turn.
What a rustlin' of bonnets there'll be!
And you'll try to smile,
But your cheeks will burn,
And your eyes'll get so dim you ken hardly see!

With your orange blossoms quiverin' in your hand,
You will stumble to the spot where the parson is,
Then your finger will be ringed with a golden band,
And you'll know the feller's yours—and you are his.

CARRIE
When I marry Mr. Snow—

GIRLS
What a day!
What a day!

CARRIE
The flowers'll be buzzin' with the hum of bees,

GIRLS
The birds'll make a racket in the churchyard trees,

CARRIE
When I marry Mr. Snow.

GIRLS
Heigh-ho!

CARRIE
Then it's off to home we'll go-—

GIRLS
Spillin' rice
On the way!

CARRIE
And both of us'll look a little dreamy-eyed,
A-drivin' to a cottage by the oceanside
Where the salty breezes blow—
   (SNOW *enters up left. He just couldn't be anyone else*)

GIRLS
You and Mr. Snow!
   (*Hearing his name,* MR. SNOW *preens*)

CARRIE
He'll carry me cross the threshold,
And I'll be as meek as a lamb.
Then he'll set me on **my** feet
And I'll say, kinda sweet:
"Well, Mr. Snow, here I am!"
   (*Now* MR. SNOW *is very pleased. He makes his presence
   known by singing*)

SNOW
Then I'll kiss her so she'll know,

CARRIE (*Mortified*)
Mr. Snow!

GIRLS (*Thrilled*)
Mr. Snow!

SNOW
That everythin'll be as right as right ken be,
A-livin' in a cottage by the sea with me,
Where the salty breezes blow!
   (CARRIE *squeals and hides her head on* JULIE'S *shoulder.
   The* GIRLS *are delighted*)

I love Miss Pipp'ridge and I aim to
Make Miss Pipp'ridge change her name to
Missus Enoch Snow!

GIRLS (*Ad lib*)
Carrie!
My lands, he give me sech a start!
Well! I never!

CARRIE (*Looking up at* JULIE)   I'll never look him in the
face again! Never!
   (*Laughs, shouts, whoops, and squeals from the* GIRLS)

GIRL   C'mon inside and leave the two iove-birds alone!
   (*They exit into the house.* CARRIE *clings to* JULIE *and won't
   let her go*)

CARRIE (*Not turning to face him yet*)   Oh, Enoch!

SNOW   Surprised?

CARRIE   Surprised? I'm mortified!

SNOW   He-he!
   (*This, we are afraid, is the way he laughs.* CARRIE *straightens out, looks at him, then beams back at* JULIE)

CARRIE   Well, this is him.
   (SNOW *bows and smiles. There is a moment of awkward
   silence*)

JULIE   Carrie told me a lot about you.
   (CARRIE *and* JULIE *nod to each other.* CARRIE *and* SNOW
   nod)

CARRIE   I told you a lot about Julie, didn't I?
   (CARRIE *and* SNOW *nod.* CARRIE *and* JULIE *nod*)

JULIE   Carrie tells me you're comin' to the clambake.
   (*He nods*)

CARRIE   Looks like we'll hev good weather fer it, too.
   (*They nod*)

JULIE   Not a cloud in the sky.

SNOW   You're right.

CARRIE (*To* JULIE)   He don't say much, but what he does
say is awful pithy! (JULIE *nods.* CARRIE *looks over toward her*

love. Still addressing JULIE) Is he anythin' like I told you he was?

JULIE   *Jest* like.

SNOW   Oh, Carrie, I near fergot. I brought you some flowers.

CARRIE   (*Thrilled*)   Flowers? Where are they? (SNOW *hands her a small envelope from his inside pocket. She reads what is written on the package*) Geranium seeds!

SNOW   (*Handing her another envelope*)   And this'n here is hydrangea. Thought we might plant 'em in front of the cottage. (*To* JULIE) They do good in the salt air.

JULIE   That'll be beautiful!

SNOW   I like diggin' around a garden in my spare time— Like t'plant flowers and take keer o' them. Does your husband like that too?

JULIE   N-no. I couldn't rightly say if Billy likes to take *keer* of flowers. He likes t'smell 'em, though.

CARRIE   Enoch's nice-lookin', ain't he?

SNOW   Oh come, Carrie!

CARRIE   Stiddy and reliable too.—Well, ain't you goin' to wish us luck?

JULIE   (*Warmly*)   Of course I wish you luck, Carrie.
   (JULIE *and* CARRIE *embrace*)

CARRIE   You ken kiss Enoch, too—us bein' sech good friends, and me bein' right here lookin' on at you.
   (JULIE *lets* ENOCH *kiss her on the cheek, which he shyly does. For a moment she clings to him, letting her head rest on his shoulder, as if it needed a shoulder very badly.* JULIE *starts to cry*)

SNOW   Why are you crying, Mrs.—er—Mrs.—

CARRIE   It's because she has such a good heart.

SNOW   We thank you for your heartfelt sympathy. We thank you Mrs.—er—Mrs.—

JULIE   Mrs. Bigelow. Mrs. Billy Bigelow. That's my name —Mrs. B— (*She breaks off and starts to run into the house, but as she gets a little right of center,* BILLY *enters. He is followed by* JIGGER. JULIE *is embarrassed, recovers, and goes mechanically through the convention of introduction*) Billy, you know Carrie. This is her intended—Mr. Snow.

(JIGGER *crosses up to the porch, standing under the arbor*)

SNOW   Mr. Bigelow! I almost feel like I know you—

BILLY   How are you? (*He starts up center*)

SNOW   I'm pretty well. Jest gettin' over a little chest cold. (*As* BILLY *gets up center*) This time of year—you know. (*He stops, seeing that* BILLY *isn't listening*)

JULIE (*Turning to* BILLY)   Billy!

BILLY (*He stops and turns to* JULIE, *crosses down to her in a defiant manner*)   Well, all right, say it. I stayed out all night—and I ain't workin'—and I'm livin' off yer Cousin Nettie.

JULIE   I didn't say anything.

BILLY   No, but it was on the tip of yer tongue! (*He starts upstage center again*)

JULIE   Billy! (*He turns*)   Be sure and come back in time to go to the clambake.

BILLY   Ain't goin' to no clambake. Come on, Jigger.
(JIGGER, *who has been slinking upstage out of the picture, joins* BILLY *and they exit upstage center and off left.* JULIE *stands watching them, turns to* CARRIE, *then darts into the house to hide her humiliation*)

CARRIE (*To* SNOW, *after a pause*)   I'm glad you ain't got no whoop-jamboree notions like Billy.

SNOW   Well, Carrie, it alw'ys seemed t'me a man had enough to worry about, gettin' a good sleep o' nights so's to get in a good day's work the next day, without goin' out an' lookin' fer any special trouble.

CARRIE   That's true, Enoch.

SNOW   A man's got to make plans fer his life—and then he's got to stick to 'em.

CARRIE   Your plans are turnin' out fine, ain't they, Enoch?

SNOW   All accordin' to schedule, so far. (*Singing*)

I own a little house,
And I sail a little boat,
And the fish I ketch I sell—
And, in a manner of speakin',
I'm doin' very well.

I love a little girl
And she's in love with me,
And soon she'll be my bride
And, in a manner of speakin',
I should be satisfied.

CARRIE (*Spoken*)   Well, ain't you?

SNOW
If I told you my plans, and the things I intend,
It'd make ev'ry curl on yer head stand on end!
    (*He takes her hand and becomes more intense, the gleam
    of ambition coming into his eye*)
When I make enough money outa one little boat,
I'll put all my money in another little boat.
I'll make twic't as much outa two little boats,
And the fust thing you know I'll hev four little boats!
Then eight little boats,
Then a fleet of little boats!
Then a great big fleet of great big boats!

All ketchin' herring,
Bringing it to shore,
Sailin' out again
And bringin' in more,
And more, and more,
And more!
    (*The music has become very operatic, rising in a cre-
    scendo far beyond what would ordinarily be justified by
    several boatloads of fish. But to this singer, boatloads of
    fish are kingdom come*)
    (*The following lines are spoken*)

CARRIE   Who's goin' t'eat all thet herring?

SNOW   They ain't goin' to *be* herring! Goin' to put 'em in
cans and call 'em sardines. Goin' to build a little sardine
cannery—then a big one—then the biggest one in the country.
Carrie, I'm goin' to get rich on sardines. I mean *we're* goin'
t'get rich—you and me. I mean you and me—and—all of us.

CARRIE *raises her eyes. Is the man bold enough to be meaning "children"?*) (SNOW *sings*)
The fust year we're married we'll hev *one* little kid,
The second year we'll go and hev *another* little kid,
You'll soon be darnin' socks fer eight little feet—

CARRIE (*Enough is enough*)   Are you buildin' up to another fleet?

SNOW (*Blissfully proceeding with his dream*)
We'll build a lot more rooms,
Our dear little house'll get bigger,
Our dear little house'll get bigger.

CARRIE (*To herself*)   And so will my figger!

SNOW (*Spoken*)   Carrie, ken y'imagine how it'll be when all the kids are upstairs in bed, and you and me sit alone by the fireside—me in my armchair, you on my knee—mebbe.

CARRIE   Mebbe.
    (*And, to his great delight,* CARRIE *sits on his knee. Both heave a deep, contented sigh, and he starts to sing softly*)

SNOW
When the children are asleep, we'll sit and dream
The things that ev'ry other
    Dad and mother dream.
When the children are asleep and lights are low,
If I still love you the way
    I love you today,
You'll pardon my saying: "I told you so!"
When the children are asleep, I'll dream with you.
We'll think: "What fun we have had!"
And be glad that it all came true.

CARRIE
When children are awake,
A-rompin' through the rooms
Or runnin' on the stairs,
Then, in a manner of speakin',
The house is really theirs.
But once they close their eyes
And we are left alone
And free from all their fuss.

Then, in a manner of speakin',
We ken be really *us*. . . .

CARRIE	SNOW

CARRIE
When the children are asleep
We'll sit and dream
The things that ev'ry other
Dad and mother dream—

SNOW

Dream all alone,

Dreams that won't be interrupted
When the children are asleep
And lights are low.

Lo and behold!
If I still love you the way
I love you today,
You'll pardon my saying:
"I told you so!"

When the children are asleep,
I'll dream with you.
We'll think: "What fun we
    hev had!"
And be glad that it all came
    true.

You'll dream with me.

When today
Is a long time ago,
You'll still hear me say
That the best dream I know
Is you. . . .

You'll still hear me say
That the best dream I know
Is—When the children are
    asleep
I'll dream with you.

("Blow High, Blow Low" starts off stage. SNOW *looks off
left, then up right, takes* CARRIE'S *chin in his hands and
kisses her gently on the forehead. As the men enter singing, he looks up, takes his hat, which he left on the bait
box. Then he and* CARRIE *exit)*

MEN (*Off stage, singing*)
Blow high, blow low!
A-whalin' we will go!
We'll go a-whalin', a-sailin' away,
Away we'll go,
Blow me high and low!
    (BILLY *and* JIGGER *enter, followed by friends from* JIGGER'S
    whaler)
For many and many a long, long day!
For many and many a long, long day!

(They sing another refrain. During this refrain BILLY *looks toward the house. He is hesitant. Maybe he should go in to* JULIE. *He crosses to center.* JIGGER *sees this, crosses over to* BILLY*)*

JIGGER Hey, Billy! (BILLY *turns*) Where are you goin'? (BILLY *looks indecisive.* JIGGER *takes his arm and brings him downstage*) Stick with me. After we get rid of my shipmates, I wanna talk to you. Got an idea, for you and me to make money.

BILLY How much?

JIGGER More'n you ever saw in yer life.

MAN Hey, Jigger, come back here!
  (BILLY *and* JIGGER *go back to the boys.* JIGGER *sings*)

JIGGER
The people who live on land
Are hard to understand.
When you're lookin' for fun they clap you into jail!
So I'm shippin' off to sea,
Where life is gay and free,
And a feller can flip
A hook in the hip of a whale.

ALL
Blow high, blow low!
A-whalin' we will go!
We'll go a-whalin', a-sailin' away,
Away we'll go,
Blow me high and low!
For many and many a long, long day!
For many and many a long, long day!

BILLY
It's wonderful just to feel
Your hands upon a wheel
And to listen to wind a-whistlin' in a sail!
Or to climb aloft and be
The very first to see
A chrysanthemum spout come out o' the snout of a whale!

ALL
Blow high, blow low!
A-whalin' we will go!

We'll go a-whalin', a-sailin' away,
Away we'll go,
Blow me high and low!
For many and many a long, long day!
For many and many a long, long day!
>   (JIGGER *draws* BILLY *and the* MEN *around him.* **They go**
>   **down to the footlights, crouch low and** JIGGER *sings an-*
>   *other verse*)

JIGGER
A-rockin' upon the sea,
Your boat will seem to be
Like a dear little baby in her bassinet,
For she hasn't learned to walk,
And she hasn't learned to talk,
And her little behind
Is kind of inclined to be wet!
>   (*During the next refrain, more* SINGERS *come on, followed*
>   *by* DANCERS)

ALL MEN
Blow high, blow low!
A-whalin' we will go!
We'll go a-whalin', a-sailin' away,
Away we'll go,
Blow me high and low!
For many and many a long, long day!
For many and many a long, long day!
>   (*Finish with big vocal climax.* JIGGER *takes* BILLY *off left,*
>   *and the* DANCERS *do:*
>   *Hornpipe.*
>   *At the finish of the number, all* DANCERS *clear the stage as*
>   BILLY *and* JIGGER *enter*)

JIGGER   I tell you it's safe as sellin' cakes.

BILLY   You say this old sideburns who owns the mill is also
the owner of your ship?

JIGGER   That's right. And tonight he'll be takin' three or four
thousands dollars down to the captain—by hisself. He'll walk
along the waterfront by himself—with all that money.
>   (*He pauses to let this sink in*)

BILLY   You'd think he'd have somebody go with him.

JIGGER Not him! Not the last three times, anyway. I watched him from the same spot and see him pass me. Once I nearly jumped him.

BILLY Why didn't you?

JIGGER Don't like to do a job less it's air-tight. This one needs two to pull it off proper. Besides, there was a moon— shinin' on him like a torch. (*Spits*) Don't like moons. (*This is good news*) Lately the nights have been runnin' to fog. And it's ten to one we'll have fog tonight. That's why I wanted you to tell yer wife we'd go to that clambake.

BILLY Clambake? Why?

JIGGER Suppose we're all over on the island and you and me get lost in the fog for a half an hour. And suppose we got in a boat and come over here and—and did whatever we had to do, and then got back? There's yer alibi! We just say we were lost on the island all that time.

BILLY Just what would we have to do? I mean me. What would *I* have to do?

JIGGER You go up to old sideburns and say: "Excuse me, sir. Could you tell me the time?"

BILLY "Excuse me, sir. Could you tell me the time?" Then what?

JIGGER Then? Well, by that time I got my knife in his ribs. Then you take *your* knife—

BILLY Me? I ain't got a knife.

JIGGER You can get one, can't you?

BILLY (*After a pause, turning to* JIGGER) Does he have to be killed?

JIGGER No, he don't have to be. He can give up the money without bein' killed. But these New Englanders are funny. They'd rather be killed— Well?

BILLY I won't do it! It's dirty.

JIGGER What's dirty about it?

BILLY The knife.

JIGGER All right. Ferget the knife. Just go up to him with a tin cup and say: "Please, sir, will you give me three thousand dollars?" See what he does fer you.

BILLY I ain't goin' to do it.

JIGGER Of course, if you got all the money you want, and don't need—

BILLY I ain't got a cent. Money thinks I'm dead.
(MRS. MULLIN *is seen entering from up left, unnoticed by* BILLY *and* JIGGER)

JIGGER That's what I thought. And you're out of a job and you got a wife to support—

BILLY Shut up about my wife. (*He sees* MRS. MULLIN) What do you want?

MRS. MULLIN Hello, Billy.

BILLY What did you come fer?

MRS. MULLIN Come to talk business.

JIGGER Business! (*He spits*)

MRS. MULLIN I see you're still hangin' around yer jailbird friend.

BILLY What's it to you who I hang around with?

JIGGER If there's one thing I can't abide, it's the common type of woman.
(*He saunters upstage left and stands looking out to sea*)

BILLY What are you doin' here? You got a new barker, ain't you?

MRS. MULLIN (*Looking him over*) Whyn't you stay home and sleep at night? You look awful!

BILLY He's as good as me, ain't he?

MRS. MULLIN Push yer hair back off yer forehead—

BILLY (*Pushing her hand away and turning away from her*) Let my hair be.

MRS. MULLIN If I told you to let it hang down over yer eyes you'd push it back. I hear you been beatin' her. If you're sick of her, why don't you leave her? No use beatin' the poor, skinny little—

BILLY   Leave her, eh? You'd like that, wouldn't you?

MRS. MULLIN   Don't flatter yourself! (*Her pride stung, she paces to center stage*) If I had any sense I wouldn't of come here. The things you got to do when you're in business! . . . I'd sell the damn carousel if I could.

BILLY   Ain't it crowded without me?

MRS. MULLIN   Those fool girls keep askin' for you. They miss you, see? Are you goin' to be sensible and come back?

BILLY   And leave Julie?

MRS. MULLIN   You beat her, don't you?

BILLY (*Exasperated*)   No, I don't beat her. What's all this damn-fool talk about beatin'? I hit her once, and now the while town is—the next one I hear—I'll smash—

MRS. MULLIN (*Backing away from him*)   All right! All right! I take it back. I don't want to get mixed up in it.

BILLY   Beatin' her! As if I'd beat her!

MRS. MULLIN   What's the odds one way er another? Look at the thing straight. You been married two months and you're sick of it. Out there's the carousel. Show booths, young girls, all the beer you want, a good livin'—and you're throwin' it all away. Know what? I got a new organ.

BILLY   I know.

MRS. MULLIN   How do you know?

BILLY (*His voice softer*)   You can hear it from here. I listen to it every night.

MRS. MULLIN   Good one, ain't it?

BILLY   Jim dandy. Got a nice tone.

MRS. MULLIN   Y'ought to come up close and hear it. Makes you think the carousel is goin' faster. . . . You belong out there and you know it. You ain't cut out fer a respectable married man. You're an artist type. You belong among artists. Tell you what: you come back and I'll give you a ruby ring my husband left me.

BILLY I dunno—I might go back. I could still go on livin' here with Julie.

MRS. MULLIN Holy Moses!

BILLY What's wrong?

MRS. MULLIN Can y'imagine how the girls'd love that? A barker who runs home to his wife every night! Why, people'd laugh theirselves sick.

BILLY I know what *you* want.

MRS. MULLIN Don't be so stuck on yerself.

BILLY I ain't happy here, and *that's* the truth.

MRS. MULLIN Course you ain't.
(She strokes his hair back off his forehead, and this time he lets her. JULIE enters from house, carrying a tray with a cup of coffee and a plate of cakes on it. MRS. MULLIN pulls her hand away. There is a slight pause)

BILLY Do you want anythin'?

JULIE I brought you your coffee.

MRS. MULLIN (*To* BILLY *in a low voice*) Whyn't you have a talk with her? She'll understand. Maybe she'll be glad to get rid of you.

BILLY (*Without conviction*) Maybe.

JULIE Billy—before I ferget. I got somethin' to tell you.

BILLY All right.

JULIE I been wantin' to tell you—in fact, I was goin' to yesterday—

BILLY Well, go ahead.

JULIE I can't—we got to be alone.

BILLY Don't you see I'm busy? Here, I'm talkin' business and—

JULIE It'll only take a minute.

BILLY Get out o' here, or—

JULIE I tell you it'll only take a minute.

BILLY Will you get out of here?

JULIE No.

BILLY What did you say?

MRS. MULLIN Let her alone, Billy. I'll drop in at Bascombe's bank and get some small change for the carousel. I'll be back in a few minutes for your answer to my proposition.
(*Exits above* JIGGER. *She looks at* JIGGER *as she goes.* JIGGER *looks at* BILLY, *then follows* MRS. MULLIN *off*)

JULIE Don't look at me like that. I ain't afraid of you—ain't afraid of anyone. I hev somethin' to tell you.

BILLY Well then, tell me, and make it quick.

JULIE I can't tell it so quick. Why don't you drink yer coffee?

BILLY That what you wanted to tell me?

JULIE No. By the time you drink it, I'll hev told you.

BILLY (*Stirs coffee and takes a quick sip*) Well?

JULIE Yesterday my head ached and you asked me—

BILLY Yes—

JULIE Well—you see—thet's what it is.

BILLY You sick?

JULIE No. It's nothin' like thet. (*He puts cup down*) It's awful hard to tell you—I'm not a bit skeered, because it's a perfectly natural thing—

BILLY What is?

JULIE Well—when two people live together—

BILLY Yes—

JULIE I'm goin' to hev a baby.
(*She turns away. He sits still and stunned. Then he rises, crosses to her, and puts his arms around her. She leans her head back on his shoulders. Then she leaves and starts for the house. As she gets to the steps,* BILLY *runs and helps her very solicitously.* JIGGER *has re-entered and calls to* BILLY)

JIGGER (*Two short whistles*) Hey, Billy!

BILLY (*Turning to* JIGGER)   Hey, Jigger! Julie—Julie's goin'
to have a baby.

JIGGER (*Calmly smoking his cigarette*) Yeh? What about it?

BILLY (*Disgusted at* JIGGER)   Nothin'. (*He goes into the
house*)

JIGGER (*Ruminating*)   My mother had a baby once.
   (*He smiles angelically and puffs on his cigarette.* MRS.
   MULLIN *enters*)

MRS. MULLIN   He in there with her? (JIGGER *ignores the
question*) They're havin' it out, I bet. (JIGGER *impudently
blows a puff of smoke in her direction*) When he comes back
to me I ain't goin' to let him hang around with you any
more. You know that, don't you?

JIGGER   Common woman.

MRS. MULLIN   Ain't goin' to let him get in your clutches.
Everybody that gets mixed up with you finishes in the jail-
house—or the grave.

JIGGER   Tut-tut-t-t-t-. Carnival blond! Comin' between a man
and his wife!

MRS. MULLIN   Comin' between nothin'! They don't belong
together. Nobody knows him like I do. And nobody is goin'
to get him away from me. And that goes fer you!

JIGGER   Who wants him? If he's goin' to let himself get tied
up to an old wobbly-hipped slut like you, what good would
he be to me?

MRS. MULLIN   He won't be *no* good to you! And he won't
end up with a perliceman's bullet in his heart—like that
Roberts boy you hung around with last year. Wisht the bullet
hadda got you—you sleek-eyed wharf rat! You keep away
from him that's all, or I'll get the cops after you.

JIGGER (*Holding his cigarette high*)   Common woman!

MRS. MULLIN   Yeh! Call names! But I got him back just the
same! And you're through!

JIGGER   Put on a new coat o' paint. You're starting to peel!
Old pleasure boat!
   (*He exits. She looks off after him, then turns right and sees*

BILLY *coming out of the house. She immediately shifts all her attention to the essential job of holding his interest. She primps and walks center. He comes down by bait box)*

BILLY (*A change has come over him. There is a strange, firm dignity in his manner*) You still here? (*He picks up tray, and sits on box, tray in his lap*)

MRS. MULLIN Didn't you tell me to come back? (*Taking money out of dress*) Here! You'll be wantin' an advance on yer salary. Well, that's only fair. You been out o' work a long time. (*She offers him money*)

BILLY (*Taking another sip of coffee*) Go home, Mrs. Mullin.

MRS. MULLIN What's the matter with you?

BILLY Can't you see I'm havin' my breakfast? Go back to your carousel.

MRS. MULLIN You mean you ain't comin' with me?

BILLY (*Still holding cup*) Get out of here. Get!

MRS. MULLIN I'll never speak to you again—not if you were dyin', I wouldn't.

BILLY That worries me a lot.

MRS. MULLIN What did she tell you in there?

BILLY (*Putting cup on tray*) She told me—

MRS. MULLIN Some lies about me, I bet!

BILLY (*Proudly*) No, Mrs. Mullin. Nothin' about you. Just about Julie and me—and— (*Looking up at her*) as a matter of fact, Mrs. Mullin—I'm goin' to be a father!

MRS. MULLIN You!—Julie—?

BILLY Good-by, Mrs. Mullin.

MRS. MULLIN You a father? (*She starts to laugh*)

BILLY (*Giving her a good push*) Get the hell away from here, Mrs. Mullin. (*She continues to laugh*) Good-by, Mrs. Mullin!

(*He pushes her again, and as she reaches the left portal, he gives her a good kick in the bustle. Then he turns, looks*

toward Nettie's house, smiles. He starts to contemplate the
future. He starts to sing softly.)

BILLY
I wonder what he'll think of me!
I guess he'll call me
"The old man."
I guess he'll think I can lick
Ev'ry other feller's father—
Well, I can!
   (*He gives his belt a hitch*)
I bet that he'll turn out to be
The spit an' image
Of his dad.
But he'll have more common sense
Than his puddin'-headed father
Ever had.
I'll teach him to wrassle
And dive through a wave,
When we go in the mornin's for our swim.
His mother can teach him
The way to behave,
But she won't make a sissy out o' him- -
Not him!
Not my boy!
Not Bill. . . .
   (*The name, coming to his lips involuntarily, pleases him*
   very much)
Bill!
   (*He loves saying it. He straightens up proudly*)
My boy, Bill!
(I will see
that he's named
After me,
I will!)
My boy, Bill—
He'll be tall
And as tough
As a tree,
Will Bill!
Like a tree he'll grow,
With his head held high

And his feet planted firm on the ground,
And you won't see no-
body dare to try
To boss him or toss him around!
No pot-bellied, baggy-eyed bully'll boss him around!
  (*Having worked himself up to a high pitch of indignation,
  he relaxes into a more philosophical manner*)
I don't give a damn what he does,
As long as he does what he likes.
He can sit on his tail
Or work on a rail
With a hammer, a-hammerin' spikes.

He can ferry a boat on the river
Or peddle a pack on his back
Or work up and down
The streets of a town
With a whip and a horse and a hack.

He can haul a scow along a canal,
Run a cow around a corral,
Or maybe bark for a carousel—
  (*This worries him*)
Of course it takes talent to do *that* well.

He might be a champ of the heavyweights
Or a feller that sells you glue,
Or President of the United States—
That'd be all right, too.
  (*Orchestra picks up the theme of "My Boy, Bill."* BILLY
  speaks over music)
His mother'd like that. But he wouldn't be President unless he
wanted to be!
  (*Singing*)
Not Bill!
My boy, Bill—
He'll be tall
And as tough
As a tree,
Will Bill!

Like a tree he'll grow,
With his head held high,
And his feet planted firm on the ground,
And you won't see no-

body dare to try
To boss him or toss him around!
No fat-bottomed, flabby-faced, pot-bellied, baggy-eyed bastard'll boss him around!
(*He paces the stage angrily*)
And I'm damned if he'll marry his boss's daughter,
A skinny-lipped virgin with blood like water,
Who'll give him a peck and call it a kiss
And look in his eyes through a lorgnette—
Say!
Why am I takin' on like this?
My kid ain't even been born yet!
(*He laughs loudly at himself, crosses up to bait box, and sits. Then he returns to more agreeable daydreaming*)
I can see him
When he's seventeen or so
And startin' in to go
With a girl.

I can give him
Lots o' pointers, very sound,
On the way to get round
Any girl.

I can tell him—
Wait a minute! Could it be—?
What the hell! What if he
Is a girl!
(*Rises in anguish*)
Bill!
Oh, Bill!
(*He sits on bait box and holds his head in his hands. The music becomes the original theme, "I Wonder What He'll Think of Me." He speaks over it in a moaning voice*)
What would I do with her? What could I do *for* her?
A bum—with no money!
(*Singing the last lines of the first stanza*)
You can have fun with a son,
But you got to be a *father*
To a girl!
(*Thinking it over, he begins to be reconciled*)
She mightn't be so bad at that—
A kid with ribbons
In her hair,

A kind o' sweet and petite
Little tintype of her mother—
What a pair!
    (*Warming up to the idea, speaking over music*)
I can just hear myself braggin' about her!
    (*Singing*)
My little girl,
Pink and white
As peaches and cream is she.
My little girl
Is half again as bright
As girls are meant to be!
Dozens of boys pursue her,
Many a likely lad
Does what he can to woo her
From her faithful dad.
She has a few
Pink and white young fellers of two or three—
But my little girl
Gets hungry ev'ry night
And she comes home to me!
My little girl!
    (*More thoughtful, and serious*)
My little girl!
    (*Suddenly panicky*)
I got to get ready before she comes!
I got to make certain that she
Won't be dragged up in slums
With a lot o' bums—
Like me!
She's got to be sheltered and fed, and dressed
In the best that money can buy!
I never knew how to get money,
But I'll try—
By God! I'll try!
I'll go out and make it
Or steal it or take it
Or die!
    (*Finishing, he stands still and thoughtful. Then he turns right and walks slowly up to the bait box and gazes off right. As he does, NETTIE comes out of the house, carrying a large jug. She crosses up center and puts the jug on the steps left center, then calls off*)

NETTIE   Hey, you roustabouts! Time to get goin'! Come and help us carry everythin' on the boats!

MAN (*Off*)   All right, Nettie, we're comin'!

2ND MAN   Don't need to have a fit about it.

NETTIE   Hey, Billy! What's this Julie says about you **not** goin' to the clambake?

BILLY   Clambake? (*Suddenly getting an idea from the word*) Mebbe I *will* go, after all! (*General laughter off stage.* JIGGER *enters down left.* BILLY *sees him. To* NETTIE) There's Jigger. I got to talk to him. Jigger! Hey, Jigger! Come here—quick!

NETTIE   I'll tell Julie you're comin'. She'll be tickled pink.
   (*She goes into the house*)

BILLY   Jigger, I changed my mind! You know—about goin' to the clambake, and— I'll do everythin' like you said. Gotta get money on account of the baby, see.

JIGGER   Sure, the baby. (*He pulls* BILLY *closer and lowers his voice*) Did you get the knife?

BILLY   Knife?

JIGGER   I only got a pocket knife. If he shows fight we'll need a real one.

BILLY   But I ain't got—

JIGGER   Go inside and take the kitchen knife.

BILLY   Somebody might see me.

JIGGER   Take it so they don't see you!
   (BILLY *looks indecisive.* JULIE *enters on the run to* BILLY *from the house*)

JULIE   Billy, is it true? Are you comin'?

BILLY   I think so. Yes.

JULIE (*Puts her arm around his waist. He puts his arms around her*)   We'll hev a barrel of fun. I'll show you all over the island. Know every inch of it. Been goin' to picnics there since I been a little girl.

JIGGER   Billy! Billy! Y'better go and get that—

JULIE   Get what, Billy?

BILLY   Why—

JIGGER   The shawl. Billy said you oughter have a shawl. Gets cold at nights. Fog comes up—ain't that what you said?
 (*People start entering with baskets, pies, jugs, etc., ready to go to the clambake*)

BILLY   Y-yes. I better go and get it—the shawl.

JULIE   Now, that was real thoughtful, Billy.
 (*We see* NETTIE *coming out of the house. The stage is pretty well crowded by now*)

BILLY   I'll go and get it.
 (*He exits into the house quickly*)

NETTIE   C'mon, all!
 (*From the house come* GIRLS *carrying cakes, pies, butter crocks;* MEN *carrying baskets.* NETTIE *sings*)
June is bustin' out all over!

ALL
The flowers are bustin' from their seed!

NETTIE
And the pleasant life of Riley
That is spoken of so highly
Is the life that ev'rybody wants to lead!

ALL
Because it's June!
June—June—June!
Jest because it's June—June—June!
 (*During this singing chorus,* SNOW *and* CARRIE *have entered from the house.* JULIE *is seen running over to* CARRIE *to tell her the good news that* BILLY *is going to the clambake.* JIGGER *crosses to* JULIE *and is introduced to* CARRIE. JIGGER *looks her over.* JULIE *also introduces* JIGGER *to* SNOW, *but* JIGGER *just brushes him off.* SNOW *tries to smile; but misses by a good margin. On the last "June" of the refrain, everyone but* JULIE *and* JIGGER *exit.* BILLY *comes out of the house carrying the shawl. He crosses to* JULIE, *who is now a little left of center and downstage.* JIGGER *is right stage. As* BILLY *is putting the shawl over* JULIE'S *shoulders,* JIGGER *works his way over to* BILLY *as if to say "Did you get the knife?"* BILLY *pantomimes that it's in the inside pocket of his vest.* JULIE *turns in time to see this.*

BILLY *quickly takes her arm and walks her off.* JIGGER *has his pocket knife in his hand and is testing the sharpness of the blade and is following* BILLY *off as*

THE CURTAIN FALLS)

ACT TWO | Scene One

SCENE: *On an island across the bay. That night.*
The backdrop depicts the bay, seen between two sand dunes.

AT RISE: *It is too dark to define the characters until a moment after the rise of the curtain when the lights start a gradual "dim-up" as if a cloud were unveiling the moon. Down left* BILLY *is seen lying stretched at full length, his head on* JULIE'S *lap. There is a small group right center dominated by* NETTIE, SNOW, *and* CARRIE. *Upstage several couples recline in chosen isolation at the edge of the trees.*
The mood of the scene is the languorous contentment that comes to people who have just had a good meal in the open air.
The curtain is up several seconds before the first speech is heard.

NETTIE (*After a loud sigh*) Dunno as I should hev et those last four dozen clams!

GIRL Look here, Orrin Peasely! You jest keep your hands in yer pockets if they're so cold.

ALL (*Softly*)
This was a real nice clambake,
We're mighty glad we came.
The vittles we et

Were good, you bet!
The company was the same.
Our hearts are warm,
Our bellies are full,
And we are feelin' prime.
This was a real nice clambake
And we all had a real good time!

NETTIE
Fust come codfish chowder,
Cooked in iron kettles,
Onions floatin' on the top,
Curlin' up in petals!

JULIE
Throwed in ribbons of salted pork.

ALL
An old New England trick.

JULIE
And lapped it all up with a clamshell,
Tied on to a bayberry stick!

ALL
Oh-h-h—
This was a real nice clambake,
We're mighty glad we came.
The vittles we et
Were good, you bet!
The company was the same.
Our hearts are warm,
Our bellies are full,
And we are feelin' prime.
This was a real nice clambake
And we all had a real good time!
   (*The memory of the delectable feast restores* SNOW'S *spirit
   and he rises and crosses to center and sings very soulfully:*)

SNOW
Remember when we raked
Them red-hot lobsters
Out of the driftwood fire?
They sizzled and crackled
And sputtered a song,
Fitten for an angels' choir.

ALL GIRLS
Fitten fer an angels',
Fitten fer an angels',
Fitten fer an angels' choir!

NETTIE
We slit 'em down the back
And peppered 'em good,
And doused 'em in melted butter—

CARRIE (*Savagely*)
Then we tore away the claws
And cracked 'em with our teeth
'Cause we weren't in the mood to putter!

ALL
Fitten fer an angels',
Fitten fer an angels',
Fitten fer an angels' choir!

MAN
Then at last come the clams—

ALL
Steamed under rockweed
And poppin' from their shells,
Jest how many of 'em
Galloped down our gullets—
We couldn't say oursel's!
Oh-h-h-h-h—
This was a real nice clambake,
We're mighty glad we came!
The vittles we et
Were good, you bet!
The company was the same.
Our hearts are warm,
Our bellies are full,
And we are feelin' prime.
This was a real nice clambake,
And we all had a real good time!

We said it afore—
And we'll say it agen—
We all had a real good time!

CARRIE   Hey, Nettie' Ain't it 'bout time the boys started their treasure-hunt?

MEN (*Ad lib*)
Sure!
Feel like I'm goin' to win it this year.
Let's get goin'.

NETTIE   Jest a minute! Nobody's goin' treasure-huntin' till we get this island cleaned up. Can't leave it like this fer the next picnickers that come.

ALL MEN   Ah, Nettie—

NETTIE   Bogue in and get to work! The whole kit and kaboodle of you! Burn that rubbish! Gather up those bottles!

ALL MEN AND WOMEN (*Ad libs*)
All right, all right.
Needn't hev a catnip fit!
(JULIE *exits. All start to leave the stage in all directions*)

NETTIE   Hey, Enoch! While they're cleanin' up, you go hide the treasure.
(*She exits*)

JIGGER   Why should *he* get out of workin'?

CARRIE (*Proudly*)   'Cause he found the treasure last year. One that finds it hides it the next year. That's the way we do!
(CARRIE *and* SNOW *cross upstage of* BILLY *and* JIGGER *and exit.* JIGGER *starts to follow*)

BILLY   Hey, Jigger!

JIGGER (*Looking off after* CARRIE)   That's a well-set-up little piece, that Carrie.

BILLY   Ain't it near time fer us to start?

JIGGER   No. We'll wait till they're ready fer that treasure-hunt. That'll be a good way fer you and me to leave. We'll be a team, see? Then we'll get lost together like I said. (BILLY *is moving about nervously*) Stop jumping from one foot to the other. Go along to yer wife—and tell that little Carrie to come and talk to me.

BILLY   Look, Jigger, you ain't got time fer girls tonight.

JIGGER   Sure I have. You know me—quick or nothin'!

BILLY Jigger—after we do it—what do we do then?

JIGGER Bury the money—and go on like nothin' happened for six months. Wait another six months and then buy passage on a ship.

BILLY The baby'll be born by then.

JIGGER We'll take it along with us.

BILLY Maybe we'll sail to San Francisco.

JIGGER Why do you keep puttin' yer hand on yer chest?

BILLY My heart's bumpin' up and down under the knife.

JIGGER Put the knife on the other side.
  (CARRIE *enters*)

CARRIE Mr. Bigelow, Julie says you should come and help her. (BILLY *exits.* CARRIE *turns to* JIGGER) Why ain't *you* workin'?

JIGGER I don't feel so well.

CARRIE It's mebbe the clams not settin' so good on yer stummick.

JIGGER Nope. It's nothin' on my stummick. It's somethin' on my mind. (*Ile takes* CARRIE'S *arm*) Sit down here with me a minute. I want yer advice.

CARRIE (*Sitting on an upturned basket*) Now, look here, Mr. Craigin, I ain't got no time fer no wharf yarns or spoondrift.

JIGGER (*Squashing out his cigarette*) I want yer advice. (*Suddenly throws his arms around her*) You're sweeter than sugar and I'm crazy fer you. Never had this feelin' before fer anyone—

CARRIE Mr. Craigin!

JIGGER Ain't nothin' I wouldn't do fer you. Why, jest to see yer lovely smile—I'd swim through beer with my mouth closed. You're the only girl fer me. How about a little kiss?

CARRIE Mr. Craigin, I couldn't.

JIGGER Didn't you hear me say I loved you?

CARRIE I'm awful sorry fer you, but what can I do? Enoch and me are goin' to be cried in church next Sunday

JIGGER   Next Sunday I'll be far out at sea lookin' at the icy gray water. Mebbe I'll jump in and drown myself!

CARRIE   Oh, don't!

JIGGER   Well, then, give me a kiss. (*Grabbing her arm. Good and sore now*) One measly little kiss!

CARRIE   (*Pushing his arm away*)   Enoch wouldn't like it.

JIGGER   I don't wanta kiss Enoch.

CARRIE   (*Drawing herself up resolutely*)   I'll thank you not to yell at me, Mr. Craigin. If you love me like you say you do, then please show me the same respect like you would if you didn't love me.
   (*She starts to stalk off left. JIGGER is a stayer and not easily shaken off. He decides to try one more method. It worked once long ago on a girl in Liverpool*)

JIGGER   (*In despair*)   Carrie! (*She stops; he crosses to her*) Miss Pipperidge! Just one word, please. (*He becomes quite humble*) I know I don't deserve yer fergiveness. Only, I couldn't help myself. Fer a few awful minutes I—I let the brute come out in me.

CARRIE   I think I understand, Mr. Craigin.

JIGGER   Thank you, Miss Pipperidge, thank you kindly. There's just one thing that worries me and it worries me a lot —it's about you.

CARRIE   About me?

JIGGER   You're such a little innercent. You had no right to stay here alone and talk with a man you hardly knew. Suppose I was a different type of feller—you know, unprincipled —a feller who'd use his physical strength to have his will— there are such men, you know.

CARRIE   I know, but—

JIGGER   Every girl ought to know how to defend herself against beasts like that. (*Proceeding slyly up to his point*) Now, there are certain grips in wrestlin' I could teach you— tricks that'll land a masher flat on his face in two minutes.

CARRIE   But I ain't strong enough—

JIGGER   It don't take strength—it's all in balance—a twist of the wrist and a dig with the elbow— Here, just let me show you a simple one. This might save yer life some day. Suppose a feller grabs you like this. (*Puts both arms around her waist*) Now you put yer two hands on my neck. (*She does*) Now pull me toward you. (*She does*) That's it. Now pull my head down. Good! Now put yer left arm all the way around my neck. Now squeeze—hard! Tighter! (*Slides his right hand down her back and pats her bustle*) Good girl!

CARRIE   (*Holding him tight*)   Does it hurt?

JIGGER   (*Having the time of his life*)   You got me helpless!

CARRIE   Show me another one! (*She lets him go*)

JIGGER   Right! Here's how you can pick a feller up and send him sprawlin'. Now I'll stand here, and you get hold of— Wait a minute. I'll do it to you first. Then you can do it to me. Stand still and relax. (*He takes her hand and foot and slings her quickly over his shoulders*) This is the way firemen carry people.

CARRIE   (*A little breathless and stunned*)   Is it?

JIGGER   See how helpless you can make a feller if he gets fresh with you? (*He starts to walk off with her*)

CARRIE   Mr. Craig— (*She stops, because something terrible has happened.* SNOW *has entered.* JIGGER *sees him and stops, still holding* CARRIE *over his shoulders, firemen style. After a terrifying pause,* CARRIE *speaks:*) Hello, Enoch. (*No answer*) This is the way firemen carry people.

SNOW   (*Grimly*)   Where's the fire?
　　(JIGGER *puts her down between* SNOW *and himself*)

CARRIE   (*Crossing to* SNOW)   He was only showin' me how to defend myself.

SNOW   It didn't look like you had learned very much by the time I came!

JIGGER   Oh, what's all the fussin' and fuzzlin' and wuzzlin' about?

SNOW   In my opinion, sir, you are as scurvy a hunk o' scum as I ever see near the water's edge at low tide!

JIGGER (*Turning his profile to* SNOW) The same—side view!

SNOW I—I never thought I'd see the woman I am engaged to bein' carried out o' the woods like a fallen deer!

CARRIE He wasn't carryin' me out o' the woods. He was carryin' me *into* the woods. No, I don't mean that!

SNOW I think we hev said all we hev to say. I can't abide women who are free, loose, and lallygaggin'—and I certainly would never marry one.

CARRIE But, Enoch!

SNOW Leave me, please. Leave me alone with my shattered dreams. They are all I hev left—memories of what didn't happen! (CARRIE *turns upstage and crosses to* JIGGER. *He puts his arms around her. She starts to whimper.* SNOW *looks out into space with pained eyes, and sings*)
Geraniums in the winder,
Hydrangeas on the lawn,
And breakfast in the kitchen
In the timid pink of dawn,
And you to blow me kisses
When I headed fer the sea—
We might hev been
A happy pair
Of lovers—
Mightn't hev we?
   (*Another sob from* CARRIE. SNOW *continues*)
And comin' home at twilight,
It might hev been so sweet
To take my ketch of herring
And lay them at your feet!
   (*Swallowing hard*)
I might hev hed a baby—

JIGGER What!

SNOW (*Glares at* JIGGER, *then out front again*)
To dandle on my knee,
But all these things
That might hev been
Are never,
Never to be!
   (*At this point* CARRIE *just lets loose and bawls, and buries*

her head in JIGGER'S *shoulder. Some people hear this and
enter as* JIGGER *consoles her*)

JIGGER
I never see it yet to fail,
I never see it fail!
A girl who's in love with a virtuous man
Is doomed to weep and wail.
  (*More people enter and get into the scene*)
Stonecutters cut it on stone,
Woodpeckers peck it on wood;
There's nothin' so bad fer a woman
As a man who thinks he's good!
  (CARRIE *bawls out one loud note. More people enter*)

SNOW   Nice talk!

JIGGER
My mother used to say to me:
"When you grow up, my son,
I hope you're a bum like yer father was,
'Cause a good man ain't no fun."

JIGGER AND CHORUS
Stonecutters cut it on stone,
Woodpeckers peck it on wood;
There's nothin' so bad for a woman
As a man who thinks he's good!
  (*From here on, the* CHORUS *takes sides*)

SNOW
'Tain't so!

JIGGER
'Tis too!

SNOW'S CHORUS
'Tain't so!

JIGGER'S CHORUS
'Tis too!
  (SNOW *crosses to right, followed by* CARRIE)

CARRIE   Enoch— Say you forgive me! Say somethin' sweet
to me, Enoch—somethin' soft and sweet. (*He remains silent
and she becomes exasperated*) Say somethin' soft and sweet!

SNOW (*Turning to* CARRIE, *fiercely*) Boston cream pie!
(*Turns and exits.* CARRIE *cries.* BILLY *enters and crosses to*
JIGGER)

BILLY Hey, Jigger—don't you think?

JIGGER Huh? (*Catches on, raises his voice to all*) When are
we goin' to start that treasure-hunt?

NETTIE Right now! Y'all got yer partners? Two men to each
team. You got half an hour to find the treasure. The winners
can kiss any girls they want!
(*A whoop and a holler goes up and all the* MEN *and the*
DANCING GIRLS *start out.* JULIE *enters from down left and
sees* BILLY *starting out with* JIGGER)

JULIE Billy—are you goin' with JIGGER? Don't you think
that's foolish?

BILLY Why?

JULIE Neither one of you knows the island good. You
ought to split up and each go with—

BILLY (*Brushing her aside*) We're partners, see? C'mon,
Jigger.

CARRIE I don't know what gets into men. Enoch put on a
new suit today and he was a different person.
(*They all group around* JULIE)

GIRL (*Singing*)
I never see it yet to fail.

ALL GIRLS
I never see it fail.
A girl who's in love with any man
Is doomed to weep and wail.

1ST GIRL (*Spoken*) And it's even worse after they marry
you.

2ND GIRL You ought to give him back that ring, Carrie.
You'd be better off.

3RD GIRL Here's Arminy—been married a year. She'll tell
you.

ARMINY (*Singing with a feeling of futility*)
The clock jest ticks yer life away,

There's no relief in sight.
It's cookin' and scrubbin' and sewin' all **day**
And Gawd-knows-whatin' all night!

ALL
Stonecutters cut it on stone,
Woodpeckers peck it on wood;
There's nothin' so bad fer a woman
As a man who's bad or good!

CARRIE (*Spoken*)   It makes you wonder, don't it?

GIRL   Now you tell her, Julie.

2ND GIRL   She's your best girl friend.

ALL GIRLS (*Singing*)
Tell it to her good, Julie,
Tell it to her good!
  (JULIE *smiles. The* GIRLS *group around her expectantly.*
  JULIE *starts singing softly and earnestly to* CARRIE, *but as
  she goes on, she quite obviously becomes autobiographical
  in her philosophy. Her singing is quiet, almost recited. The
  orchestration is light. The* GIRLS *hold the picture, perfectly
  still, like figures in a painting*)

JULIE (*Singing*)
What's the use of wond'rin'
If he's good or if he's bad,
Or if you like the way he wears his hat?
Oh, what's the use of wond'rin'
If he's good or if he's bad?
He's your feller and you love him—
That's all there is to that.

Common sense may tell you
That the endin' will be sad
And now's the time to break and run away.
But what's the use of wond'rin'
If the endin' will be sad?
He's your feller and you love him—
There's nothin' more to say.

Somethin' made him the way that he is,
Whether he's false or true.
And somethin' gave him the things that are his—

One of those things is you.
So
When he wants your kisses
You will give them to the lad,
And anywhere he leads you, you will walk.
And anytime he needs you,
You'll go runnin' there like mad!
You're his girl and he's your feller—
And all the rest is talk.

>   (*As* JULIE *finishes her song, we see* BILLY *and* JIGGER
>   *entering, crouching behind the sand dunes.* JULIE *turns
>   just in time to see them as they get up center.* JULIE *crosses
>   to* BILLY)

JULIE   Billy! Billy! Where you goin'?

BILLY   Where we goin'?

JIGGER   We're looking for the treasure.

JULIE   I don't want you to, Billy. Let me come with you.

JIGGER   No.

JULIE (*Putting her hands to his chest and feeling the knife*)
Billy!

BILLY   I got no time to fool with women. Get out of my
way!
>   (*He succeeds in shoving her aside*)

JULIE   Let me have that. Oh, Billy. Please—
>   (*He exits.* JIGGER *follows.* NETTIE *puts her arms around*
>   JULIE *to comfort her. The* GIRLS *group around them*)

GIRLS
Common sense may tell you
That the endin' will be sad
And now's the time to break and run away,
But what's the use of wond'rin'
If the endin' will be sad?
He's your feller and you love him—
There's nothin' more to say.
>   (*The lights dim and the curtains close*)

ACT TWO | Scene Two

SCENE: *Mainland Waterfront. An hour later. Extreme left there is an upright pile, a box, and a bale. At center is a longer bale. Up right center is an assorted heap consisting of a crate, a trunk, a sack, and other wharfside oddments.*

AT RISE: JIGGER *is seated on the pile extreme left, smoking.* BILLY *is pacing back and forth, right center.*

BILLY   Suppose he don't come.

JIGGER   He'll come. What will you say to him?

BILLY   I say: "Good evening, sir. Excuse me, sir. Can you tell me the time?" And suppose he answers me. What do I say?

JIGGER   He won't answer you.
(JIGGER *throws his knife into the top of the box so that the point sticks and the knife quivers there*)

BILLY   Have you ever—killed a man before?

JIGGER   If I did, I wouldn't be likely to say so, would I?

BILLY   No, guess you wouldn't. If you did—if tonight we—I mean—suppose some day when *we* die we'll have to come up before—before—

JIGGER   Before who?

BILLY   Well—before God.

JIGGER   You and me? Not a chance!

BILLY   Why not?

JIGGER What's the highest court they ever dragged you into?

BILLY Just perlice magistrates, I guess.

JIGGER Sure. Never been before a supreme-court judge, have you?

BILLY No.

JIGGER Same thing in the next world. For rich folks, the heavenly court and the high judge. For you and me, perlice magistrates. Fer the rich, fine music and chubby little angels—

BILLY Won't we get any music?

JIGGER Not a note. All we'll get is justice! There'll be plenty of that for you and me. Yes, sir! Nothin' but justice.

BILLY It's gettin' late—they'll be comin' back from the clambake. I wish he'd come.—Suppose he don't.

JIGGER He will. What do you say we play some cards while we're waitin'? Time'll pass quicker that way.

BILLY All right.

JIGGER Got any money?

BILLY Eighty cents.
(*Crosses to* JIGGER, *sits on small bale, and puts his money on table.* JIGGER *takes out cards and his change*)

JIGGER (*Puts money on box top, shuffles cards*) All right, eighty cents. We'll play twenty-one. I'll bank. (*Deals the necessary cards out*)

BILLY (*Looking at his cards*) I'll bet the bank.

JIGGER (*Aloud, to himself*) Sounds like he's got an ace.

BILLY I'll take another. (JIGGER *deals another card to* BILL) Come again! (JIGGER *deals a fourth card*) Over! (*Throws cards down.* JIGGER *gathers in the money.* BILLY *rises, crosses right center, looks off right*) Wish old sideburns would come and have it over with.

JIGGER He's a little late. (*Looking up at* BILLY) Don't you want to go on with the game?

BILLY Ain't got any more money. I told you.

JIGGER   Want to play on credit?

BILLY   You mean you'll trust me?

JIGGER   No—but I'll deduct it.

BILLY   From what?

JIGGER   From your share of the money. If you win, you deduct it from my share.

BILLY (*Crossing and sitting on bale*)   All right. Can't wait here doin' nothin'. Drive a feller crazy. How much is the bank?

JIGGER   Sideburns'll have three thousand on him. That's what he always brings the captain. Tonight the captain don't get it. We get it. Fifteen hundred to you. Fifteen hundred to me.

BILLY   Go ahead and deal. (JIGGER *deals*) Fifty dollars. (*Looks at his card*) No, a hundred dollars. (JIGGER *gives him a card*) Enough.

JIGGER (*Laying down stack and looking at his own cards*) Twenty-one.

BILLY   All right! This time double or nothin'!

JIGGER (*Dealing*)   Double or nothin' it is.

BILLY (*Looking at cards*)   Enough.

JIGGER (*Laying down his cards*)   Twenty-one.

BILLY   Hey—are you cheatin'?

JIGGER (*So innocent*)   Me? Do I look like a cheat?

BILLY (BILLY *raps the box impatiently.* JIGGER *deals*)   Five hundred!

JIGGER   Dollars?

BILLY   Dollars.

JIGGER   Say, you're a plunger, ain't you? Yes, sir.

BILLY (*Getting a card*)   Another. (*He gets it*) Too much.

JIGGER   That makes seven hundred you owe me.

BILLY   Seven hundred! Double or nothin'. (JIGGER *deals*) I'll stand pat!

JIGGER (*Laying down his cards in pretended amazement*)
Twenty-one! A natural!

BILLY (*Rising and taking hold of* JIGGER *by the coat lapels*)
You—you—damn you, you're a dirty crook! You— (BAS-
COMBE *enters from left.* JIGGER *coughs, warning* BILLY, *and
then nudges* BILLY *into action as* BASCOMBE *crosses to right
center.* JIGGER *runs behind crates.* BILLY *addresses* BASCOMBE)
Excuse me, sir. Can you tell me the time?
   (BASCOMBE *turns to* BILLY, *and* JIGGER *leaps out from
   behind the crates and tries to stab* BASCOMBE. BASCOMBE
   gets hold of JIGGER'S *knife hand and twists his wrist,
   forcing him into a helpless position.* BASCOMBE *takes his
   gun from its holster with his free hand, holding* BILLY *off*)

BASCOMBE   Now don't budge, either one of you. (*To* JIGGER)
Drop that knife. (JIGGER *drops the knife*) Ahoy, up there on
the *Nancy B*! Captain Watson! Anybody up there?

CAPTAIN (*Off*)   Ahoy, down there!
   (JIGGER *twists himself loose and runs off right. A* SAILOR
   enters from left. BASCOMBE *turns and fires a shot at* JIGGER
   as he runs, then turns, holding BILLY *off, as the* SAILOR *gets
   to* BASCOMBE)

BASCOMBE (*To the* SAILOR)   Go after that one. He's runnin'
up Maple Street. I'll cover the other one. (*The* SAILOR *runs off
after* JIGGER) There's another bullet in here. Don't forget
that—you. Look behind you! What do you see comin'?

BILLY (*Slowly turning and looking off left*)   Two perlicemen.

BASCOMBE   You wanted to know what time it was. I'll tell
you—the time for you will be ten or twenty years in prison.
   (*The* TWO POLICEMEN *enter from left*)

BILLY   Oh, no it won't.
   (*He clambers up on the pile with his knife drawn*)

BASCOMBE (*Jeering and covering him with his pistol*)   Where
do you think you're escapin' to—the sky?

BILLY   They won't put me in no prison.
   (*He raises the knife high in air*)

POLICEMAN   Stop him!

BILLY (*Stabbing himself in the stomach*)   Julie!
(*He topples off the pile of crates, falling behind them. The* TWO POLICEMEN, *who have made a vain attempt to stop him, rush behind the crates, where they proceed to remove his coat, which is later to be used for his pillow. The* CAPTAIN *and* ANOTHER SAILOR *come on the run from left. The* CAPTAIN *is carrying a lantern, which he puts on the pile, right center*)

CAPTAIN (*To* BASCOMBE)   How about you, Mr. Bascombe? You all right?

BASCOMBE   Yes, I'm all right. Lucky, though. Very lucky. This is the first time I ever took a pistol with me.

CAPTAIN (*Looking over crates at* BILLY)   Is he dead?

1ST POLICEMAN   I don't think so, he's still breathing.

CAPTAIN   Bring him out here where we can lay him out flat. (*The* CAPTAIN *looks around to see what can be used for a bed for* BILLY. *He spots the bales, crosses to left, takes the small bale, and puts it end to end with a larger one. The* TWO POLICEMEN *and the* SAILOR *carry* BILLY *out and lay him on the bales. The* CAPTAIN *speaks to the* SAILOR) You go for a doctor. (*To the* POLICEMAN *who is holding* BILLY'S *coat*) Put that under his head.
(*The* POLICEMAN *does this. When* BILLY *is set, the* TWO POLICEMEN *rise; one stands left end of bale, the other right end*)

BASCOMBE   The fools—the silly fools. They didn't even notice I was comin' from the ship, not to it.
(*The* CAPTAIN *is covering* BILLY *with a tarpaulin he found on the top of crates at right center*)

CAPTAIN   The money they tried to kill you for is locked up in my desk!
(*Voices off left are heard to be singing "June Is Bustin' Out All Over," very softly, as if in the distance*)

BASCOMBE   The fools.

1ST SAILOR (*The one who chased* JIGGER, *returning*)   He got away.

BASCOMBE (*Hearing the offstage singing as it has become louder*)   What's that?

CAPTAIN   The folks comin' back from the clambake.
  (*The people enter left*)

BASCOMBE (*To the* POLICEMEN)   You'd better stop them.
  (BASCOMBE *exits*)

POLICEMAN   Yes, sir. (*They cross over and stop the crowd
from reaching* BILLY, *but one or two get through and see the
tragedy, and they recognize* BILLY. *The* POLICEMEN *get to
these and speak. The singing stops*) Get back there. Stand
back.
  (*A voice is heard from behind the crowd*)

1ST VOICE   Who is it?

2ND VOICE   Billy.

3RD VOICE   Billy Bigelow.

4TH VOICE   Poor Julie.
  (*The crowd opens up for* JULIE, *who goes straight to*
BILLY, *up behind the bales.* NETTIE *and the* POLICEMEN
hurry the crowd off quietly. They exit left. The CAPTAIN
remains on right of the crates looking upstage. The POLICE-
MEN *and* NETTIE *also remain*)

JULIE (*As she is crossing to him*)   Billy—

BILLY   Little Julie—somethin' I want to tell you— (*Pause*)
I couldn't see anythin' ahead, and Jigger told me how we
could get a hold of a lot of money—and maybe sail to San
Francisco.—See?

JULIE   Yes.

BILLY   Tell the baby, if you want, say I had this idea about
San Francisco. (*His voice grows weaker*) Julie—

JULIE   Yes.

BILLY   Hold my hand tight.

JULIE   I am holdin' it tight—all the time.

BILLY   Tighter—still tighter! (*Pause*) Julie!

JULIE   Good-by.
  (*He sinks back.* JULIE *kisses his hand. The* CAPTAIN *crosses
over, picks* JULIE *up gently. He then bends down and
inspects* BILLY. *He rises, looks at* JULIE)

CAPTAIN   The good Lord will help him now, ma'am.
   (CARRIE *enters, followed by* SNOW. *They cross to* JULIE'S *left*)

CARRIE   Julie—don't be mad at me fer sayin' it—but you're better off this way.

SNOW   Carrie's right.

CARRIE   Julie, tell me, am I right?

JULIE   You're right, Carrie.

CARRIE (*Looking down at* BILLY)   He's better off too, poor feller. Believe me, Julie, he's better off too. (*She embraces* JULIE, *weeping*)

JULIE   Don't cry, Carrie.

CARRIE   God be with you, Julie.
   (JULIE *smiles at her wearily.* SNOW *takes* CARRIE *by the arm and leads her off down left. We hear voices off left*)

MRS. MULLIN (*Off left*)   Where is he? No, no, please.
   (MRS. MULLIN *comes in on the run from left, followed by* TWO GIRLS, *who try to stop her*)

GIRL   Don't let her!
   (MRS. MULLIN *stops left center, looks at* BILLY, *then at* JULIE *questioningly.* JULIE *steps back—a silent invitation to come and pass in front of her.* MRS. MULLIN *walks slowly to where* BILLY *lies. After a moment she brushes* BILLY'S *hair off his forehead, as she used to do. Then* NETTIE, *the* POLICEMAN *and all exit, leaving only* JULIE *and* MRS. MULLIN *on the stage with* BILLY. MRS. MULLIN *gets up and turns slowly to look at* JULIE, *who looks back at her.* MRS. MULLIN *tries a faint little smile, then turns and exits left.* JULIE *returns to* BILLY, *leans over, and restores the stray lock to where it was before* MRS. MULLIN *took the liberty to brush it back*)

JULIE   Sleep, Billy—sleep. Sleep peaceful, like a good boy. I knew why you hit me. You were quick-tempered and unhappy. I always knew everythin' you were thinkin'. But you didn't always know what I was thinkin'. One thing I never told you--skeered you'd laugh at me. I'll tell you now— (*Even now she has to make an effort to overcome her shyness in saying it*) I love you. I love you. (*In a whisper*) I love—

you. (*Smiles*) I was always ashamed to say it out loud. But now I said it. Didn't I? (*She takes the shawl off her shoulders and drapes it over* BILLY. NETTIE *comes in from left.* JULIE *looks up and sees her, lets out a cry, and runs to her*) What am I goin' to do?

NETTIE   Do? Why, you gotta stay on here with me—so's I ken be with you when you hev the baby. (JULIE *buries her head in* NETTIE'S *shoulder and holds tightly to her*) Main thing is to keep on *livin'*—keep on *keerin'* what's goin' to happen. 'Member that sampler you gave me? 'Member what it says?

JULIE   The words? Sure. Used to sing 'em in school.

NETTIE   Sing 'em now—see if you know what they mean.

JULIE (*Singing*)
When you walk
Through a storm
Keep your chin up high,
And don't be afraid—of—the—dar—
   (JULIE *breaks off, sobbing.* NETTIE *starts the song*)

NETTIE (*Singing*)
When you walk
Through a storm
Keep your chin up high,
And don't be afraid of the dark.
At the end
Of the storm
Is a golden sky
And the sweet
Silver song
Of a lark.

Walk on
Through the wind,
Walk on
Through the rain,
Though your dreams be tossed and blown,
Walk on, walk on,
With hope in your heart,
And you'll never walk alone!
   (JULIE *and* NETTIE *kneel in prayer. The* TWO HEAVENLY
   FRIENDS *enter from right and cross to* BILLY)

1ST HEAVENLY FRIEND Get up, Billy.

BILLY Huh?

1ST HEAVENLY FRIEND Get up.

BILLY (*Straightening up*) Who are you?

2ND HEAVENLY FRIEND Shake yourself up. Got to get goin'.

BILLY (*Looking up at them and turning front, still sitting*)
Goin'? Where?

1ST HEAVENLY FRIEND Never mind where. Important thing
is you can't stay here.

BILLY (*Turning left, looks at* JULIE) Julie!
    (*The lights dim, and a cloud gauze drop comes in behind*
    BILLY *and the* HEAVENLY FRIENDS)

1ST HEAVENLY FRIEND She can't hear you.

BILLY Who decided that?

1ST HEAVENLY FRIEND You did. When you killed yourself.

BILLY I see! So it's over!

1ST HEAVENLY FRIEND It isn't as simple as that. As long as
there is one person on earth who remembers you—it isn't
over.

BILLY What're you goin' to do to me?

1ST HEAVENLY FRIEND We aren't going to do anything. We
jest came down to fetch you—take you up to the jedge.

BILLY Judge! Am I goin' before the Lord God Himself?

1ST HEAVENLY FRIEND What hev you ever done thet you
should come before Him?

BILLY (*His anger rising*) So that's it. Just like Jigger said;
"No supreme court for little people—just perlice magistrates"!

1ST HEAVENLY FRIEND Who said anythin' about—

BILLY I tell you if they kick me around up there like they
did on earth, I'm goin' to do somethin' about it! I'm dead
and I got nothin' to lose. I'm goin' to stand up for my rights!
I tell you I'm goin' before the Lord God Himself—straight to
the top! Y'hear?

1ST HEAVENLY FRIEND Simmer down, Billy.

BILLY (*Singing*)
Take me beyond the pearly gates
Through a beautiful marble hall.
Take me before the highest throne
And let me judged by the highest Judge of all!

Let the Lord shout and yell,
Let His eyes flash flame,
I promise not to quiver when He calls my name,
Let Him send me to hell,
But before I go,
I feel that I'm entitled to a hell of a show!
Want pink-faced angels on a purple cloud,
Twangin' on their harps till their fingers get red,
Want organ music—let it roll out loud,
Rollin' like a wave, washin' over my head!
Want ev'ry star in heaven
Hangin' in the room,
Shinin' in my eyes
When I hear my doom!

Reckon my sins are good big sins,
And the punishment won't be small;
So take me before the highest throne
And let me judged by the highest Judge of all.
  (1ST HEAVENLY FRIEND *gestures to* BILLY *to follow. They
  exit*)

ACT TWO | Scene Three

SCENE: *Up there.*
  *A celestial clothes-line is seen stretching back through
infinity, but one portion of it is strung across as far downstage as possible. There is a celestial stepladder standing*

right center upstage of the line. It resembles our own step-ladders except that it shimmers with a silvery light. The clothes-line is quite full of shimmering stars. There is a basket full of stars on the shelf behind the ladder.

AT RISE: *The* STARKEEPER *is seated on the top of the step-ladder, and as the lights come up, he can be seen hanging out stars and dusting them with a silver-handled white feather duster.*

    BILLY *and the* TWO HEAVENLY FRIENDS *are seen making their way through the clouds from stage left to right, emerging a moment later through entrance down right into the back yard. The* 1ST HEAVENLY FRIEND *enters, He stops, stage right center, faces front, and speaks.*

1ST HEAVENLY FRIEND Billy!

BILLY (*Entering*) Hey, what is this! (*Crossing and speaking to* STARKEEPER) Who are you?

STARKEEPER Never mind who I am, Bigelow.

BILLY (*To* FRIEND) Where am I?

STARKEEPER (*Although question was not addressed to him*) You're in the back yard of heaven. (*Pointing off right*) There's the gates over there.

BILLY The pearly gates!

STARKEEPER Nope. The pearly gates are in front. Those are the back gates. They're just mother-of-pearly.

BILLY I don't wanta go in no back gate. I wanta go before the highest—

STARKEEPER You'll go where we send you, young man.

BILLY Now look here!

STARKEEPER Don't yell.

BILLY I didn't yell.

STARKEEPER Well, don't. (*He takes a star off the line. To* FRIEND) This one's finished. Brother Joshua, please hang it over Salem, Mass.

1ST HEAVENLY FRIEND (*Crossing over and taking star*)
A-yah. (*Exits off left*)

STARKEEPER (*Taking a notebook out of his pocket*) Now,
this is a routine question I gotta ask everybody. Is there
anythin' on earth you left unfinished? The reason I ask you
is you're entitled to go back fer one day—if you want to.

BILLY   I don't know. (*Doggedly*) Guess as long as I'm here,
I won't go back.

STARKEEPER (*Jotting down in a notebook*)   "Waives his right
to go back."

BILLY   Can I ask you somethin'? I'd like to know if the baby
will be a boy or a girl.

STARKEEPER   We'll come to that later.

BILLY   But I'm only askin'—

STARKEEPER   Jest let me do the askin'—you do the answerin'.
I got my orders.—You left yer wife hevin' thet baby comin'
—with nothin' fer 'em to live on. Why'd you do thet?

BILLY   I couldn't get work and I couldn't bear to see her—
(*Pause*)

STARKEEPER   You couldn't bear to see her cry. Why not
come right out and say it? Why are you afraid of sayin' the
right word? Why are you ashamed you loved Julie?

BILLY   I ain't ashamed of anything.

STARKEEPER   Why'd you beat her?

BILLY   I didn't beat her—I wouldn't beat a little thing like
that—I hit her.

STARKEEPER   Why?

BILLY   Well, y'see—we'd argue. And she'd say this and I'd
say that—and she'd be right—so I'd hit her.

STARKEEPER   Hmm! Are you sorry you hit her?

BILLY   Ain't sorry fer anythin'.

STARKEEPER (*Taking his basket and coming down off the
ladder*)   You ken be as sot and pernicketty as you want. Up
here patience is as endless as time. We ken wait. (*He turns*

to BILLY *in a more friendly way*) Now look here, son, it's only fair to tell you—you're in a pretty tight corner. Fact is you haven't done enough good in yer life to get in there—not even through the back door.

BILLY (*Turning away*)   All right. If I can't get in—I can't.

STARKEEPER (*Testily*)   I didn't say you can't. Said you ain't done enough so *far*. You might still make it—if you tried hard enough.

BILLY   How?

STARKEEPER   Why don't you go down to earth fer a day like I said you could. Do somethin' real fine fer someone.

BILLY   Aw—what could I do?

STARKEEPER   Well, fer one thing you might do yer little daughter some good.

BILLY (*Turning to* STARKEEPER, *elated*)   A daughter! It's a girl—my baby!

STARKEEPER   Ain't a baby any more. She's fifteen years old.

BILLY   How could that be? I just come from there.

STARKEEPER   You got to get used to a new way of tellin' time, Billy. A year on earth is just a minute up here. Would you like to look down and see her?

BILLY   Could I? Could I see her from here?

STARKEEPER   Sure could. Follow me.
(STARKEEPER *and* BILLY *cross down right. The lights dim and the gauze cloud curtain descends behind them*)

BILLY   Tell me—is she happy?

STARKEEPER   No, she ain't, Billy. She's a lot like you. That's why I figure you're the one could help her most—if you was there.

BILLY   If she ain't happy, I don't want to look.

STARKEEPER (*Looking off left, as if toward the earth*)   Well, right this minute she appears to be hevin' a fine time. Yes, sir! There she is, runnin' on the beach. Got her shoes and stockin's off.

BILLY   Like I used to do!

STARKEEPER   Don't you think you better take a look?

BILLY   Where is she? What do I have to do to see her?

STARKEEPER   Jest look and wait. The power to see her will come to you. (*He puts his hand lightly on* BILLY's *shoulder*)

BILLY   Is that her? Little kid with straw-colored hair?
(*The lights dim. The curtain goes up on a dark stage*)

STARKEEPER (*As the lights are dimming*)   Pretty—ain't she?

BILLY   My little girl!
(BILLY *and the* STARKEEPER *back off down right and the entire stage is suddenly flooded with light*)

ACT TWO | Scene Four

SCENE: *Down here. On a beach. Fifteen years later.*

AT RISE: LOUISE *is romping on the beach. Two little* RUFFIAN BOYS *join her. Presently* ENOCH SNOW *enters, leading his six very well-behaved* CHILDREN. LOUISE *invites them to join in her play, but, taking their cue from their father's horrified face, they snub her. They exit with their father, all except one little horror in a big hat who remains to taunt* LOUISE.

SNOW'S DAUGHTER   My father bought me my pretty dress.

LOUISE   My father would have bought me a pretty dress, too. He was a barker on a carousel.

SNOW'S DAUGHTER   Your father was a thief.

(*Her nasty work accomplished, she assumes an impish, satisfied look and starts away.* LOUISE *goes after her. Their pace increases.* LOUISE *finally chasing her off, returning soon with a trophy—the big hat.*
(*Now a* CARNIVAL TROUPE *dances on. The* RUFFIANS *are frightened by them. Failing to persuade* LOUISE *to run away with them, they leave her there. One of the carnival boys is the type* LOUISE'S *father was when he was young. Of all this fascinating group, he interests her most. After the others dance off, he returns to her for a flirtation. It is much more than this to* LOUISE. *It is a first experience, overwhelmingly beautiful, painful and passionate. He leaves her abruptly. She's too young. Thwarted, humiliated, she weeps alone.*
(*Now a group of* CHILDREN *enter, dressed for a party.* LOUISE *seeks consolation with them. She tries to join in their dancing. They reject her and make fun of her. She turns on them so viciously that they are frozen with awe and fear as she speaks to them in a voice full of deep injury and the fury of a hopeless outcast*)

LOUISE I hate you—I hate all of you!
(*They back away, then dance away, leaving her heartbroken and alone—terribly alone.*
(*The gauze cloud curtain falls, revealing* BILLY *and the* STARKEEPER, *who have been watching all this from "up there."*)

BILLY Why did you make me look?

STARKEEPER You said you wanted to.

BILLY I know what she's goin' through.

STARKEEPER Somethin' like what happened to you when you was a kid, ain't it?

BILLY Somebody ought to help her.

STARKEEPER Ay-ah. Somebody ought to. You ken go down any time. Offer's still open.
(*The* 1ST HEAVENLY FRIEND *enters to guide* BILLY *if he wants to go.* BILLY *starts toward him; then, getting a sudden idea, he turns back and stealthily takes a star from the* STARKEEPER'S *basket. Both the* STARKEEPER *and the* HEAV-

ENLY FRIEND *are aware of this, but pretend not to notice.*
BILLY *waves an elaborate good-by to the* STARKEEPER *and,
whistling casually to quell suspicion, he starts away with
the* HEAVENLY FRIEND)

ACT TWO | Scene Five

SCENE: *Outside Julie's cottage.*
AT RISE: JULIE *and* CARRIE *are seated outside the cottage,
having coffee.*

CARRIE (*Seated left of* JULIE, *continuing a narrative*) —and
so the next day we all climbed to the top of the Statue of
Liberty—Enoch and me and the nine kids.

JULIE   Did you go to any theayters in New York?

CARRIE   Course we did!

JULIE   Did you see any of them there "extravaganzas"?

CARRIE   Enoch took me to one of them things. The curtain
went up and the fust thing y'see is twelve hussies with nothin'
on their legs but tights!

JULIE   What happened then?

CARRIE   Well! Enoch jest grabbed hold o' my arm and
dragged me out of the theayter! But I went back the next day
—to a matinee—to see how the story come out.

JULIE   All by yerself? (CARRIE *nods*) Lucky you didn't see
anybody you know.

CARRIE   I did.

JULIE   Who?

CARRIE Enoch!

(JULIE *clasps her hand over her mouth to keep from laugh-ing. Then she gets the cups together.* CARRIE *gets up*)

CARRIE (*Animatedly*) There was one girl who sung an aw-ful ketchy song. (*She walks to the back of her chair.* LOUISE *enters from the house, unnoticed*) She threw her leg over a fence like this— (*As she is swinging her leg over the chair, she sees* LOUISE *and hastily puts her leg down*)—and it rained all day!

(JULIE, *her back toward* LOUISE, *stares at* CARRIE *in won-der. She gathers that something is up, turns right, and sees* LOUISE)

JULIE Oh-h-h. Louise, take these cups right into the kitchen, dear. That's a good girl.

(LOUISE *takes the cups into the house*)

CARRIE She threw her leg over a fence like this— (*She swings her leg over the chair and pulls her skirt up over her knee*) and she sung: (*She sings:*)
I'm a tomboy,
Jest a tomboy!
I'm a madcap maiden from Broadway!

(ENOCH *enters, followed by their* ELDEST SON, *but* CARRIE *does not see them.* JULIE *tries to warn her*)
I'm a tomboy,
A merry tomboy!

ENOCH (*Taking his son by the shoulders*) Turn yer eyes away, Junior! (*Turns his son's face away*)

CARRIE (*Taking her leg off the chair and standing there guiltily*) I was jest tellin' Julie about thet show—*Madcap Maidens.*

ENOCH We also saw *Julius Cæsar.* Wouldn't thet be a better play to quote from?

CARRIE I don't remember much of thet one. All the men was dressed in nightgowns and it made me sleepy.

JULIE (*Trying to change the subject*) Won't you set down and visit with us?

ENOCH Afeared we hevn't time. Mrs. Snow and I hev to stop at the minister's on our way to the graduation. (*To*

CARRIE) And I'll thank you not to sing "I'm a tomboy" to the minister's wife.

CARRIE I already did.

ENOCH (*Giving his son a good slap on the back with right hand*) Come, Junior!
(LOUISE *comes out of the house just as* JUNIOR *turns to his father.* JUNIOR *sees* LOUISE *and gets a new idea*)

ENOCH, JR. Pa, ken I stay and talk to Louise? (ENOCH *looks stern.* CARRIE *crosses to* ENOCH) Jest fer five minutes.

ENOCH No!

CARRIE (*Slapping* ENOCH'S *back in the same manner as* ENOCH *slapped* JUNIOR) Aw, let him!

ENOCH All right. Five minutes. No more.

JULIE (*Going into house*) Good-by.

CARRIE See you at the graduation.
(JULIE *exits into house*)

ENOCH (*Taking* CARRIE *to exit*) Still lallygaggin'. You'd think a woman with nine children'd hev more sense.

CARRIE If I hed more sense I wouldn't hev nine children!
(*She crosses in front of* ENOCH *and exits. He follows*)

LOUISE I wish I could go to New York.

ENOCH, JR. What are you goin' to do after you graduate?

LOUISE (*Lowering her voice, as* BILLY *and* FRIEND *enter left*) Listen, Enoch—ken you keep a secret?
(JUNIOR *solemnly crosses his heart and spits*)

BILLY (*To* HEAVENLY FRIEND) Can she see me?

1ST HEAVENLY FRIEND Only if you want her to.
(*They remain silent observers of the scene,* BILLY *standing by the trellis,* HEAVENLY FRIEND *extreme downstage left*)

ENOCH, JR. Well, what's the secret?

LOUISE I'm goin' to be an actress. There's a troupe comin' through here next week. I met a feller—says he's the advance man, or somethin'—says he'll help me!

ENOCH, JR. (*Horrified*) You mean run away? (*She puts her fingers to her lips to shush him.* BILLY *winces.* 1ST HEAVENLY FRIEND *watches* BILLY) I won't let you do it, Louise.

LOUISE How'll you stop me?

ENOCH, JR. I'll marry you. That's how. The hardest thing'll be to persuade Papa to let me marry beneath my station.

LOUISE You needn't bother about marryin' beneath your station! I wouldn't have you. And I wouldn't have that stuck-up buzzard for a father-in-law if you give me a million dollars!
(BILLY *looks at* FRIEND *and smiles, happy over this*)

ENOCH, JR. (*Outraged, hit in a tender spot*) You're a fine one to talk about my father! What about yer own? A cheap barker on a carousel—and he beat your mother!

LOUISE (*Giving* JUNIOR *a good punch*) You get out of here! You sleeky little la-de-da! (*Spins him around, gives him a well-directed kick.* BILLY, *seeing all this, puts out his foot and trips* JUNIOR *just as he is passing him*) I'll—I'll kill you—you—
(JUNIOR *runs off left.* LOUISE *suddenly turns, crosses to her chair, sinks on it, and sobs.* BILLY *looks over at* LOUISE, *who is a very heartbroken little girl. He turns to the* HEAVENLY FRIEND)

BILLY If I want her to see me, she will? (*The* HEAVENLY FRIEND *nods.* BILLY *approaches* LOUISE *timidly*) Little girl— Louise!
(*She looks up through her tears*)

LOUISE Who are you?

BILLY I—I— (*He's nearly as rattled as he was the night he suddenly faced* BASCOMBE *on the wharf*)

LOUISE How did you know my name?

BILLY Somebody told me you lived here. I knew your father.

LOUISE My father!

BILLY I heard what that little whippersnapper said. It ain't true—any of it.

LOUISE It is true—all of it.
  (*Pause. He is stunned*)

BILLY Did your mother tell you that?

LOUISE No, but every kid in town knows it. They've been throwin' it up at me ever since I kin remember. I wish I was dead. (*She looks away to hide her tears*)

BILLY (*Softly*) What—what did yer *mother* say about—him?

LOUISE Oh, she's told me a lot of fairy stories about how he died in San Francisco—and she's always sayin' what a handsome fellow he was—

BILLY Well, he was!

LOUISE (*Hopefully, rising*) Was he—really?

BILLY He was the handsomest feller around here.

LOUISE You really knew him, did you? And he was handsome. (*He nods his head*) What else about him? Know anythin' else *good* about him?

BILLY (*Passing right hand through his hair*) Well-ll—he used to tell funny jokes at the carousel and make people laugh.

LOUISE (*Her face lighting up*) Did he? (*They both laugh*) What else?
  (*Pause. He's stuck and changes the subject*)

BILLY Look—I want to give you a present.

LOUISE (*Backing up right, immediately suspicious*) Don't come in, mister. My mother wouldn't like it.

BILLY I don't mean you any harm, child. I want to give you somethin'.

LOUISE Don't you come any closer. You go 'way with yer white face. You scare me.

BILLY Don't chase me away. I want to give you a present —somethin' pretty—somethin' wonderful—
  (*He looks at* HEAVENLY FRIEND, *who turns front and smiles.* BILLY *takes the star from his inside vest pocket.* LOUISE *looks at star, then at* BILLY)

LOUISE What's that?

BILLY Pst! A star.
(*He points up to the sky with right hand to indicate whence it came.* LOUISE *is terrified now*)

LOUISE (*Backing up right*) Go away!

BILLY (*Growing panicky and taking her arm*) Darling, please—I want to help you.

LOUISE (*Trying to pull arm away*) Don't call me darling. Let go my arm!

BILLY I want to make you happy. Take this—

LOUISE No!

BILLY Please! (*She pulls away from him, holding out her right hand to keep him away from her*) Please—dear—
(*Impulsively, involuntarily, he slaps her hand. She is startled*)

LOUISE Mother! (*She runs into the house*) Mother!
(BILLY *puts star on the chair nearest center. Then he looks at* FRIEND *guiltily*)

1ST HEAVENLY FRIEND Failure! You struck out blindly again. All you ever do to get out of a difficulty—hit someone you love! Failure!

JULIE (*Coming out of house, agitated*) Where is he?
(*She stops suddenly.* BILLY *turns to her. She stares at him*)

BILLY (*To* HEAVENLY FRIEND, *but looking at* JULIE) I don't want her to see me.

1ST HEAVENLY FRIEND Then she doesn't.

BILLY She looks like she saw me before I said that.

LOUISE (*Coming out of the house and crossing downstage of* BILLY, *almost touching him*) Oh, he's gone! (*Turning to* JULIE) I didn't make it up, Mother. Honest there was a strange man here and he hit me—hard—I heard the sound of it—but it didn't hurt, Mother! It didn't hurt at all—it was jest as if he—kissed my hand!

JULIE Go into the house, child.

LOUISE What's happened, Mother? (JULIE *just stares at the same place*) Don't you believe me?

JULIE Yes, I believe you.

LOUISE (*Coming closer to* JULIE) Then why don't you tell me why you're actin' so funny?

JULIE It's nothin', darlin'.

LOUISE But is it possible, Mother, fer someone to hit you hard like that—real loud and hard—and not hurt you at all?

JULIE It is possible, dear—fer someone to hit you—hit you hard—and not hurt at all.

(JULIE *and* LOUISE *embrace and start for the house.*
LOUISE *exits into house, but* JULIE *sees the star that* BILLY *had placed on the chair and goes toward it. As she does so, the lights dim slowly. She picks up the star and holds it to her breast*)

BILLY Julie—Julie! (*She stands transfixed. He sings:*)
Longing to tell you,
But afraid and shy,
I let my golden chances pass me by.
Now I've lost you;
Soon I will go in the mist of day,
And you never will know
How I loved you,
How I loved you.

(*The lights fade out as* JULIE *goes into the house. As* BILLY *crosses to the* HEAVENLY FRIEND, *the cloud curtain falls behind him*)

She took the star—she took it! Seems like she knew I was here.

1ST HEAVENLY FRIEND Julie would always know.

BILLY She never changes.

1ST HEAVENLY FRIEND No, Julie never changes.

BILLY But my little girl—my Louise—I gotta do somethin' fer her.

1ST HEAVENLY FRIEND So far you haven't done much.

BILLY I know. I know.

1ST HEAVENLY FRIEND   Time's running out.

BILLY   But it ain't over yet. I want an extension! I gotta see her graduation.

1ST HEAVENLY FRIEND   All right, Billy.
   (*They exit. The blue lights dim on the curtain. The curtain rises in the dark. The lights flash up on the next scene*)

ACT TWO | Scene Six

SCENE: *Outside a schoolhouse. Same day.*

AT RISE: *The graduating class sits massed on three rows of benches. The* GIRLS, *all dressed alike in white, are seated on the first two benches. The* BOYS, *wearing blue serge suits, sit on the third bench. The* BOYS *who cannot be seated on the third bench are standing on the steps of the schoolhouse, behind the benches. Stage left is a bench standing at an angle.* JULIE *is seated on the downstage end of this bench,* NETTIE *is seated alongside of her. There are two other persons on this bench and other relatives of the graduating class are lined up behind it. Stage right, there is a small platform on which is a speakers' stand. Upstage of this stand,* DR. SELDON *is seated on a chair.* MR. BASCOMBE *is seated on a chair downstage of the stand.* MR. AND MRS. SNOW *and their entire family are standing downstage right.* LOUISE *is seated on the extreme left end of the first bench with the graduating* GIRLS.

   As the lights come up, the PRINCIPAL *is standing behind the speakers' stand. All are applauding and* A YOUNG GIRL *has just received her diploma. She goes up and joins the others.*

PRINCIPAL   Enoch Snow, Junior!
   (ENOCH, JR., *comes up. His applause is led by his not in-*
   considerable family—ENOCH, SR., CARRIE *and his* BROTHERS
   and SISTERS. *They form a solid cheering section. As* ENOCH
   returns to his place, one of the girls sitting in the first row
   puts out her foot and trips him. He looks around, and she
   applauds vigorously. He walks on)

BABY SISTER   Yah!
   (CARRIE *pulls her back in line with rest of family*)

PRINCIPAL   Miss Louise Bigelow. (JULIE *steps out and ap-*
   plauds. CARRIE *claps her hands a few times, and there is not*
   much more. LOUISE *walks up, receives her diploma sullenly,*
   and joins the group again. BILLY *and the* HEAVENLY FRIEND
   have come in, down right, in time to see this. The PRINCIPAL
   introduces the doctor) Our speaker this year is the most
   popular, best-loved man in our town—Dr. Seldon.
   (*The* PRINCIPAL *steps down from the speakers' stand and*
   stands behind MR. BASCOMBE. DR. SELDON *now takes his*
   place on the stand. He adjusts his spectacles, and as he
   does so, BILLY *speaks to the* HEAVENLY FRIEND)

BILLY   Say! He reminds me of that feller up on the ladder.

HEAVENLY FRIEND   Yes, a lot of these country doctors and
ministers remind you of him.

DOCTOR   It's the custom at these graduations to pick out some
old duck like me to preach at the kids. (*Laughter*) I can't
preach at you. Know you all too well. Brought most of you
into the world. Rubbed liniment on yer backs, poured castor
oil down yer throats. (*A shudder runs through them, and a*
girl laughs. All look at her and she is mortified) Well, all I
hope is that now I got you this far, you'll turn out to be worth
all the trouble I took with you! (*He pauses, looks steadily at*
them, his voice more earnest) I can't tell you any sure way
to happiness. All I know is you got to go out and find it fer
yourselves. (BILLY *goes over to* LOUISE) You can't lean on the
success of your parents. That's their success. (*Directing his*
words to LOUISE) And don't be held back by their failures!
Makes no difference what they did or didn't do. You jest
stand on yer own two feet.

BILLY (*To* LOUISE)   Listen to him. Believe him.
   (*She looks up suddenly*)

DOCTOR   The world belongs to you as much as to the next feller. Don't give it up! And try not to be skeered o' people not likin' you—jest you try likin' *them*. Jest keep yer faith and courage, and you'll come out all right. It's like what we used to sing every mornin' when I went to school. Mebbe you still sing it—I dunno. (*He recites*)
"When you walk through a storm,
Keep yer chin up high—"
(*To the kids*) Know thet one?
  (*They nod eagerly and go on with the song*)

ALL
And don't be afraid of the dark.

BILLY (*To* LOUISE)   Believe him, darling! Believe.
  (LOUISE *joins the others as they sing*)

ALL
At the end of the storm
Is a golden sky
And the sweet silver song
Of the lark.
  (BILLY *crosses back of bench left and stands behind* JULIE)
Walk on
Through the wind,
Walk on
Through the rain,
Though your dreams be tossed and blown.

BILLY (*To* JULIE)   I loved you, Julie. Know that I loved you!
  (JULIE'S *face lights up and she starts singing with the rest*)

ALL
Walk on,
Walk on,
With hope in your heart,
And you'll never walk alone.
  (LOUISE *moves in closer to the group. The girl to her right puts her arm around her. Her eyes shine. The* HEAVENLY FRIEND *smiles and beckons* BILLY *to follow him.* BILLY *does. As they pass the* DOCTOR, *he watches and smiles wisely*)
You'll never walk alone.

CURTAIN

♡

Allegro

♥

Cast

MARJORIE TAYLOR	Annamary Dickey
DR. JOSEPH TAYLOR	William Ching
MAYOR	Edward Platt
GRANDMA TAYLOR	Muriel O'Malley
FRIENDS OF JOEY	Ray Harrison
	Frank Westbrook
JENNY BRINKER	Roberta Jonay
PRINCIPAL	Robert Byrn
MABEL	Evelyn Taylor
BICYCLE BOY	Stanley Simmons
GEORGIE	Harrison Muller
HAZEL	Kathryn Lee
CHARLIE TOWNSEND	John Conte
JOSEPH TAYLOR, JR.	John Battles
MISS LIPSCOMB	Susan Svetlik
CHEER LEADERS	Charles Tate
	Sam Steen
COACH	Wilson Smith
NED BRINKER	Paul Parks
ENGLISH PROFESSOR	David Collyer
CHEMISTRY PROFESSOR	William McCully
GREEK PROFESSOR	Raymond Keast
BIOLOGY PROFESSOR	Robert Byrn
PHILOSOPHY PROFESSOR	Blake Ritter
SHAKESPEARE STUDENT	Susan Svetlik
BERTRAM WOOLHAVEN	Ray Harrison
MOLLY	Katrina van Oss
BEULAH	Gloria Wills
MINISTER	Edward Platt
MILLIE	Julie Humphries
DOT	Sylvia Karlton

ADDIE	Patricia Bybell
DR. BIGBY DENBY	Lawrence Fletcher
MRS. MULHOUSE	Frances Rainer
MRS. LANSDALE	Lily Paget
JARMAN, *a butler*	Bill Bradley
MAID	Jean Houloose
EMILY	Lisa Kirk
DOORMAN	Tom Perkins
BROOK LANSDALE	Stephen Chase
BUCKLEY	Wilson Smith

DIRECTION AND CHOREOGRAPHY BY Agnes de Mille
SETTINGS AND LIGHTING BY Jo Mielziner
COSTUMES BY Lucinda Ballard
PRODUCTION SUPERVISED BY Lawrence Langner and
    Theresa Helburn
ORCHESTRATIONS BY Russell Bennett
ORCHESTRA DIRECTED BY Salvatore Dell'Isola

The Story starts in 1905 on the day Joseph Taylor, Jr., is born, and follows his life to his thirty-fifth year.

The three major locations of action are in his home town, his college town, and a large city, all in the same Midwestern state.

There are no stage "sets" in the conventional sense, but backgrounds for action are achieved by small scenic pieces on a moving stage, by light projections, and by drops.

The singing chorus is used frequently to interpret the mental and emotional reactions of the principal characters, after the manner of a Greek chorus.

ACT ONE

Marjorie's Bedroom

As in all the succeeding scenes, there is no detailed stage set—no walls, no windows, no other furniture except the bed itself.

The lights come up slowly and are concentrated only on the bed where MARJORIE *lies, looking dreamily contented.*

Soon another light comes up on the opposite side of the stage, revealing a CHORUS *group.*

CHORUS (*Singing*)
The lady in bed is Marjorie Taylor,
Doctor Joseph Taylor's wife.
Except for the day when she married Joe,
This is the happiest day of her life!

TAYLOR (*Entering*)   You awake, dear?

MARJORIE   Where've you been, Joe?

TAYLOR (*Putting down his doctor's bag*)   Making rounds. You were asleep when I left. How do you feel?

MARJORIE   Feel like jumping out of bed and dancing.

TAYLOR   Well, don't. (*He kisses her*) How's old Skeezicks? (*Gently he lifts the bedcover beside* MARJORIE)

MARJORIE   Old Skeezicks is asleep.
(MARJORIE *and* JOE *gaze down fondly at their first born*)

CHORUS (*Soft and staccato*)
His hair is fuzzy,
His eyes are blue.
His eyes may change—
They often do.
He weighs eight pounds
And an ounce or two—
Joseph Taylor, Junior!

When he wakes up
He wants to eat.

And when he sleeps he wets his seat,
But you'd forgive anyone as sweet
As Joseph Taylor, Junior!
>   (TAYLOR *takes a thermometer out of his pocket*)

MARJORIE   Do many people know yet?

TAYLOR   About him? (*He shakes the thermometer as doctors do*) Do they know! Why the whole town is in an uproar! (*He puts the thermometer in her mouth and sits on her bed, speaking with extravagant gestures*) Women are rushing to church! Men are pouring into the saloons! Early this morning the townspeople gathered in front of Elks Hall! His Honor the Mayor addressed them!
>   (*The* CHORUS *group scatters and runs out to join others who now come out from all sides, shouting and chattering excitedly*)

GIRL   Have you heard the news?
>   (*Streamers of confetti are projected on the backdrop*)

ANOTHER GIRL   It's a boy!

ALDERMEN (*Quieting the crowd*)   Hear ye! Hear ye!
>   (*The façade of Elks Hall is projected on the backdrop*)

MAYOR   The birthday of Joseph Taylor, Jr., is bound to be a legal holiday some day, so we might as well start on his first birthday. Close the bank! (*Cheers*) And tell the kids no *school today!* (*Cheers from the* KIDS) (*Entering with Moxie wagon*) Moxie —Free Moxie—Free Moxie—
>   (*A group of* DRUNKS *reel on, singing*)

DRUNKS
His hair is fuzzy
His eyes are blue
His eyes may change—
They often do.
He weighs eight pounds
And an ounce or two—
Joseph Taylor—hic—Junior!
>   (*The* DRUNKS *stop and take off their hats reverently as a church* CHOIR *walks on slowly*)

CHOIR
Ring out, ring out,

Oh bells of joy,
And all the ships at sea, ahoy!
The doctor's wife
Has a bouncing boy,
Joseph Taylor, Junior.

CHILDREN (*Lifting high their exalted and very squeaky voices*)
See what Mrs. Taylor's done!
Had herself an eight-pound son!
Hail him, hail him, ev'ryone!
Joseph Taylor, Junior!

ENSEMBLE
Jo-o-se-eph Tay-ay-lor, Jun-i-or!
Ring, oh bells of joy
For Jo-o-se-eph Tay-ay-lor, Junior,
Marjorie's eight-pound boy!
   (*Their impressive vocal climax attained, a curtain is drawn in front of them, leaving only* MARJORIE *in her bed, with* TAYLOR *beside her*)

TAYLOR
Jo-o-se-eph Tay-ay-lor, Junior,
Marjorie's eight-pound boy!
   (*With a flourish he takes the thermometer out of her mouth*)

MARJORIE (*Laughing*)   You fool!

GRANDMA (*Off*)   Joe! (*Nearer*) Joe!

TAYLOR   Here I am, Mother.

GRANDMA (*Entering*)   Ned Brinker just drove up in his buckboard. He says Jenny has started and you better go right over there with him. Don't forget you got to stop in to see old man McCoy too. That's on your way back.

TAYLOR   Gosh! Is everybody going to have their babies today? (*Testily*) This town needs about ten more doctors. (*He picks up his satchel*) I wish old Skeezicks would hurry and grow up so's he could help me.
   (*He takes another peek at the baby*)

MARJORIE   What makes you think he's going to be a doctor?

TAYLOR I dunno. He—he *looks* like a doctor. (*He kisses her and starts out, calling back over his shoulder:*) See that the old lady gets a rest, Mother.
  (*Exit*)

GRANDMA I'll take the young man into his crib. (*She picks up the baby, holding him up high on her shoulder*) Oops! Did you hear that?

MARJORIE What?

GRANDMA He brought up a bubble.

MARJORIE Isn't he clever!

GRANDMA That's Grandma's good boy!

MARJORIE Mother Taylor—

GRANDMA What?

MARJORIE Do you think he'll ever get to look any better?

GRANDMA Sure he will. He'll look younger when he's older!
  (MARJORIE'S *bed "riaes" off left on the moving stage, and*
  GRANDMA *carries the baby to a bassinet, placing him in it
  tenderly*)

GRANDMA You don't look any worse than your father did when he was a baby. Maybe you will grow up to be a doctor like him. But looking at you now it doesn't seem possible.
(*Singing*)
Starting out, so foolishly small,
It's hard to believe you will grow at all.
It's hard to believe that things like you
Can ever turn out to be men,
But I've seen it happen before,
So I know it can happen again.

Food and sleep and plenty of soap,
Molasses and sulphur, and love, and hope,
The winters go by, the summers fly,
And all of a sudden you're men!
I have seen it happen before
  (*To baby*)
And I know it can happen again.
  (*The lights dim on her. Loud voices are heard*)

MAN'S VOICE Pretty baby! Close your eyes and go to sleep.

WOMAN'S VOICE   Open your eyes. Say goo goo!
   (*A chorus group has entered*)

CHORUS (*Speaking in unison*)   A funny place to be coming to life in.
   (*They speak straight out at the audience and in the ensuing sequences the audience is made to feel that it is Joseph Taylor, Junior, experiencing the first stages of consciousness and then being whirled through the swift adventures of his infancy and childhood*)

MAN'S VOICE   Papa's boy!

WOMAN'S VOICE   Mama's precious! Grandma's good boy! Say goo goo! Say ga ga! Coochie, coochie, coochie.

MAN'S VOICE   Wanta play with the rattle?
   (*The sound of a rattle is heard, very loud, followed by the sharp, protesting wail of a baby*)

WOMAN'S VOICE   Coochie, coochie, coochie . . .
   (*A large head is projected on the backdrop*)

CHORUS
It's a funny place.
And those things with the big heads
Don't help to clear things up.
Nobody helps you.
You have to puzzle it out for yourself.

GRANDMA'S VOICE   Ipecac—Ipecac

CHORUS
Now there's a sound you've begun to know
It means they try to put something
Into your mouth.
   (*A large spoon is seen on the dackdrop*)
Sometimes you give them a fight.
   (*Sound of a baby's wail*)
You spit it out.
But they keep giving you more.

MARJORIE (*Entering*)   Open your mouth for Mother. That's a good boy.

CHORUS
Another sound you're getting to know.
A face goes with it.

MARJORIE (*Looking out at audience*) Please, Joey. Like a good boy.

CHORUS
All right.
Might as well take the darn stuff—
If *she* wants you to.

MARJORIE That's Mother's beautiful, big, brave man!

CHORUS
Knows how to make you feel good, that one.

TAYLOR (*Entering, putting his arm around* MARJORIE *and talking straight out at audience*) That's how they get you, Skeezicks! Call you their big, brave, beautiful man. That's how they make you do all the things you don't want to do— take your ipecac, comb your hair, buy them wedding rings—

CHORUS
You're getting to know that one, too.
The one with the loud, rough voice,
When he holds you against him
He doesn't feel soft like the other one . . .
He doesn't smell as sweet, either.

TAYLOR Well, so long, you two. Got to go out and kill a few patients.
    (*He picks up his bag*)

CHORUS
He's leaving.
When he picks up that black thing
He always goes.
    (TAYLOR *takes* MARJORIE *in his arms and kisses her*)
Look! He's hurting the little one!
Don't let him do that!
Stop him!
    (*The sound of a baby's wail*)
    (TAYLOR *releases* MARJORIE *quickly*)

MARJORIE (*Laughing, talking to audience*) What's the matter, Joey? Are you crying because your daddy's going?

TAYLOR Take it easy, Skeezicks. I'll be back soon.
    (*Exit*)

CHORUS
There he goes. . . . Good!
(MARJORIE *waves upstage through imaginary window*)
Look!
She's waving at the big one.
Why does she do that? . . .
Why isn't she looking at *you* instead of him? . . .
Make her look at you!
(*A loud wail.* MARJORIE *turns*)
That's getting her!
(*A louder wail.* MARJORIE *comes forward anxiously*)
You've got her!
(*The lights go out on* MARJORIE)

CHORUS (*Singing*)
Pudgy legs begin to grow long
And one sunny day, when you're feeling strong,
You straighten a knee and suddenly
You're struck with a daring idea! . . .
(GRANDMA *enters and stands transfixed, fascinated by something she sees as she looks straight out at the audience. She calls off in a hoarse whisper*)

GRANDMA Marjorie!
(MARJORIE *runs on, looks out, and stops, astounded. She whispers to* GRANDMA)

MARJORIE He's standing up! (*A sudden look of worry on her face and pity in her voice*) Ah! He fell down!
(*She starts forward but* GRANDMA *stops her*)

GRANDMA Let him try to get up by himself.

MARJORIE Come on, Joey. Try again.

CHORUS
Wonder if she knows how dangerous it is!
You're sorry you started now.
What got into you today, anyway?
All of a sudden crawling wasn't good enough!
Well, there they are watching you.
Go to it!

GRANDMA That's Grandma's good boy!

CHORUS
Grandma's good boy!

But what do you do now that you're up?
As usual nobody helps.
You've got to puzzle everything out for yourself . . .
Whoops!
Almost fell again.
Hey! Wait!
Do you realize what happened just then?
(*The voices of the* CHORUS *are charged with the excitement of discovery*)
You felt yourself falling
And you put one foot out to save yourself,
And you didn't fall! . . .
Say! Maybe if you keep taking steps,
One after the other—
One after the other . . .
Maybe going forward is easier than standing still!
(*Slowly and significantly*)
Maybe going forward is easier than standing still!
Come on!
Step out!
(MARJORIE *and* GRANDMA *in unison with the* CHORUS *plead and exhort while projections on the drop convey the thrills of* JOE'S *hazardous trip*)
One foot, other foot,
One foot, other foot,
One foot, other foot,
Faster
Faster
Faster
Faster
Ah-h-h-h-h-h-h-h!
(*The lights go out on* MARJORIE *and* GRANDMA *as they open their arms to catch* JOE. *The* CHORUS *spreads out across the stage and sings, to express* JOE'S *first big conquest*)

CHORUS
One foot, other foot,
One foot, other foot,
One foot, other foot,
One foot, other foot,

Now you can go
Wherever you want,
Wherever you want to go.

One foot out
And the other foot out—
That's all you need to know!

Now you can do
Whatever you want,
Whatever you want to do,
Here you are
In a wonderful world
Especially made for you,
Especially made for you!

   Now you can march around the yard,
   Shout to all the neighborhood,
   Tell the folks you're feeling good
   (Folks ought to know when boys feel good)

   Now you can imitate a dog,
   Chase a bird around a tree,
   You can chase a bumble bee
   (Once is enough to chase a bee)

   Now you can play among the flow'rs,
   Grab yourself a hunk o' dirt,
   Smudge it on your mother's skirt
   (*That little dirt won't hurt a skirt*)

One foot, other foot,
One foot, other foot,
   (*From here they sing with mounting triumph*)
Now you can do
Whatever you want
Whatever you want to do.
Here you are
In a wonderful world,
Especially made for you,
Especially made for you!
Especially made for you
To walk in, to run in,
To play in the sun in,
Especially made for you!
For now you can walk,
You taught yourself to walk!
You puzzled it out yourself
And now you can walk!

One foot, other foot,
One foot, other foot,
One foot, other foot,
One foot, other foot

Now you can go
Wherever you want
Wherever you want to go!
One foot out
And the other foot out,
One foot out
And the other foot out
One foot out
And the other foot out
And the world belongs to Joe! . . .
And the world belongs to Joe!
(*Now the dancing ensemble, representing* JOE'S *playmates, scamper on, shouting, romping, playing children's games, "growing up" exuberantly. In the course of this ballet a new principal is introduced, "Joey Taylor's girl,"* JENNY BRINKER. *She tries to emulate the feats of the tomboy girls, but she loses her nerve. She then resorts to dancing for the boys, striking pretty poses and flattering them. She is that kind of "girly" girl, and always will be.*

At the end of the ballet the light dims, the children bid one another good night and drift away.

GRANDMA *enters, troubled, trying to smile in spite of her worry*)

GRANDMA (*Singing*)
Food and sleep, and plenty of soap,
Molasses and sulphur, and love and hope—
The winters go by,
The summers fly,
And all of a sudden . . .
(*A cloud crosses her face*)
All of a sudden. . . .
(*Exit. The lights change, becoming bright again. Two* BOYS *run on and shout out to the audience*)

FIRST BOY   C'mon out, Joey. Race you down to the picture house.

SECOND BOY   Jo-ey! It's a Broncho Billy!

CHORUS   But you can't go today.

FIRST BOY   Gee! That's right. I forgot— (*Whispering to* SECOND BOY) His grandma!

SECOND BOY   Oh, yeh. Gee!
  (*They wave timidly and walk away*)
  (TAYLOR *enters, putting on his black gloves*)

TAYLOR   Ready, Marge?

MARJORIE (*Entering*)   Yes, darling. (*Speaking out to audience*) Joey, stay in the house till we get back, like a good boy. (*To* TAYLOR) Ned Brinker's bringing little Jenny over to keep him company.

TAYLOR   That's good. These things are nothing for kids. Nothing for anybody. (*His voice breaks huskily*) She was a good old lady, wasn't she?
  (MARJORIE *takes his arm and they go off. A new* CHORUS *group enters on the right.* GRANDMA *is among them*)

CHORUS
"These things are nothing for kids." . . .
But it *did* happen to you
You're a kid,
And yet here you are,
And suddenly you have no grandma.

GRANDMA
It'll be funny without me,
Hard to imagine the house without me.

JENNY (*Entering, carrying a rag doll and candy apples in a paper bag*)   G'morning Joseph. I'm sorry about your Grandma.
  (*She sits down, takes two candy apples from a paper bag, compares them, then offers the smaller to* JOE. *He is apparently not interested. She withdraws it and starts licking the other one*)

GRANDMA
Death is a sad thing.
People cry and sob,
Grown people.
You haven't seen your father cry.
He just looks kind of angry.

CHORUS
Grandma was his mother—
Gosh!
Suppose your mother ever—
Oh, well, *that* isn't going to happen
Just stop thinking things like that!
Get back to Grandma,
Quick!

GRANDMA
Look out, Joey,
Your eyes are watery.
Blow your nose.
   (JENNY *holds out her handkerchief*)
If Jenny sees you crying,
She'll cry too.
Try to smile,
Ah—that's Grandma's good boy.
   (JENNY *smiles and puts her handkerchief away. Then she*
   gets up and goes off as the CHORUS *starts to sing.* GRANDMA
   retires soon after)

CHORUS
The winters go by
The summers fly,
And soon you're a student in "High!"
And now your clothes are spotlessly clean,
Your head is anointed with brilliantine!
You're brimming with hope,
But can't quite cope
With problems that vex and perplex,
For you don't quite know how to treat
The bewilderingly opposite sex!
   (JENNY *enters. She is sixteen now and wears a party dress.*
   She faces the audience)

JENNY   G'night, Joseph. I had a lovely time . . . er . . .
g'night. . . .
   (*She looks up with an expression that would make it*
   obvious to a more sophisticated escort that she expected to
   be kissed)

CHORUS (*Whispering*)   What do you suppose Jenny would do
if you kissed her?

JENNY (*Putting all the sex she can into her voice*)   G'night.

CHORUS (*Singing*)
Poor Joe!
The older you grow,
The harder it is to know,
What to think,
        What to do,
            Where to go!

JENNY   Well . . . g'night, Joseph.

CHORUS (*Speaking*)
Jenny is so innocent, so frail!
You could crush her in your strong, manly arms . . .
But that wouldn't be right.
Besides she might get sore—
Might yell, and wake up her old man!

JENNY (*In a flat, discouraged voice*)   Yeh. See you in school
tomorrer.
    (*The light fades on a girl with a frustrated heart and a
    disgusted face*)

CHORUS
Heigh-ho! It would have been nice . . .
Think about it as you walk home.
Make believe you did it,
And make out she wasn't mad
When you kissed her.
Gee, wouldn't it be wonderful
If girls liked it too! . . .
    (*Singing*)
Your love for Jenny
Becomes more keen,
Your arms get long,
Your legs get lean,
And all at once you are seventeen!

SCHOOL PRINCIPAL (*Stepping out from* CHORUS, *a sealed and
ribboned diploma in his hand*)   Joseph Taylor, Junior.
    (*He hands the diploma out toward audience*)

                                            THE LIGHTS FADE

The Taylors' Porch
    (TAYLOR *and* MARJORIE *sit side by side in the moonlight.
    She is darning socks*)

TAYLOR (*Looking up and out*)   Do you suppose he's asleep?

MARJORIE (*Pointing up toward height of theater's balcony as if at another wing or ell of their house*)   Must be. His light's out.

JOE'S VOICE
I'm too excited to be asleep,
Leaving for college in the morning.
Leaving home—

TAYLOR (*To* MARJORIE)   Don't look so mopey. The boy isn't going away forever.

MARJORIE   You're not his mother.

TAYLOR   That's the most unnecessary statement you've made this year.

MARJORIE   You know very well what I mean, Joseph Taylor. I'm losing him. When he comes back from college he'll be a different boy. I won't know him.

TAYLOR   I'll point him out to you.

MARJORIE (*Ignoring this as husband humor*)   I've had the feeling—all the time I was getting his things ready, sewing his name on his shirts, helping him pack. "This is the end of me," I thought. Mother's job is over.

JOE'S VOICE
If I closed my window
They'd know I had heard all that!
Anyway I'm too interested to stop listening.
They're talking about me.
Gee, I'm pretty important to them!

MARJORIE (*Who has been studying* TAYLOR)   You look kind of mopey yourself.

TAYLOR   I had another tough day.

MARJORIE   How's Mrs. Mason doing?

TAYLOR   Worse since yesterday.

MARJORIE (*Fully understanding what this means to him*)   Ah, Joe! And last night you came home and said you thought you had the case licked.

TAYLOR (*Sighing*)   That's what I thought.

MARJORIE   You'll pull her through. I have a feeling.

TAYLOR   Well, Marge—I'll tell this to *you*—at this moment I haven't the faintest idea what to do for the old lady. Every diagnosis I've made so far I've had to throw out. I tell you I'm stumped.

MARJORIE (*Putting her hand on his*)   You'll beat it. I have a feeling about it.

JOE'S VOICE   I've been hearing this kind of talk ever since I can remember. Dad always has one case that stumps him, and Mother always has a "feeling" he'll beat it.

MARJORIE   Do you think Joe takes to medicine?

TAYLOR   He's a born doctor! Could tell when he made rounds with me this summer. Could tell by the questions he asked, by the way he looked when he asked them.

MARJORIE   He was telling me how he helped you with the Jacobs boy.

TAYLOR   Yep. That was a quick one.

JOE'S VOICE   Dad had to use the kitchen table to operate on the kid. Boy, was I scared! Nothing in the world mattered except saving a ten-year-old boy I'd never seen before. Gosh! Who would want to be anything else but a doctor!

MARJORIE   How you coming along with the hospital fund?

TAYLOR   I don't know, Marge. It's hard raising money when people can give you only five and ten dollar gifts—some of 'em give fifty cents.

MARJORIE   You'll have your hospital some day, Joe. I just know it.

TAYLOR (*Smiling at her*)   Got a feeling about it?

MARJORIE   Yes. I have a feeling.

TAYLOR   I hope Joe marries a girl who gets "feelings" about things.

MARJORIE   I hope he gets a girl with good sense.

TAYLOR   Y-y-yes. Good sense is all right too, if she doesn't overdo it. . . . D'you suppose he'll marry Jenny Brinker?

MARJORIE   Oh, it's hard to say. He'll be meeting a lot of new girls at college.

JOE'S VOICE   But not like Jenny! No other girl could ever be like her. She's so—unusual!

TAYLOR   I hope he doesn't pick a lemon. It's only dumb luck when a boy picks the right girl—the way I did.

MARJORIE   You say that to make me feel good.

TAYLOR   Well, doesn't it?

MARJORIE (*Laughing*)   Fool!

TAYLOR (*Singing*)
A fellow needs a girl
To sit by his side
At the end of a weary day,
To sit by his side
And listen to him talk
And agree with the things he'll say.

A fellow needs a girl
To hold in his arms
When the rest of his world goes wrong,
To hold in his arms,
And know that she believes
That her fellow is wise and strong.

When things go right
And his job's well done,
He wants to share
The prize he's won.
If no one shares,
And no one cares,
Where's the fun
Of a job well done—
Or a prize you've won?

A fellow needs a home,
(His own kind of home)
But to make this dream come true,
A fellow needs a girl,
His own kind of girl . . .
My kind of girl is you.

(*The music continues. The light remains on* MARJORIE *and* TAYLOR *as they sit contentedly together*)

JOE'S VOICE They're funny when they're by themselves—not like a mother and a father. A fellow and a girl—like Jenny and me—almost.

MARJORIE (*Singing*)
My fellow needs a girl
To sit by his side
At the end of a weary day,
So I sit by his side
And listen to him talk
And agree with the things he'll say

My fellow needs a girl
To hold in his arms
When the rest of his world goes wrong,
To hold in his arms
And know that she believes
That her fellow is wise and strong.

When things go right
And his job's well done,
He wants to share
The prize he's won,
If no one shares,
And no one cares,
Where's the fun
Of a job well done?

TAYLOR
Or a prize you've won?

MARJORIE
My fellow needs a home,
(His own kind of home)
But to make his dreams come true,

TAYLOR
A fellow needs to love,

MARJORIE
His one only love

BOTH
My only love is you.

THE LIGHTS FADE

ʀoe's voice (*In the dark*)   "Dear Mother and Dad: Tonight
I am going to the Freshman Get-Together Dance in the col-
lege gym."
   (*Strains of a jazz band steal in*)

The College Gym
   (*Japanese lanterns are projected on the backdrop. A tacky
   crowd of boys and girls, gauche but gay, give some painful
   illustrations of what were considered snappy dance steps in
   1921. Presently they come to a sudden stop and stand still
   in a frozen picture*)

chorus (*Addressing the audience*)   This is how we look
when we are dancing—
But we feel much better than we look.
We feel that we are floating and flying.
Look at our dreamy faces! . . .

Here is how we think we are dancing—
   (*They move again, but now the dancers float and fly as
   they imagine they were doing. The gymnasium lanterns
   become silver stars and planets in a dazzling firmament.
   The clothes of the dancers are filmy and graceful, the Dixieland Jazz Band now sounds like a symphony orchestra.
   After several minutes of this fulfilled illusion the picture
   dissolves back to the way it was—accomplished by sub-
   stitution of dancers—the gymnasium lanterns are back, the
   Dixieland jazz blares out again*)

a voice   You are about to get your first look at yourself.
Joseph Taylor, Jr. is one of these boys. Shall we try to pick
him out?
   (*A spotlight is turned on a likely looking couple*)

girl   What're you going to be when you get out of college?

boy   I don't know. A doctor, I guess. What're you going to
be when you get out of college?

girl   I don't go to college. I just came up for the dance.

boy   Well, what're you going to be anyway?

girl   I don't know. Somebody's wife, I guess.

boy   How'd you like to be a doctor's wife?

GIRL You've got some line, Charlie. . . .
  (*They dance off*)

VOICE Charlie? Well, let's try another.
  (*The spotlight is turned to a fancy dancing couple. The*
  BOY *is too fancy for his partner's taste*)

GIRL (*Struggling to yank herself free*) You're the limit!
Stop it! You're pulling me to pieces! Georgie! Stop it!
Georgie. . . .

VOICE Georgie! Wrong again!
  (*The spotlight is again shifted to another couple, just as*
  the BOY *steps on the* GIRL's *toe. She winces*)

BOY I'm sorry if I step on your feet every once in a while.
You see, I never had any dancing lessons until six months ago.

GIRL You mean to say this is not the first time you've ever
danced?

BOY N-no. I'm all right—I mean I'm better if I count to
keep with the music. I have my own way figured out.

GIRL Well, if it helps you, go ahead and count.

BOY It's not exactly counting. I go like this:
One foot, other foot,
One foot, other foot,
One foot, other foot.

CHORUS That's our boy!
  (JOE, *at last! The* CHORUS *points to him as they sing*)
You must forgive him
If he looks new.
He may grow older—
They often do.
He weighs one hundred and fifty-two—
Joseph Taylor, Junior!
  (*The* CHORUS *retires.* JOE *is alone, gazing about him, awed*)

JOE I had no idea it was such a big college . . . sure is
big. (*Singing with assumed bravery*)
It's a darn nice campus,
With ivy on the walls,
Friendly maples
Outside the lecture halls,

A new gymnasium,
A chapel with a dome—
It's a darn nice campus . . .
And I wish I were home.
   (CHARLIE *enters.* JOE *greets him timidly*)
Hiya, Townsend!

CHARLIE 'Lo there, feller.
   (*Two girls enter and gape at* CHARLIE *as he passes them and
   exits. One girl was* JOE'S PARTNER *at the dance*)

JOE'S PARTNER (*To the other girl*) That's Charlie Townsend.
Only Freshman to make the Varsity.
   (*They turn and go past* JOE)

JOE Good morning, Miss Lipscomb.

JOE'S PARTNER (*With no interest whatever*) Hello.
   (*After they pass him she whispers to her companion who
   looks back at him and giggles. They quicken their pace and
   exit, stifling their laughter*)

JOE (*Pretending to himself that he hasn't noticed this*)
It's a darn nice campus,
I'm going to like it fine!
Darn cute coeds,
They have a snappy line;
Darn nice fellers,
As far as I can tell—
It's a darn nice campus . . .
And I'm lonely as hell!
   (*Cheers and applause. Lights up on*)

The Football Field
   (*The* FRESHMEN *are being led in the college cheer*)

FRESHMEN S-T-A-T-E—
   (*They spell it out several times, "locomotive" fashion.
   Then a* COACH *steps out from a group of players. Cheers.
   He stops them with his uplifted hand*)

COACH (*Starting quietly*) I'm just a football coach. I'm not
much on making speeches. . . . (*Sailing into it suddenly*)
But I wanta say this to you! You people up in the stands
have got to do your part tomorrow. You've got to let the
Wildcats know you're behind them! Yell! Yell till you're
hoarse! Then yell some more. (*His voice dropping dramat-*

ically) This is your college—your team— (*His voice rising dramatically*) The Wildcats! (*He points to the team, a tired, injured, bedraggled group of young men*) Don't let 'em down!
(*Thunderous applause. The* CHEERLEADER *rushes out*)

CHEERLEADER Get out your songbooks, Freshmen! Page three. *The Football Song.* Show 'em what you're goin' to do tomorrow. Hip! Hip! One—two—three!
(*As they start,* JOE *is still fumbling for page three, and is a little behind the others all the way*)

ALL
The Wildcats are on a rampage!
Hear those Wildcats yell—*Yow!*
(JOE, *unprepared for this shout, gives a start*)
The Wildcats are out to beat you,
To beat you to a fare-thee-well—*Wow!*
(*Surprised again*)
Wow! Wow! Wow! Go the Wildcats
And another team goes down—
(JOE *puts in an extra wow here, but he is all alone. The* CHEERLEADERS *glare at him*)
It's another day of victory
For the *purple and brown!*
(JOE *goes off in disgrace*)

The Campus
(CHARLIE *enters with three gaping girls*)

CHARLIE Did you see me in football practice? See me give that guy the old straight arm? (*Looking off, seeing* JOE *approach*) Beat it girls. I've got to talk to this fellow.
(*With disappointed and protesting murmurs they accept their dismissal.* CHARLIE *turns and greets* JOE, *obviously having some ax to grind*)

CHARLIE We seem to be taking the same courses. Premedical?

JOE (*So pleased to be addressed by the Freshman football star that if he were a dog, he would wag his tail*) Yes. Are you?

CHARLIE Yep. Don't know why exactly. I got an uncle in Chicago who juggles pills. Says he'll take me in with him if

I'm any good. (*Getting down to the real business of the conversation*) Say—could I have a look at your notebook?

JOE   Sure. (*He hands* CHARLIE *his notebook.* CHARLIE *looks at it*) I've got a father who juggles pills. (*He can't help laughing as he repeats this witty and picturesque expression*) He might take me in with him, he says.

CHARLIE (*Whistling in admiration*) Say! You take *some* notes! Don't miss a thing, do you? Would you let me borrow them?

JOE   Sure.

CHARLIE   Know what I've been reading all through the lecture? This.
   (*He takes a magazine from inside his notebook and passes it to* JOE)

JOE (*Reading cover*)   *Snappy Stories.*

CHARLIE   Ever read it? Hot stuff. I'll lend it to you. (*He gives it to* JOE) Want to come over to the house for lunch?

JOE (*Great awe in his voice*)   House? Fraternity house?

CHARLIE   Sure. Have you been pledged to one yet?

JOE   No.

CHARLIE   I just joined one. Nice crowd. Want to come?

JOE (*Does he want to come!*)   Why, sure!
   (*Exeunt as*)

                              THE LIGHTS FADE

Jenny's Garden
   (JENNY *is sitting in a swing, reading a letter to her friend* HAZEL, *who lies on the lawn, eating chocolates*)

JENNY
"It's a darn nice campus,
With ivy on the walls,
Friendly maples
Outside the lecture halls.

I like my roommate
And you would like him too—
It's a darn nice campus
But I'm lonely for you."

HAZEL That's beautiful!
   (HAZEL *takes a chocolate. Jenny's father,* NED BRINKER, *enters*)

NED Good evening, Hazel.

HAZEL Hello, Mr. Brinker.

NED (*He kisses* JENNY) See you got another letter from Romeo. What's in it? A lot of lovey-dovey stuff?

JENNY Oh, Popper! Honestly!

NED Let's see—only two and a half more years in college—then four years in medical school—then two years as an intern—then God knows how long before he can get enough paying patients to support a wife! You're making a brilliant match, my girl. Brilliant!

JENNY Popper! *Honestly!*
   (NED *exits, chuckling*)

HAZEL Jenny, all fooling aside, don't you ever worry about you and Joe having to wait so long?

JENNY 'Course I worry.

HAZEL Why does he have to be a doctor?

JENNY Because his *mother* wants him to be. Her father was a doctor and her husband is a doctor, and if her darling son Joey isn't a doctor this whole town will get sick and die!

HAZEL Gosh, I don't envy *you!* With his mother against you there isn't much you can do.

JENNY (*Wisely*) Oh, I wouldn't say that, Hazel. There might be a lot I can do. Might take a little time. . . . But I think there's a *lot* I can do.

HAZEL Gosh, Jenny, what goes on in that little head of yours is nobody's business!
   (*She takes another chocolate.* JENNY *smiles smugly and goes on swinging*)

                                          THE LIGHTS FADE

Joe's Study
   (JOE *sits at the desk reading a letter from* JENNY)

JENNIE'S VOICE "Remember Hazel Skinner? She was over to see me today and I bet *your* ears burned. (*He smiles con-*

tentedly) "Hazel is going to marry a man named Bobby Martin. He is only one year older than you, but he is making lots of money selling automobiles. (JOE's *smile starts to fade*) "His family wanted him to be a lawyer, but he says the trouble with professions is that you study years and you're an old man before you make any money. (JOE *swallows hard as he turns the page*) "I guess that's all the news.

Fondly,
Jenny"

(*He puts the letter down on his desk and slowly takes up his Latin book and reads*)

JOE (*Reading in meter*) *Persicos odi puer, apparatus*— (*Starting to translate*) *"Odi"*—I hate—

(*The slam of a door is heard and* CHARLIE *comes into the room like a whirlwind. During the following scene he never stops doing what he came in to do: change his shirt, collar, and tie*)

CHARLIE   'Lo, Joe.

JOE   'Lo. What's your hurry?

CHARLIE   Late for a date. Wanta come along? I think she's got an older sister. I dunno how *much* older.

JOE   No, thanks, Charlie. I got a lot of Latin to translate.

CHARLIE   Okay, boy. You take the dead language. I'll take my live woman.

JOE   Only one I care about is back home. Just got a letter from her.

CHARLIE   Got a clean shirt?

JOE   Y-yes. But I've only got one.

CHARLIE   Swell! (*Fishing it out of a bureau drawer*) That the dame you want to marry?

JOE (*Looking down at Jenny's letter*)   If she'll wait for me. . . . I don't know if I ever told you this, Charlie, but she's the only girl I ever had a date with. . . . I suppose you think I'm crazy.

CHARLIE   Well-ll, you're something like a guy who goes fishing for the first time in his life and decides to quit after he's caught his first fish. For all you know the waters might be filled with gorgeous and tasty tuna, and you may be settling for a sardine—I'm taking your tie. You don't mind, do you?

JOE (*Sore*) I'm not settling for any sardine.
  (*He goes back to his Latin*)

CHARLIE 'Course you're not. She's probably a wonderful girl Only thing I say is— (*Pointing to a dollar bill on the bureau*) Is that dollar bill yours or mine?

JOE (*Snappily*) Mine!

CHARLIE (*Taking it*) I'll pay you tomorrow when I get my check. Only thing I say is it's all right to get married eventually, but I want to have plenty of fun first.

JOE People can have fun after they're married.

CHARLIE What people?

JOE My father and mother. They have lots of fun. Don yours?

CHARLIE I guess so. But not with each other, I don't think. (*Putting on his coat, starting to go*) Sure you don't want to come? Relax?

JOE Uh-uh.

CHARLIE Leave that translation out so I can copy it when I get back.

JOE (*Not looking up*) Okay.

CHARLIE Thanks. S'long.

JOE So long. (*Noticing that* CHARLIE *has forgotten to tuck his shirt in his trousers*) Hey—put my shirt in!
                              THE LIGHTS FADE

Classroom
  (*This is a composite of all the classrooms. Five* PROFESSORS *stand in a large semicircle, each behind his own lectern, each spouting his respective subject, in competition with* JOE'S *dreams of* JENNY *and the worries caused by her letters.* JOE *sits at a classroom armchair.* CHARLIE *sits behind him*)

CHEMISTRY PROF. An acid is monobasic, dibasic, or tribasic, according to the number of replaceable hydrogen atoms. (*His voice drones off*) Thus HNO_3 is monobasic, H_2SO_4 is dibasic, H_3PO is tribasic—

GREEK PROF. (*Overlapping his predecessor*)　Book two of the Odyssey where we left off yesterday, Mr. Taylor—
　　(JOE *does not hear because* JENNY *and her last letter glide through his thoughts*)

JENNY　"Dear Joe: Hazel and Bob have the cutest white stucco house. They are living together there like two love-birds. The lucky bums!"

GREEK PROF.　Mr. Taylor!
　　(JOE *awakens and gingerly finds the place*)

JOE (*Rising and reading*)　"Thus did Telemachus invoke Zeus. And the all powerful answering his prayer, sent forth two eagles from his mountain. Swift as the wind of a storm they flew—wing tip to wing—in lordly—"
　　(JENNY *glides across stage*, JOE'S *lips continue to move but he is drowned out by the singing of the* CHORUS)

CHORUS (*Singing*)
She is never away,
From her home in your heart,
In your heart, every day,
She is playing her part.

BIOLOGY PROF.　All living matter proceeds from pre-existing living matter. The new form takes on the character of that from which it came.
　　(*Again* JOE'S *mind is on a new letter*)

JENNY　"Hazel is going to have a baby. How I envy her. That's all the news. Fondly, Jenny."
　　(JENNY *glides away*)

PHILOSOPHY PROF.　The aim of philosophy is to exhibit the universe as a rational system in the harmony of its parts.

JENNY (*Dashing on again*)　"Dear Joe! Popper is taking me to Europe. He wants me to meet new friends!"
　　(JENNY *puts on a "steamer" coat and a hat and runs off*)

CHORUS
New friends! Get that, Joe?
Her father wants her to find a husband—

Some lousy nobleman perhaps!
Where does that leave you?

CHEMISTRY PROF. A molecule is the smallest part of a
substance which can exist—*alone!*

JOE   *Alone!*

CHORUS
You'll never get her back
Think of the men she'll meet on the steamer,
And when she gets to England and Paris!
  (JENNY *enters from one side, a* BOY *enters from another.
  They proceed to dance a passionate tango*)

JENNY (*While dancing*) I met a charming boy named
Bertram Woolhaven.

CHORUS
She wants to get married!
She's tired of waiting for you.

JOE (*Very annoyed, he throws his book on the floor, and
collapses in seat*)   Damn her! *Damn her!!*

JENNY   Bertram's father is in the coal and lumber business
too!

CHORUS
That's the end Joe!
An alliance between two big lumber families!
It's the handwriting on the wall!

ENGLISH PROF. (*Reading Keats's* "Eve of St. Agnes")
"Unclasps her warmed jewels one by one;
Loosens her fragrant bodice;"
  (CHARLIE *sits back in his seat, doing some imagining of his
  own. Two* GIRLS *enter his dream and stand on either side of
  him, disrobing as Madeleine does in the poem*)
              . . . "by degrees
Her rich attire creeps rustling to her knees;
Half-hidden like a mermaid in seaweed,
Pensive awhile, she dreams awake, and sees
In fancy, fair St. Agnes in her bed,"
  (CHARLIE'S *smile has become beatific. The* GIRLS *stoop
  down and pick up their discarded clothing*)

"But dares not look behind,
Or all the charm is fled."
> (*The* GIRLS *drift away. One of them as she leaves his dream
> passes her hand lightly over* CHARLIE'S *face and through
> his hair. He "awakes" with a start, rubs his face, then sits
> back and smiles with rapturous memory of the lovely vision.
> Now our interest reverts to* JOE)

PHILOSOPHY PROF.   The pragmatic philosopher searches for
the hypothesis which can best serve him.

CHORUS (*To* JOE)   Philosophy, hell! You'll never drive her
out of your mind! (*Singing*)
In your heart every day
She is playing her part.

JENNY (*Entering with the same* BOY. *They are both in bathing
suits*)
Bertram is teaching me to swim!
We're learning a new stroke.
> (BERTRAM *carries her off*)

CHORUS
She is never away
And you'll never be free!

PHILOSOPHY PROF.   The Greek philosophers finally rebelled
against fatalism. We need not be dominated, they said—

CHORUS (*Breaking in*)
We need not submit, Joe!
We need not be dominated—
To hell with her!
Lots of good fish in the sea!

JOE (*To* CHARLIE *with sudden determination*)   Did you say
that girl friend of yours had a friend?

CHARLIE   I'll say she has!

JOE   Then get her! I'm on the loose!
> (*He takes* CHARLIE'S *arm, and they go out*)
                                    THE LIGHTS FADE
Woodland
> (CHARLIE *sits on an automobile seat he has placed on the
> ground. A reclining female companion rests her head on*

his lap. CHARLIE *looks bored. The romance of the evening obviously has gone beyond its climax*)

CHARLIE (*Looking at his wrist watch*)   I wonder what happened to the other two.

MOLLY   Oh, they won't get lost. My girl friend knows every inch of these woods. Wouldn't it be funny if she and Joe fell in love, like you and me?

CHARLIE   Yeh. Only I hope they don't take too long to fall in love. I've got an eight-o'clock class.

MOLLY   Well, goodness, it was your idea to drive out here after the movie. You said it'd be romantic to sit in the woods, in the moonlight.

CHARLIE   Well, it was for a while, wasn't it?

MOLLY   Why do you say "wasn't it" like it was all over? Sometimes I think these nights don't mean to you what they mean to me— Do they?

CHARLIE   Absolutely!
   (*He puts her arm in an unconvincing manner*)

MOLLY   You aren't just kidding around with me, are you, Charlie?

CHARLIE   Absolutely not. What gives you ideas like that?

MOLLY   Oh, I don't know. Sometimes I think this is just a college romance. And when you graduate you'll go away and forget all about me—just like all the other boys.

CHARLIE   Like all what other boys?

MOLLY (*After a pause while she recovers her wits*)   I mean like all the other boys with all the other girls.

CHARLIE   Let's go and look for Joe and that friend of yours.
   (*They rise. He picks up the automobile seat, and they walk off*)

Another Part of the Woodland
   (JOE *lies on his back. Molly's friend* BEULAH *looks at him ruefully*)

BEULAH   Do you go out with girls much?

JOE   What makes you ask?

BEULAH   I was just thinking. You meet all kinds of fellows, don't you—I mean don't I?

JOE   What kind would you say I am?

BEULAH   I don't know. You're a problem.

JOE (*With a pleased smirk*)   A problem, eh? (*He takes out a flask*) Let's pep up the party.

BEULAH   O.K. with me. (*He passes her the flask*) Here's looking at you, Blue Eyes!
    (*She passes it back to him*)

JOE   Here's looking at you—Blue Eyes! (*He drinks, gives the flask a shake, and hands it back to her*) Here, finish it up. (*She takes it*) Do you know you're a hell of an attractive girl?

BEULAH (*Passing flask back to him*)   *You* finish it up.
    (*He does*)

JOE   Beulah, what would you do if—suppose I was the kind of a class of a type of fellow that would suddenly grab you and kiss you— What would you do?

BEULAH   But you're not that type.

JOE   No, I'm not.

BEULAH   That's what I thought.

JOE   And you're not that type of girl. You're romantic— like me.

BEULAH   Yeh— (*A light dawning on her*) Say! I'm just beginning to get you! (*She fluffs out her hair and proceeds to be "romantic."*) Look at the starlight! Falling down like rain! And you and me bathing together in it—that's just an expression.

JOE   You and me, on the threshold of the unknown!

BEULAH (*Uncertainly*)   Yeh, the unknown!

JOE   A new secret to learn, a new flower to pluck— (*She gives him an incredulous look*) A blank page to write on!

BEULAH   Yeh, you and me both! (*She sings*)
No keepsakes have we
For days that are gone,
No fond recollections to look back upon,
No song that we love,
No scene to recall
We have no traditions at all. . . .

We have nothing to remember so far, so far,
So far, we haven't walked by night
And shared the light of a star.
So far, your heart has never fluttered so near, so near,
That my own heart alone could hear it.
We haven't gone beyond the very beginning,
We've just begun to know how lucky we are,
So we have nothing to remember, so far, so far—
But now I'm face to face with you,
And now at last we've met
And now we can look forward to
The things we'll never forget. . . .

> (*After the first refrain the music of the second is picked up. She puts her head on his knees. He makes up his mind to kiss her.* JENNY *appears in his thoughts*)

JENNY   Joe! (*He draws away, then* BERTRAM *appears at* JENNY'S *side*) Bertram!
> (*That does it.* JOE *kisses* BEULAH)

BEULAH   Joe!

JOE   (*Afraid he has offended her*)   I'm sorry, Beulah. I couldn't help—

BEULAH   Joe! (*She throws her arms around him and kisses him with such verve that he is thrown flat on his back. Slowly he edges away from under her. Fondly she looks at him and sings the second part of the refrain.* JOE, *exhausted, lies prone, his head on his arm.* BEULAH *finishes her song and calls to him seductively*) Joe! (*No answer. She leans over and looks at him tenderly. Then she frowns and in a voice at once humiliated and indignant she cries*) The little louse is asleep!
> (*She yanks the blanket from under him, throws it over her own shoulders, and stalks off*)

THE LIGHTS FADE

The Campus
   (JOE, *walking by himself, is met by a* FELLOW STUDENT,
   who hands him a letter)

JOE'S FELLOW STUDENT   Letter for you, Taylor. Got mixed
up with my mail.

JOE (*Taking it*)   Thanks. (*He looks at the envelope*) From
her! (*Opening it feverishly, muttering bitterly*) Probably announcing her engagement to Bertram! As if I cared!

CHARLIE (*Entering, followed by* GIRLS)   Hey, Joe! I fixed up
another date tonight!

JOE (*Reading—shouting*)   She's coming home!

CHARLIE   Who?

JOE   Jenny! She's through with Bertram! Says she can't
stand the sight of him! She gets home in July! Oh, how can I
wait?

CHARLIE   I thought you said you were on the loose?

JOE   I'm through with that—philandering.

CHARLIE   Okay, I'll carry on for you.
   (*He rejoins the* GIRLS *and exits*)

JOE   What'll I say when I see her? (*Frowning*) First I'll give
her a piece of my mind about this Bertram business. Shall I
tell her about that girl last night? No. Let bygones be bygones. Oh, boy, July! Get away, May! Hurry up, June! Come
on, you July!

                                    THE LIGHTS FADE

Jenny's Garden
   (JENNY *stands beside a bench, looking like an angel in the
   moonlight.* JOE *gazes upon her in awed rapture*)

CHORUS
There she is!
Waiting for you—the way you hoped she would be.

JENNY   Hello, Joe.

JOE   Hello, Jenny.

CHORUS
Say something wonderful to her—

JOE I noticed your house has a new coat of paint.

JENNY Popper cabled ahead to have it done.

JOE It looks nice.

CHORUS
Get the conversation around to her—
To her and you!

JOE You look different too.

JENNY Older?

JOE Prettier.

CHORUS
That's it! Go on!

JENNY Want to sit down?

JOE Yes, I would.

CHORUS
Oh, yes, yes, yes, Jenny—darling.
I want to sit next to you,
To be near you,
To touch you—
   (*They sit*)

JOE Nice night.

JENNY It's just the kind of night I hoped it would be.

JOE Did you—did you think much about tonight—too?
   (JENNY *nods her head*)

JENNY Did you?

JOE Quite a lot.

CHORUS
You are never away from your home in my heart.

JOE I always think of you—quite a lot.

CHORUS
There is never a day—

JOE There is never a day when you— (*Emotion coming into his voice*) Jenny, I think about you all the time.

JENNY Do you, Joe?

JOE   Every minute!
   (*She nestles close to him. Timidly, he steals his arm around
   her. The* CHORUS *hums softly. Then* JOE *starts to sing*)
You are never away
From your home in my heart;
There is never a day
When you don't play a part
In a word that I say
Or a sight that I see—
   You are never away
   And I'll never be free.

You're the smile on my face,
Or a song that I sing!
You're a rainbow I chase
On a morning in spring;
You're a star in the lace
Of a wild, willow tree—
   In the green, leafy lace
   Of a wild, willow tree.

But tonight you're no star,
Nor a song that I sing;
In my arms, where you are
You are sweeter than spring;
In my arms, where you are,
Clinging closely to me,
   You are lovelier, by far,
   Than I dreamed you could be—
      You are lovelier, my darling,
      Than I dreamed you could be! . . .
(*He can manage only to whisper it*) I love you.

JENNY   I love you. (*A pause. Then* JENNY *opens up reality*)
Going to medical school next year?

JOE   Yep. I've been working a lot with Dad this summer.
Gosh, it's exciting watching sick people get better!

JENNY (*Flatly*)   Is it?

JOE   You know, a doctor doesn't always know what to do at
first. He tries this or that, and it doesn't do any good. Then
he hits it. And you see the patient get better every day. Well
then you know it's about the best thing a man can be—is a
doctor. (JENNY *sits on the bench.* JOE, *sensing her disappoint-*

ment, goes to her) I'm not going to wait till I get out of medical school. We've got to get married sooner than that. I'm going to speak to my dad about it—I guess I better speak to your father too. Do you know if he likes me?

JENNY   He likes you a lot. Only he's going to ask you about how you're going to support me.

JOE   He is?

JENNY   The other night on the boat he was saying how he needs a young man to help him in his coal and lumber business. It's getting awful big. And now he wants to go in for farm machinery too. He might say something to you about whether you'd like to—to go in with him.

JOE   You mean instead of being a doctor?

JENNY   Well, he'll tell you how rich we could— (*Afraid she has started this line too quickly*) But whatever happens, Joey, it's got to be you who decides. I'd never influence one way or the other— (*She slides down on to* JOE's *lap and nestles in his arms*) You have to make up your own mind—my darling.

CHORUS (*Off*)
Poor Joe!
The older you grow,
The harder it is to know
What to think,
        What to do,
                Where to go!

THE LIGHTS FADE

The Taylors' Porch
    (TAYLOR, MARJORIE, NED, *and* JENNY *sip lemonade and pass the time of a summer evening*)

NED   Joe, this local hospital you're trying to build—know why you're having so much trouble raising money?

TAYLOR   Well if I—

NED (*Breaking in*)   It's because people don't want a little hospital. They'd rather put money into a big skyscraper hospital in the nearest big town.

TAYLOR   But we need small hospitals, Ned.

MARJORIE   My father used to say he hoped the automobile would bring the patient to the doctor, instead of the doctor

having to go to the patient the way he had to do with his
horse and buggy.

TAYLOR   When the snows were deep he used to have an awful
time getting out to the farmers' wives when they were having
their babies.

MARJORIE   That's why he built that ell on the house.
   (MARJORIE *and* TAYLOR *look out front as if the ell were
   there*)

TAYLOR   We put three beds in there. That was the start of
our hospital. Never got any further with it. But I'm going to
—when I have Joe to help me.

NED   Well, I wouldn't count on Joe too much if I were you.
A young fellow like him might be too ambitious to be a
small-town doctor. What do you say, Jenny?
   (*There is a moment of loud silence.* MARJORIE *and* TAYLOR
   exchange a look)

JENNY (*A note of warning in her voice*)   Pop, aren't you
late getting started for your meeting?

NED (*Looking at watch*)   So I am! I was due down at the
Elks five minutes ago!

JENNY   How long'll you be?

NED   Oh, not long. I'll pick you up here in about an hour.
Good night, Marge. Thanks for the supper.

MARJORIE   Good night, Ned.

NED (*As* TAYLOR *sees him out*)   Say, Joe, I got one on you.
That stock I told you about has gone up twenty-two points
You were a sucker not to buy.

TAYLOR   Know what a smart man once said? If you get ten
per cent on your money you can eat better.

NED   Right.

TAYLOR   And if you get two per cent on your money you can
sleep better.

NED   Whoever said that didn't know much about business
Who was he?

TAYLOR   J. P. Morgan.

NED Oh!
(*Exit*)

TAYLOR Marge, if you and Jenny'll excuse me I'd like to go upstairs and get some reading done.

MARJORIE Of course, Joe.

TAYLOR Good night, Jenny.

JENNY Good night, Doctor Taylor.

TAYLOR (*About to go, he turns back*) Oh Marge—feeling better, darling?

MARJORIE Yes, dear.
(TAYLOR *exits*)

MARJORIE (*Who hasn't taken her eyes off* JENNY'S *face*) What did your father mean by that, Jenny?

JENNY (*Innocently*) By what, Mrs. Taylor?

MARJORIE About Joe being too ambitious to be a small-town doctor. Has Joe said anything about that?

JENNY No. It's just that Pop thinks—well, he thinks it's awful for us to have to struggle along for years like—like you and Doctor Taylor.

MARJORIE And do you agree with him?

JENNY Well, it seems a shame with a wonderful business like Pop's—he has no son—and he says he could teach it to Joe in a couple of years. Pop thinks Joe is smart.

MARJORIE So do I. Joe's good at anything he likes to do. Joe's good at medicine, Jenny. His father says he's a born doctor.

JENNY (*Beginning to show her fangs, but sweetly*) Oh, I don't think anybody is a born anything, do you, Mrs. Taylor?

MARJORIE Perhaps not. But when you've watched a boy grow up, you know a lot about what—what's inside him. I don't think Joe would be happy selling coal and lumber.

JENNY Well. I don't think I'd be happy as the wife of a starving doctor. I've got things inside of me too.

MARJORIE I know you have, Jenny, but— (*Pausing, then giving the question real importance*) Jenny, what would you do if Joe refused to give up medicine?

JENNY What would I do? I'd see to it that he became a **real** doctor, a rich one. We'd go to some big city. I'd help him **get** to be the most successful doctor in town. I guess I'm **more** ambitious than you.

MARJORIE Jenny, I think my husband is a very successful man. He's doing work he likes for people he likes—and **he** has the kind of home he needs.

JENNY You think I'm the wrong kind of wife for Joe, don't you? (MARJORIE *doesn't answer*) Have you told him that?

MARJORIE I haven't said a word to Joe about this. This ıs between you and me.

JENNY You don't like me and you never did—and I always knew it. (MARJORIE *does not deny this*) If you're trying to get Joe away from me, all I can say is you're going to have some fight on your hands! And you may wind up by losing him altogether!

MARJORIE I know that. But I don't think I can stand by without at least trying to save him—

JENNY From me?

MARJORIE Yes.

JENNY When my father calls for me tell him I got tired and went home. (*She starts off, then comes back*) You know, I feel better now that war's declared.
   (*Pause*)

MARJORIE (*Coolly*) So do I, Jenny.

JENNY Try and get him away from me! You just try!
   (*Exit. Once she has gone,* MARJORIE *loses the outward strength she has been assuming. Thoughtful and worried, she walks to a chair. Then suddenly she clutches it for support, her other hand going to her chest*)

MARJORIE (*Calling off, her voice growing progressively weaker*) Joe—Joe, I'm out on the porch—hurry— (*She tries to get to the door*) Hurry—sweetheart—

THE LIGHTS FADE

Joe's Study at College
   (JOE *stands tense and still.* CHARLIE *enters.* JOE *passes him
   a telegram.* CHARLIE *reads it, looks at* JOE *with great pity
   and sympathy, puts his arm around him, and leads him off
   as*)

                                            THE LIGHTS FADE

The Taylors' Porch
   (TAYLOR *sits beside* MARJORIE'S *empty chair, looking
   straight ahead of him, silent, grim, stunned. The theme of
   "A Fellow Needs a Girl" is played.* JOE *enters, a suitcase
   in his hand. He walks over and stands before his father.
   Neither can trust himself to say anything.* TAYLOR *looks up,
   smiles sadly, and motions* JOE *to sit in his mother's chair.*
   JOE *obeys. The two lost men sit mute, and strange with
   each other. Then* JOE *reaches over and timidly places his
   hand on his father's hand*)

                                            THE LIGHTS FADE

Outside the Church
   (*The wedding* GUESTS *pour in*)

GUESTS (*Singing*)
What a lovely day for a wedding!
Not a cloud to darken the sky.
It's a treat to meet at a wedding,
To laugh and to gossip and to cry.

What a lovely day for a wedding!
What a day for two to be tied!

NED
It's a lovely day for a wedding,
But not for the father of the bride.
   What I'm about to get
   I don't exactly need—
   A doctor for a son-in-law
   Another mouth to feed!

GUESTS
   What he's about to get
   He doesn't really need
   A doctor for a son-in-law
   Another mouth to feed.

What a lovely day for a wedding!
There's a lively tang in the air.

It's a treat to meet at a wedding
When families are letting down their hair.
What a lovely day for a wedding!
We have come by motor and shay.
It's a treat to meet at a wedding
And say what we usually say.

THE TAYLOR GROUP
  What can he see in her?

THE BRINKER GROUP
  What can she see in him?

THE TAYLOR GROUP
  The Brinkers all are stinkers!

THE BRINKER GROUP
  All the Taylor crowd is grim!
  What can she see in him?

THE TAYLOR GROUP
  What can he see in her?

ALL
  In many ways we differ
  But in one thing we concur:

  It's a lovely day for a wedding!
  What a day for two to be tied!

NED
It's a lovely day for a wedding
But not for the father of the bride.
    (*Exeunt* NED *and others. Only the* BRIDESMAIDS *and a few*
    SINGERS *remain on as* CHARLIE *enters*)

GIRLS (*Singing to* CHARLIE *slowly and suggestively*)
It's a lovely day for a wedding,
Not a cloud to darken the sky,
It's a lovely day for a wedding—

CHARLIE
As long as the bridegroom isn't I.

BRIDESMAIDS (*Disappointed in him*)   Why?

CHARLIE
It may be a good idea for Joe.
But it wouldn't be good for me

To sit in a mortgaged bungalow
With my little ones on my knee.
I'd much rather go and blow my dough
On a casual chickadee.
I don't want a mark that I'll have to toe;
My toe can go where it wants to go;
It wants to go where the wild girls grow
In extravagant quantity!
To bask in the warm and peaceful glow
Of connubial constancy
May be awfully good for good old Joe
But it wouldn't be good for me!

THE LIGHTS FADE

Inside the Church
   (*The* GUESTS *are assembled. The* CHOIR *marches slowly down the center aisle. The* BRIDESMAIDS *follow the* CHOIR. JOE *enters from the side,* CHARLIE, *his best man, behind him. They await* JENNY *who comes down the aisle on the arm of* NED. MARJORIE, *in* JENNY'S *mind today, enters and stands behind* JENNY)

CHOIR (*Singing*)
Let the church light up with the glory
That belongs to every bride and groom,
May the first bright day of their story
Be a flower that will ever bloom.

CHORUS (*Speaking softly*)
What happens in a church
During the wedding march?
What suddenly rises in our hearts, and hurts us?
Is it the effect of the music?
Or is it the sight of two lovers,
Two lovers,
Looking like two very serious children?
   (GRANDMA *enters* JOE'S *memory and stands behind him*)

JOE   I hope I'll make Jenny a good husband.

GRANDMA   You were always a good boy.

JOE   Funny—I've been thinking a lot about Grandma lately.

MINISTER   Dearly beloved, we are gathered together here in the sight of God, and in the face of this company, to join together this man and this woman in holy matrimony.

(*His lips continue to move as the* CHORUS *speak their thoughts*)

CHORUS (*Speaking softly, earnestly*)
A change has come over us.
The simple words,
The commonplace words,
And the two serious children listening—
A change has come over us!
The whispered jokes,
The "cracks" that seemed funny
A few moments ago,
Aren't funny any more!
This is no time for the humorous skeptic,
Or the gloomy prophet.
This is a time for hope.
These children desperately
Need our hope!

MINISTER   —If any man can show just cause why they may not be lawfully joined together, let him now speak, or else hereafter forever hold his peace.
(*His lips continue to move as* CHARLIE, HAZEL, *and* NED *speak their thoughts*)

CHARLIE   I hardly know the girl. She may turn out swell.

HAZEL
I know she loves him.
She fought his mother,
She fought her own father.
She loves him all right!

NED   The boy has a right to try medicine if he wants. He could always come in with me later, as Jenny says.

MINISTER   Joseph, wilt thou have this woman to thy wedded wife, to live together—
(*His lips continue to move as* GRANDMA *sings*)

GRANDMA (*Looking at* JOE)
Starting out so foolishly small,
It's hard to believe they will grow at all,
But winters go by and summers fly,
And all of a sudden they're men! . . .

JOE (*Answering the* MINISTER) I will.

MINISTER Janet—

MARJORIE Jenny! Listen!

MINISTER Janet, wilt thou have this man to thy wedded hus,
band, to live together after God's ordinance in the holy estate
of matrimony?
(*His lips continue to move, but it is* MARJORIE'S *insistent
voice that* JENNY *hears*)

MARJORIE Wilt thou love him, comfort him, honor, and
keep him in sickness and in health; and forsaking all others,
keep thee only unto him, so long as ye both shall live?—
Jenny?

JENNY (*Deeply affected*) I will.

MINISTER Who giveth this woman to be married to this
man?

NED I do.

MINISTER I, Joseph, take thee, Janet, to my wedded wife—

JOE I, Joseph, take thee, Janet, to my wedded wife—

MINISTER To have and to hold from this day forward—

CHORUS (*Singing*)
To have and to hold
From this day forward
For better, for worse,
For richer, for poorer,
In sickness and in health,
To love and to cherish,
'Till death do us part,
'Till death do us part.
(*As they sing,* MARJORIE *walks slowly over to* TAYLOR *and
stands before him as if she longed to touch him, to be
alive with him for a moment.* TAYLOR *puts his hand to his
forehead, hurt by a sudden memory*)
(CHARLIE *steps forward and hands the ring to the* MINIS-
TER)

MINISTER (*Placing the ring on* JENNY'S *finger*) With this
ring I thee wed.

JOE With this ring I thee wed.

(*The* MINISTER'S *lips continue to move, delivering the balance of the service as the* CHORUS *sings*)

CHORUS
Two more lovers
Were married today.
Wish them well!
Wish them well!
Wish them well!
Brave and happy,
They start on their way,
Wish them well!
Wish them well!
Wish them well!

(JOE *raises* JENNY'S *veil and kisses her*)
They have faith in the future
And joy in their hearts,
If you look in their eyes
You can tell
How brave and happy,
And hopeful are they.
Wish them well, wish them well,
Wish them well, wish them well, wish them well.

(JENNY *and* JOE, *married, walk up the aisle together as the* CHORUS *sings exultantly.* MARJORIE *covers her eyes with her hands, afraid of what she can foresee*)

CURTAIN

ACT TWO

Backyard of the Taylor Home

(JENNY *in a very plain house dress, her hair in curlers, stands between a clothesline and a wash basket, a clothespin held to her mouth reflectively.* NED *enters carrying a garden hose and a newspaper. He walks slowly, tired and without spirit*)

NED   Working hard, baby?

JENNY (*Awakened and annoyed*)   Oh . . . hello, Pop.

NED   Joe out making calls?

JENNY   No, he went up to State College for a fraternity reunion.

NED   Know what I saw just now?

JENNY (*Resuming her work*)   No, what?
(*There is something subtly disrespectful in her voice, something that goes with* NED *now. He looks shabby. He has lost his bounce*)

NED   I was passing my old place, and that fool was taking my name off! After he bought the right to use it! What do you think of that?

JENNY   I don't know. What do *you* think of it?

NED   I think he's crazy. "Brinker's Coal and Lumber"—that's a name been known around here for years. And he puts his own name up—Ramazotti! "Ramazotti's Coal and Lumber"—what the hell does that mean?

JENNY   It means Ramazotti owns your business.

NED   The ignorant dumbbell!

JENNY   He also happens to own our old house. He isn't such a dumbbell.

NED   Meaning I am! (JENNY *goes about her work in eloquent silence*) I'm the only one got caught in the crash, I suppose. (*He opens his paper to read*) If this government would only do something, a man'd have a chance to get back on his feet.

JENNY   What could the government do?

NED   Well, it could do something! That's what a government is for. . . . That Hoover!

MILLIE (*Off*)   Jenny.

JENNY   Hello. Millie.

MILLIE (*Off*)   Come on over and see the chinchilla coat.

JENNY I've got to hang my wash. You and the girls come over here.

MILLIE All right.

NED Who's got a chinchilla coat?

JENNY Nobody. It's a picture of one in *Vogue*.

NED I was going to say! What women can afford expensive furs these days?

JENNY Lots of women—Mrs. Ramazotti, for instance.

NED You're always throwing that up to me. Damn it! Everybody's poor these days. You're lucky your husband is a professional man who makes a decent living. Gives you a roof over your head.

JENNY He gives you a roof over *your* head too.

NED (*Hurt*) It's—all in the family, isn't it?
　(*Exit*)

JENNY I'm sorry. (*Muttering to herself as she works*) Decent living! If I thought that was all we'd ever have, I'd just as soon die!
　(HAZEL *enters with* ADDIE)

HAZEL Here it is.
　(*She hands the magazine to* JENNY, *who gazes at the turned page, dumbfounded.* MILLIE *and* DOT *enter. All the girls wear cheap print dresses, young housewives like* JENNY, *and as poor*)

ADDIE Isn't that the dreamiest coat you ever saw?

MILLIE Terrific!

JENNY To think some girls actually get things like this!

HAZEL And they're the kind who don't do any housework.

DOT All they do is try to look beautiful.

HAZEL And men think they're wonderful.

MILLIE (*Laughing*) Look. On the opposite page is an article: "Money Isn't Everything."

JENNY Well, fine! I don't want everything. I'll just take money.

(The rest of the scene is sung)

MILLIE (*Reading*)
"Money isn't everything!
What can money buy?"

ADDIE *and* DOT
An automobile, so you won't get wet—
Champagne, so you won't get dry!

MILLIE (*Reading*)
"Money isn't everything!
What have rich folks got?"

ADDIE *and* DOT
A Florida home, so you won't get cold—
A yacht so you won't get hot!

DOT
An orchid or two
So you won't feel blue
If you have to go out at night—

ADDIE
And maybe a jar
Of caviar
So your appetite won't be light!

MILLIE (*Reading again*)
"Oil tycoon and cattle king,
Radio troubadour,
Belittle the fun that their fortunes bring,
And tell you that they are sure
Money isn't everything!"

MILLIE, ADDIE, DOT
Money isn't everything,
Money isn't everything—

JENNY *and* HAZEL
Unless you're very poor!

MILLIE (*Reading*)
"Can money make you honest?
Can it teach you right from wrong?
Can money keep you healthy?
Can it make your muscles strong?"

ADDIE
Can money make your eyes get red,
The way they do from sewing?
Can money make your back get sore,
The way it gets from mowing?

DOT
Can money make your hands get rough,
As washing dishes does?

JENNY *and* HAZEL
Can money make you smell the way
That cooking fishes does?

MILLIE
"It may buy you gems and fancy clothes
And juicy steaks to carve,
But it cannot build your character—"

JENNY, HAZEL, ADDIE *and* DOT
Or teach you how to starve!

MILLIE
"Money isn't everything!
If you're rich, you pay—"

ADDIE *and* DOT
Elizabeth Arden to do your face
The night you attend a play!

ADDIE, DOT, MILLIE (*Singing dreamily, while* JENNY *and*
HAZEL *pantomime the thrilling event*)
Feeling like the bloom of spring,
Down the aisle you float!
A Tiffany ring, and a Cartier string
Of pearls to adorn your throat!
Your Carnegie dress
Will be more or less
Of a handkerchief round your hip,
Sewed on to you so
That your slip won't show—

JENNY *and* HAZEL
And whatever you show won't slip!

ADDIE, DOT, MILLIE
To your creamy shoulders cling

Ermines white as snow.
Then on to cafés where they sway and swing
You go with your wealthy beau.
There you'll hear a crooner sing:
   (*Imitating Vallee*)
"Money isn't everything!"

ALL
Money isn't everything,
As long . . . as . . . you . . . have . . . dough!
   (HAZEL *dances here to depict the life of an idly rich and self-centered woman*)

THE LIGHTS FADE

Bedroom
   (JENNY *sits up in bed glaring at* JOE, *who stands before her*)

JENNY (*Extreme irritation in her voice*)   This isn't true. You're trying to be funny.

JOE   No, I'm not. Charlie's uncle came to the reunion especially to talk to me.

JENNY   And you were offered a chance to be his partner? A partner of Dr. Denby?

JOE   Well, you see, I was a kind of a white-haired boy of Denby's when I was an intern at his hospital, and—

JENNY   And you have the nerve to stand there and tell me you turned him down! Turned down a partnership in his office and—

JOE   I've got to think of my father. I'm just beginning to be some help to him.

JENNY   What it gets down to is this: you care more about your father than you do about me.

JOE (*Out of patience*)   It's got nothing to do with caring about anybody. I'm just not going to walk out on my father. For you, or Charlie, or anybody. I'm not going to do it, that's all!
   (*Exit. A door slams. . . . Silence.* JENNY *puffs at her cigarette thoughtfully*)

CHORUS (*All women*)
Go easy, Jenny!

When a man slams a bathroom door like that.
You're in trouble! . . .
Use your head!
This is the biggest chance you'll ever have—
Maybe the *only* chance
To get the kind of life you want.
Don't throw it away with a few angry words.
Use your head.
This is the most important night of your life!
>   (JOE *enters, his coat off and his tie loosened. He sits in a chair*)

Be clever!
>   (JENNY *looks over at him and sniffles softly. Then she looks away. But he doesn't react. Then she sniffles louder. No reaction from* JOE)

He must have heard you.
Lord knows, you sniffled loud enough.
He didn't even ask what you were crying about.
That's bad!
Better do something
Or say something—quick!

JENNY (*Stifling a childish little sob*)   Have you got a hanky?
(JOE *gives her his handkerchief*) Thankee!
>   (*She looks up sidewise to see if he grins. No grin*)

CHORUS
There's a wall between you.
You'll have to do something more—
Well—radical!
Don't you think you'd better—
Sort of—
Go to him?
>   (JENNY *immediately rises, throws a robe over her night-gown without wrapping it around her, and patters in her bare feet over to* JOE. *She slips down on to his lap, puts her arms around him, buries her head in his chest, and sobs. He is touched. He holds her tighter*)

JOE   Don't cry, Jenny. Nothing to cry about.

JENNY   I'm a mean, selfish girl! I wasn't thinking of you.
I was only thinking of myself and how wonderful it would be
to have a beautiful house in Chicago, and servants and lovely

dresses to wear so I could look pretty for you when you came home at night.

CHORUS
Good!
(*They retire*)

JOE   I know how tough it's been for you, Jenny. Gosh, cooking three meals a day is bad enough, without the rest of the housework.

JENNY   Three meals for four people—that's twelve meals a day, you silly!

JOE   I wish I could explain just how I feel about this Chicago thing. It's—I don't know—

JENNY (*Rising*)   Don't worry about it, darling—you're a better judge of what you can do than I am.

JOE   What do you mean?

JENNY   Well, I suppose you're worried about whether you could handle a big city practice.

JOE   Me? Oh, I could handle it all right! Why do you suppose they want me?

JENNY (*Craftily*)   Well, I— Goodness! *I* think you're the best doctor in the world. Only it looked to me as if you might be afraid to tackle—

JOE   Afraid! Of course not! I just feel—if I *did* want to go I don't know how I could ever break it to Dad. Don't know how I could even open up the subject. (JENNY *chuckles*) What're you laughing at?

JENNY   The way my mind rushes on when I get excited. When you told me about this, I thought of a million things all at once! First thing I thought of was we'd soon be so rich you could give your father that old ten thousand dollars he needs to complete the hospital. (JOE *looks thoughtful.* JENNY *is quick to follow with another ace*) Know what else I was thinking? I was thinking now at last we could afford something—something I've wanted ever since we were married—even before we were married. He'd be—or she'd be—the most important thing in my life, next to you.
(*She patters over to him, kneels at his feet, and presses her head to his knee in pretty shyness*)

VOICES OF UNSEEN CHORUS (*Men*)
Poor Joe!
The older you grow,
The harder it is to know
What to think,
> What to do,
>> Where to go!

JENNY   I'm home alone so much—I have a lot of time to
think and dream. You're so busy, you don't have a chance.

JOE   Oh, yes, I do. What do you suppose I think of all day,
in between calls, driving from one house to the other?

JENNY   What?

JOE   Same girl I've been thinking about since I was eight
years old.
   (*He sings a reprise of "You Are Never Away." After he
   finishes,* JENNY *looks up at him and blinks her eyes like a
   little child*)

JENNY   Baby's sleepy.
   (JOE *kisses her, picks her up, and starts to carry her back
   to the bed*)

VOICES OF UNSEEN CHORUS (*All men*)
That's all, brother!

> THE LIGHTS FADE

Taylor's Office
   (TAYLOR *stands looking at two diplomas that hang side by
   side—his own and* JOE'S)

JOE'S VOICE (*Off*)   Dad! (TAYLOR *gingerly slips back to his
desk, not wanting* JOE *to come in and find him looking at the
diplomas*) . . . Dad!
   (JOE *enters*)

TAYLOR   Hello, Joe. Just looking over your parting instructions.

JOE (*Tactfully*)   Not instructions, Dad. Just a few—er—
suggestions about the people I've been taking care of. I par-
ticularly wanted to talk about that Reilly kid.
   (*He points over his father's shoulder to the top page of
   notes*)

TAYLOR (*Looking down at it*) Oh, I know Vincent. Works on a farm all day and studies all night. Wants to be a priest.

JOE That's the one.

TAYLOR Put on any weight? (JOE *shakes his head*) What are you doing for him?

JOE Well, yesterday I called in a vet. I had him take a look at the Reilly's cow.
    (*Pause.* TAYLOR *looks up at* JOE)

TAYLOR T.B.? (JOE *nods*) Well, if Vincent's tubercular I'll call up the commissioner and get him put on the list for the state sanitarium.

JOE That'll mean giving up his studies, won't it?

TAYLOR 'Course it will. He oughtn't to do anything for a couple of years.

JOE Well you see that's our biggest worry, Dad. He's going to think he'll be too old to go back to his studies. The only reason he wants to live is to be a priest. We've got to—you've got to see that he doesn't lose hope.

TAYLOR (*Looking at* JOE *with an understanding smile*) Well, I'll do what I can, Joe. (*He picks up another paper*) Jan Malinowski—the old Polish fellow with a chronic catarrh?

JOE Well, the only note I made about him is that I haven't been charging him anything—

TAYLOR We'll continue that policy.

JOE He's out of work now.

TAYLOR (*Studying* JOE) Get kind of wrapped up in these people don't you?

JOE (*Self-consciously*) Yes—you do—don't you?

TAYLOR One night—I was about fourteen I guess—I was out in the barn hitching the mare to your grandfather's sleigh. He had a bad chest cold—probably running a fever—but he was going to drive twelve miles through a blizzard on a call. I asked him why—asked him if it was because he loved people so much. He said "Hell no!" Didn't give a hoot about

them—didn't really like anybody till after he had done something for them. After that he figured he had a stake in them.

JOE I see what he meant.
　(MARJORIE *enters*)

MARJORIE Of course you do. They're your people after
you've helped them. . . . (*Coming up close behind* JOE)
Why does your heart feel so heavy?
If it is so fine to go to Chicago
To be rich and successful and famous—
Why does your heart feel heavy?
You could still change your mind!
Let the train go without you!
　(*Sound of an auto horn*)

TAYLOR I guess that's Jenny in the car.

MARJORIE Lean out the window and tell her it's all off.
　(JOE *starts for window.* CHARLIE'S *face appears before
　him, dimly lit*)

CHARLIE You going nuts? People will think you are crazy.
Not just Jenny. Me. Everybody.
　(CHARLIE *disappears.* JOE *turns back from the window*)

TAYLOR (*Holding out his hand*) Well— Good luck, son.

JOE (*Blurting it all out*) I'm doing this for Jenny, Father.
It'll be easier for her, and it's a wonderful practice—wonderful people—I even figured in a few years I might be able to
give you the ten grand you need to finish the hospital.

TAYLOR Fine, Joe! Just fine!

JOE And another thing. Now, Jenny and I can afford to
have a baby.

MARJORIE Your father and I didn't know whether we could
afford you or not. We just wanted you.
　(*Automobile horn off*)

JOE Well—so long, Dad. (*He turns to go, then suddenly
stops and wheels around.* MARJORIE *and* TAYLOR *stand transfixed with wild hope*) I forgot my diploma.
　(JOE *crosses and takes down his diploma.* MARJORIE *goes
　to* TAYLOR, *throws her arms around him from behind, and
　holds both hands on his heart*)

MARJORIE You're hurt!

JOE Guess I can get this in the big suitcase.

MARJORIE
I'm here with you, darling,
I love you.
Don't let him hurt you.

TAYLOR (*His voice hoarse as he attempts to throw the thing off lightly*) Lucky you remembered that. A doc isn't much good without his shingle. They'd think you were a horse doctor or something. No room for horse doctors in a fancy office like that. (JOE *and* TAYLOR *force a laugh*) (JOE *gulps and fearing to trust his voice further, waves at his father as he starts out.* TAYLOR *calls to him, a tired smile on his face*) Don't take any wooden nickels.

    (JOE *is gone.* TAYLOR *sinks down at his desk.* MARJORIE *sings part of "A Fellow Needs a Girl."* TAYLOR'S *head falls to his arms*)

THE LIGHTS FADE

Jenny's Salon, Chicago
    (*A mass of chattering people packed close together. A butler and maid carrying drinks hold their trays aloft so they can worm in and out of the crowd.* JENNY *glides from one guest to another with the manner of an assured hostess*)

ALL
Yatata yatata yatata yatata
Yatata yatata yatata yatata

GIRL (*To* ANOTHER GIRL, *with great expression*) Broccoli!

A MAN (*Answering in the same gushing manner*) Hogwash!

MAN (*To* GIRL) Balderdash!

ANOTHER MAN (*To* ANOTHER GIRL) Phoney baloney!

GIRL (*Answering*) Tripe and trash!

ALL
Yatata yatata yatata yatata
Yatata yatata yatata yatata
Yatata yatata yatata yatata
Yatata yatata yatata yatata

GIRL (*To two* OTHER GIRLS)
Busy!
Busy!
I'm busy as a bee!
I start the day at half past one!
When I am finished phoning
It's time to dress for tea.

ALL THREE GIRLS
Nothing we have to do gets done!

CHARLIE (*To himself, reflectively*)
The deep-thinking gentlemen and ladies
Who keep a metropolis alive,
Drink cocktails
And knock tails
  (*Which they all do in two beats*)
Ev'ry afternoon at five.

ALL
Yatata yatata yatata yatata
Yatata yatata yatata yatata

MAN (*To* GIRL, *indicating a new arrival, a distinguished-look-ing gentleman with white hair*)   There goes Dr. Denby!

ANOTHER MAN (*To his companion*)   Doctor Bigby Denby!

ALL   Bigby Denby Bigby Denby Bigby Denby Bigby Denby!

A GROUP OF LADIES (*Surrounding Denby*)
Doctor!
Doctor!
I need another shot!

A SECOND GROUP (*Explaining to a* THIRD GROUP)
The shots he gives are too divine!
He fills a little needle and he gives you all it's got!
Your fanny hurts but you feel fine!

ALL
Yatata yatata yatata yatata
Yatata yatata yatata yatata
Yatata yatata yatata yatata
Yatata yatata yatata yatata

Broccoli Hogwash Balderdash
Phoney Baloney Tripe and Trash!

Goodness knows where the day has gone!
The days come fast and are quickly gone,
But the talk talk talk goes on and on
And on and on and on!

MEN (*Indicating* LANSDALE *who is telling a story to a sychophantic group that includes* JENNY)
Lansdale!
Lansdale!
The multimillionaire!
He manufactures Lansdale soap!

CHARLIE
So when he tells a story
His listeners declare;
He's twice as comical as Bob Hope!
    (LANSDALE'S *listeners smack their thighs and bend over as they laugh*)

ALL
Yatata yatata yatata yatata
Yatata yatata yatata yatata
    (*The following speeches are not in meter but the "yatata yatata yatata" continues softly underneath:*)

MRS. LANSDALE (*Shouting right in the face of a friend*)   I can't sleep at night!

MAN (*To a sympathetic young woman*)   When I was four years old I tried to murder my nurse. My psychiatrist says my wife is taking her place.

DENBY (*To an extremely* HEALTHY LOOKING WOMAN)   What you need little lady is a good rest! One month at Hot Springs for you! Golf, dancing!

HEALTHY ONE   Oh, thank you, doctor!

DENBY   And when you come back I'll give you some shots.
    (*He gives her an assuring pat on the shoulder and a pinch on the cheek*)

MRS. LANSDALE (*Telling it to someone else*)   Not one wink!

CHARLIE (*To a* FAIR PATIENT)   Hot Springs for you, little lady.

FAIR PATIENT   I just came from Hot Springs.

CHARLIE   All right then. Palm Springs!
   (*He gives her the same pat and pinch that his uncle gave his patient.* NED *appears in the crowd, well dressed and with his old assurance returned*)

NED (*To* LANSDALE)   If the government would only let us alone— That Roosevelt!

MRS. LANSDALE (*Yelling at another friend*)   I've tried reading a book!

GIRL (*Pointing across the room*)   Look at Mrs. Mulhouse! She simply doesn't know how to drink!
   (MRS. MULHOUSE *has the goofy faraway look of someone about to pass out*)

JENNY (*Summoning the* BUTLER)   Jarman!
   (JARMAN *passes his tray to* JENNY, *hoists* MRS. MULHOUSE *over his shoulder as if this were all a part of his normal routine, and starts out with her*)

CHARLIE
The deep-thinking gentlemen and ladies
Who keep a metropolis alive,
Drink cocktails
And knock tails
Ev'ry afternoon at five!

NED (*To a* MAN)   All I ever see those WPA guys do is lean on their shovels.

LANSDALE (*To a* GIRL, *finishing a story with an impressive gesture*)   And I sank a ten-foot putt.
   (JOE *appears, carrying a tray of cocktails, looking as silly as he feels. He passes them to a* MAID, *but* JENNY *comes along immediately with a fresh tray, which she presses into* JOE'S *hands, pantomiming instructions as to where he must go with it. He starts off but is quickly intercepted by the sleepless* MRS. LANSDALE)

MRS. LANSDALE   Barbital, nembutal, luminal, tuinal— (*With a helpless gesture*) Wide awake!

JOE (*His manner just like* BIGBY DENBY'S *and* CHARLIE'S)
Little lady, my advice to you is a good long rest. Lake Louise, Canada! The smell of the pines will put you to sleep.

MRS. LANSDALE (*She'll be damned if anything is going to put her to sleep*) Suppose it doesn't?

JOE Then come home and we'll try giving you some—

ALL (*Breaking in*)
Broccoli hogwash balderdash
Phoney baloney tripe and trash.

DENBY
Goodness knows where the years have gone!

ALL
The years of a life are quickly gone,
But the talk talk talk goes on and on,
The prattle and the tattle,
The gab and the gush,
The chatter and the patter
And the twaddle and the tush
Go on and on and on and on and on!
   (*They resume their eternal chant*)
Yatata yatata yatata yatata yatata yatata yatata.

THE LIGHTS FADE

Foyer of the Taylor Apartment
   (EMILY, *a neatly dressed young woman, is discovered seated at small table. She has a brief case on her lap.* JARMAN *crosses with* MRS. MULHOUSE *over his shoulder*)

EMILY Good evening, Jarman. Is that Mrs. Mulhouse you've got there?

JARMAN (*Laconically*) Yes.
   (*Exit*)

JOE (*Entering with a highball in his hand*) Hello, Emily. What's on your mind?

EMILY (*Taking an X-ray film from her brief case*) I won't keep you long.

JOE I brought along a drink for you.

EMILY Thanks, doctor, I don't feel like one just now.

JOE (*Putting the drink on the table*) What have you got there?

EMILY X-ray films. Gilbert Martin's.

JOE (*In a tone of mild rebuke*)   But I've already looked at them. You were there, Emily. Don't you remember? I told you to phone him and tell him there was nothing to worry about.

EMILY   I remember.

JOE   Did you phone him?

EMILY   N—no.

JOE (*Irritated*)   Why not?

EMILY   After you left I took a squint at it.
    (*Handing him the X-ray films*)

JOE   Think the aging doctor's eyes are going back on him, eh?
    (*He holds the films up to the lamplight*)

EMILY   You were in such a hurry to leave this afternoon! Don't blame you of course, with fifty guests here—all high-bracket patients, and hospital trustees— (JOE *gives her a quick look, not sure if she is ribbing him or not. She dodges that issue by getting back to the film*) See what I mean, doctor? (*She points to a spot on the film*) Couldn't that be an ulcer crater?

JENNY (*Entering*)   Darling! You must come inside! Mrs. Lansdale is just leaving and she wants to talk to you. (*To* EMILY, *impressively*) Mrs. Brook Lansdale.

EMILY   I know. Twenty million dollars, and she can't sleep.

JENNY   She wants to talk to my husband about donating three hundred thousand dollars toward our new private pavilion. (*To* JOE, *whose eyes have not left the X-ray film*) I guess that's about as important to you as anything else can be right now, isn't it, Joe?
    (*She gives* EMILY *a sharp look*)

JOE   I'll go right in to her.

EMILY   Shall I phone Mr. Martin and tell him that his stomach is fine and dandy?
    (JOE *is now pretty sure he was wrong about the X-ray, but he hasn't quite got around to admitting it*)

JOE   Er—no. I'd like to look at it in the office. I don't trust this light.

JENNY   Hurry, Joe! She'll be gone! I'll stay here and talk to Miss West.

EMILY   I'm just going.

JOE   Good night, Emily.

EMILY   Good night, doctor.

JOE   And thanks for calling this to my attention. It was nice of you to come all the way up in this kind of weather.

JENNY   Joe! Don't dawdle! She'll be gone!

JOE   All right, dear, all right!
  (*Exit*)

JENNY   Forgive me for taking him away from you. Social contacts play such an important part in a practice like ours.

EMILY   Half the battle.

JENNY   Exactly.

EMILY   A big medical practice is like any other big business. If you want to be an important doctor with important patients, you've got to give time to them, play golf with them, go to their homes for dinner, have them at your house for cocktails. (*She makes a gesture that indicates the present party.* JENNY *smiles and nods her agreement*) Of course you haven't got time to do that with every stumblebum who gets sick, so you concentrate on the big ones— (JENNY *knits her brows, not quite sure of* EMILY) The leaders of the community!

JENNY (*Caught*)   That's just what I tell the doctor—just the phrase I use! The leaders of the community!

EMILY   You're so right, Mrs. Taylor!

JENNY   Of course I'm not criticizing my husband, but he isn't the most practical man in the world.

EMILY   Kind of a softy.

JENNY   That's right. And he's inclined to give too *much* time to the little things and not enough to the things that count.

EMILY   Oh, I think he's learning, Mrs. Taylor . . . He's learning fast.

JENNY (*Picking up* EMILY'S *drink from the table where* JOE *left it*)   He left his drink. I'll take it to him.

EMILY (*With sudden, impulsive bluntness*)   That's mine!

JENNY   Oh—sorry.

EMILY (*Taking it from her*)   Thank you. (*She finishes the glass in one swallow*) Good night!
    (*And she leaves the astonished* JENNY)

                                              THE LIGHTS FADE
Street Entrance of the Apartment Building
    (*Two* COUPLES *and a uniformed* DOORMAN *stand in the rain. The* DOORMAN *blows a whistle several times.* EMILY *enters and after waiting a few seconds, addresses him*)

EMILY   Are all these people ahead of me?

DOORMAN   They are, miss.

EMILY   I'll go around to the avenue and take my chance.

DOORMAN   Please yourself.
    (*He didn't expect much of a tip from her anyway. He leads the others off to a taxi.* EMILY *walks in the other direction. Her eyes follow an imaginary cab as it whizzes by. She puts her collar up*)

EMILY   Taxi—taxi— (*Mumbling to herself*) This is what I get for being a Girl Scout. Save the doc, save the patient, and get pneumonia myself— Way I feel now, I wouldn't care much. That wife of his leads him around by the nose— Well, if a man lets himself be led by the nose, that's all **he rates!**
(*Continuing her mumbling, but now to music*)
The boss gets on my nerves.
I've got a good mind to quit.
I've taken all I can,
It's time to get up and git,
And move to another job—
Or maybe another town!
The gentleman burns me up!
The gentleman gets me down . . .

The gentleman is a dope,
A man of many faults,
A clumsy Joe

Who wouldn't know
A rumba from a waltz.
The gentleman is a dope,
And not my cup of tea—
  (Why do I get in a dither?
  He doesn't belong to me!)

The gentleman isn't bright,
He doesn't know the score;
A cake will come,
He'll take a crumb
And never ask for more!
The gentleman's eyes are blue,
But little do they see—
  (Why am I beating my brains out?
  He doesn't belong to me!)
    He's somebody's else's problem,
    She's welcome to the guy!
    She'll never understand him
    Half as well as I.

The gentleman is a dope,
He isn't very smart.
He's just a lug
You'd like to hug
And hold against your heart.
The gentleman doesn't know
How happy he could be—
  (Look at me, crying my eyes out
  As if he belonged to me . . .
  He'll never belong to me!)
  (*She stops singing and her eyes resume searching the
streets for a cab. She continues to hail them, alternating
with her repeated comment about the "gentleman."*)
Hey, taxi! . . .
  (The gentleman is a dope)
Taxi! . . .
  (The gentleman is a dope)
Hey, ta— Oh, hell, I'll walk!
  (*She digs her hands into her raincoat pockets and stamps
off*)

Bigby Denby's Private Office

(DENBY *is alone, letting his fingers run idly over the piano keyboard*)
(JOE *enters*)

JOE   You sent for me, doctor?

DENBY   Oh, yes, come in. Sit down, doctor. Two things. First about yourself. I am very pleased with you, Joseph. Not only because of your work here at the office, but at the hospital—you—well you have won the regard of Brook Lansdale and the approval of our—ha! ha! biggest trustee is even more important than *my* approval—hmm? (*Changing quickly*) Now I come to my second topic: Charlie, my nephew—in this recent—ah—rebellion at the hospital—the nurses demanding eight-hour duty—he actually took their side! You don't think he's been drinking too much, do you?

JOE   Well, no. As a matter of fact, Doctor Denby—
   (*Telephone bell*)

DENBY   Excuse me. (*Into phone*) Mr. Tubb? Chairman of what Committee? (*Bored*) Yes, I know. It's the worst slum in the city. Quite right, Mr. Tubb! A cesspool—a disease hatchery. I agree— No, I will not go to the mayor— No, Mr. Tubb, our policy at the hospital is to keep out of politics— (*Suddenly infuriated*) And I say to you— (*His face in horrified*) What!— You— You— What? (*He bangs down the receiver and paces the room angrily*) Do you know what that man called me? An old vitamin pot! (CHARLIE *enters*) This *fellow!* Do you know what else he called me? A—

CHARLIE   A mechanical bottom jabber!
   (BIGBY DENBY *turns on* CHARLIE)

DENBY   Was that you on the phone just now?

CHARLIE   Just my little joke for the day, Uncle.
   (*He starts to pour a glass of brandy*)

DENBY   Joke! Is that all you have to do? Because if it is, we can get along without you. We want doctors here not jokers Put that brandy down at once!

CHARLIE   Down at once—yes, Uncle!
   (*He puts it down his throat*)

LANSDALE (*Off*)   I'll go right in.

(LANSDALE *enters and* BIGBY DENBY *practically clicks his heels at attention*)

DENBY Why, Brook! This is an unexpected pleasure. We were just—

LANSDALE (*Gruff and decisive*) I'm catching a train. Sorry to break in on you, but this couldn't wait. It's about the trouble we've been having with the nurses.

DENBY But I squelched that, old boy! They're continuing on the old basis of twelve-hour duty.

LANSDALE (*Impatiently*) I know that, but I've got the name of the agitator who started the whole thing. I've been doing a little investigating. I want to get rid of this woman.

DENBY Well, naturally! We'll have to make an example of her.

LANSDALE Name of the woman is Carrie Middleton.

DENBY (*Stunned*) Carrie!

JOE You mean old Carrie Middleton on the fifth floor?

LANSDALE That's the one. Been with us for thirty years and then turns traitor! Take her name off the registry. (*To* BIGBY DENBY) I want her out of the hospital when I get back here. That'll be day after tomorrow. (*To others*) Good day, gentlemen.
   (*Exit*)
   (*A pause, then* DENBY *picks up the phone*)

DENBY (*In phone*) Miss West, will you come in here a moment?

CHARLIE (*Looking hard at his uncle*) I seem to remember an old photograph at home. You and Carrie at the Chicago World's Fair when she was a student nurse. (*To* JOE) Carrie had a big sailor straw hat, and her waist was pulled in like this.
   (*He looks back quickly at Denby*)

EMILY (*Entering*) You wanted me, Doctor Denby?

DENBY Call up the Nurses' Registry and have them strike off the name of Carrie Middleton.
   (*He starts off grimly*)

EMILY   But, doctor! Carrie's never worked anywhere else.

JOE   Don't you think this is pretty hard on her? A lot of people favor the eight-hour shift. It isn't any crime to—

DENBY   Ah, my boy, but there's such a thing as discipline— loyalty! We must do many things we don't want to do. Duty — We must be good soldiers!
(*Exit*)

CHARLIE (*Uneasy under the gaze of* JOE *and* EMILY)   He's only my uncle by marriage.

JOE   I wonder if Carrie would go down and help my father out. He's up to his neck in a flu epidemic.

CHARLIE   Good idea! But don't tell Lansdale. Mustn't be friendly with anybody he doesn't like. My uncle *never* is. That's why he's Physician-in-Chief at the hospital.

JOE   Well, to hell with Lansdale!

CHARLIE (*Imitating his uncle's voice and manner*)   Tut, tut, my boy! There are many things that one would like to do that one does not. Duty—
(*He strikes a chord on the piano*)

EMILY   You must be good soldiers!
(CHARLIE *strikes another chord*)

CHARLIE   This is a big-time medical practice, Joe.

JOE (*Bitterly*)   Sure! Through the portals of this office pass the biggest screwballs in town.

CHARLIE   *And* the most repulsive.
(CHARLIE, *playing his own accompaniment, starts singing ironically*)
Our world is for the forceful,
And not for sentimental folk,
But brilliant and resourceful
And paranoiac gentle folk!

JOE (*To* EMILY)
Not soft and sentimental folk!

CHARLIE
"Allegro," a musician
Would so describe the speed of it,

The clash and competition
Of counterpoint—

EMILY
The need of it?

CHARLIE
We cannot prove the need of it!
   (*Faster and crisper*)
We know no other way
Of living out a day.
Our music must be galloping and gay!

JOE
We muffle all the undertones,
The minor blood-and-thunder tones,
The overtones are all we care to play!

ALL THREE
Hysterically frantic,
We are stubbornly romantic
And doggedly determined to be gay!

EMILY
Brisk, lively,
Merry and bright!
Allegro!
Same tempo
Morning and night!
Allegro!
Don't stop whatever you do
Do something dizzy and new,
Keep up the hullabaloo!

CHORUS (*Off, alternates with* EMILY)
Allegro!   Allegro!
Allegro!   Allegro!
Allegro!   Allegro!
   (*Now the singing* CHORUS *is faintly seen through a gauze
   curtain.* DANCERS *are also seen spinning across the stage*)

JOE
We spin and we spin and we spin and we spin,
Playing a game no one can win,
The men who corner wheat,
The men who corner gin.

The men who rule the air waves,
The denizens of din—

CHORUS
They spin and they spin
They spin and they spin.

CHARLIE
The girls who dig for gold,
And won't give in for tin,
The lilies of the field,
So femininely thin,
They toil not, they toil not,
But oh, how they spin!

CHORUS
Oh, how they spin!
Oh, how they spin!

JOE
May's in love with Kay's husband,
He's in love with Sue!
Sue's in love with May's husband,
What are they to do?
Tom's in love with Tim's wife,
She's in love with Sam!
Sam's in love with Tom's wife,
So they're in a jam!

CHARLIE
They are smart little sheep
Who have lost their way,

CHARLIE, JOE, *and* EMILY
Blah! Blah! Blah!
(*The gauze curtain opens, disclosing full* SINGING *and*
DANCING ENSEMBLES)

CHARLIE, JOE, EMILY *and* CHORUS
Brisk, lively,
Merry and bright!
Allegro!
Same tempo
Morning and night!
Allegro!
Don't stop whatever you do

Do something dizzy and new
Keep up the hullabaloo!
Allegro! Allegro!
Allegro! Allegro!
Allegro! Allegro!

(*The stage is now left to the* DANCERS, *who in their own medium depict the confusion and the futility that pervade the society in which* JOE *practices medicine. A curtain comes down on this ballet while it is still going its frenzied way*)

Joe's Office

(JOE *is seated at his desk looking over the day's engagements*)

EMILY (*Entering briskly*)   'Morning, doctor.

JOE   Anybody waiting?

EMILY   The zoo is packed. Mrs. Mulhouse is in the recovery room waiting for her stomach pump.

JOE   Did you give that night-club singer her ultraviolet ray?

EMILY   I was just going to when Doctor Charlie came in. He saw her and immediately decided he would personally administer the ultraviolet ray! (*Looking off*) The lady has probably been ultraviolated by now. (*He doesn't smile at her sally*) You seem kind of low today, boss.

JOE   I am. I just had a letter from a boy who used to be a patient of mine. He was going to study for the priesthood at one time. It was a sad, hopeless little letter.

EMILY   The T.B. case. You told me about him.

JOE   I did?

EMILY   Several times.

JOE   I guess I feel guilty about him. I can't get rid of the feeling that if I'd spent the last five years on one boy like Vincent, I'd have done the world more good than I could do in a lifetime here.

EMILY   Getting sour on rich city people?

JOE   No, I'm not, Emily. There's nothing wrong with people just because they have money or live in the city—nothing wrong with being a city doctor—but this crowd that we get! (*He shakes his head and sighs*) Who else is out there now?

EMILY Harry Buckley on his way through from California. Mrs. Lansdale is there too. She came in last, but she insists on being seen first.

JOE All right, let her in— No, wait! I'm damned if I'll let these Lansdales walk all over me. Send Buckley in first.

EMILY You mean I can look the empress right in the puss and tell her she has to wait?

JOE You bet you can.

MRS. LANSDALE (*Dashing in*) I knew you must be in by now. (*Glaring at* EMILY) Why didn't you tell me he was here? (*To* JOE) What I've got to say won't take long. The other night I nearly got to sleep.

JOE Well, fine!

MRS. LANSDALE I was just dozing off about two in the morning when the phone rang. It was my husband to say that he'd be home late. It then occurred to me that most nights I lie awake wondering when and if he is coming home.

JOE He works too hard. He—

MRS. LANSDALE So I put a detective on him! (*Taking a typewritten report from her bag*) It seems my husband has got himself a girl. (*Throwing paper on* JOE'S *desk*) Here's a carbon copy of the report. (JOE'S *eyes shift to* EMILY) Oh, she can hear. The papers'll have it tomorrow when I fly to Nevada.

JOE Don't you think you're jumping at this too quickly? Why not think it over? Sleep on it—

MRS. LANSDALE Sleep! Me?

JOE Well, is there anything you want me to do? Want anything to quiet your nerves?

MRS. LANSDALE Hell, no! I want to enjoy this! So long! (*Indicating the report on his desk*) Read that little blue paper when you get time. It'll give you quite a kick. Good afternoon.
  (*She sweeps out*)
  (JOE *is thoughtful and silent*)

EMILY   Shall I send Buckley in?

JOE   What's that? (*Coming out of it*) Oh, yes—yes, send him in.

EMILY (*Calling off as she exits*)   Mr. Buckley.
  (JOE *picks up* MRS. LANSDALE's *detective report, but has time only to glance at it idly before* BUCKLEY *enters. He is almost too well dressed. Nervous mannerisms belie his self-assurance*)

BUCKLEY   Hiya, doc?

JOE (*As they shake hands*)   Good to see you, Harry.

BUCKLEY   You're busy and I've got to make a connection for New York, so I'll go right to it. I've decided I've got a low metabolism, and I want you to give me some thyroid pills.

JOE   Did you have your California doctor do your metabolism?

BUCKLEY   No. Haven't had a minute's extra time for anything like that.

JOE   What makes you think you have a thyroid deficiency?

BUCKLEY   Well, you know how it is in southern California. I keep in shape. We've got a gymnasium right in the studio—massage too and Turkish bath. I play a lot of tennis and I get a lot of sun. I'm always in marvelous condition, and I feel lousy!

JOE   I didn't know they had gymnasiums in studios.

BUCKLEY   Just for producers.

JOE   But you went out there as a writer.

BUCKLEY   I'm a producer now.

JOE   More money?

BUCKLEY   Plenty more, and do I earn it! I live at that studio! Start at the crack of dawn and get home in the middle of the night.

JOE   How does your wife like it?

BUCKLEY   Lola? She hates it. But what are you going to do? If you're successful, you're successful.

JOE You're successful, and you feel lousy. Do you like this better than writing?

BUCKLEY Gosh, I've got to run!
(*He rises, and so does* JOE)

JOE Why don't you get back to writing? Seems to me writers are the lucky fellows. You can work at home. You have no special hours, and you have time for your wife.

BUCKLEY (*A cloud of worry crossing his face*) I'm having a little trouble with Lola right now. Somebody wrote her a letter giving her information about me when I was on location with a picture. I don't know what to do.

JOE Don't let a thing like that hang over you, Harry. Get it behind you. Make an honest confession.

BUCKLEY Yes. But I don't know what to confess. She won't tell me what's in the letter. Good-bye.
(*Exit.* JOE *paces his office angrily. He picks up the telephone instrument and bangs it on his desk.* EMILY *enters*)

JOE Emily! Is there anyone out there with a broken arm or a gallstone? Is there anybody out there worth a doctor's time and knowledge? Can't you scare us up a ruptured appendix or a pair of infected tonsils. . . . What the hell kind of practice is this anyhow? (*He picks up the detective's report again*) All we seem to attract is. . . .
(*His voice drops off as he becomes interested in what he's reading.* EMILY *looking worried, speaks to him*)

EMILY Dr. Denby wants me to remind you that you all have to leave the office in a few minutes and go over to the dedication of the new private pavilion. They're going to unveil the bronze plaque. (JOE *frowns at what he is reading and doesn't seem to have heard her*) Mr. Lansdale will come in his car and pick you up at—

JOE Mr. Lansdale, you say? Why he's the very man I'm reading about! This paper tells all about how he meets his girl and where he takes her— (*Looking up*) And Emily, do you know who Mr. Lansdale's girl is?
(*Pause. She lowers her eyes*)

EMILY Yes. I do.

JOE Does everybody know?

EMILY   They seem to.

JOE   Well, that's the way it is I guess— (*Rising from his desk and walking away*) Do you know what is very sad about this? The heart-breaking part of it is that I don't give a damn! (*Thoughtfully*) I must have stopped loving her some time ago and I didn't know it—not until this minute! Somewhere in this rat race, somewhere along the line, we lost each other. But I don't know when it happened. (EMILY *sits very still and listens*) What became of her? The dream girl of my college days! There was a time when if she danced with another boy and he held her close, there would be murder in my heart. . . . Now she's Lansdale's girl, and it means no more to me than just another cheap little setup, like so many that pass through this office every day. . . . These benzedrine romances! They have no faint resemblance to love. There's nothing real about any of it—nothing real about the whole damn place. What the hell am I doing here! What the hell am I doing!

> (*He sits at his desk and drops his head on his arms. The lights come up slowly behind the gauze curtain revealing* JOE'S FATHER *surrounded by a* GROUP *of his friends from home. He sees them in his mind and hears them sing*)

GROUP
We are the friends that you left behind.

TAYLOR
You need us, Joe—

GROUP
And we need you,
We can bring happiness and peace to your mind.

TAYLOR
We want you, Joe.

GROUP
We want you to
Come home—come home. . . .

> (MARJORIE *enters, comes softly and quietly toward* JOE *and sings*)

MARJORIE
Come home, come home,
Where the brown birds fly
Through a pale, blue sky

To a tall green tree,
There is no finer sight for a man to see—
Come home, Joe, come home!
Come home and lie
By a laughing spring,
Where the breezes sing
And caress your ear.
There is no sweeter sound for a man to hear—
Come home, Joe, come home.
You will find a world of honest friends who miss you,
You will shake the hands of men whose hands are strong,
And when all their wives and kids run up and kiss you,
You will know that you are back where you belong.
You'll know you're back
Where there's work to do,
Where there's love for you
For the love you give,
There is no better life for a man to live—
     Come home, Joe, come home
     Come home, son, come home!
     (MARJORIE *drifts off out of* JOE's *mind. He lifts his head,
     becomes conscious of* EMILY's *presence again, and averts
     his eyes*)

EMILY   Feeling better?

JOE   Yes—I'm sorry—I went kind of haywire, I guess.

EMILY   I liked it fine.

BIGBY DENBY (*Off*)   Joe!—Joe! (*He enters with* LANSDALE)
Heavens, boy, aren't you ready? Brook and I have been
waiting for you in my office.

LANSDALE   Hurry up. I've got the car downstairs.

DENBY (*Beaming*)   Shall we tell him now, Brook?

LANSDALE (*Grinning*)   Might as well. Give him time to compose a speech on the way over.

JOE   Speech?
     (CHARLIE *enters and stands watching*)

LANSDALE   An acceptance speech. (*Putting his hand on* JOE's
shoulder affectionately) Joe, my boy, you're about to be made
Physician-in-Chief to the hospital—youngest man ever ap

pointed! (JOE *looks dazed*) You'll be the head man. We are making Bigby President of the Medical Board.

DENBY (*The hearty, good-fellow characterization*) I'm being kicked upstairs. Ha! Ha!
(*He looks around at* EMILY *and she responds with a laugh of bare acknowledgment*)

LANSDALE What do you say?

JOE Well, I'm knocked over. I don't know what to say!

DENBY What do *you* say, Emily?

EMILY (*Drily*) Well, gee whillikers!

LANSDALE (*To* DENBY) Hope he isn't so tongue-tied when he gets in front of the trustees! (*He puts his arm through* JOE'S *and leads him off*) Come on, we're late!

DENBY (*Following them off gaily*) I know one little lady who'll be proud of her husband today!
(*All three are off.* EMILY *looks after them.* CHARLIE *comes down, nearer to her*)

CHARLIE What're you thinking about, nursie?

EMILY Just thinking how hard it is for a man to get off a merry-go-round after it gets going fast.

CHARLIE You couldn't expect him to turn down a plum like this. Being head man at our hospital makes a fellow one of the biggest men in medicine.

EMILY Big politician, big social lion, and banquet man— not much of a doctor. He could've been, though. When he first came here, I thought—I hoped— (*She swallows hard*) He could've been a hell of a doctor!

CHARLIE There's something about Joe—something so *good* about him that you want him to be even better. I can understand a girl getting stuck on a fellow like that. Wouldn't blame her.

EMILY Thanks, pal.
(*Pause*)

CHARLIE Want to take the day off and go to a burlesque show?

EMILY   I don't know. I think the dedication ceremony will be funnier.

CHARLIE   Okay. We'll go there.

EMILY   Can we stop on the way and have a drink?

CHARLIE   A drink? We'll get cockeyed! How else can you go to such things?
(*Exeunt*)

The Lobby of the New Private Pavilion
(LANSDALE *stands before a bronze plaque dedicated to* BIGBY DENBY. *He addresses a group of trustees and guests on the right. Behind him, on the left, stand a* CHORUS *of simply dressed people, representing opposing spirits,* JOE'S *memories, the principles he has forgotten, his roots*)

LANSDALE   (*Oratorically*)   Bigby Denby, M.D.—physician, scientist, humanitarian— (*Applause*) And better than all these —an *executive!* (*Applause*) To use a phrase of his own, he has been a "good soldier." Bigby Denby has for years—
(*His mouth continues to move but the words are drowned out by the* CHORUS)

CHORUS
Broccoli Hogwash Balderdash,
Phoney Baloney Tripe and Trash,
No one knows where his youth has gone,
No one knows where his heart has gone,
But the talk talk talk goes on and on and on and on and on
Yatata yatata yatata yatata
Yatata yatata yatata yatata
(*They continue softly as* DENBY *starts his speech*)

DENBY   Mr. Chairman, trustees, friends—the cup of my happiness runneth over. My heart is so full, words fail me. And yet—
(*He proceeds to prove that words do not fail him, but we do not hear them, being spared by the* CHORUS)

CHORUS
The prattle and the tattle,
The gab and the gush,
The chatter and the patter
And the twaddle and the tush
Go on and on and on and on and on!

DENBY (*Finishing his speech, indicating* JOE) My co-worker, my young but very talented friend, Joseph Taylor, Junior— the youngest man ever to receive this appointment.

CHORUS (*In cadence*) Joseph Taylor, Junior!
(*Applause.* CHARLIE *and* EMILY *enter and applaud and cheer too loudly. Midday Martinis have done their work. As* JOE *rises to face his audience, the applause continues and he continues bowing. The clapping hands, however, never meet each other; they clap only "in dumb show," while the following conflict in* JOE'S *mind is audible:*)

CHORUS
Look out, Joe!
Once you cross this threshold
The door will close behind you.

TRUSTEES *and* GUESTS (*As their hands continue to indicate applause, but noiselessly*) Don't be a fool! Think what other doctors would give to be up there in your place.

CHORUS
Lansdale is the real boss of the hospital.
You'll be a stooge like Bigby Denby!

TRUSTEES *and* GUESTS But think what it means to be a Physician-in-Chief! You can't turn down such an honor. You'd be a sap. (*A reporter takes a flash-bulb photo*) See that! The *Chicago Tribune!* Make a good speech. It will be in the papers!

JOE Ladies and Gentlemen. This comes to me as a complete surprise. I look upon this appointment as a challenge. One must approach with deep humility the task of succeeding so illustrious a predecessor as Doctor Bigby Denby! (*Applause*)
He has been an ornament to medicine,
An ornament to his city,
An ornament—
(JOE *and the entire company suddenly "freeze" in a still picture and remain motionless during the following speech*)

CHORUS
"Ornament"—
A man's brain is sometimes cleared
By the sudden light of one word.
In the flash of a split second

He sees a signpost, pointing down a new road,
And he may take a new turning
That will affect the rest of his life.
　　(*Pause. They speak in a hushed tone*)
The split second is over.
　　(*The company relaxes from its frozen tableau*)

JOE (*A different note in his voice*)
It takes a special talent to be an ornament . . .
I am not blessed with this talent!

GRANDMA (*Entering, seeing* JOE, *then calling off to his mother just as she did on the day he learned to walk*)　Marjorie!
　　(MARJORIE *rushes on, stands with* GRANDMA, *and listens to* JOE *"learn to walk" again*)

CHORUS (*Starting quietly but with exhortation in their voices*)
One foot, other foot,
One foot, other foot—
　　(*They keep this up under* JOE'S *speech*)

JOE　I must therefore . . . (*With a sudden burst of courage*) I decline the appointment! As a matter of fact I have another offer, in a smaller hospital, where my father is Physician-in-Chief. I'll be his assistant. I want to practice medicine again, among people I understand . . . I'm going home.

CHORUS (*Singing to him, happily*)
Come home, come home
Where the brown birds fly,
Through a pale blue sky
To a tall green tree.
　　(*The* TRUSTEES, GUESTS, LANSDALE, *et al. laugh in derision at* JOE)

JOE (*Shouting them down*)
There is no finer sight
For a man to see!
　　(JENNY *glares at* JOE *and goes to the shelter of* LANSDALE'S *consoling arms*)

CHORUS
Come home, Joe, come home!

DENBY　You can't do this! What'll I tell the papers?

LANSDALE　Tell the papers he's sick!

JOE   Tell them I'm just getting well!
   (JOE *starts to go*)

CHORUS (*Singing ecstatically, triumphantly*)
Now you can do whatever you want,
Whatever you want to do—

EMILY (*Shouting to* JOE)   Doctor Taylor! Can you use a
nurse back there?
   (JOE *turns and holds out his hand to welcome her. She
   joins him*)

CHORUS
Here you are in a wonderful world
Especially made for you!

CHARLIE   Hey! What about me?

DENBY   Charlie!

JOE (*To* CHARLIE)   Come on!
   (CHARLIE *staggers forward*)

EMILY (*As she supports* CHARLIE *and helps him walk steadily*)
One foot, other foot,
One foot, other foot—

ALL (*With increasing volume and spirit*)
One foot, other foot,
One foot, other foot,
Now you can do whatever you want,
Whatever you want to do—
One foot out and the other foot out,
One foot out and the other foot out,
One foot out and the other foot out—
And the world belongs to you!
   (JOE *walks away, out into the sunlight.* EMILY *and* CHARLIE
   follow)

                                        CURTAIN

♡

South Pacific

♥

BOOK BY *Oscar Hammerstein, II,*
and Joshua Logan

ADAPTED FROM
James A. Michener's
Pulitzer Prize-Winning

TALES OF THE SOUTH PACIFIC

to our patient

DOROTHY AND NEDDA,

who liked it even
when all the parts were
sung and acted by us.

South Pacific *was first produced by Richard Rodgers and Oscar Hammerstein, II, in association with Leland Hayward and Joshua Logan, on April 7, 1949, at the Majestic Theatre, New York City, with the following cast:*

IN ORDER OF THEIR APPEARANCE

NGANA	Barbara Luna
JEROME or	Michael De Leon / Noel De Leon
HENRY	Richard Silvera
ENSIGN NELLIE FORBUSH	Mary Martin
EMILE DE BECQUE	Ezio Pinza
BLOODY MARY	Juanita Hall
BLOODY MARY'S ASSISTANT	Musa Williams
ABNER	Archie Savage
STEWPOT	Henry Slate
LUTHER BILLIS	Myron McCormick
PROFESSOR	Fred Sadoff
LT. JOSEPH CABLE, U.S.M.C.	William Tabbert
CAPT. GEORGE BRACKETT, U.S.N.	Martin Wolfson
CMDR. WILLIAM HARBISON, U.S.N.	Harvey Stephens
YEOMAN HERBERT QUALE	Alan Gilbert
SGT. KENNETH JOHNSON	Thomas Gleason
SEABEE RICHARD WEST	Dickinson Eastham
SEABEE MORTON WISE	Henry Michel
SEAMAN TOM O'BRIEN	Bill Dwyer
RADIO OPERATOR BOB MC CAFFREY	Biff McGuire
MARINE CPL. HAMILTON STEEVES	Jim Hawthorne
STAFF SGT. THOMAS HASSINGER	Jack Fontan
SEAMAN JAMES HAYES	Beau Tilden
LT. GENEVIEVE MARSHALL	Jacqueline Fisher
ENSIGN DINAH MURPHY	Roslyn Lowe
ENSIGN JANET MAC GREGOR	Sandra Deel
ENSIGN CORA MAC RAE	Bernice Saunders
ENSIGN SUE YAEGER	Pat Northrop
ENSIGN LISA MINELLI	Gloria Meli
ENSIGN CONNIE WALEWSKA	Mardi Bayne
ENSIGN PAMELA WHITMORE	Evelyn Colby
ENSIGN BESSIE NOONAN	Helena Schurgot
LIAT	Betta St. John
MARCEL, Henry's Assistant	Richard Loo
LT. BUZZ ADAMS	Don Fellows

Islanders, Sailors, Marines, Officers: Mary Ann Reeve, Chin Yu, Alex Nicol, Eugene Smith, Richard Loo, William Ferguson

BOOK AND MUSICAL NUMBERS STAGED BY Joshua Logan
SCENERY AND LIGHTING BY Jo Mielziner
COSTUMES BY Motley
ORCHESTRA DIRECTED BY Salvatore Dell'Isola
ORCHESTRATIONS BY Robert Russell Bennett

The action of the play takes place on two islands in the South Pacific during the recent war. There is a week's lapse of time between the two acts.

Musical Numbers

ACT
ONE

Dites-Moi Pourquoi   Ngana and Jerome
A Cockeyed Optimist   Nellie
Some Enchanted Evening   Emile
Bloody Mary Is the Girl I Love   Sailors, Seabees,
   Marines
There Is Nothing Like a Dame   Billis, Sailors, Seabees,
   Marines
Bali Ha'i   Bloody Mary
I'm Gonna Wash That Man Right Outa My Hair
   Nellie and Nurses
I'm in Love with a Wonderful Guy   Nellie and Nurses
Younger Than Springtime   Cable
Finale   Nellie and Emile

ACT
TWO

Soft Shoe Dance   Nurses and Seabees
Happy Talk   Bloody Mary, Liat and Cable
Honey Bun   Nellie and Billis
You've Got to Be Taught   Cable
This Nearly Was Mine   Emile
Reprise: Some Enchanted Evening   Nellie
Finale

ACT ONE | Scene One

SCENE: EMILE DE BECQUE'S *plantation home on an island in the South Pacific.*

On your right as you look at the stage is a one-storied residence. On your left is a teakwood pagoda at the edge of the cacao grove. House and pagoda are bordered and decked in the bright tropical colors of the flaming hibiscus, the purple bougainvillaea, and the more pale and delicate frangipani. Between the house and the pagoda you can see the bay below and an island on the open sea beyond the bay. Twin volcanoes rise from the island.

AT RISE: *As the curtain rises, two Eurasian children,* NGANA, *a girl about eleven, and* JEROME, *a boy about eight, are, with humorous dignity, dancing an impromptu minuet. A bird call is heard in the tree above.* JEROME *looks up and imitates the sound. The eyes of both children follow the flight of the bird.* NGANA *runs over to the pagoda and climbs up on a table and poses on it as if it were a stage.* JEROME *lifts his hands and solemnly conducts her as she sings.*

NGANA
Dites-moi
Pourquoi
La vie est belle,
Dites-moi
Pourquoi
La vie est gai!
Dites-moi
Pourquoi,
Chère mad'moiselle,
Est-ce que
Parce que
Vous m'aimez?
    (HENRY, *a servant, enters and scolds them*)

HENRY   Allez-vous! Vite! Dans la maison!

NGANA   Non, Henri!

JEROME   (*Mischievously delivering an ultimatum*)   Moi, je reste ici!

HENRY   Oh, oui? Nous verrons bien . . . (*He chases* JEROME *around the giggling* NGANA) Viens, petit moustique!
(HENRY *catches* JEROME. *He is not as angry as he pretends to be, but he grabs* JEROME *by the ear and leads him off squealing, followed by* NGANA, *who protests violently*)

NGANA   Non, Henri . . . non . . . non!
(*As she runs off,* NELLIE *and* EMILE *are heard offstage from around the corner of the house*)

NELLIE'S VOICE   What's this one?

EMILE'S VOICE   That is frangipani.

NELLIE'S VOICE   But what a color!

EMILE'S VOICE   You will find many more flowers out here.
(NELLIE *enters, looking around her, entranced by the beauty of the scene. She turns upstage to gaze out over the bay.* HENRY *comes on from downstage with a tray which he takes over to the coffee table.* EMILE, *entering a few paces behind* NELLIE, *comes down briskly and addresses* HENRY)

EMILE   Je servirai le café.

HENRY   Oui, Monsieur.

EMILE   C'est tout.

HENRY   Oui, Monsieur de Becque.
(HENRY *exits.* NELLIE *comes down, still under the spell of the surrounding wonder*)

NELLIE   Well, I'm just speechless! . . . And that lunch! Wild chicken— I didn't know it was ever wild. Gosh! I had no idea people lived like this right out in the middle of the Pacific Ocean.

EMILE   (*Pouring coffee*)   Sugar?

NELLIE   Thanks.

EMILE   One?

NELLIE   Three. (EMILE *smiles*) I know it's a big load for a demitasse to carry. All right, I'm a hick. You know so many American words, do you know what a hick is?

EMILE   A hick is one who lives in a stick.

NELLIE   Sticks. Plural. The sticks.

EMILE   Pardon. The sticks. I remember now.

NELLIE   How long did it take you to build up a plantation like this?

EMILE   I came to the Pacific when I was a young man.
     (NELLIE *studies him for a moment*)

NELLIE   Emile, is it true that all the planters on these islands —are they all running away from something?

EMILE (*Pausing cautiously before he answers*)   Who is not running away from something? There are fugitives every-where—Paris, New York, even in Small Rock— (NELLIE *looks puzzled*) Where you come from . . .
     (NELLIE *suddenly understands what he means and bursts out laughing*)

NELLIE   Oh, Little Rock!

EMILE (EMILE, *laughing with her and shouting the correction*) Little Rock! . . . You know fugitives there?
     (NELLIE *runs over to where she has left her bag*)

NELLIE   I'll show you a picture of a Little Rock fugitive. (*Taking a clipping from an envelope in the bag*) I got this clipping from my mother today.
     (*She hands it to* EMILE *who reads:*)

EMILE   "Ensign Nellie Forbush, Arkansas' own Florence Nightingale . . ."

NELLIE (*Apologetically*)   That was written by Mrs. Leeming, the Social Editor. She went to school with my mother. To read her, you would think that I'm practically the most im-portant nurse in the entire Navy and that I run the fleet hospital all by myself, and it's only a matter of time before I'll be a Lady Admiral.

EMILE   In this picture you do not look much like an Admiral.

NELLIE   Oh, that was taken before I knew what rain and heat and mud could do to your disposition. But it isn't rainy

today. Gosh, it's beautiful here. Just look at that yellow sun! You know, I don't think it's the end of the world like everyone else thinks. I can't work myself up to getting that low. (*He smiles*) Do you think I'm crazy too? They all do over at the fleet hospital. You know what they call me? Knucklehead Nellie. I suppose I am, but I can't help it. (*She sings*)
When the sky is a bright canary yellow
I forget every cloud I've ever seen—
So they call me a cockeyed optimist,
Immature and incurably green!

I have heard people rant and rave and bellow
That we're done and we might as well be dead—
But I'm only a cockeyed optimist
And I can't get it into my head.

I hear the human race
Is falling on its face
And hasn't very far to go,
But every whippoorwill
Is selling me a bill
And telling me it just ain't so!

I could say life is just a bowl of jello
And appear more intelligent and smart
But I'm stuck
(Like a dope!)
With a thing called hope,
And I can't get it out of my heart . . . Not this heart!
    (*She walks over to him, speaking the next line*)
Want to know anything else about me?

EMILE   Yes. You say you are a fugitive. When you joined the Navy, what were you running away from?
    (*He returns the clipping to her*)

NELLIE   Gosh, I don't know. It was more like running *to* something. I wanted to see what the world was like—outside Little Rock, I mean. And I wanted to meet different kinds of people and find out if I like them better. And I'm finding out.
    (*She suddenly becomes self-conscious*)

EMILE (*Tactful*)   Would you like some cognac?

NELLIE (*Relieved*)   I'd love some.
    (EMILE *goes to the table and pours the brandy. In the tol-*

lowing verses, EMILE *and* NELLIE *are not singing to each other. Each is soliloquizing)*

NELLIE (*Thoughtfully watching* EMILE)
Wonder how I'd feel,
Living on a hillside,
Looking on an ocean,
Beautiful and still.

EMILE (*Pouring the cognac*)
This is what I need,
This is what I've longed for,
Someone young and smiling
Climbing up my hill!

NELLIE
We are not alike;
Probably I'd bore him.
He's a cultured Frenchman—
I'm a little hick.

EMILE (*Pausing as he starts to pour the second glass*)
Younger men than I,
Officers and doctors,
Probably pursue her—
She could have her pick.

NELLIE (*She catches his eye. Each averts his eyes from the other*)
Wonder why I feel
Jittery and jumpy!
I am like a schoolgirl,
Waiting for a dance.

EMILE (*Carrying the two filled brandy glasses, he approaches* NELLIE)
Can I ask her now?
I am like a schoolboy!
What will be her answer?
Do I have a chance?
(*He passes* NELLIE *her brandy glass. It is a large snifter type of glass. She has apparently never drunk from one before. She watches him carefully as he lifts his to his lips, and does the same. As they drink, the music rises to great ecstatic heights. One is made aware that in this simple act*

of two people who are falling in love, each drinking brandy, there are turbulent thoughts and feelings going on in their hearts and brains. They lower their glasses. The music dies down. EMILE *struggles to say something. He plunges into the middle of his subject as if continuing a thought which he assumes she has sensed)*

EMILE   In peacetime, the boat from America comes once a month. The ladies—the wives of the planters—often go to Australia during the hot months. It can get very hot here.

NELLIE   It can get hot in Arkansas, too.
     (She takes another quick swallow after this one)

EMILE   Ah, yes?

NELLIE *(Nodding her head)*   Uh-huh.

EMILE *(He puts his glass down on the table)*   I have many books here . . . Marcel Proust? *(She looks blank)* Anatole France? *(This evokes a faint smile of half-recognition from her)* Did you study French in school?

NELLIE   Oh, yes.

EMILE   Ah, then you can read French?

NELLIE *(As though saying, "Of course not")*   No! *(Fearful of having disappointed him, she makes a feeble attempt to add a note of hope)* I can conjugate a few verbs. *(Realizing how silly this must sound to him, she changes the subject)* I bet you read a lot.

EMILE   Out here, one becomes hungry to learn everything. *(He rises and paces nervously)* Not to miss anything, not to let anything good pass by.
     (He pauses and looks down at her, unable to go on. She, feeling he is coming closer to his point, looks up with a sudden encouraging smile)

NELLIE   Yes?

EMILE   One waits so long for what is good . . . and when at last it comes, one cannot risk to lose. *(He turns away, searching for more words)* So . . . so one must speak and act quickly even—even if it seems almost foolish to be so quick. *(He looks at her, worried . . . has he gone too far . . . how will she accept any advance at all he may make to her? She can only smile helplessly back at him. He goes on, speaking quickly*) I know it is only two weeks. A dinner given at your Officers' Club. Do you remember?

NELLIE   Yes.

EMILE   That is the way things happen sometimes. . . . Isn't it, Nellie?

NELLIE (*Swallowing hard*)   Yes, it is . . . Emile.

EMILE (*Singing*)
Some enchanted evening
You may see a stranger,
You may see a stranger
Across a crowded room—
And somehow you know
(You know even then)
That somewhere you'll see her again and again.

Some enchanted evening
Someone may be laughing,
You may hear her laughing
Across a crowded room—
And night after night
(As strange as it seems)
The sound of her laughter will sing in your dreams.

  Who can explain it?
  Who can tell you why?
  Fools give you reasons—
  Wise men never try.

Some enchanted evening
When you find your true love,
When you feel her call you
Across a crowded room—
Then fly to her side,
And make her your own,
Or all through your life you may dream all alone. . . .

  Once you have found her
  Never let her go,
  Once you have found her
  Never let her go!
(*There follow several seconds of silence. Neither moves.*

EMILE *speaks*)

I am older than you. If we have children, when I die they will be growing up. You could afford to take them back to America—if you like. Think about it.

(HENRY *enters*)

HENRY   Monsieur de Becque, la jeep de Mademoiselle est ici. (NELLIE *and* EMILE *turn as if awakened from a dream*) La jeep de Mademoiselle. (HENRY *smiles, a wide toothy smile, at* NELLIE) Votre jeep!

NELLIE   Oh, my jeep! (*She looks at her watch*) Gosh! Thank you, Henry. I'm on duty in ten minutes!

(HENRY *exits.* NELLIE *holds out her hand to* EMILE)

EMILE   Before you leave, Nellie, I want to tell you something. A while ago, you asked me a question—why did I leave France?

NELLIE   Oh, Emile, that was none of my business.

EMILE   But I want to tell you. I had to leave France. I killed a man.

(*Pause*)

NELLIE   Why did you kill him?

EMILE   He was a wicked man, a bully. Everyone in our village was glad to see him die, and it was not to my discredit. Do you believe me, Nellie?

(*Another pause—unbearable to him*)

NELLIE   You have just told me that you killed a man and that it's all right. I hardly know you, and yet I know it's all right.

EMILE (*Deeply moved*)   Thank you, Nellie. (*His voice suddenly gay and exultant*) And you like my place?

NELLIE   Yes.

EMILE   You will think?

NELLIE (*Smiling up at him*)   I will think.

(*They are silent and motionless for a moment. Then she turns suddenly and walks off very quickly. He looks after her and starts to hum softly. He picks up the coffee cup she has left on the fountain and smiles down at it. He holds the cup up so he can examine its rim*)

EMILE   Lipstick! . . . Three lumps of sugar in this little cup! (*He laughs aloud, then resumes his humming and walks, almost dances, across the stage in time to his own music.* NGANA *and* JEROME *enter and walk behind him across the stage, imitating his happy stride. As* EMILE *puts down the cup, the children join him, humming the same melody. He turns quickly and frowns down on them with mock sternness. They giggle*) Eh bien!

JEROME   Bravo, Papa!
  (*The children both applaud*)

EMILE   Merci, Monsieur!

NGANA   Nous chantons bien, aussi.

EMILE   Ah, oui?

NGANA   Attends, Papa!

JEROME (*Parroting* NGANA)   Attends, Papa!
  (*He looks at* NGANA *for the signal to start the song. They sing . . .* EMILE *conducting them*)

NGANA *and* JEROME
Dites moi
Pourquoi
La vie est belle—
  (EMILE *joins them*)
Dites moi
Pourquoi
La vie est gai!
Dites moi
Pourquoi,
  (EMILE *and* JEROME *make a deep bow to* NGANA)
Chère Mad'moiselle,
  (EMILE *picks them up, one under each arm, and starts to carry them off as they finish singing the refrain together*)
Est-ce que
Parce que
Vous m'aimez?
  (*The lights fade out and a transparent curtain closes in on them. Before they are out of sight, the characters of the next scene have entered downstage in front of the curtain. All transitions from one scene to another in the play are achieved in this manner so that the effect is of one picture dissolving into the next*)

ACT ONE | Scene Two

The curtain depicts no specific place but represents the abstract pattern of a large tapa-cloth. In front of this, lounge a group of Seabees, sailors and Marines. As the lights come up on them and go out on the previous scene, they are singing.

MEN
Bloody Mary is the girl I love,
Bloody Mary is the girl I love,
Bloody Mary is the girl I love—
Now ain't that too damn bad!
Her skin is as tender as DiMaggio's glove,
Her skin is as tender as DiMaggio's glove,
Her skin is as tender as Di Maggio's glove—
Now ain't that too damn bad!
(*The object of this serenade who has been hidden during the song, by two sailors, is now revealed as they move away. This is* BLOODY MARY. *She is small, yellow, with Oriental eyes. She wears black sateen trousers, and a white blouse over which is an old Marine's tunic. On her head is a peach-basket hat. Around her neck is a G.I. identification chain from which hangs a silver Marine emblem. At the end of the singing, she gives out a shrill cackle of laughter with which we shall soon learn to identify her*)

MARY (*Looking straight out at the audience*)   Hallo, G.I.! (*She holds up a grass skirt*) Grass skirt? Very saxy! Fo' dolla'? Saxy grass skirt. Fo' dolla'! Send home Chicago. You like? You buy? (*Her eyes scan the audience as if following a passer-by. Her crafty smile fades to a quick scowl as he apparently passes without buying. She calls after him)* Where you go? Come back! Chipskate! Crummy G.I.! Sadsack. Droopy-drawers!

MARINE   Tell 'em good, Mary!

MARY   What is good?

MARINE   Tell him he's a stingy bastard!

MARY (*Delighted at the sound of these new words*)   Stingy bastard! (*She turns back toward the MARINE for approval*) That good?

MARINE   That's great, Mary! You're learning fast.

MARY (*Calling off again*)   Stingy bastard! (*She cackles gaily and turns back to the MARINE*) I learn fast. . . . Pretty soon I talk English good as any crummy Marine. (*Calling off once more*) Stingy bastard!
   (*She laughs very loud but the Marines, Seabees and sailors laugh louder and cheer her. They then resume their serenade*)

MEN
Bloody Mary's chewing betel nuts,
She is always chewing betel nuts,
Bloody Mary's chewing betel nuts—
And she don't use Pepsodent.
   (*She grins and shows her betel-stained teeth*)
Now ain't that too damn bad!
   (*While this is being sung, the lights come up behind the tapa-cloth transparent curtain revealing*)

ACT ONE | Scene Three

SCENE: *The edge of a palm grove near the beach. Beyond the beach in the bay can be seen the same twin-peaked island that was evident from* EMILE'S *hillside. On your left, as you look at the stage, is* BLOODY MARY'S *kiosk. This is made of bamboo and canvas. Her merchandise, laid out in front, comprises shells, native hats, local dress material, outrigger canoes and hookahs. Several grass skirts are hanging up around the kiosk. On the right, at first making a puzzling silhouette, then as the lights come up, resolving itself into a contraption of weird detail, is a G.I. homemade washing machine. It looks partly like a giant ice-cream freezer, partly like a windmill. In front of it there is a sign which reads:*

> TWISTED AIR HAND LAUNDRY
> LUTHER BILLIS ENTERPRISES
> SPECIAL RATES FOR SEABEES

As the lights come up, the washing machine is being operated by Carpenter's Mate, Second Class, George Watts, better known as "STEWPOT." *Seabees, sailors, Marines and some Army men lounge around the scene waiting for whatever diversion* BLOODY MARY *may provide. During the singing which covers this change,* BLOODY MARY *takes a strange-looking object out of her pocket and dangles it in front of a* MARINE.

MARINE   What is that thing?

MARY (*Holding the small object in her hand*)   Is head. Fifty dolla'.

MARINE (*Revolted*)   What's it *made* of?

MARY   Made outa head! Is real human.

MARINE (*Fascinated*)   What makes it so small?

MARY   Shlunk! Only way to keep human head is shlink 'em.

MARINE   No, thanks.
  (*He leaves quickly*)

MARY (*To a new customer as she holds a grass skirt up to her waist and starts to dance*) Fo' dolla'. Send home Chicago to saxy sweetheart! She make wave like this.
  (*She starts to dance. One of the sailors grabs her and goes into an impromptu jitterbug dance with her. Others join, and soon the beach is alive with gyrating gentlemen of the United States Armed Services. As this spontaneous festivity is at its height,* LUTHER BILLIS *enters, followed by the* PRO-FESSOR, *both loaded with grass skirts. They come down in front of* BLOODY MARY *and throw the grass skirts at her feet*)

BILLIS   Here you are, Sweaty Pie! Put them down, Professor. These beautiful skirts were made by myself, the Professor here, and three other Seabees in half the time it takes your native workers to make 'em. (*He picks up a skirt and demonstrates*) See? No stretch! (*Throwing the skirt back on the ground*) Look 'em over, Sweaty Pie, and give me your price.
  (*At this point, an altercation starts upstage near the washing machine*)

SAILOR   Look at that shirt!

STEWPOT   Take it up with the manager.
  (*He points down to* BILLIS)

SAILOR (*Coming down to him*) Hey, Big Dealer! Hey, Luther Billis!

BILLIS (*Smoothly*)   What can I do for you, my boy? What's the trouble?

SAILOR (*Holding up his shirt which has been laundered and is in tatters*)   Look at that shirt!

BILLIS   The Billis Laundry is not responsible for minor burns and tears. (*He turns back laconically to* MARY) What do you say, Sweatso? What am I offered?
  (*The* SAILOR *storms off. The* PROFESSOR, *meanwhile, is*

showing the beautiful work they do to some other sailors and Seabees)

PROFESSOR (*Holding up a skirt*)   All hand sewn!

SAILOR   Gee, that's mighty nice work!

BILLIS (*To* BLOODY MARY)   Do you hear that, Sweaty Pie? You can probably sell these to the chumps for five or six dollars apiece. Now, I'll let you have the whole bunch for . . . say . . . eighty bucks.

MARY   Give you ten dolla'.

BILLIS   What?

MARY   Not enough?

BILLIS   You're damn well right, not enough!

MARY (*Dropping the skirt at his feet*)   Den you damn well keep.
    (*She goes down to another sailor and takes from her pocket a boar's tooth bracelet which she holds up to tempt him*)

BILLIS (*Following* BLOODY MARY)   Now look here, Dragon Lady— (*Whatever he was about to say is knocked out of his head by the sight of the bracelet.* BILLIS *is an inveterate and passionate souvenir hunter*)   What's that you got there, a boar's tooth bracelet? Where'd you get that? (*He points to the twin-peaked island*)   Over there on Bali Ha'i?

MARY (*Smiling craftily*)   You like?

BILLIS (*Taking bracelet and showing to G.I.'s who have huddled around him*)   You know what that is? A bracelet made out of a single boar's tooth. They cut the tooth from the boar's mouth in a big ceremonial over there on Bali Ha'i. There ain't a souvenir you can pick up in the South Pacific as valuable as this . . . What do you want for it, Mary?

MARY   Hundred dolla'!

BILLIS   Hundred dollars! (*Shocked, but realizing he will pay it, turns to the boys and justifies himself in advance*)   That's cheap. I thought it would be more.
    (*He takes the money from his pocket*)

PROFESSOR   I don't see how she can do it.

MARY   Make you special offer Big Deala'. I trade you boar's tooth bracelet for all grass skirts.

BILLIS   It's a deal.

MARY   Wait a minute. Is no deal till you throw in something for good luck.

BILLIS   Okay. What do you want me to throw in?

MARY (*Taking money from his hand*)   Hundred dolla'.

BILLIS   Well, for the love of . . .

MARY (*Shaking his hand, grinning a big Oriental grin*)   Good luck.
  (*She exits with grass skirts. The men all crowd around* BILLIS, *shaking his hand in ironic "congratulation."*)

BILLIS   You don't run into these things every day. They're scarce as hens' teeth.

PROFESSOR   They're bigger, too.

BILLIS   That damned Bali Ha'i! (*Turning and looking toward the twin-peaked island*) Why does it have to be off limits? You can get everything over there. Shrunken heads, bracelets, old ivory—

SAILOR   Young French women!

BILLIS   Knock off! I'm talking about souvenirs.

PROFESSOR   So's he.

BILLIS (*Pacing restlessly*)   We got to get a boat and get over there. I'm feeling held down again. I need to take a trip.

STEWPOT   Only officers can sign out boats.

BILLIS   I'll get a boat all right. I'll latch onto some officer who's got some imagination . . . that would like to see that Boar's Tooth ceremonial as much as I would . . . It's a hell of a ceremonial! Dancin', drinkin' . . . everything!

SAILOR   Why, you big phony. We all know why you want to go to Bali Ha'i.

BILLIS   Why?

SAILOR   Because the French planters put all their young

women over there when they heard the G.I.'s were coming.
That's why! It ain't boar's teeth . . . it's women!

BILLIS   It is boar's teeth . . . *and* women!
(*A long pause. All the men are still and thoughtful, each
dreaming a similar dream—but his own. Music starts.* A
SEABEE *breaks the silence*)

SEABEE (*Singing*)
We got sunlight on the sand,
We got moonlight on the sea.

SAILOR
We got mangoes and bananas
You can pick right off a tree.

MARINE
We got volley ball and ping pong
And a lot of dandy games—

BILLIS
What ain't we got?

ALL
We ain't got dames!

MARINE
We get packages from home,

SAILOR
We get movies, we get shows,

STEWPOT
We get speeches from our skipper

SOLDIER
And advice from Tokyo Rose

SEABEE
We get letters doused wit' poifume,

SAILOR
We get dizzy from the smell—

BILLIS
What don't we get?

ALL
You know damn well!

BILLIS
We have nothin' to put on a clean, white suit for.
What we need is what there ain't no substitute for!

ALL
There is nothin' like a dame
Nothin' in the world.
There is nothin' you can name
That is anythin' like a dame.

MARINE
We feel restless,
We feel blue.

SEABEE
We feel lonely and, in brief,
We feel every kind of feelin'

PROFESSOR
But the feelin' of relief.

SAILOR
We feel hungry as the wolf felt
When he met Red Riding Hood—

ALL
What don't we feel?

STEWPOT
We don't feel good!

SAILOR
Lots of things in life are beautiful, but brother—
There is one particular thing that is nothin' whatsoever in any
     way shape or form like any other!

ALL
There is nothin' like a dame—
Nothin' in the world.
There is nothin' you can name
That is anythin' like a dame.

Nothin' else is built the same,
Nothin' in the world
Has a soft and wavy frame
Like the silhouette of a dame.

MARINE (*With a deep bass voice*)
There is absolutely nothin' like the frame of a dame!

(*The music continues throughout the following dialogue and action*)

GIRL'S VOICE   Hut, two, three, four! Get—your—exercise!
(*A husky* NURSE *enters, leading several other* NURSES, *all dressed in bathing suits. playsuits, or fatigues.* NELLIE *is among them. They jog across the stage, their* LEADER *continuing the military count. The men's eyes follow them*)

A TIRED NURSE   Can't we rest a while?

HUSKY LEADER   Come on you nurses, pick it up!
(NELLIE *drops out of line as the others run off*)

NELLIE (*Beckoning to* BILLIS)   Hey, Luther!

STEWPOT (*Nudging* BILLIS)   Luther!
(BILLIS *turns and goes shyly to* NELLIE, *terribly embarrassed that the men are watching him. He is a different* BILLIS *in front of* NELLIE. *He is unassured and has lost all of his brashness. For him,* NELLIE FORBUSH *has "class."*)

BILLIS   Yes, Miss Forbush.
(*All eyes follow him*)

NELLIE   Have you done what you promised?

BILLIS   Yes, Miss Forbush. (*He pulls out a newspaper package from a hiding place in the roots of a tree and hands it to her*) I did it all last night. (*With an alarmed look at his comrades, as she starts to unwrap it*) You don't have to open it now!
(*But* NELLIE *opens the package, much to* BILLIS' *embarrassment. It is her laundry, neatly folded*)

NELLIE   Oh. You do beautiful work, Luther! (*Two men painfully cling to each other and turn their heads away.* BILLIS *tries to outglare the others in defensive defiance*) You've even done the pleats in my shorts!

BILLIS   Aw, pleats aren't hard. You better run along now and catch up to your gang.

NELLIE   Pleats are *very* hard. How do you do such delicate work at night, in the dark?

BILLIS   There was a moon!

STEWPOT (*In a syrupy voice*)   There was a moon!

BILLIS (*He turns to the men, realizing that they have heard this, and shouts defiantly*)   A full moon!

NELLIE (*She is wrapping up the package*)   How much, Luther!

BILLIS (*Earnestly*)   Oh, no, not from you.

NELLIE   Gosh, I guess I'm just about the luckiest nurse on this island to have found you. You're a treasure. (*She turns and runs off*) Well, good-bye, Luther. Hut, two, three, four!
   (*She has gone!* BILLIS *turns and faces the men, trying to bluff it out. He walks belligerently over to* STEWPOT *who with the* PROFESSOR *whistles* "There's Nothin' Like a Dame." *Then he walks over to another group and they join* STEWPOT *and* PROFESSOR *in whistling. Soon all are whistling.* BILLIS *whistles too. After the refrain is finished,* STEWPOT *looks off reflectively at the departing* NELLIE)

STEWPOT   She's a nice little girl, but some of them nurses—the officers can have them.

PROFESSOR   They got them!

STEWPOT   Well, they can have them!

MARINE (*Singing*)
So suppose a dame ain't bright,
Or completely free from flaws,

SAILOR
Or as faithful as a bird dog,

SEABEE
Or as kind as Santa Claus,

SOLDIER
It's a waste of time to worry
Over things that they have not

SAILOR
Be thankful for

ALL
The things they got!

HUSKY LEADER (*Entering*)   Hut, two, three, four. Hut, two, three, four!
   (*The exercising* NURSES *enter upstage, jogging in the op-*

posite direction to their previous course. NELLIE *is again with them. She turns and waves to* BILLIS *and points to the laundry under her arm. The boys all rise and turn upstage, their heads following the girls until they're off. Then the boys continue to turn until they're facing front again)*

ALL
There is nothin' you can name
That is anythin' like a dame!
There are no books like a dame,
And nothin' looks like a dame,
There are no drinks like a dame,
And nothin' thinks like a dame,
Nothin' acts like a dame
Or attracts like a dame.
There ain't a thing that's wrong with any man here
That can't be cured by puttin' him near
A girly, womanly, female, feminine dame!
(BLOODY MARY *enters and starts humming the song, as she proceeds to rearrange her new stock of grass skirts.* LT. JOSEPH CABLE *enters. He wears suntans, overseas cap, and carries a musette bag in his hand.* BLOODY MARY *sees him and stops singing. They stand for a moment, looking at each other—she, suspicious and frightened, and he, puzzled and curious)*

MARY   Hallo.

CABLE   Hello.
(*Music of "Bali Ha'i" is played softly*)

MARY   You mak' trouble for me?

CABLE   Hunh?

MARY   Are you crummy major?

CABLE   No, I'm even crummier than that. I'm a lieutenant.

MARY   Lootellan?

CABLE (*Laughing*)   Lootellan.
(*He strolls away from her, toward the men*)

BILLIS   Hiya, Lootellan. New on the rock?

CABLE   Just came in on that PBY.

BILLIS   Yeah? Where from?

CABLE   A little island south of Marie Louise.

STEWPOT   Then you been up where they use real bullets!

CABLE   Unh-huh.

MARY (*Who has been looking adoringly at* CABLE)   Hey, Lootellan. You damn saxy man!

CABLE (*Rocked off his balance for a moment*)   Thanks. You're looking pretty—er—fit yourself.
  (*She grins happily at him, showing her betel-stained teeth and crosses, beaming, to her assistant*)

MARY (*To assistant*)   Damn saxy!

CABLE (*To* BILLIS)   Who is she?

BILLIS   She's Tonkinese—used to work for a French planter.

MARY   French planters stingy bastards!
  (*She laughs*)

CABLE   Say, I wonder if any of you know a French planter named de Becque?

BILLIS   Emile de Becque? I think he's the guy lives on top of that hill . . . Do you know him?

CABLE (*Looking off toward the hill, thoughtfully*)   No, but I'm going to.
  (MARY *follows* CABLE, *taking the shrunken head from her pocket*)

MARY   Hey, Lootellan! Real human head! . . . You got sweetheart? Send home Chicago to saxy sweetheart!

CABLE   No—er—she's a Philadelphia girl.

MARY   Whazzat, Philadelia girl? Whazzat mean? No saxy? (*With a sudden impulse*) You like I give you free?

BILLIS   Free! You never give *me* anything free.

MARY   You not saxy like Lootellan. (*To* CABLE, *proffering the shrunken head*) Take!

CABLE   No, thanks. Where'd you get that anyway?

MARY   Bali Ha'i.

STEWPOT (*Nudging* BILLIS, *pointing to* CABLE, *as he whispers*)   There's your officer! There's your officer!

BILLIS   That's that island over there with the two volcanoes.
(*Significantly*) *Officers* can get launches and go over there.

CABLE (*Looking out at island*)   Bali Ha'i . . . What does
that mean?

MARY   Bali Ha'i mean "I am your special Island" . . . mean
. . . "Here I am." Bali Ha'i is *your* special Island, Lootellan.
I know! You listen! You hear island call to you. Listen! You
no hear something? Listen!

CABLE (*After listening for a moment*)   I hear the sound of
the wind and the waves, that's all.

MARY   You no hear something calling? Listen!
   (*Silence.* ALL *listen*)

STEWPOT (*Trying to be helpful*)   I think *I* hear something.

BILLIS (*In a harsh, threatening whisper*)   Shut your big fat
mouth!

MARY   Hear voice? (*She sings to* CABLE, *as he gazes out at
the mysterious island*)
Mos' people live on a lonely island,
Lost in de middle of a foggy sea.
Mos' people long fo' anudder island
One where dey know dey would lak to be . . .

Bali Ha'i
May call you,
Any night, any day.
In your heart
You'll hear it call you
"Come away, come away."

Bali Ha'i
Will whisper
On de wind of de sea,
"Here am I,
Your special island!
Come to me, come to me!"

Your own special hopes,
Your own special dreams
Bloom on de hillside
And shine in de streams.

If you try,

You'll find me
Where de sky meets de sea,
"Here am I,
Your special island!
Come to me, come to me!"

Bali Ha'i!
   Bali Ha'i!
      Bali Ha'i!

Some day, you'll see me,
Floatin' in de sunshine,
My head stickin' out
F'um a low-flyin' cloud.
You'll hear me call you,
Singin' through de sunshine,
Sweet and clear as can be,
"Come to me,
Here am I,
Come to me!"

If you try,
You'll find me
Where de sky meets de sea,
"Here am I,
Your special island!
Come to me, come to me!"

Bali Ha'i!
   Bali Ha'i!
      Bali Ha'i!
      (BLOODY MARY *exits.* CABLE *seems spellbound by her words.*
      BILLIS *follows up with a more earthy form of salesman-
      ship*)

BILLIS Of course, Lieutenant, right now that island is off
limits due to the fact that the French planters have all their
young women running around over there. (*He pauses to observe the effect of these significant words*) Of course, you
being an officer, you could get a launch. I'd even be willing to
requisition a boat for you. What do you say, Lieutenant?
(*Singing throatily*)
   Bali Ha'i may call you
   Any night any day.
   In your heart you'll

Hear it call you—
Bali Ha'i—Bali Ha'i . . .
Hunh, Lieutenant?
(*Pause*)

CABLE No.

BILLIS (*Making a quick shift*) I see what you mean, being off limits and all. It would take a lot of persuading to get *me* to go over there . . . But, another thing goes on over there— the ceremonial of the boar's tooth. After they kill the boar they pass around some of that coconut liquor and women dance with just skirts on . . . (*His voice becoming evil*) and everybody gets to know everybody pretty well . . . (*He sings*)
Bali Ha'i will whisper—
(BILLIS *starts dance as he hums the melody seductively. Then he stops and talks*) It's just a little tribal ceremonial and I thought you being up in the shooting war for such a long time without getting any—recreation—I thought you might be interested.

CABLE I am. But right now I've got to report to the Island Commander.

BILLIS Oh. (*Shouting officiously*) Professor! Take the Lieutenant up in the truck.

CABLE Professor?

BILLIS That's because he went to college. You go to college?

CABLE Er—yes.

BILLIS Where?

CABLE A place in New Jersey.

BILLIS Where? Rutgers?

CABLE No . . . Princeton.

BILLIS Oh. Folks got money, eh, Lieutenant? (*He leers wisely*) Don't be ashamed of it. We understand. Say! Maybe you'd like to hear the Professor talk some language. What would you like to hear? Latin? Grecian? (*Grabbing the unwilling* PROFESSOR *by the arm and leading him over to* CABLE) Aw, give him some Latin!

PROFESSOR (*The* PROFESSOR *feels pretty silly, but proceeds*)
"Rectius vives Licini—"

BILLIS   Ain't that beautiful!

PROFESSOR
". . . neque altum
Semper urgendo dum procellas . . ."
  (*A crowd gathers around the* PROFESSOR. BILLIS *beams at*
  CABLE)

BILLIS   Now, Lieutenant, what did he say?

CABLE   I'm afraid I haven't the slightest idea.

BILLIS   What's the matter, didn't you graduate? (*Disgusted,
to the* PROFESSOR) Take the Lieutenant to the buildings.
  (CABLE *and the* PROFESSOR *start to go*)

PROFESSOR   Aye, aye!

BILLIS (*To* STEWPOT)   He'll never make Captain.
  (*The* PROFESSOR, *suddenly alarmed by something he sees
  offstage, turns back and starts to make strange signal-
  noises of warning*)

PROFESSOR   Whoop-whoop-whoop! (*In a hoarse whisper*)
Iron Belly!
  (*The men assume casual and innocent attitudes. Some
  make bird sounds.* MARY *looks off and walks back to her
  kiosk to stand defiantly in front of it.* CABLE, *puzzled,
  stands by to await developments. What develops is that
  "Iron Belly,"* CAPTAIN BRACKETT, *enters, followed by his
  executive officer,* COMMANDER HARBISON)

HARBISON (*A brusque man*)   Here she is, sir.
  (*He points to* BLOODY MARY, *who is standing her ground
  doggedly in front of her kiosk.* BRACKETT *walks slowly over
  to her.* HARBISON *takes a few steps toward the men and they
  move away.* BRACKETT *glares at* MARY. *Undaunted, she
  glares right back*)

BRACKETT   You are causing an economic revolution on this
island. These French planters can't find a native to pick a
coconut or milk a cow because you're paying them ten times
as much to make these ridiculous grass skirts.

MARY   French planters stingy bastards!
  (STEWPOT *drops a tin bucket. The men control themselves*

by great efforts, their faces contorted queerly. BRACKETT *scowls and for the moment can think of no answer.* BILLIS *approaches him, with a snappy salute)*

BILLIS   Sir! May I make a suggestion, sir?

BRACKETT   (*Returning salute*)   Who are you?

BILLIS   Billis, sir, Luther Billis. (*Making an impressive announcement*) The natives can now go back to work on the farms. The demand for grass skirts can now be met bv us Seabees!

BRACKETT   Dressmakers! (*Starting to blow up*) Do you mean to tell me the Seabees of the United States Navy are now a lot of—

BILLIS   If you don't like the idea, sir, we can drop it right here, sir. Just say the word. Just pretend I never brought it up.

HARBISON   (*Reflectively*)   Luther Billis.

BILLIS   Yes, sir?

HARBISON   Nothing. Just making a mental note. I want to be sure not to forget your name.
   (*Pause, during which* BILLIS *slowly and dejectedly retires.* BRACKETT *turns to* MARY)

BRACKETT   I want to see you pick up every scrap of this paraphernalia now! And, for the last time, carry it way down there beyond that fence off Navy property.
   (MARY *stands firmly planted and immovable!* . . . CABLE *walks to the kiosk and collapses it)*

CABLE   (*With decisive authority*)   Come on, everybody. Take all this stuff and throw it over that fence.
   (*The men quickly obey,* BILLIS *ostentatiously taking charge in front of the two officers)*

BILLIS   (*To men*)   All right—take it way down there. Off Navy property!

CABLE   (*Strides over to* MARY *and points off*)   You go too!

MARY   (CABLE *can do no wrong in her eyes*)   All right, Lootellan. Thank you.
   (*She exits. By this time, all the men have gone, taking her kiosk with them.* BRACKETT, CABLE *and* HARBISON *are left.*

BRACKETT *looks at* HARBISON *as if to ask who* CABLE *is.* HARBISON *shrugs his shoulders.* CABLE *turns and exchanges salutes with* BRACKETT)

BRACKETT   Lieutenant, who are you, anyway?

CABLE   I'm Lieutenant Joseph Cable, sir. I just flew in on that PBY.

BRACKET   A joy ride?

CABLE   No, sir. Orders.

BRACKETT   A Marine under orders to me?

CABLE   Yes, sir.

BRACKETT   I'm Captain Brackett.

CABLE   How do you do, sir?

BRACKETT   This is Commander Harbison, my Executive Officer. (CABLE *and* HARBISON *exchange hellos, salutes and handshakes*) Well, what's it all about?

CABLE   My Colonel feels that all these islands are in danger because none of us has been getting first-hand intelligence, and what we need is a coast watch.

HARBISON   A coast watch?

CABLE   A man with a radio hiding out on one of those Jap-held islands, where he could watch for Jap ships when they start down the bottleneck . . . down this way.

BRACKETT (*Turning to* HARBISON)   What do you think, Bill?

HARBISON   Well, sir, our pilots could do a hell of a lot to Jap convoys with information like that.

BRACKETT   You'd have to sneak this man ashore at night from a submarine.

CABLE   Yes, sir.

HARBISON   Who's going to do it?

CABLE   Well, sir . . . *I've* been elected.
   (*Pause*)

BRACKETT (*After exchanging a look with* HARBISON)   You've got quite an assignment, son.

HARBISON How long do you think you could last there, sending out messages, before the Japs found you?

CABLE I think I'd be okay if I could take a man with me who really knew the country. Headquarters has found out there's a French civilian here who used to have a plantation on Marie Louise Island.

HARBISON Marie Louise! That's a good spot. Right on the bottleneck.

BRACKETT What's this Frenchman's name?

CABLE Emile de Becque.

BRACKETT (*Suddenly excited*)   Meet me in my office in about half an hour, Cable.
  (*He starts off, followed by* HARBISON)

CABLE Yes, sir.

BRACKETT Come on, Bill! Maybe we'll get in this war yet!
  (*They exit.* CABLE *watches them off, then picks up his musette bag and starts off himself. The music of "Bali Ha'i" is played.* CABLE *stops in his tracks and listens. Then he turns and looks across at the island. . . . Softly, he starts to sing*)

CABLE
Bali Ha'i may call you
Any night,
Any day,
In your heart you'll hear it call you,
Come away, come away.
Bali Ha'i, Bali Ha'i, Bali Ha'i.

ACT ONE | Scene Four

As CABLE *sings, the lights fade slowly. A transparent curtain closes across him.*

Downstage, several G.I.'s enter carrying bales and various articles of equipment. The lights dim out on CABLE *behind the curtain and now, illuminating the forestage, reveal the curtain as depicting a company street.*

SAILOR (*Crossing stage*)   When are you guys going to get that lumber down in our area?

SEABEE (*Passing him*)   Aw, knock it off!

SAILOR   We'll never get it finished by Thanksgiving.
(*By this time, the lights are higher on the company street. Natives and G.I.'s are constantly crossing, carrying equipment. Natives are seen sometimes wearing G.I. uniforms and sometimes just native clothes. Two nurses in white uniforms cross. Then* BILLIS *enters, in earnest conversation with* STEWPOT *and the* PROFESSOR)

BILLIS   Did you tell those guys at the shop to stop making those grass skirts?

STEWPOT   Sure, they just turned out one of these. (*He hands him a small, dark object*) What do you think of it?

BILLIS (*Studying it a moment*)   That don't look like a dried-up human head. It looks like an old orange painted with shoe-polish.

STEWPOT   That's what it is.

BILLIS   Go back to the shop and tell them to try again. If

I order a dried-up human head, I want a human head . . .
dried up!

(*He puts the orange in his pocket*)

STEWPOT   But—

BILLIS   Fade. Here he comes. (STEWPOT *and the* PROFESSOR
move away as CABLE *enters.* BILLIS *crosses to him and speaks
to him in a low voice, right in* CABLE'S *ear, as he walks alongside him*) Don't change your expression, Lieutenant. Just act
like we're talking casual. I got the boat.

CABLE (*Stops*)   What boat?

BILLIS   Keep walking down the company street. Keep your
voice down. (CABLE *walks slowly and uncertainly*) I signed
out a boat in your name. We're shoving off for Bali Ha'i in
forty-five minutes.

CABLE (*Stopping*)   No, we're not. I've got to see Captain
Brackett.

BILLIS (*An injured man*)   Lieutenant! What are you doing to
me? I signed this boat out in your name.

CABLE   Then you're just the man to go back and cancel it.
(*Very firmly*) Forget the whole thing. Okay?

(CABLE *walks off.* BILLIS *looks after him with narrowing
eyes and jaw thrust forward*)

BILLIS   Lieutenant, you and me are going on a boat trip
whether you like it or not.

(*He pulls the orange, covered with shoe polish, out of his
pocket, and wishing to vent his rage somehow, he turns
and hurls it off in the direction opposite that taken by*
CABLE)

A FURIOUS VOICE (*Offstage*)   Hey! Who the hell threw that?

BILLIS (*Spoiling for a fight with anyone at all*)   I threw it!
What are you gonna do about it?

(*He strides off pugnaciously in the direction of the voice.
Before he is off, the curtains have parted on the succeeding
scene*)

ACT ONE | Scene Five

Inside the Island Commander's OFFICE. BRACKETT *is sitting at his desk, reading some papers.* HARBISON *stands above him.* CABLE *sits on a chair facing the desk.*

BRACKETT (*As curtains part*) Cable . . . we've got some dope on your Frenchman. (*He reads a paper before him*) Marie Louise Island . . . moved down here sixteen years ago . . . lived with a Polynesian woman for about five years . . . two children by her. She died . . . Here's one thing we've got to clear up. Seems he left France in a hurry. Killed a guy. What do you think of that?

CABLE Might be a handy man to have around.
  (*The phone rings*)

HARBISON (*Beckoning to* CABLE) Cable.
  (CABLE *joins him and they inspect a map on the wall*)

BRACKETT (*In phone*) Good . . . send her in. No, we haven't got time for her to change into her uniform. Tell her to come in. (*The men exchange looks and face the doorway where presently* NELLIE *appears*) Come in, Miss Forbush.

NELLIE Captain Brackett, please excuse the way . . .

BRACKETT You look fine. May I present Commander Harbison?

HARBISON I have the pleasure of meeting Miss Forbush twice a week. (BRACKETT *looks at him, surprised and curious*) We serve together on the G.I. Entertainment Committee.

BRACKETT Oh. May I also present Lt. Joseph Cable . . . Miss Forbush. Sit down, Miss Forbush. (*The three men rush to help her sit.* CABLE *gets there first.* NELLIE *sits.* BRACKETT *sits on his desk facing her.* CABLE *drops upstage.* BRACKETT *starts off with light conversation*) How's the Thanksgiving Entertainment coming along?

NELLIE   Very well, thank you, sir. We practice whenever we get a chance.

(*She wonders why she has been sent for*)

BRACKETT   About a week ago, you had lunch with a French planter . . . Emile de Becque.

NELLIE   Yes, sir.

BRACKETT   What do you know about him?

NELLIE (*Thrown off balance*)   Well, I er . . . what do I know about him?

BRACKETT   That's right.

NELLIE   I . . . we . . . met at the Officers' Club dance. He was there and I . . . met him. (*She stops, hoping they will help her along, but they say nothing, so she has to continue*) Then I had lunch with him that day. . . .

BRACKETT (*Quickly*)   Yes! Now, what kind of a man is he?

NELLIE   He's very nice . . . He's kind . . . He's attractive. I—er—I just don't know what you want to know, sir.

HARBISON   Miss Forbush, Captain Brackett wants to know, did you discuss politics?

NELLIE   No, sir.

BRACKETT (*After a long, pitying look at* HARBISON)   Would you have discussed politics, Commander? (*Turning back to* NELLIE) Now, what we are specifically interested in is—er—when these fellows come out from France, it's generally because they've had some trouble. (NELLIE *looks worried*) Now . . . has he ever told you anything about that? (NELLIE *hesitates a moment, deliberating just how far to go in her answer.* BRACKETT *tries to help her out, sensing her embarrassment*) What do you know about his family?

NELLIE (*Glad to be able to answer a simple specific question without incriminating* EMILE)   He has no family—no wife. nobody.

HARBISON He hasn't any children?
(CABLE *and* HARBISON *exchange looks*)

NELLIE No, sir!

BRACKETT And you say he's never told you why he left France?
(*Pause. Then* NELLIE *answers as a Navy Ensign should*)

NELLIE Yes, sir. He left France because he killed a man.
(*A sigh of relief from* BRACKETT)

HARBISON Did he tell you why?

NELLIE No. But he will if I ask him.

HARBISON Well, Miss Forbush, that's exactly what we'd like to have you do. Find out as much as you can about him, his background, his opinions, and why he killed this man in France.

NELLIE In other words, you want me to spy on him.

BRACKETT Well, I'm afraid it *is* something like that.

NELLIE Why? (*Alarmed, she rises and faces* BRACKETT *across his desk*) Do you suspect him of anything?

BRACKETT (*Lies do not come easy to him*) No, it's just that we don't know very much about him and he's—er . . . Will you help us, Miss Forbush?
(*Pause*)

NELLIE I'll try.

BRACKETT Thank you. You may go now if you wish.
(*She starts toward the door, then turns, thoughtfully, as if asking the question of herself*)

NELLIE I don't know very much about him really—do I?
(*Slowly, she goes out. For a moment, the men are silent*)

CABLE He's kept a few secrets from her, hasn't he?

BRACKETT Well, you don't spring a couple of Polynesian kids on a woman right off the bat!

HARBISON I'm afraid we aren't going to get much out of her. She's obviously in love with him.

CABLE (*To* HARBISON) That's hard to believe, sir. They tell me he's a middle-aged man.

BRACKETT (*Rising from his desk chair. Smoldering*) Cable! It is a common mistake for boys of your age and athletic ability to underestimate men who have reached their maturity.

CABLE I didn't mean, sir . . .

BRACKETT Young women frequently find a grown man attractive, strange as it may seem to you. I myself am over fifty. I am a bachelor and, Cable, I do not, by any means, consider myself—through. (*To* HARBISON *who is suppressing laughter*) What's the matter, Bill?

HARBISON Nothing, evidently!

BRACKETT O.K., Cable. See you at chow. Do you play bridge?

CABLE Yes, sir.

BRACKETT Got any money?

CABLE Yes, sir.

BRACKETT I'll take it away from you.

CABLE Yes, sir.
(*He goes out.* BRACKETT *darts a penetrating look at* HARBISON)

BRACKETT What makes you so *damn sure* this mission won't work out?

HARBISON (*Looking at the map*) Marie Louise Island is twenty-four miles long and three miles wide. Let's say that every time they send out a message they move to another hill. It seems to me, looking at this thing—

BRACKETT Realistically.

HARBISON . . . realistically (*Measuring his words*), they could last about a week.
(*Pause.* BRACKETT *considers this*)

BRACKETT Of course, it would be worth it, if it were the right week. With decent information, our side might get moving. Operation Alligator might get off its can.

YEOMAN (*Entering with large cardboard box*) Here it is, sir, I got it.

BRACKETT (*To* HARBISON) Okay, Bill. See you at chow.

(HARBISON *looks at the package curiously*) *See you at chow, Bill.*

HARBISON (*Snapping out of it*) Oh, see you at chow.
(*He goes out*)

BRACKETT Got the address right?

YEOMAN I think so, sir. (*Reading the box lid*) Mrs. Amelia Fortuna. Three twenty-five Euclid Avenue, Shaker Heights, Cleveland, Ohio.

BRACKETT That's right. I want to pack it myself.

YEOMAN Yes, sir.
(YEOMAN *exits.* BRACKETT *starts to whistle. He opens the package and takes out a bright yellow grass skirt and shakes it out.* HARBISON *re-enters, stands in doorway, unseen by* BRACKETT, *nods as if his suspicions were confirmed and exits as the lights fade*)

ACT ONE | Scene Six

As the lights are fading on the captain's hut, the company-street curtain closes in and the activity seen here before is resumed.
G.I.'s and natives cross, carrying various items of equipment. NELLIE *enters, walking slowly as she reads a letter. Another* NURSE *in working uniform has some letters in her hand and is moving off.*

NURSE Going back to the beach, Nellie?
(NELLIE *nods.* NURSE *exits.* CABLE *enters and watches* NELLIE *for a moment.* NELLIE *is now standing still, reading*

*a part of her letter that evokes an occasional groan of
irritation from her.* CABLE *grins at her*)

CABLE   Letter from home?
(NELLIE *looks up, startled by his voice, then grins back at
him*)

NELLIE   Yes. Do you get letters from your mother, telling
you that everything you do is wrong?

CABLE   No. My mother thinks everything I do is right. . . .
Of course, I don't tell her everything I do.

NELLIE   My mother's so prejudiced.

CABLE   Against Frenchmen?
(*She smiles to acknowledge that she gets the allusion then
pursues her anti-maternal tirade*)

NELLIE   Against anyone outside of Little Rock. She makes a
big thing out of two people having different backgrounds.

CABLE (*Rather hopefully*)   Ages?

NELLIE   Oh, no. Mother says older men are better for girls
than younger men.

CABLE (*Remembering his recent lecture from* BRACKETT *on
this subject*)   This has been a discouraging day for me.

NELLIE   Do you agree with Mother about people having
things in common? For instance, if the man likes symphony
music and the girl likes Dinah Shore—and he reads Marcel
Proust and she doesn't read anything . . . Well, what do *you*
think? Do you think Mother's right?

CABLE   Well, she might be.

NELLIE   Well, I don't think she is.

CABLE   Well, maybe she's not.

NELLIE   Well, good-bye, Lieutenant. You've helped a lot.

CABLE   Listen, you don't know so much about that guy. You
better read that letter over two or three times . . .

NELLIE   I'll show you what I think of that idea.
(*She crumples the letter and throws it on the ground*)

CABLE   Well, don't say I didn't warn you.
(*He exits.* NELLIE *comes back and picks up the letter and starts reading as she walks off*)

ACT ONE | Scene Seven

Before NELLIE *is off the lights come up on:*
The beach. Several nurses are lounging about before taking their swim. More enter. One of them, DINAH, is washing an evening dress in a tin tub. Upstage is a home-made shower bath, bearing a sign:

BILLIS BATH CLUB
SHOWER 15¢
USE OF SOAP 5¢
NO TOWELS SUPPLIED

Two or three SEABEES *stand in attendance, part of* BILLIS' *business empire, no doubt.*

BILLIS (*Entering*)   Oh, I thought Miss Forbush was here. I brought some hot water for her. (*He goes to shower, climbs a ladder and pours a bucket of water into the tank on top*) She likes to take a shampoo Fridays.

NELLIE (*Entering*)   Hello, Luther.

BILLIS   Hello, Miss Forbush. I brought some hot water for you.

NELLIE   Thanks. It'll do me a lot of good to get some of this sand out of my hair.

BILLIS   If you need some extra water for rinsing your hair, my bath-club concession boys will take care of you. When you're ready for the shower, just pull this chain, just like you was . . . Like you was pulling down a window shade. Take care of her, boys.

(*He exits.* NELLIE *enters the shower*)

NURSE   What'd he want?

NELLIE   Huh?

NURSE   What'd he want?

NELLIE   Who?

NURSE   Iron Belly.

NELLIE   Captain Brackett? Oh, nothing—nothing important. Something about the Thanksgiving show.

SECOND NURSE   Then what's the trouble, Knucklehead?

NELLIE   Huh?
  (*She is now soaking her hair and it is difficult for her to hear*)

SECOND NURSE   I said, what's the trouble?

NELLIE   Oh, nothing. (*The girls look at one another.* NELLIE *comes out of the shower enclosure*) There's not going to be any trouble any more because I've made up my mind about one thing. (*She takes a deep breath and looks at them dramatically*) It's all off.
  (*She goes back into the shower enclosure*)

THIRD NURSE   With him?

NELLIE (*Coming right out again through the swinging doors*) Unh-hunh. (*She starts back, then stops and turns*) I'm going to break it off clean before it's too late.

FOURTH NURSE   Knucklehead, what's happened? What'd he do?

NELLIE   *He* didn't do anything. It's just that . . . Well, I guess I don't know anything about him really and before I go any further with this thing—I just better not get started! Don't you think so, too? Diney?

DINAH   Yes, I do.

NELLIE (*Unprepared for such prompt and unequivocal agreement*)   You do? Well, I guess I do, too. (*She turns to the other girls*) Well, don't look so dramatic about it. Things like this happen every day. (*She sings*)

I'm gonna wash that man right outa my hair,
I'm gonna wash that man right outa my hair,
I'm gonna wash that man right outa my hair,
And send him on his way!
   (*She struts around splashing soap out of her hair*)
Get the picture?

I'm gonna wave that man right outa my arms,
I'm gonna wave that man right outa my arms,
I'm gonna wave that man right outa my arms,
And send him on his way!

Don't try to patch it up—

NURSES
Tear it up, tear it up!

NELLIE
Wash him out, dry him out—

NURSES
Push him out, fly him out!

NELLIE
Cancel him and let him go—

NURSES
Yea, sister!

I'm gonna wash that man right outa my hair,
I'm gonna wash that man right outa my hair,
I'm gonna wash that man right outa my hair,
And send him on his way!

NELLIE
If the man don't understand you,
If you fly on separate beams,
Waste no time!
Make a change,
Ride that man right off your range,
Rub him outa the roll call
And drum him outa your dreams!

NURSES
Oh-ho!

DINAH
If you laugh at different comics,

ANOTHER NURSE
If you root for different teams,

NELLIE, DINAH, SECOND NURSE
Waste no time,
Weep no more,
Show him what the door is for!

NURSES
Rub him outa the roll call
And drum him outa your dreams!

NELLIE
You can't light a fire when the wood's all wet,

GIRLS
No!

NELLIE
You can't make a butterfly strong,

GIRLS
Uh-uh!

NELLIE
You can't fix an egg when it ain't quite good,

NURSES
And you can't fix a man when he's wrong!

NELLIE
You can't put back a petal when it falls from a flower,
Or sweeten up a feller when he starts turning sour—
    (NELLIE *goes back into the shower, turns on the water and
    rinses the soap out of her hair*)

NURSES
Oh no, Oh no!
If his eyes get dull and fishy
When you look for glints and gleams,
Waste no time,
Make a switch,
Drop him in the nearest ditch!
Rub him outa the roll call
And drum him outa your dreams!
Oh-ho! Oh-ho!

NELLIE (*Poking her head out from the shower, then dancing
down to the nurses, as she sings*)

I went and washed that man right outa my hair,
I went and washed that man right outa my hair,
I went and washed that man right outa my hair,
And sent him on his way!

NURSES
She went and washed that man right outa her hair,
She went and washed that man right outa her hair,
She went and washed that man right outa her hair,
    (NELLIE *joining them in a triumphant finish*)
And sent him on his way!

 (NELLIE *starts to dry her hair with a towel.* EMILE *enters. She cannot see him because the towel covers her eyes. The other girls quickly slip away to leave them alone, all except* DINAH, *who goes to her tin tub and takes out her evening dress.* NELLIE *is humming and dancing as she dries her hair. Suddenly, she stops. She has seen something on the ground*—EMILE'S *shoe tops! She moves closer to them, holding the towel forward, as a photographer holds his cloth. She patters over to* DINAH *for confirmation, still holding the towel in this manner.* DINAH *nods, as if to say: "That's him, all right."* NELLIE *makes a dash for the shower. While* NELLIE *is putting a top-piece on over her bathing bra,* DINAH *stands in front of the shower enclosure, blocking the way, and trying to make conversation with* EMILE. *She looks and feels very silly*)

DINAH   You'd never think this was an evening dress, would you? We're only allowed to bring two of them—evening dresses . . . only two . . . I brought . . . Yeah, sister!
    (*She retreats offstage, with no grace whatever.* NELLIE *comes out of the shower and makes a naive attempt to appear surprised*)

NELLIE   Hello!

EMILE   Hello. . . . That song . . . is it a new American song?

NELLIE   It's an American type song. We were kind of putting in our own words. (*Looking around*) Where *is* everybody?

EMILE   It is strange with your American songs. In all of them one is either desirous to get rid of one's lover, or one weeps for a man one cannot have.

NELLIE   That's right.

EMILE   I like a song that says: "I love you and you love me
. . . And isn't that fine?"

NELLIE (*Not very bright at the moment*)   Yes . . . that's
fine.

EMILE   I left a note for you at the hospital. It was to ask
you to my home for dinner next Friday.

NELLIE   Well, I don't think I'll be able to come, Emile, I—

EMILE   I have asked all my friends. The planters' colony.

NELLIE (*Determined to wash him out of her hair*)   A big
party. Well then, if I can't come, you won't miss me.

EMILE   But it is *for* you. It is for my friends to meet you
and—more important—for you to meet them; to give you an
idea of what your life would be like here. I want you to know
more about me . . . how I live and think—

NELLIE (*Suddenly remembering her promise to "spy on him"*)
More about you?

EMILE   Yes. You know very little about me.

NELLIE   That's right! (*Getting down to business*) Would you
sit down? (EMILE *sits.* NELLIE *paces like a cross-examiner*)
Do you think about politics much . . . And if so what do
you think about politics?

EMILE   Do you mean my political philosophy?

NELLIE   I think that's what I mean.

EMILE   Well, to begin with, I believe in the free life—in
freedom for everyone.

NELLIE (*Eagerly*)   Like in the Declaration of Independence?

EMILE   C'est ça. All men are created equal, isn't it?

NELLIE   Emile! You really believe that?

EMILE   Yes.

NELLIE (*With great relief*)   Well, thank goodness!

EMILE   It is why I am here. . . . Why I killed a man.

NELLIE (*Brought back to her mission*)   Oh, yes. I meant to
ask you about that too . . . I don't want you to think I'm

prying into your private life, asking a lot of questions. But
. . . I always think it's interesting why a person . . . kills
another person.

(EMILE *smiles understandingly*)

EMILE Of course, Nellie. That has worried you. (*He turns
away to compose his story. Then he begins by stating what
he considers the explanation and excuse for the whole thing*)
When I was a boy, I carried my heart in my hand. . . . So
. . . when this man came to our town—though my father
said he was good—I thought he was bad. (*With a shrug and
a smile*) I was young . . . He attracted all the mean and
cruel people to him. Soon he was running our town! He could
do anything—take anything . . . I did not like that. I was
young. (NELLIE *nods, understanding*) I stood up in the public
square and made a speech. I called upon everyone to stand
with me against this man.

NELLIE What did they do?

EMILE (*Letting his hands fall helplessly to his side*) They
walked away!

NELLIE Why?

EMILE Because they saw him standing behind me. I turned,
and he said to me, "I am going to kill you now." We fought.
I was never so strong. I knocked him to the ground. And
when he fell, his head struck a stone and . . . (*He turns
away and lets* NELLIE *imagine the rest*) I ran to the waterfront and joined a cargo boat. I didn't even know where it
was going. I stepped off that boat into another world . . .
(*He looks around him, loving all he sees*) where I am now
. . . and where I want to stay. (*He turns to* NELLIE *and
impulsively steps toward her, deep sincerity and anxiety in
his voice*) Nellie, will you marry me? . . . There are so few
days in our life, Nellie. The time I have with you now is
precious to me . . . Have you been thinking?

NELLIE I have been thinking. (*Singing, thoughtful, con-
sidering*)
Born on the opposite sides of the sea,
We are as different as people can be,

EMILE
It's true.

NELLIE
And yet you want to marry me. . . .

EMILE
I do.

NELLIE
I've known you a few short weeks and yet
Somehow you've made my heart forget
All other men I have ever met
But you . . . but you . . .

EMILE
Some enchanted evening
You may see a stranger,
You may see a stranger
Across a crowded room,
And somehow you know,
You know even then
That somewhere you'll see her
Again and again. . . .

NELLIE
Who can explain it?
Who can tell you why?

EMILE
Fools give you reasons,
Wise men never try . . .
Some enchanted evening,
When you find your true love,
When you feel her call you
Across a crowded room,
Then fly to her side
And make her your own,
Or all through your life you may dream all alone!

NELLIE (*Clinging to him*)
Once you have found him
Never let him go.

EMILE
Once you have found her
Never let her go.
   (*They kiss*)
Will you come next Friday?

NELLIE (*Somewhere, from out of the ether, she hears her voice murmur an inarticulate but automatic assent*)   Uh-huh.
   (EMILE *kisses her again and leaves. There is the sound of a girl's laughter offstage and a voice is heard*)

GIRL'S VOICE (*Offstage*)   Well, she sure washed him out of her hair!
   (*More laughter.* NELLIE *looks defiantly off in the direction of her mocking friends*)

NELLIE (*Singing*)
I expect every one
Of my crowd to make fun
Of my proud protestations of faith in romance,
And they'll say I'm naive
As a babe to believe
Any fable I hear from a person in pants! . . .

Fearlessly I'll face them and argue their doubts away,
Loudly I'll sing about flowers and spring!
Flatly I'll stand on my little flat feet and say,
"Love is a grand and a beautiful thing!"
I'm not ashamed to reveal the world-famous feeling I feel.

I'm as corny as Kansas in August,
I'm as normal as blueberry pie.
No more a smart
Little girl with no heart,
I have found me a wonderful guy.

I am in a conventional dither
With a conventional star in my eye
And, you will note,
There's a lump in my throat
When I speak of that wonderful guy.

I'm as trite and as gay
As a daisy in May
(A cliché coming true!)
I'm bromidic and bright
As a moon-happy night
Pouring light on the dew.

I'm as corny as Kansas in August,
High as a flag on the Fourth of July!
If you'll excuse

An expression I use,
I'm in love
I'm in love
I'm in love
I'm in love
I'm in love with a wonderful guy!

(*The other nurses enter and join in her song; each obviously thinking of her own wonderful guy. The "company street" curtain closes as they sing, and before the light on the girls fades out, the men are seen pursuing the activities which have characterized previous company street scenes. The music of "I'm in Love with a Wonderful Guy" has continued and now the nurses enter and resume singing it.* NELLIE *running on last and finishing in a triumphant coda to the amusement of the G.I.'s. The lights fade on them all as they exit and the next scene is revealed*)

ACT ONE | Scene Eight

This is BRACKETT'S *office again.*

BRACKETT, HARBISON *and* CABLE *are all looking intently at* EMILE . . .

BRACKETT   Now, before you give us your answer, I want to impress you with three things. First, you are a civilian and you don't have to go. There's no way of our making you go. Second, this is a very dangerous mission and there's no guarantee that you'll survive—or that it will do any good. Third, that it might do a great good. It might be the means of turning the tide of war in this area.

EMILE   I understand all these things.

BRACKETT   Are you ready to give us your answer?

EMILE   Yes, I am. (*Pause*) My answer must be no. (CABLE's *foot comes down from the top of the wastebasket, on which it was resting.* HARBISON *uncrosses his arms.* BRACKETT *and* HARBISON *exchange looks*) When a man faces death, he must weigh values very carefully. He must weigh the sweetness of his life against the thing he is asked to die for. The probability of death is very great—for both of us. I know that island well, Lieutenant Cable. I am not certain that I believe that what you ask me to do is . . . is—

BRACKETT   We're asking you to help us lick the Japs. It's as simple as that. We're against the Japs.

EMILE   I know what you're against. What are you for? (*He waits for an answer. They have none*) When I was twenty-two, I thought the world hated bullies as much as I did. 1 was foolish—I killed one. And I was forced to flee to an island. Since then, I have asked no help from anyone or any country. I have seen these bullies multiply and grow strong. The world sat by and watched.

CABLE   Aw, to hell with this, de Becque, let's be honest! Aren't you just a guy in love with a girl and you're putting her above everything else in the world?
      (EMILE *looks at* CABLE *for a moment before answering*)

EMILE   Yes, I do care about my life with her more than anything else in the world. It is the only thing that is important to me. This I believe in. This I am sure of. This I have. I cannot risk to lose it. Good day, gentlemen.
      (*He goes out. There is a pause. All three men have been rocked off their balance*)

HARBISON   (*Thoughtfully*)   He's an honest man, but he's wrong. Of course, we can't guarantee him a better world if we win. Point is, we can be damned sure it'll be worse if we lose. Can't we? . . . (*Hotly*) Well, can't we?

BRACKETT   (*Rising*)   Of course. Cable, there's a bottle of Scotch in my bottom drawer. See you tomorrow.
      (*He exits quickly.* HARBISON *goes to the desk and takes a bottle from a drawer*)

HARBISON   This is the one he means.
      (*He takes two glasses and starts to pour the Scotch. A* YEOMAN *enters holding a sheaf of papers to be signed*)

YEOMAN (*Querulously*) Commander Harbison! The Old Man walked right out on me with all these orders to be signed! And there's another delegation of French planters here, complaining about that stolen pig—the one the Seabees took and barbecued. And Commander Hutton's here—

HARBISON (*Grabbing papers from him, irritably*) Okay, okay! . . . I'll take care of it!

YEOMAN Well, all right, sir!

CABLE (*As he takes his glass of Scotch*) What should I do, Commander Harbison? Go back to my outfit tonight?

HARBISON (*With his drink in his hand*) No, take a couple days off and unwind.

CABLE Unwind?

HARBISON Sure. Take a boat. Go fishing.

CABLE (*A light dawning on him, a memory of* BILLIS' *offer and* BLOODY MARY'S *song about Bali Ha'i*) Boat!
(*He puts his glass down and exits suddenly—as if pulled out of the room!* HARBISON *takes a swallow of Scotch, puts down his glass, looks around for* CABLE, *but* CABLE *has disappeared.* HARBISON *rubs his face with the gesture of a weary man, and starts to go to work on the papers as the lights fade*)

ACT ONE | Scene Nine

As BRACKETT'S *office recedes upstage, the tapa-cloth curtain closes and groups of French girls and native girls enter. They sing softly:*

GIRLS
Bali ha'i t'appele

Dans le jour,
Dans la nuit.
Dans ton coeur,
Toujours resonne,
Par ici,
Me voici.
Si tu veux,
Tu me trouvera
Ou le ciel
Trouve la mer.
Me voici,
Laisse moi te prendre
Par ici,
Me voici,
Bali ha'i,
  Bali ha'i,
    Bali ha'i!

(*There is a bell ringing offstage. A native* KID *shouts excitedly, "Boat! Boat! Boat!" He runs off left. The girls back away a few steps as* BILLIS, CABLE *and* BLOODY MARY *walk on*)

CABLE (*As he enters*)   Look, Billis, I didn't come over here to Bali Ha'i to see anybody cut any boar's teeth out.

BILLIS   It ain't the cutting of the boar's tooth exactly. It's what comes afterwards.

(*During these lines,* MARY *has whispered into a small boy's ear and sent him running off.* CABLE *has crossed the girls and looks back over his shoulder at them*)

MARY (*Smiling, understanding perfectly*)   I take you with me. Come, Lootellan. You have good time. (*Calling to a native*) Marcel! Come here! Billis, Marcel take you to boar ceremony. Lootellan come later. (*Two French girls have caught* CABLE'S *eye, and he has about made up his mind to approach them. He takes a couple of steps toward them, but now two* NUNS *enter and engage them in conversation. Thwarted by this unhappy development,* CABLE *becomes more receptive to* MARY, *who now says*) Lootellan, come with me. You have good time. Come!

(*She leads him off as the lights fade*)

ACT ONE | Scene Ten

The music swells. A concentration of light in the center of the stage reveals:
> *The interior of a native hut.*
> BLOODY MARY *comes in. Even she has to bend low to get through the doorway.* CABLE, *following her, finds himself in the darkness, blinking.*

CABLE   What's this?

MARY   You wait.

CABLE   There's nobody around here.

MARY   You wait, Lootellan.

CABLE   What's going on, Mary? What—
(He doesn't finish because a small figure has appeared in the doorway. A girl, perhaps seventeen. Her black hair is drawn smooth over her head. Like BLOODY MARY, *she wears a white blouse and black trousers. Barefooted, she stands, silent, shy and motionless against the wattled wall, looking at* CABLE *with the honest curiosity and admiration of a child)*

MARY *(To* CABLE, *with a sly smile)*   You like?

CABLE *(Never taking his eyes from the girl)*   Who is she?

MARY   Liat.

LIAT *(Nodding her head and repeating it in a small voice)* Liat.

MARY   Is French name.

CABLE *(Still stunned, still gazing at the girl)*   Liat.

MARY But she no French girl. She Tonkinese like me. We
are ver' pretty people— No? . . .
  (*She goes closer to* CABLE *and looks at him. She turns to*
  LIAT *and then back to* CABLE. *The two young people continue to regard each other with silent, longing interest*)

CABLE (*Over* MARY'S *head, to* LIAT) Do you speak English?

MARY Only a few word. She talk French. (*To* LIAT)
Français!

LIAT (*Smiling shyly*) Je parle Français—un peu.
  (*She holds her forefinger and thumb close together to show
  how very little French she speaks*)

CABLE (*Grinning, nearly as shy as she*) Moi, aussi—un peu.
(*He holds up his forefinger and thumb, just as she did. They
both laugh, and in some strange way,* BLOODY MARY *seems to
have been forgotten by both of them. She looks from one to
the other. Then, with the air of one who has accomplished a
purpose, she waddles to the doorway. As she goes out, she
lets the bamboo curtain roll down across the opening, re-
ducing the light inside the hut. There is a long moment of
silence*) Are you afraid of me? (LIAT *looks puzzled. He remembers she knows only a few words of English*) Oh . . .
er . . . avez-vous peur?

LIAT (*Her young face serious*) Non. (*He takes a step toward
her. She backs closer to the wall*) Oui! (*He stops and looks
at her, worried and hurt. This sign of gentleness wins her.
She smiles*) . . . Non.
  (*Now it is she who walks slowly toward him. The music
  builds in a rapturous upsurge.* CABLE *gathers* LIAT *in his
  arms. She reaches her small arms up to his neck. He lifts
  her off her feet. The lights fade slowly as his hand slides
  her blouse up her back toward her shoulders. The lights
  dim to complete darkness. Light projections of large and
  lovely Oriental blossoms are thrown against the drop.
  Native couples stroll across the stage, only dimly seen. The
  music mounts ecstatically, then diminishes. The stage is
  clear. The light comes up on the hut again and moonlight
  now comes through the opened doorway where* CABLE
  stands. He has no shirt on. LIAT *is seated on the floor,
  gazing up at him silently; her hair hangs loose down her
  back.* CABLE *smiles down at her*)

CABLE (*Trying to puzzle something out in his mind*) But you're just a kid . . . How did that Bloody Mary get a kid like you to come here and . . . I don't get it! (*Suddenly realizing that she has not understood*) Cette vielle femme . . . votre amie?

LIAT Ma mère.

CABLE (*Horrified*) Your mother! Bloody Mary is your mother! But she didn't tell me.
 (LIAT, *to divert him from unpleasant thoughts, suddenly throws herself in his lap; they kiss. The sound of a ship's bell is heard in the distance. They sit up.* LIAT *looks panic-stricken*)

LIAT Non, Non!
 (*She covers his ears with her hands*)

CABLE (*Looking off*) It's the boat all right. (*He turns back to her, sees her little face below his, her eyes pleading with him to stay*) Aw, let them wait. (*He sings*)
I touch your hand
And my arms grow strong,
Like a pair of birds
That burst with song.
My eyes look down
At your lovely face
And I hold the world
In my embrace.

Younger than springtime are you,
Softer than starlight are you,
Warmer than winds of June are the gentle lips you gave me.
Gayer than laughter are you,
Sweeter than music are you,
Angel and lover, heaven and earth are you to me,
And when your youth and joy invade my arms
And fill my heart as now they do,
Then,
Younger than springtime am I,
Gayer than laughter am I,
Angel and lover, heaven and earth am I with you . . .
 (*He releases her, goes to the door, looks off, then comes back to her. He stoops to pick up his shirt. She tries to get it first. Each has hold of one end of it. He looks down at her and repeats, softly*)

And when your youth and joy invade my arms
And fill my heart as now they do,
Then, younger than springtime am I,
Gayer than laughter am I,
Angel and lover, heaven and earth am I with you.

(*He starts. She clings to her end of his shirt for a moment, then lets it slide through her sad little fingers, and watches him go through the door—out of her life, perhaps. She sinks to her knees. The lights fade. Now, again in front of the tapa-cloth curtain, native girls bearing trays of tropical flowers and French girls are gathered in several groups*)

ACT ONE | Scene Eleven

The girls sing and hum "Bali Ha'i" softly under the scene, as Hawaiians sing "Aloha" to all departing craft. BLOODY MARY *and* BILLIS *are looking off, anxiously awaiting* CABLE.

BILLIS (*Shouting off*) Ring the bell again! Ring the bell again! (*Taking a lei from a* FLOWER-SELLER) I'll have another one of those.

(*He drapes the lei around his neck where he already has three others*)

MARY He come. He come. He be here soon. Don't worry, Billis.

BILLIS Hey, Mary— Please ask those Boar Tooth ceremonial fellows not to be sore at me. I didn't think those girls would do a religious dance with only skirts on. If somebody had told me it was a religious dance, I wouldn't have gotten up and danced with them. (*Looking off*) Oh! Here he comes! Here he comes.

(BILLIS *exits toward the boat.* CABLE *enters and crosses the stage in a kind of dream.* MARY *smiles, ecstatic, as she sees*

his face. Several of the French girls try to flirt with CABLE,
but he doesn't know they're alive. He goes right by them.
MARY *then walks past them, her chin in the air, very
proudly and triumphantly. The girls' voices rise, singing the
final measures of "Bali Ha'i." They throw flowers offstage
where* BILLIS *and* CABLE *made their exit. Cries of "Au
revoir" and laughter are heard over the singing)*

MARY (*Throwing flower garland she has taken from a native
girl and shouting to the others*)   Is gonna be my son-in-law.
(*Calling off*) Goo' bye! Come back soon, Lootellan! Bali Ha'i!
Come back soon!

The lights fade

ACT ONE | Scene Twelve

And other lights come up slowly on EMILE'S *terrace.*
    *The good-byes continue through the darkness and other
good-byes from other voices blend in with these . . . all
in French.*
    HENRY *enters with another* SERVANT. *They start to clear
glasses, champagne bottles and other left-overs of a gay
party which clutter the scene.*

FRENCHMAN (*Offstage*)   Bali Ha'i . . . Bon soir!

FRENCHWOMAN (*Offstage*)   Merci, Emile. Merci, mille fois!
    (EMILE *enters and addresses* HENRY)

EMILE   Pas maintenant . . . demain!

FRENCHMAN (*Offstage*)   A bientot! Bali Ha'i.
    (HENRY *and the other* SERVANT *exit*)

FRENCHWOMAN (*Offstage*)   Quelle charmante soirée.

NELLIE (*Offstage*) Good night . . . everybody . . . Good night.

FRENCHMAN (*Offstage*) Non, Non . . . Nellie . . . en Français . . . en Français.

NELLIE (*Offstage, laboring with her French*) Je . . . suis . . . enchantée . . . de faire . . . votre . . . connaissance! (EMILE, *looking off, smiles with amusement and pride. Voices offstage shout "Bravo!" "Formidable!" EMILE exits*)

FRENCHMAN (*Offstage*) Bon soir, de Becque.

FRENCHWOMAN (*Offstage*) Merci mille fois!!! (*There is the sound of a motor starting loud, then growing fainter. EMILE and NELLIE enter and turn back to wave good-bye to the last guests. Then NELLIE turns to EMILE, who has been gently urging her farther into the garden. There is high excitement in her voice and she speaks very rapidly*)

NELLIE Emile, you know I can't stay. And I've got to get that jeep back. I stole it. Or rather, I borrowed it. Or rather a fellow stole it for me. A wonderful man named Billis. I'll have to sneak around behind the hospital as it is.

EMILE In that case, I forbid you to go! If you have to sneak back without anyone seeing you, you might just as well sneak back later. (NELLIE *thinks for an instant, then comes to a quick decision*)

NELLIE (*Taking off her coat*) You're absolutely right! (*She looks guiltily at EMILE and screams with laughter. So does he. She puts her coat on the back of a chair*) I never had such a wonderful time in my whole life. All these lovely people and that cute old man who spoke French with me and made believe he understood me. And that exciting native couple who danced for us. Oh, it's so different from Little Rock! (*She screams the last line passionately, as if she hopes Little Rock would hear. EMILE laughs uproariously. She suddenly becomes quiet*) What on earth are you laughing at? Am I drunk?

EMILE (*Still laughing*) Oh, no.

NELLIE Yes, I am. But it isn't the champagne—it's because I'm in love with a wonderful guy! (*She sings this last line.*

They waltz to the music of "I'm in Love with a Wonderful Guy!" NELLIE *resumes singing*)
If you'll excuse an expression I use,
I'm in love, I'm in love, I'm in love—

EMILE (*Also singing*)
I'm in love, I'm in love and the girl that I love—She thinks I'm a wonderful guy!
(*They stop, exhausted and laughing. She turns and notices a half-filled glass of champagne which has been left by one of the guests. She takes it up and drinks it*)

NELLIE   Imagine leaving all this wonderful champagne! (*She drinks out of this one, then takes another one. She hands it to* EMILE) Here, Emile. You have some, too. It's such a waste!

EMILE   Here—here's another bottle.
(*He goes over to a long table which is under the windows on the porch. There are several buckets of champagne there. He takes one and fills two clean glasses and brings them to* NELLIE. *Meanwhile, she leans back, stretching her arms behind her head. Dreamily, she sings*)

NELLIE
This is how it feels,
Living on a hillside . . .
(*She speaks as the melody in the orchestra continues*)
Here we are just like two old married people. Our guests have gone home and we're alone.

EMILE (*Handing her the glass of champagne, singing*)
This is what I need,
This is what I've longed for—
Someone young and smiling,
Here upon my hill—
(*The orchestra starts the music of "A Cockeyed Optimist."* NELLIE *has been thinking*)

NELLIE   Emile, you know, my mother says we have nothing in common. But she's wrong. We have something very important in common—very much in common.

EMILE   Yes, we're both in love.

NELLIE   Yes, but more than that. We're—we're the same kind of people fundamentally—you and me. We appreciate things! We get enthusiastic about things. It's really quite exciting when two people are like that. We're not blasé. You know what I mean?

EMILE   We're both knuckleheads, cockeyed optimists.
   (*They both laugh and start to sing*)

NELLIE
I hear the human race
Is falling on its face . . .

EMILE
And hasn't very far to go!

NELLIE
But every whippoorwill
Is selling me a bill
And telling me it just ain't so.

BOTH (*Harmonizing—"Sweet Adeline" fashion*)
I could say life is just a bowl of jello
And appear more intelligent and smart,
But I'm stuck,
Like a dope,
With a thing called hope,
And I can't get it out of my heart . . .
   (*Dwelling on the fancy ending*)
Not this heart!
   (*They smile in each other's eyes.* EMILE *suddenly gets an idea and rises*)

EMILE   Nellie, I have a surprise for you. You sit over there —something that I have been preparing for two days. Close your eyes. No peeking. (EMILE *looks around first for a prop, sees her coat, then makes her go over and sit by the fountain.* NELLIE *is mystified, but excited, like a child waiting for a surprise.* EMILE *takes her coat and throwing it over his head, using it to simulate a towel, he imitates her as he found her on the beach the other day*)
I'm going to wash that man right out of my hair,
I'm going to wash that man right out of my hair,

NELLIE   Oh, no! No!
   (*She writhes with embarrassment and laughter as he continues*)

EMILE
I'm going to wash that man right out of my hair
And send him on his way! . . .
   (*She covers her eyes*)
Don't try to patch it up,
Tear it up, tear it up,
Wash him out, dry him out,
Push him out, fly him out,
Cancel him, and let him go—
Yea, Sister!
   (*He finishes, waving his arms wildly*)

NELLIE (*Applauding*)   That's wonderful, **Emile.**
   (EMILE *lifts the coat and, looking off, sees* NGANA *and*
   JEROME *as they enter in their nightgowns, followed by*
   HENRY)

EMILE   Bon soir!
   (NELLIE *turns, looks at the children and is immediately enchanted. She kneels before the two of them, holding them
   at arm's length*)

NELLIE   You're the cutest things I ever saw in my whole life!
What are your names? You probably can't understand a word
I'm saying, but, oh, my goodness, you're cute.

EMILE   Nellie, I want you to meet Ngana and Jerome.
Ngana and Jerome, Nellie.

NGANA AND JEROME   Nellie . . .

EMILE (*To the children*)   Maintenant au lit . . . vite!

HENRY   Venez, Petits!

NGANA   Bon soir, Nellie.

JEROME   Bon soir, Nellie.
   (*They wave to* NELLIE, *as* HENRY *leads them out*)

NELLIE   Bon soir! (*Turning to* EMILE) Oh, aren't they ador-
able! Those big black eyes staring at you out of those sweet
little faces! Are they Henry's?

EMILE   They're mine.

NELLIE (*Carrying out what she thinks is a joke*)   Oh, of
course, they look exactly like you, don't they? Where did you
hide their mother?

EMILE She's dead, Nellie.

NELLIE She's— (*She turns*) Emile, they *are* yours!

EMILE Yes, Nellie. I'm their father.

NELLIE And—their mother . . . was a . . . was . . . a . . .

EMILE Polynesian. (NELLIE *is stunned. She turns away, trying to collect herself*) And she was beautiful, Nellie, and charming, too.

NELLIE But you and she . . .

EMILE I want you to know I have no apologies. I came here as a young man. I lived as I could.

NELLIE Of course.

EMILE But I have not been selfish. No woman ever hated me or tried to hurt me.

NELLIE No woman could ever want to hurt you, Emile. (*Suddenly, feeling she must get away as quickly as she can*) Oh, what time is it? I promised to get that jeep back! (*She looks at her wrist watch*) Oh, this is awful. Look at the time!
  (*She grabs her coat.* EMILE *tries to stop her*)

EMILE Nellie, wait, please. I'll drive you home.

NELLIE You will do no such thing. Anyway, I couldn't leave the jeep here. I've got to get it back by—

EMILE Don't go now, Nellie. Don't go yet, please.

NELLIE (*Rattling on very fast*) Yes, I must go now This is terrible! I won't be able to face the girls at the hospital. You can't imagine the way they look at you when you come in late . . . I'll call you, Emile. I'll come by tomorrow. (*Suddenly remembering*) Oh, no! Oh, dear! There are those awful rehearsals for Thanksgiving Day—I'm teaching them a dance and they want to rehearse night and day—but after that— (*Shifting quickly*) Oh, thank you for tonight, Emile. I had a wonderful time. It was the nicest party and you're a perfect host. Good-bye. Please stay here, Emile. Don't go out to the jeep, please.

EMILE (*Grabbing her arms, feeling her slipping away from him*) Nellie, I love you. Do you hear me, Nellie? I love you!

NELLIE   And I love you, too. Honestly I do— Please let me go! Please let me go!

(NELLIE *goes off. She runs as fast as she can.* EMILE *watches for a second. The motor of the jeep starts and fades away quickly, as though the jeep were driven away very, very fast. The music of "Some Enchanted Evening" swells as* EMILE *looks down and picks up a coffee cup that has been left on the fountain*)

EMILE (*Singing, as he looks down at the cup*)
Once you have found her,
Never let her go.
Once you have found her,
Never let her go!

Curtain

ACT TWO | Scene One

The stage during a performance of "The Thanksgiving Follies."

A dance is in progress, four girls and four boys. NELLIE *is one of the girls. They meticulously perform the steps and evolutions of a dance routine no more distinguished or original than any that might be produced by a Navy nurse who had been the moving spirit in the amateur theatre of Little Rock. Not one of the dancers makes a single mistake. Nobody smiles. Tense concentration is evident in this laboriously perfect performance. During the course of the dance, there are solo "step-outs" after which each soloist soberly steps back into place. The most complicated unison step is saved for the exit, which they execute with vigorous precision.*

On either side, in the downstage corners of the stage, G.I.'s are sitting as if there had not been enough seats and the audience overflowed up onto the stage. There are no chairs. They are seated and sprawled on the floor of the stage.

NELLIE *returns to the stage, a sheaf of notes in her hand and talks into the microphone.*

NELLIE It has been called to our attention that owing to some trouble with the mimeograph, the last part of the program is kind of blurry, so I will read off who did the last number. (*Reading*) The hand-stand was by Marine Sergeant Johnson. (*Applause*) The Barrel Roll was done by Lieutenant J. G. Bessie May Sue Ellie Jaeger. (*Applause*) The solo featuring the hitch-kick and scissors . . . those are the names of the steps . . . was by Ensign Cora McRae. (*Applause*) The Pin Wheel . . . you know— (*She demonstrates by waving her leg in imitation of* STEWPOT) was by Stewpot . . . I mean George Watts, Carpenter's Mate, Third Class.

(*Applause.* STEWPOT'S *head protrudes from the wings*)

STEWPOT Second class.
(*Applause*)

NELLIE The multiple revolutions and— (NELLIE *becomes self-consciously modest*) incidentally the dance steps were by Ensign Nellie Forbush. (*She bows. Applause*) Now the next is a most unusual treat. An exhibition of weight lifting by Marine Staff Sergeant Thomas Hassinger.

(HASSINGER *enters from right. He flexes muscles. Applause and shouts from "audience" on the corner of the stage*)

SAILOR Atta boy, Muscles!
(*The lights start fading*)

NELLIE . . . and Sergeant Johnson . . . (JOHNSON *enters*) Marine Corporal . . .
(*The lights are out*)

VOICE IN DARK Hey, lights . . . the lights are out . . . Billis!

NELLIE Bill-is . . . what the heck happened to the lights?

OTHER VOICES "It's the generator." "Generator ran out of gas." "Switch over to the other one." "Mike . . . turn on the truck lights."

NELLIE   Keep your seats, everybody! There's nothing wrong except that the lights went out.

VOICES   "Look where you're going." "How the hell can I look when I can't see?"
   (*The lights come up. The set has been changed in the darkness. We are now in*)

ACT TWO | Scene Two

In back of the stage.

SEABEE   We'll have that other generator on in a minute.

BILLIS   They got the truck lights on. That's something.
   (*Applause offstage, right*)

STEWPOT (*Looking off toward "stage"*)   The weight-lifting act got started.

BILLIS   Good . . . (*He notices two Seabees who are pushing a large roll of cable*) What I can't understand is how some guys ain't got the artistic imagination to put gas in a generator so a show can be a success . . . especially when they're on the committee.

FIRST SEABEE   You're on the committee, too. Why didn't you tell us it wasn't gassed up?

BILLIS   I'm acting in the show and I'm stage manager and producer. I can't figure out everything, can I?

SECOND SEABEE   Sure you can. Just put your two heads together.
   (*He and his companion exit, pushing the roll of cable before them*)

BILLIS (*Calling off*) Look, jerk! I got a production on my hands. (*Turning to* STEWPOT) How's the weight-lifting act going?

STEWPOT I can't tell. Nobody's clapping.

BILLIS If nobody's clapping, they ain't going good. You ought to be able to figure that out. Put your two heads together.

STEWPOT You was the one with two heads.
(EMILE *enters. He carries a bunch of flowers in his hand. He has a serious "set" expression in his eyes*)

EMILE Pardon, can you tell me where I can find Miss For-bush?

BILLIS (*Shrewdly sensing trouble and determined to protect* NELLIE) She's on stage now. She's the Emcee. She can't talk to nobody right now. Do you want me to take the flowers in to her?

EMILE No. I would prefer to give them to her myself.

BILLIS Are you Mister de Becque?

EMILE Yes.

BILLIS Look, Mister de Becque. Do me a favor, will you? Don't try and see her tonight.

EMILE Why?

BILLIS We got her in a great mood tonight and I don't want anything to upset her again.

EMILE She has been upset?

BILLIS Upset! She's asked for a transfer to another island. And day before yesterday, she busted out crying right in the middle of rehearsal. Said she couldn't go on with the show. And she wouldn't have either unless Captain Brackett talked to her and told her how important it was to the Base. So do us all a favor—don't try to see her now.

EMILE She's asked for a transfer?

BILLIS Don't tell her I told you. Nobody's supposed to know.

EMILE I must see her. Tonight!

BILLIS   Then stay out of sight till after the show. I'll take the flowers to her.
   (EMILE *gives him the flowers.* BILLIS *and* STEWPOT *exit,* CABLE *enters. He doesn't see* EMILE *at first*)

CABLE   Hey, Billis— Billis!

EMILE   (*Peering through the semi-darkness*) Lieutenant Cable?

CABLE   (*Putting his fingers to his lips in a mocking gesture*) Ssh! Lieutenant Cable is supposed to be in his little bed over at the hospital.

EMILE   You have not been well?

CABLE   I'm okay now. Fever gone. They can't hold me in that damned place any longer. I'm looking for a guy named Billis, a great guy for getting boats. (*His voice rising, tense and shrill*) And I need a boat right now. I've got to get to my island.

EMILE (*Worried by* CABLE'S *strangeness*)   What?

CABLE   That damned island with the two volcanoes on it. You ever been over there?

EMILE   Why, yes, I—

CABLE   I went over there every day till this damned malaria stopped me. Have you sailed over early in the morning? With warm rain playing across your face? (LIAT *enters. He sees her, but doesn't believe his eyes*) Beginning to see her again like last night.

LIAT (*Calling offstage*)   Ma mère! C'est lui!
   (*She turns and, like a young deer, glides over to the amazed* CABLE *and embraces him before the equally amazed* EMILE. MARY *waddles on*)

CABLE (*Holding* LIAT *tight*)   I thought I was dreaming.

LIAT (*Laughing*)   Non.
   (*She holds him tighter*)

CABLE (*He holds her away from him and looks at her*) What are you doing over here?

MARY (*Grimly*)   She come in big white boat—bigger than your boat. Belong Jacques Barrere. He want to marry Liat.

(*To* EMILE) You know him. (EMILE *nods. She turns back to* CABLE) Is white man, too. And very rich!

CABLE (*To* LIAT)   Is that the old planter you told me about? The one who drinks? (*His eye catches* EMILE'S. EMILE *nods.* CABLE *cries out as if hurt*) Oh, my God! (*He turns angrily to* MARY) You can't let her marry a man like that.

MARY   Hokay! Then *you* marry her.

EMILE (*Angrily, to* MARY)   Tais-toi! Il est malade! . . . Tu comprends? (MARY *is temporarily silenced.* EMILE *turns to* CABLE *and his voice becomes gentle and sympathetic*) Lieutenant, I am worried about you. You are ill. Will you allow me to see you back to the hospital?

CABLE   You're worried about me! That's funny. The fellow who says he lives on an island all by himself and doesn't worry about anybody—Japs, Americans, Germans—anybody. Why pick out *me* to worry about?

EMILE (*Stiffly*)   Forgive me. I'm sorry, Lieutenant.
   (*He leaves.* MARY *goes to* CABLE *to make one last plea for her daughter's dream*)

MARY   Lootellan, you like Liat. . . . Marry Liat! You have good life here. Look, Lootellan, I am rich. I save six hundred dolla' before war. Since war I make two thousand dolla' . . . war go on I make maybe more. Sell grass skirts, boar's teeth, real human heads. Give all de money to you an' Liat. You no have to work. I work for you. . . . (*Soft music is played*) All day long, you and Liat be together! Walk through woods, swim in sea, sing, dance, talk happy. No think about Philadelia. Is no good. Talk about beautiful things and make love all day long. You like? You buy? (*She sings. Throughout the song,* LIAT *performs what seem to be traditional gestures*)
Happy Talk,
Keep talkin' Happy Talk!
Talk about tings you'd like to do.
You got to have a dream—
If you don' have a dream
How you gonna have a dream come true?

Talk about a moon
Floatin' in de sky,
Lookin' like a lily on a lake:
Talk about a bird

Learnin' how to fly,
Makin' all de music he can make.

Happy Talk,
Keep talkin' Happy Talk!
Talk about tings you'd like to do.
You got to have a dream—
If you don' have a dream
How you gonna have a dream come true?

Talk about a star
Lookin' like a toy,
Peekin' through de branches of a tree.
Talk about a girl,
Talk about a boy
Countin' all de ripples on de sea.

Happy Talk,
Keep talkin' Happy Talk!
Talk about tings you'd like to do.
You got to have a dream—
If you don' have a dream
How you gonna have a dream come true?
     (LIAT *now performs a gentle, childish dance. At the end of
     it, she returns to* CABLE'S *side and* MARY *resumes her song*)
Talk about a boy
Sayin' to de girl,
"Golly, baby, I'm a lucky cuss!"
Talk about a girl
Saying to de boy,
"You an' me is lucky to be us."
     (LIAT *and* CABLE *kiss.* MARY'S *voice becomes triumphant*)

Happy Talk,
Keep talkin' Happy Talk!
Talk about tings you'd like to do.
You got to have a dream—
If you don' have a dream
How you gonna have a dream come true?

If you don' talk happy
An' you never have a dream
Den you'll never have a dream come true.
     (*Speaking eagerly*)
Is good idea . . . you like?
     (*She laughs gaily and looks in* CABLE'S *eyes, anxious to see*

the answer. CABLE *is deeply disturbed. He takes a gold watch from his pocket and puts it in* LIAT'S *hand*)

CABLE   Liat, I want you to have this. It's a man's watch but it's a good one —belonged to my grandfather. It's kind of a lucky piece, too. My dad carried it all through the last war. Beautiful, isn't it?
   (LIAT *has taken the watch, her eyes gleaming with pride*)

MARY   When I see you firs' time. I know you good man for Liat. And she good girl for you. You have special good babies.
   (*Pause.* CABLE *looks tortured*)

CABLE (*Forcing the words out*)   Mary, I can't . . . marry . . . Liat.

MARY (*Letting out her rage and disappointment in a shout, as she grabs* LIAT'S *arm*)   Was your las' chance! Now she marry Jacques Barrere. Come, Liat! (LIAT *runs to* CABLE. MARY *pulls her away*) Give me watch. (LIAT *clasps it tight in her hands.* MARY *wrests it from her and yells at* CABLE) Stingy bastard!
   (*She throws it on the ground and it smashes.* CABLE *looks on, dazed, stunned.* MARY *pulls* LIAT *off.* CABLE *kneels down, gathers up the pieces and puts them in his pocket. Meanwhile, several of the men come on, dressed for the finale of the show. They are looking back over their shoulders at* LIAT *and* MARY *whom they must have just passed*)

PROFESSOR   Hey! Did you get a load of that little Tonkinese girl?
   (*They continue up to the stage door as they speak*)

MARINE   Yeah.
   (*Applause off.* NELLIE'S *voice is heard through the loudspeaker*)

NELLIE (*Offstage*)   Now, boys, before we come to the last act of our show, it is my great pleasure to bring you our skipper, Captain George Brackett.
   (*Applause.* CABLE *looks off at* LIAT *as she passes out of his life*)

CABLE (*Singing*)
Younger than springtime were you,
Softer than starlight were you,
Angel and lover, heaven and earth
Were you to me. . . .

ACT TWO | Scene Three

The lights fade to complete darkness. BRACKETT'S *voice is heard in the loudspeaker. During his speech, the lights come up, revealing:*
The G.I. Stage, as before. BRACKETT *is speaking into a microphone.*

BRACKETT   Up to now, our side has been having the hell beat out of it in two hemispheres and we're not going to get to go home until that situation is reversed. It may take a long time before we can get any big operation under way, so it's things like this, like this show tonight, that keep us going. Now I understand that I am not generally considered a sentimental type. (*Laughter and cries of "Oh, boy!" "Check," "You can say that again," etc., from the boys on the corners of the stage*) Once or twice I understand I have been referred to as "Old Iron Belly."

VOICES   "Once or twice." "Just about a million times."
(*Loud laughter*)

BRACKETT   I resent that very much because I had already chosen that as my private name for our Executive Officer, Commander Harbison. (*Big laugh. Applause.* BRACKETT *calls into the wings*) Take a bow, Commander.
(*Two of the girls pull* COMMANDER HARBISON *out*)

SAILOR   I wish I was a commander!
(HARBISON, *flanked by the two girls, stands beside* BRACKETT *as he continues*)

BRACKETT   I want you to know that both "Old Iron Bellies" sat here tonight and had a hell of a good time. And we want to thank that hard working committee of Nurses and Seabees

who made the costumes out of rope and mosquito nets, comic
books and newspapers . . .
  (*He fingers the comic-paper skirt of one of the girls*)

SAILOR Ah, ah—captain!
  (BRACKETT *frowns, but pulls himself together*)
BRACKETT   . . . and thought up these jokes and these grand
songs. And I just want to say on this Thanksgiving Day, to all
of them from all of us, thank you. (*Applause from the boys,
but it is comically feeble. Obviously, they'd like to get on with
the show*) And now I'm going to ask Commander Harbison
to announce the next act which is the Finale of our Thanksgiving entertainment.
  (*He hands* HARBISON *a paper.* HARBISON *reads from a small
  card*)

HARBISON   The next and last will be a song sung by Bosun
Butch Forbush . . . (*He looks kind of puzzled*) . . . and
that Siren of the Coral Sea . . . gorgeous, voluptuous and
petite Mademoiselle Lutheria . . . (*Ending in a high, surprised voice, as he reads the name of his pet abomination*)
. . . Billis!

BRACKETT (*Laughing*)   Come on, Bill.
  (*He leads off* HARBISON, *who is looking at the paper,
  puzzled. The music of "Honey-Bun" starts and* NELLIE
  *enters, dressed as a sailor, in a borrowed white sailor suit,
  three times too big for her*)

NELLIE (*Singing*)
My doll is as dainty as a sparrow,
Her figure is something to applaud.
Where she's narrow, she's as narrow as an arrow
And she's broad where a broad should be broad!

A hundred and one
Pounds of fun—
That's my little Honey-Bun!
Get a load of Honey-Bun tonight!

I'm speakin' of my
Sweetie Pie,
Only sixty inches high—
Ev'ry inch is packed with dynamite!

Her hair is blonde and curly,
Her curls are hurly-burly.

Her lips are pips!
I call her hips:
"Twirly"
And "Whirly."
She's my baby,
I'm her Pap!
I'm her booby,
She's my trap!
I am caught and I don't wanta run
'Cause I'm havin' so much fun with Honey-Bun!

> (NELLIE *starts a second refrain, meanwhile having con-siderable difficulty with her sagging trousers. Now* BILLIS *enters, dressed as a South Sea siren in a straw-colored wig, long lashes fantastically painted on his eyelids, lips painted in bright carmine, two coconut shells on his chest to simu-late "femininity" and a battleship tatooed on his bare midriff. He and* NELLIE *dance. For an exit, she leads him off, singing a special ending)*

NELLIE

She's my baby,
I'm her Pap!
I'm her booby,
She's my trap!
I am caught and I don't wanta run
'Cause I'm havin' so much fun with Honey-Bun!
(Believe me, sonny)
She's a cookie who can cook you till you're done,
(Ain't bein' funny)
Sonny,
Put your money
On my Honey-Bun!

> (*After they exit,* NELLIE *returns for a bow. Then* BILLIS *enters with* EMILE'S *flowers and presents them to her. Thinking they are from* BILLIS, *she kisses him. He exits in a delirious daze. She exits as the girls enter, singing)*

GIRLS

A hundred and one
Pounds of fun—
That's my little Honey-Bun
Get a load of Honey-Bun tonight.

I'm speakin' of my
Sweetie Pie,

Only sixty inches high—
Every inch is packed with dynamite.

(*The girls are dressed in home-made costumes representing island natives. The materials are fish-net, parachute cloth, large tropical leaves and flowers—anything they could find and sew together. At the end of their line is* BILLIS *still dressed as a girl. As the song proceeds, he is the butt of many a slur from his comrades. While passing one of them, he is shocked and infuriated to feel a hand thrust up his skirt. He turns to swing on him, but he can't get out of line and spoil the number; "On with the show!" He is grim and stoic—even when another boy lifts one of the coconuts in his "brassiere" and steals a package of cigarettes therefrom. The girls and* BILLIS *continue singing through these impromptu shenanigans*)

GIRLS
Her hair is blonde and curly,
Her curls are hurly-burly.
Her lips are pips!
I call her hips:
"Twirly" and "Whirly."

She's my baby,
I'm her Pap!
I'm her booby,
She's my trap!
I am caught and I don't wanta run
'Cause I'm havin' so much fun with **Honey-Bun!**
    (*All lining up for finale*)
And that's the finish,
And it's time to go for now the show is done.
    (*Balance of* "COMPANY" *comes on*)
We hope you liked us,
And we hope that when you leave your seat and run
Down to the Mess Hall
You'll enjoy your dinner each and every one.
    (NELLIE *makes a special entrance, now wearing a* **new** *costume*)

NELLIE (*Very brightly*)   Enjoy your turkey.

ALL (*Pointing to* BILLIS)
And put some chestnut dressing on our **Honey-Bun!**
    (*The curtain is slow.* NELLIE *signals for it and jumps up to*

help pull it down. The lights are off. Boys on the stage wave their flashlights out at the audience, addressing them as if they were all G.I.'s. "See you down at the mess hall," etc. When the clamor dies down, two lines are distinguishable)

SAILOR How d'ye like the show?

MARINE It stunk!

ACT TWO | Scene Four

Now the lights come up on the scene behind the stage.

The girls come off the stage and file into their dressing shack. BILLIS follows them in. After a few moments, he comes hurtling out, minus his wig. A few seconds later, the wig is thrown out by one of the girls in the dressing room.

BILLIS Oh, I beg your pardon.
(*At this moment, he turns and faces NELLIE, who has just come down the steps from the stage with another girl*)

NELLIE (*Seeing BILLIS*) Oh, Luther, you really are a honey-bun! These beautiful flowers! I needed someone to think of me tonight. I appreciate it, Luther—you don't know how much.

BILLIS (*Very emotionally*) Miss Forbush, I would like you to know I consider you the most wonderful woman in the entire world—officer and all. And I just can't go on being such a heel as to let you think I thought of giving you those flowers.

NELLIE But you did give them to me and I—

BILLIS (*Shoving a card at NELLIE*) Here's the card that came with them. (*She reads the card, then turns away—*

deeply affected) Are you all right, Miss Forbush? (*She nods her head*) I'll be waiting around the area here in case you need me. Just—just sing out.

(*He exits.* NELLIE *is on the point of tears.* CABLE, *who has been sitting on a bench below the ladies' dressing shack, now rises and approaches* NELLIE)

CABLE (*Sympathetically, but taking a light tone*)   What's the matter, Nellie the nurse? Having diplomatic difficulties with France?

(NELLIE *turns, startled*)

NELLIE (*Immediately becoming the professional nurse*)   Joe Cable! Who let you out of the hospital?

CABLE   Me. I'm okay.

(*She leads him to the bench and feels his forehead and pulse*)

NELLIE (*Accusingly*)   Joe! You're trying to get over to Bali Ha'i. That little girl you told me about!

CABLE (*Nodding thoughtfully*)   Liat. I've just seen her for the last time, I guess. I love her and yet I just heard myself saying I can't marry her. What's the matter with me, Nellie? What kind of a guy am I, anyway?

NELLIE   You're all right. You're just far away from home. We're both so far away from home.

(*She looks at the card. He takes her hand.* EMILE *enters. He is earnest and importunate*)

EMILE   Nellie! I must see you.

NELLIE   Emile! I—

EMILE   Will you excuse us, Lieutenant Cable?

(CABLE *starts to leave*)

NELLIE   No, wait a minute, Joe. Stay. Please! (*To* EMILE) I've been meaning to call you but—

EMILE   You have asked for a transfer, why? What does it mean?

NELLIE   I'll explain it to you tomorrow, Emile. I'm—

EMILE   No. Now. What does it mean, Nellie?

NELLIE   It means that I can't marry you. Do you understand?
I can't marry you.

EMILE   Nellie— Because of my children?

NELLIE   Not because of your children. They're sweet.

EMILE   It is their Polynesian mother then—their mother
and I.

NELLIE   . . . Yes. I can't help it. It isn't as if I could give
you a good reason. There is no reason. This is emotional. This
is something that is born in me.

EMILE (*Shouting the words in bitter protest*)   It is not. I do
not believe this is born in you.

NELLIE   Then why do I feel the way I do? All I know is that
I can't help it. I can't help it! Explain how we feel, Joe—
    (JOE *gives her no help. She runs up to the door of the
    dressing shack*)

EMILE   Nellie!

NELLIE (*Calling in*)   Dinah, are you ready?

NURSE   Yes, Nellie.

NELLIE   I'll go with you.
    (*The other nurse comes out and they exit quickly.* EMILE
    turns angrily to CABLE)

EMILE   What makes her talk like that? Why do you have this
feeling, you and she? I do not believe it is born in you. I do
not believe it.

CABLE   It's not born in you! It happens *after* you're born . . .
    (CABLE *sings the following words, as if figuring this whole
    question out for the first time*)
You've got to be taught to hate and fear,
You've got to be taught from year to year,
It's got to be drummed in your dear little ear—
You've got to be carefully taught!

You've got to be taught to be afraid
Of people whose eyes are oddly made,
And people whose skin is a different shade—
You've got to be carefully taught.

You've got to be taught before it's too late,
Before you are six or seven or eight,
To hate all the people your relatives hate—
You've got to be carefully taught!
You've got to be carefully taught!

(*Speaking, going close to* EMILE, *his voice filled with the emotion of discovery and firm in a new determination*)
You've got the right idea, de Becque—live on an island. Yes, sir, if I get out of this thing alive, I'm not going back there! I'm coming here. All I care about is right here. To hell with the rest.

EMILE (*Thoughtfully*)   When all you care about is here . . . this is a good place to be. When all you care about is taken away from you, there is no place . . . (*Walking away from* CABLE, *now talking to himself*) I came so close to it . . . so close. (*Singing*)
One dream in my heart,
One love to be living for,
One love to be living for—
This nearly was mine.

One girl for my dreams,
One partner in Paradise,
This promise of Paradise—
This nearly was mine.

Close to my heart she came,
Only to fly away,
Only to fly as day
Flies from moonlight!

Now, now I'm alone,
Still dreaming of Paradise.
Still saying that Paradise
Once nearly was mine.

So clear and deep are my fancies
Of things I wish were true,
I'll keep remembering evenings
I wish I'd spent with you.
I'll keep remembering kisses
From lips I'll never own
And all the lovely adventures
That we have never known.

One dream in my heart
One love to be living for
One love to be living for—
This nearly was mine.

One girl for my dreams,
One partner in Paradise.
This promise of Paradise—
This nearly was mine.

Close to my heart she came,
Only to fly away,
Only to fly as day
Flies from moonlight!

Now . . . now I'm alone,
Still dreaming of Paradise,
Still saying that Paradise
Once nearly was mine.

(*He drops to the bench, a lonely and disconsolate figure*)

CABLE (*Going to him*) De Becque, would you reconsider going up there with me to Marie Louise Island? I mean, now that you haven't got so much to lose? We could do a good job, I think—you and I. (EMILE *doesn't answer*) You know, back home when *I* used to get in a jam, I used to go hunting. That's what I think I'll do now. Good hunting up there around Marie Louise. Jap carriers . . . cargo boats . . . troopships . . . big game. (*He looks at* EMILE, *craftily considering how much headway he has made.* EMILE *smiles a little*) When I go up, what side of the island should I land on?

EMILE The south side.

CABLE Why?

EMILE There's a cove there . . . and rocks. I have sailed in behind these rocks many times.

CABLE Could a submarine get in between those rocks without being observed?

EMILE Yes. If you know the channel.

CABLE And after I land, what will I do?

EMILE You will get in touch with my friends, Basile and Inato—two black men—wonderful hunters. They will hide us in the hills.

CABLE (*His eyes lighting up*)   Us? Are you going with me?

EMILE (*A new strength in his voice*)   Of course. You are too young to be out alone. Let's go and find Captain Brackett.

CABLE (*Delirious*)   Wait till that old bastard Brackett hears this. He'll jump out of his skin!

EMILE   I would like to see this kind of a jump. Come on! (*They go off quickly together.* BILLIS *rushes on and looks after them. Obviously, he's been listening. He thinks it over for a moment, "dopes it out." Then, with sudden decision, he takes one last puff on a cigarette butt, flings it away, and follows after them*)

ACT TWO | Scene Five

The lights go out and almost immediately the sound of an airplane motor is heard, revving up, ready for the take-off. The lights come up between the tapa-cloth and the dark-green drop.

    Several Naval Aircraft mechanics are standing with their backs to the audience— They look off, watching tensely. As the plane is heard taking off, they raise their hands and shout in an exultant, defiant manner.

    The music reaches a climax and the lights fade out on them, as they exit.

    Lights in center come on simultaneously, revealing:

ACT TWO | Scene Six

This is the communications office or radio room. The back wall is covered with communications equipment of all sorts: boards, lights, switches. There is a speaker, a small table with a receiving set, various telephones and sending equipment. A COMMUNICATIONS ENLISTED MAN *is sitting at the table with earphones. He is working the dials in front of him.* CAPTAIN BRACKETT *is seated on an upturned wastebasket. On the floor are several empty Coca-Cola bottles and several full ones. He is eating a sandwich and alternately guzzling from a bottle of Coca-Cola. There are a couple of empty Coca-Cola bottles on the* ENLISTED MAN'S *desk, too.* BRACKETT *is listening avidly for any possible sound that might come from the loudspeaker. After a moment, there is a crackle.*

BRACKETT (*Excitedly*) What's that? What's that? (*The* ENLISTED MAN *cannot hear him, because he has earphones.* BRACKETT *suddenly becomes conscious of this. He pokes the* ENLISTED MAN *in the back. The* ENLISTED MAN, *controlling himself, turns and looks at* BRACKETT, *as a nurse would at an anxious, complaining patient. He pulls the earphones away from his ear*) What was that?

ENLISTED MAN (*Quietly*) That was . . . nothing, sir.
(*He readjusts his earphones and turns to his dials again.* BRACKETT, *unsatisfied by this, pokes the* ENLISTED MAN *again. The* ENLISTED MAN *winces, then patiently takes the earphones from his ears*)

BRACKETT Sounded to me like someone trying to send a message . . . sounded like code.

ENLISTED MAN   That was not code, sir. That sound you just heard was the contraction of the tin roof. It's the metal, cooling off at night.

BRACKETT   Oh.

ENLISTED MAN   Sir, if you'd like to go back to your office, I'll let you know as soon as . . .

BRACKETT   No, no, I'll stay right here. I don't want to add to your problems.

ENLISTED MAN (*He turns back to his dials*)   Yes, sir.
   (BRACKETT *impatiently looks at his watch and compares it with the watch on the* ENLISTED MAN'S *desk. He talks to the* ENLISTED MAN *who cannot hear him*)

BRACKETT   We ought to be getting a message now. We ought to be getting a message, that's all. They'd have time to land and establish some sort of an observation post by now, don't you think so? (*He realizes that the* ENLISTED MAN *cannot hear*) Oh.
   (*He sits back in a position of listening.* HARBISON *enters. He is very stern, more upset than we have ever seen him*)

HARBISON   Captain Brackett?

BRACKETT   Yeah, what is it? What is it? Don't interrupt me now, Bill. I'm very busy.

HARBISON   It's about this Seabee out here, sir, Billis! Commander Perkins over at Operations estimates that Billis' act this morning cost the Navy over six hundred thousand dollars!

BRACKETT   Six hundred— By God, I'm going to chew that guy's—send him in here!

HARBISON   Yes, sir.
   (*He exits.* BRACKETT *goes over and taps the* ENLISTED MAN *on the shoulder. The* ENLISTED MAN *removes earphones*)

BRACKETT   Let me know the moment you get any word. No matter what I'm doing, you just break right in.

ENLISTED MAN   Yes, sir.
   (*He goes back to his work.* BRACKETT *paces another second and then* BILLIS *enters, wary, on guard; his face is flaming red, his nose is a white triangle, covered with zinc-oxide.*

He wears an undershirt. His arms are red, except for two patches of zinc-oxide on his shoulders. He is followed by LIEUTENANT BUS ADAMS *and* COMMANDER HARBISON, *who closes the door*)

HARBISON (*Pushing* BILLIS *in*) Get in there! Captain Brackett, this is Lieutenant Bus Adams, who flew the mission.

BRACKETT H'y'a, Adams.

ADAMS Captain.
   (BRACKETT *beckons* BILLIS *to him.* BILLIS *walks over to him slowly, not knowing what may hit him*)

BRACKETT One man like you in an outfit is like a rotten apple in a barrel. Just what did you feel like—sitting down there all day long in that rubber boat in the middle of Empress Augusta Bay with the whole damn Navy Air Force trying to rescue you? And how the hell can you fall out of a PBY anyway?

BILLIS Well, sir, the Jap anti-aircraft busted a hole in the side of the plane and—I fell through . . . the wind just sucked me out.

BRACKETT So I'm to understand that you deliberately hid in the baggage compartment of a plane that you knew was taking off on a very dangerous mission. You had sand enough to do that all right. And then the moment an anti-aircraft gun hit the plane you fell out. The wind just sucked you out . . . you and your little parachute! I don't think you fell out, Billis, I think you jumped out. Which did you do?

BILLIS Well, sir . . . er . . . it was sort of half and half . . . if you get the picture.

BRACKETT This is one of the most humiliating things that ever happened to me. Adams, when did you discover he was on the plane?

ADAMS Well, sir, we'd been out about an hour—it was still dark, I know. Well, we were flying across Marie Louise. The Jap anti-aircraft spotted us and made that hit. That's when Luther . . . er . . . this fellow here . . . that's when he . . . left the ship. I just circled once . . . time enough to drop him a rubber boat. Some New Zealanders in P-40s spotted him though and kept circling around him while I flew across the island and landed alongside the sub, let Joe and the Frenchman off. By the time I got back to the other side of the island, our Navy planes were flying around in the air above this guy like a thick swarm of bees. (*He turns to grin at* HARBISON, *who gives him no returning grin. He clears his throat and turns back to* BRACKETT) They kept the Jap guns occupied while I slipped down and scooped him off the rubber boat. You'd have thought this guy was a ninety-million-dollar cruiser they were out to protect. There must have been fifty-five or sixty planes.

BILLIS   Sixty-two.

BRACKETT   You're not far off, Adams. Harbison tells me this thing cost the Navy about six hundred thousand dollars.

BILLIS (*His face lighting up*)   Six hundred thous . . . !

BRACKETT   What the hell are you so happy about?

BILLIS   I was just thinking about my uncle. (*To* ADAMS) Remember my uncle I was telling you about? He used to tell my old man I'd never be worth a dime! Him and his lousy slot machines. . . . Can you imagine a guy . . .
    (*He catches sight of* HARBISON'S *scowl and shuts up quickly*)

BRACKETT   Why the hell did you do this anyway, Billis? What would make a man do a thing like this?

BILLIS   Well, sir, a fellow has to keep moving. You know . . . you get kind of held down. If you're itching to take a trip to pick up a few souvenirs, you got to kind of horn in . . . if you get the picture.

BRACKETT   How did you know about it?

BILLIS   I didn't know about it, exactly. It's just when I heard Lieutenant Cable talking to that fellow de Becque, right away I know something's in the air. A project. That's what I like, Captain. Projects. Don't you?

HARBISON   Billis, you've broken every regulation in the book. And, by God, Captain Brackett and I are going to throw it at you.

ADAMS   Sir. May I barge in? My co-pilot watched this whole thing, you know, and he thinks that this fellow Billis down there in the rubber boat with all those planes over him caused a kind of diversionary action. While all those Japs were busy shooting at the planes and at Billis on the other side of the island, that sub was sliding into that little cove and depositing the Frenchman and Joe Cable in behind those rocks.

BRACKETT   What the hell do you want me to do? Give this guy a Bronze Star?

BILLIS   I don't want any Bronze Star, Captain. But I could use a little freedom. A little room to swing around in . . . if you know what I mean. If you get the picture.

BRACKETT   Get out of here. Get the hell out of here!
    (*Moving up after* BILLIS. BILLIS *flees through the door*)

HARBISON   I'd have thrown him in the brig. And I will too, if I get the ghost of a chance.
    (*Suddenly, the* RADIO OPERATOR *becomes very excited and waves his arm at* CAPTAIN BRACKETT. *We begin to hear squeaks and static from the loudspeaker and through it we hear* EMILE DE BECQUE'S *voice. Everyone on the stage turns. All eyes and ears are focused on the loudspeaker*)

EMILE'S VOICE   —And so we are here. This is our first chance to send news to you. We have made contact with former friends of mine. We have set up quarters in a mango tree—no room but a lovely view. . . . First the weather: rain clouds over Bougainville, The Treasuries, Choiseul and New Georgia. We expect rain in this region from nine o'clock to two o'clock. Pardon? Oh—my friend Joe corrects me. Oh—nine hundred to fourteen hundred. And now, our military expert, Joe.

CABLE'S VOICE   All you Navy, Marine and Army Pilots write this down. (ADAMS *whips out his notebook and writes it as* CABLE *speaks*) Surface craft—nineteen troop barges headed down the bottle neck; speed about eleven knots. Ought to pass Banika at about twenty hundred tonight, escorted by heavy warships. (BRACKETT *and* HARBISON *smile triumphantly*) There ought to be some way to knock off a few of these.
    (CABLE'S *voice continues under the following speeches*)

ADAMS   Oh, boy!
    (*He goes to door*)

HARBISON   Where you going?

ADAMS   Don't want to miss that take off. We'll be going out in waves tonight—waves—

(*He exits quickly.* BRACKETT *sits down on wastebasket and opens another Coke*)

BRACKETT   Sit down, Bill. (HARBISON *sits, listening intently.* BRACKETT *hands him a Coca-Cola.* HARBISON *takes it*) Here.

HARBISON   Thanks.

BRACKETT   You know what I like, Bill? Projects—don't you? (*Lights start to fade*)

CABLE'S VOICE (*Which has been continuing over above dialogue*)   As for aircraft, there is little indication of activity at the moment. But twenty-two bombers—Bettys—went by at 0600, headed southwest. There was fighter escort, not heavy . . . They should reach—
   (*The lights are now off the scene, but another part of the stage is lighted, revealing a group of pilots around a radio set, being briefed by an* OPERATIONS OFFICER)

ACT TWO | Scene Seven

OPERATIONS OFFICER   Listen carefully.

EMILE'S VOICE   Ceiling today unlimited. Thirty-three fighters —Zeros—have moved in from Bougainville. Their course is approximately 23 degrees— Undoubtedly, heavy bombers will follow.

OFFICER (*To pilots who are writing*)   Got that?
   (*Lights out. Light hits another group*)

NAVY PILOT (*To a group of officers*)   Well, gentlemen, here's the hot tip for today. Joe and the Frenchman have sighted twenty surface craft heading southeast from Vella Lavella. Christmas is just two weeks away. Let's give those two characters a present—a beautiful view of no ships coming back

AN OFFICER Okay, that's all right with me.
(*They exit. Lights fade off and return to center of stage, revealing*)

ACT TWO | Scene Eight

The Radio Shack again.
    BRACKETT *is pacing up and down.* HARBISON *is standing near the door, a pleading expression on his face.*

HARBISON Sir, you just have to tell her something some time. She hasn't seen him for two weeks. She might as well know it now.

BRACKETT Okay. Send her in. Send her in. I always have to do the tough jobs.
    (HARBISON *exits. A second later,* NELLIE *enters, followed by* HARBISON. *She goes to* BRACKETT *and immediately plunges into the subject closest to her heart. Her speech is unplanned. She knows she has no right to ask her question, but she must have an answer*)

NELLIE Captain Brackett, I know this isn't regular. . . . It's about Emile de Becque. I went to his house a week ago to . . . You know how people have arguments and then days later you think of a good answer. . . . Well, I went to his house, and he wasn't there. I even asked the children . . . he has two little children . . . and they didn't seem to know where he'd gone. At least, I think that's what they said—they only speak French. And then tonight while I was on duty in the ward—we have a lot of fighter pilots over there, the boys who knocked out that convoy yesterday—you know how fighter pilots talk—about "Immelmanns" and "wingovers" and things. I never listen usually but they kept talking about a

Frenchman—the Frenchman said this, and the Frenchman said that . . . and I was wondering if this Frenchman they were talking about could be—*my* Frenchman.
(*Pause*)

BRACKETT   Yes, Miss Forbush, it is. I couldn't tell you before but . . . As a matter of fact, if you wait here a few minutes, you can hear his voice.

NELLIE   His voice? Where is he?

BRACKETT   With Lieutenant Cable behind enemy lines.

NELLIE   Behind . . . !
(*The* RADIO OPERATOR *snaps his fingers. All heads turn up toward the loudspeaker. They listen to* EMILE'S *voice on the radio*)

EMILE'S VOICE   Hello. Hello, my friends and allies. My message today must be brief . . . and sad. Lieutenant Cable, my friend, Joe, died last night. He died from wounds he received three days ago. I will never know a finer man. I wish he could have told you the good news. The Japanese are pulling out and there is great confusion. Our guess is that the Japs will try to evacuate troops from Cape Esperance tonight. You may not hear from us for several days. We must move again. Two planes are overhead. They are looking for us, we think. We believe that . . . (*His speech is interrupted. There is the sound of a plane motor.* EMILE'S *voice is heard shouting excitedly "off mike"*) What? . . . What? (*"In mike"*) Good-bye!
(*There is a moment's silence. The* RADIO OPERATOR *works the dials*)

BRACKETT   Is that all? Is that all? Can't you get them back?

RADIO OPERATOR   No, sir. They're cut off.

NELLIE   (*Tears in her eyes*)   Poor Joe. Poor little Joe Cable. (*She grabs* BRACKETT *and holds tightly to his arms*) Captain Brackett . . . Do you think there's a chance I'll ever see Emile de Becque again? If you don't think so, will you tell me?

BRACKETT   There's a chance . . . of course there's a chance.

NELLIE   (*Turning to* HARBISON)   I didn't know he was going

BRACKETT   Of course not. How could he tell you he was going? Now don't blame Emile de Becque. He's okay . . . he's a wonderful guy!
   (NELLIE *tries to answer, swallows hard, and can make only an inarticulate sound of assent*)

NELLIE   Uh-huh!
   (*She exits quickly*)

BRACKETT   He has got a chance, hasn't he, Bill?

HARBISON (*Hoarsely*)   Of course. There's always a chance!

BRACKETT   Come on! Let's get out of here!
   (*Both exit, as the shack recedes upstage and a group of officers and nurses enter downstage to walk across the company street*)

ACT TWO | Scene Nine

The officers and nurses are singing the refrain of "I'm in Love with a Wonderful Guy."
   NELLIE *walks on from the opposite side, looking straight ahead of her, a set expression on her face.*

NURSE (*As they pass her*)   Coming to the dance, Nellie?
   (NELLIE *just shakes her head and passes them*)

A LIEUTENANT   What's the matter with her?
   (*Three girls in a trio and in a spirit of kidding* NELLIE, *sing back over their shoulders at her,* "She's in love, she's in love, she's in love, she's in love with a wonderful guy." *Even before they have reached the end of this, the lights have started to dim. Now the lights come up in back, revealing*)

ACT TWO | Scene Ten

The Beach.
    NELLIE *walks on. The strain of "I'm in love, I'm in love, I'm in love" ringing in her ears and cutting deeply into her heart.* NELLIE *walks up and looks over the sea.*
    Pause. Then she speaks softly.

NELLIE   Come back so I can tell you something. I know what counts now. You. All those other things—the woman you had before—her color . . . (*She laughs bitterly*) What piffle! What a pinhead I was! Come back so I can tell you. Oh, my God, don't die until I can tell you! All that matters is you and I being together. That's all! Just together— The way we wanted it to be the first night we met! Remember? . . . Remember?
    (*She sings*)
Some enchanted evening
When you find your true love,
When you feel him call you
Across a crowded room—
Then fly to his side,
And make him your own,
Or all through your life you may dream all alone . . .
    (*Music continues. She speaks*)
Don't die, Emile.
    (*As the last line of the refrain is played,* BLOODY MARY *walks on and addresses* NELLIE, *timidly*)

MARY   Miss Nurse! (NELLIE, *shocked by the sudden sound of an intruding voice, turns and emits a startled scream*) Please, please, Miss Nurse?

NELLIE   Who are you? What do you want?

MARY   Where is Lootellan Cable?

NELLIE   Who *are* you?

MARY   I am mother of Liat.

NELLIE   Who?

MARY   Liat. She won't marry no one but Lootellan Cable.
(LIAT *walks on slowly.* MARY *moves her forward and shows
her to* NELLIE. NELLIE *looks at this girl and realizes who
she is*)

NELLIE   Oh. (NELLIE *rushes to her impulsively and embraces
her*) Oh, my darling!
(*As she clasps* LIAT *in her arms, the noises of the company street burst harshly as the curtains close and we are
plunged abruptly into*)

ACT TWO | Scene Eleven

*The company street is crowded with members of all Forces,
ready to embark. There are sounds of truck convoys passing. Over the loudspeaker the following is heard:*

VOICE ON LOUDSPEAKER   All right, hear this. All those outfits
that are waiting for loading, please keep in position. We'll
get to you as soon as your boat is ready for you.
(BILLIS, STEWPOT *and the* PROFESSOR *enter*)

STEWPOT   Hey, Billis, let's head back, huh? Our gang's about
a mile back down the beach. Suppose they call our names?

PROFESSOR   Yeah! They may be ready for us to go aboard.

BILLIS   They won't be ready for hours yet . . . this is the
Navy. (*He turns and regards the scene offstage*) Eager
Beavers! Look at that beach . . . swarmin' with 10,000 guys

—all jerks! (*Picking out a likely "jerk"*) Hey, are you a Marine?

MARINE (*Turning*)   Yeah!

BILLIS   Are you booked on one of those LCT's?

MARINE   I guess so, why?

BILLIS   They'll shake the belly off you, you know. (*He takes out a small package*) Five bucks and you can have it.

MARINE   What is it?

BILLIS   Seasick remedy. You'll be needing it.

MARINE   Aw, knock off! (*Pulls out a handful of packages from his pocket*) That stuff's issued. We all got it. Who are you tryin' to fool?

BILLIS (*Turning to* STEWPOT)   These Marines are getting smarter every day.

OFFICER (*Passing through*)   All right, all right. Stay with your own unit. (*To a nurse in combat uniform*) Ensign, you too. For Heaven's sake, don't get spread out over here. We're trying to get this thing organized as quickly as possible, so for God's sake, stay with your outfit! (*To* BILLIS) Say, Seabee . . . you belong down the beach.

BILLIS (*Saluting officer*)   Excuse me, sir, could you tell me where we could find Captain Brackett?

OFFICER   He's up at the head of the company street. He'll be along any minute now.

BILLIS (*Saluting*)   Thank you, sir. That's all, sir.
(*The* OFFICER, *having started off, stops in his tracks, stunned and rocked off his balance by being thus "dismissed" by* BILLIS. *Oh, well—too many important things to be done right now! He goes on his way, shouting*)

OFFICER   All right! Stay in line! How many times have I told you . . .
(*He is off. A* NURSE *comes by*)

BILLIS   Hello, Miss McGregor. You nurses going too?

NURSE   Only a few of us. We're going to fly back some wounded.

BILLIS Is Miss Forbush going with you?

NURSE I don't know. She may be staying here with the hospital.
   (*She starts to leave*)

BILLIS Oh, Miss McGregor . . . you don't get airsick, do you? I was thinking maybe if you got three bucks handy, you might be able to use this little package I got here.

NURSE (*Looking down at it*) Oh, that stuff's no good . . . we gave that up last month.

BILLIS (*Turning to* STEWPOT) That's a female jerk! (BRACK-ETT *and* HARBISON *enter*) I beg pardon, sir . . . could I speak to you a minute?

BRACKETT (*Peering through the semi-darkness*) Who's that?

BILLIS Billis, sir . . . Luther Billis.

BRACKETT Oh. What do you want, Billis? We're moving out pretty soon.

BILLIS Yes, sir, I know. I'd like to do something for Miss Forbush, sir. Stewpot and the Professor and me was wondering if anything is being done about rescuing the Frenchman off that island. We hereby volunteer for such a project . . . a triple diversionary activity, like I done to get 'em on there. You could drop us in three rubber boats on three different sides of the island . . . confuse the hell out of the Japs. . . . Get the picture?

BRACKETT It's very fine of you, Billis . . . but you're too late for diversionary activity. That started this morning before the sun came up. Operation Alligator got under way. Landings were made on fourteen Japanese-held islands.

BILLIS I think that's very unfair, sir. The first thing they should have done was try to rescue that Frenchman.

HARBISON The Admiral agrees with you, Billis. Marie Louise was the first island they hit.

BILLIS Did they get him? Is he alive?

BRACKETT We don't know. Lieutenant Bus Adams flew up there to find out. He hasn't come back. But if the French-man's dead, it *is* unfair. It's too damned bad if a part of this

huge operation couldn't have saved one of the two guys who
made it all possible.

HARBISON (*Gazing off*)   Look at the beach . . . far as you
can see . . . men waiting to board ships. The whole picture
of the South Pacific has changed. We're going the other way.

OFFICER   Captain Brackett, sir . . . the launch is ready to
take you to your ship.

BILLIS   You got a ship, sir?

BRACKETT   Yes, Harbison and I've got a ship. I'm no longer
a lousy Island Commander. Come on, Bill.

BILLIS   Good-bye, Commander Harbison.

HARBISON   Good-bye, Billis. Oh, by the way, I never did get
you in the brig . . . did I?

BILLIS (*Laughing almost too heartily at his triumph*)   No!
Ha-ha.

HARBISON   Oh, I forgot!

BILLIS (*Still laughing*)   Forgot what, sir?

HARBISON   Your unit'll be on our ship. I'll be seeing all of
you.
  (*Dismay from* BILLIS, STEWPOT *and the* PROFESSOR)

BRACKETT   Come on, Bill.
  (BRACKETT *and* HARBISON *exit*)

OFFICER (*Entering*)   All right . . . let's start those trucks
moving out—all units on the company street. We're ready to
load you. All Nurses will board assigned planes—Seabees to
embark on Carrier 6. All Marines to board LCT's. Any
questions? MOVE OUT!
  (*The sound trucks roar. The music which has been playing
  under the scene mounts in volume. The men march off.
  Nurses in hospital uniforms stand waving to the men and
  the nurses in combat uniform who leave with them. Soon
  the groups are all dispersed and lights come up in back,
  revealing*)

ACT TWO | Scene Twelve

EMILE'S *terrace.*

It is late afternoon. Sunset—reddish light. The drone of planes can be heard. JEROME *stands on a table.* NELLIE *holds him.* NGANA *is beside her. All look off.*

NELLIE (*Pointing off*) The big ones are battleships and the little ones are destroyers—or cruisers— I never can tell the difference. (*She looks up in the air*) And what on earth are those?

JEROME P-40s.

NELLIE Oh, that's right. They're all moving out, you see, because, well . . . there's been a big change. They won't be around here much any more, just off and on, a few of us. Did you understand anything I said? Vous ne comprenez pas?

NGANA Oui, oui, nous comprenons.
   (JEROME *nods his head*)

JEROME Oui.

NELLIE Now, while I'm down at the hospital, you've got to promise me to mangez everything—everything that's put before you on the table—sur le tobler. Sur la tobler?

NGANA (*Smiling patiently*) Sur la table.

NELLIE (*She smiles, congratulating herself*) Now come back here, Jerome, and sit down. (*She starts to place the children at the table, on which a bowl of soup and some plates have been set. At this point,* BUS ADAMS *appears upstage—a weary figure. Behind him comes* EMILE *in dirt-stained uniform, helmet, paratroop boots and musette bag.* BUS *calls his attention to the planes droning above. Neither sees* NELLIE *or the children.* NELLIE *pushes the kids down, on the bench, as they playfully balk at being seated)* Ass—say—yay—voo. *(They sit.* EMILE *turns sharply at the sound of her voice)* Now you have to learn to mind me when I talk to you and be nice to me too. Because I love you very much. Now, *mangez.*

(EMILE'S *face lights up with grateful happiness.* BUS *knows it's time for him to shove off, and he does.* NELLIE *proceeds to ladle soup from the large bowl into three small bowls)*

JEROME *(His eyes twinkling mischievously)*   Chantez, Nellie.

NELLIE   I will not sing that song. You just want to laugh at my French accent. *(The kids put their spoons down—on strike)* All right, but you've got to help me.

NELLIE, NGANA AND JEROME
Dites moi
Pourquoi
     (NELLIE *is stuck. The children sing the next line without her)*
La vie est belle.

NELLIE *(Repeating, quickly, to catch up to them)*
La vie est belle.
     (Meanwhile EMILE *has crossed behind them.* NELLIE *is looking out front, not seeing him, trying to remember the lyrics, continues to sing with the children)*
Dites moi
Pourquoi . . .
     (She turns to the children)
Pourquoi what?
     (She sees EMILE)

EMILE *(Answering her, singing)*
La vie est gai!
     (NELLIE *gazes at him, hypnotized—her voice gone. The children rush to embrace him)*

EMILE, NGANA AND JEROME
Dites moi
Pourquoi,
Chère mad'moiselle—
     (EMILE *leans forward and sings straight at* NELLIE)

EMILE
Est-ce que

Parce que
Vous m'aimez—

> (*The music continues. The children drink their soup.* NELLIE *comes back to consciousness enough to realize that* EMILE *must be hungry. She leans over and hands him the large bowl of soup with an air of "nothing's-too-good-for-the-boss!" Then she passes him the soup ladle! But he doesn't use it. Instead he thrusts his hand forward.* NELLIE *clasps it. Looking into each other's eyes, they hold this position as the curtain falls*)

♡

The King and I

♥

BASED ON THE BOOK

ANNA AND THE KING OF SIAM

by Margaret Landon

The King and I *was first produced by Richard Rodgers and Oscar Hammerstein, II, on March 29, 1951, at the St. James Theatre, New York City, with the following cast:*

CAPTAIN ORTON	Charles Francis
LOUIS LEONOWENS	Sandy Kennedy
ANNA LEONOWENS	Gertrude Lawrence
THE INTERPRETER	Leonard Graves
THE KRALAHOME	John Juliano
THE KING	Yul Brynner
PHRA ALACK	Len Mence
TUPTIM	Doretta Morrow
LADY THIANG	Dorothy Sarnoff
PRINCE CHULALONGKORN	Johnny Stewart
PRINCESS YING YAOWALAK	Baayork Lee
LUN THA	Larry Douglas
SIR EDWARD RAMSAY	Robin Craven

PRINCESSES AND PRINCES: Crisanta Cornejo, Andrea Del Rosario, Carol Percy, Barbara Luna, Nora Baez, Corrine St. Denis, Bunny Warner, Rodolfo Cornejo, Robert Cortazal, Thomas Griffin, Alfonso Maribo, James Maribo, Orlando Rodriguez

THE ROYAL DANCERS: Jamie Bauer, Lee Becker, Mary Burr, Gemze DeLappe, Shellie Farrell, Marilyn Gennaro, Evelyn Giles, Ina Kurland, Nancy Lynch, Michiko, Helen Murielle, Prue Ward, Dusty Worrall and Yuriko

WIVES: Stephanie Augustine, Marcia James, Ruth Korda, Suzanne Lake, Carolyn Maye, Helen Merritt, Phyllis Wilcox

AMAZONS: Geraldine Hamburg, Maribel Hammer, Norma Larkin, Miriam Lawrence

PRIESTS: Duane Camp, Joseph Caruso, Leonard Graves, Jack Matthew, Ed Preston

SLAVES: Doria Avila, Otis Bigelow, Beau Cunningham, Tommy Gomez

DIRECTED BY John van Druten
CHOREOGRAPHY BY Jerome Robbins
SETTINGS AND LIGHTING BY Jo Mielziner
COSTUMES DESIGNED BY Irene Sharaff
ORCHESTRATIONS BY *Robert Russell Bennett*
MUSICAL DIRECTOR, Frederick Dvonch

The play is divided into two acts. The action takes place in and around the King's palace, Bangkok, Siam.

TIME: *Early eighteen sixties.*

ACT ONE | Scene One

Deck of the Chow Phya, a ship that has sailed from Singapore, up the Gulf of Siam, and is now making its way slowly along the winding river that approaches Bangkok.
CAPTAIN ORTON, a middle-aged Englishman, is leaning on the binnacle, smoking a pipe. The deck is crowded with boxes and crates of furniture.
As soon as the curtain is up LOUIS runs on.

ORTON   Hello, laddy.

LOUIS   (*Mounting the steps of the gangway, to look out on the river*)   How near are we to Bangkok, Captain?

ORTON   See that cluster of lights jutting out into the river? That's it. That's Bangkok.

LOUIS   (*Seeing the crates and boxes*)   Oh, look! All our boxes!

ORTON   Aye, and a fair lot they are.

LOUIS   We packed everything we had in our Singapore house —furniture and everything.

ANNA   (*Offstage*)   Louis! Where are you?

LOUIS   (*Running to meet her as she enters*)   Mother! Mother, look!   There's Bangkok! Do you see, Mother? That cluster of lights that sticks out into the river. You see, Mother? That's Bangkok!

ANNA   (*Laughing*)   I see, Louis. I see them. It's exciting, isn't it?

LOUIS   Will the King of Siam come down to the dock to meet us?

ANNA   The King himself? I don't think so. Kings don't as a rule.

ORTON (*With earnest concern*) I wonder if you know what you're facing, Ma'am—an Englishwoman here in the East . . .

LOUIS (*Running down right, looking out toward the audience, and pointing over the imaginary rail*) Look, Mother! Look at that boat! Look at the dragon's head in the bow, and all the men standing up, carrying torches.

ORTON That's the Royal Barge!

LOUIS Do you suppose that's the King, the man sitting under the gold canopy?

ORTON That's the Kralahome. (*Explaining to* ANNA) Sort of "Prime Minister"—the King's right-hand man, you might say.

ANNA Do you suppose he's coming out to meet us?

ORTON No doubt of it. They'll be waiting till we pass them. Then they'll come around our stern. (*He starts to go, then turns back*) Ma'am . . . if I might be allowed to offer you a word of warning . . .

ANNA What is it, Captain?

ORTON (*Indicating the barge*) That man has power, and he can use it *for* you or *against* you.

ANNA (*Laughing*) Oh.

ORTON I think you should know.
    (*He goes off. A sound comes from the river, a snarling sound in rhythm, oarsmen marking the cadence of their stroke*)

LOUIS Look, Mother! They're closer! (*With amazement, as he gets a better view*) Mother! The Prime Minister is naked!

ANNA Hush, Louis, that's not a nice word. He's not naked. (*She looks again*) Well, he's half naked.

LOUIS They all look rather horrible, don't they, Mother? (*He draws a little closer to her*) Father would not have liked us to be afraid, would he?

ANNA No, Louis. Father would not have liked us to be afraid.

LOUIS Mother, does anything ever frighten you?

ANNA   Sometimes.

LOUIS   What do you do?

ANNA   I whistle.

LOUIS   Oh, that's why you whistle!

ANNA   (*Laughing*)   Yes, that's why I whistle . . . (*She sings*)
Whenever I feel afraid
I hold my head erect
And whistle a happy tune,
So no one will suspect
    I'm afraid.

While shivering in my shoes
I strike a careless pose
And whistle a happy tune,
And no one ever knows
    I'm afraid.

The result of this deception
Is very strange to tell,
For when I fool the people I fear
I fool myself as well!

I whistle a happy tune,
And ev'ry single time
The happiness in the tune
Convinces me that I'm
    Not afraid.

Make believe you're brave
And the trick will take you far;
You may be as brave
As you make believe you are.
    (LOUIS *whistles this strain, then they both sing*)

ANNA AND LOUIS
You may be as brave
As you make believe you are.

LOUIS   (*After a moment's reflection*)   I think that's a very good idea, Mother. A *very* good idea.

ANNA   It *is* a good idea, isn't it?

LOUIS   I don't think I shall ever be afraid again.

ANNA   Good!
(LOUIS *resumes singing the refrain.* ANNA *joins in. They do
not see four Siamese slaves, naked from the waist up, with
knives in their belts, come over the rail, down the gangway, and line up, center. As they are happily singing the
last eight measures* ANNA *turns, sees the formidable-looking
Siamese, and gasps in terror.* LOUIS *sees them, too, and
clutches his mother's arm. Then they face the men and
whistle—as casually as they can*)

ORTON (*Coming on hurriedly, followed by two deckhands*)
Clear that away! (*The deckhands remove a trunk*) Ma'am, I
wouldn't whistle. He might think it disrespectful.

ANNA   Oh, was I whistling? Sorry, I didn't realize.
(*The* INTERPRETER *comes over the rail and down the steps*)

INTERPRETER (*Rather insolently, to* ANNA)   Good evening,
sir. Welcome to Siam.
(*He turns his back on her and prostrates himself, toad-
like, as do the four slaves*)

LOUIS   He called you sir!

ANNA   Hush, dear! Hush!
(*The* KRALAHOME *comes over the rail slowly and with
terrifying majesty. He is naked from the waist up, except
for several necklaces. Now he addresses the* INTERPRETER
in Siamese)

(AT THIS POINT, AND THROUGHOUT THE PLAY, THE SIAMESE
LANGUAGE WILL BE REPRESENTED BY CERTAIN SOUNDS
MADE IN THE ORCHESTRA. SIAMESE WORDS WILL NEVER BE
LITERALLY PRONOUNCED. MUSIC WILL SYMBOLIZE THEM)

INTERPRETER (*Turning to* ANNA, *still crouching like a toad,
relaying the* KRALAHOME'S *questions*)   Sir, His Excellency
wishes to know—are you lady who will be schoolmistress of
royal children?

ANNA (*In a small, frightened voice*)   Yes.

INTERPRETER   Have you friends in Bangkok?

ANNA   I know no one in Bangkok at all.
(*The* INTERPRETER *delivers her answers and the* KRALA-
HOME *directs him to ask further questions*)

INTERPRETER   Are you married, sir?

ANNA   I am a widow.

INTERPRETER   What manner of man your deceased husband?

ANNA   My husband was an officer of Her Majesty's Army in
. . . (*She suddenly stiffens*) Tell your master his business
with me is in my capacity of schoolteacher to the royal children. He has no right to pry into my personal affairs. (ORTON
tries to signal a warning, but she turns to him impatiently)
Well, he hasn't, Captain Orton!
   (*The* INTERPRETER *gives the* KRALAHOME *her message. The*
   KRALAHOME *gives the* INTERPRETER *a kick on the shoulder*
   which sends him sprawling out of the way)

LOUIS (*To* ANNA, *pointing toward the* KRALAHOME)   I don't
like that man!

KRALAHOME   In foreign country is best you like everyone—
until you leave.

ANNA (*Startled*)   Your Excellency, I had no idea you spoke
English.

KRALAHOME   It is not necessary for you to know everything
at once. You come with me now. Your boxes are carried to
palace—later.

ANNA   No. Not to the palace. I am not living at the palace.

KRALAHOME   Who say?

ANNA   The King say . . . Says! The King has promised me
twenty pounds a month and a house of my own.

KRALAHOME   King do not always remember what he promise.
If I tell him he break his promise, I will make anger in him.
I think it is better I make anger in him about larger matters.

ANNA   But all I want is ten minutes' audience with him.

KRALAHOME   King very busy now. New Year's celebrations
just finishing. Fireworks every night. Cremation of late Queen
just starting.

ANNA   Oh. You have lost your Queen. I am so sorry. When
did she die?

KRALAHOME   Four years ago . . . With cremation ceremony
comes also fireworks

ANNA   And what am I to do in the meantime?

KRALAHOME   In the meantime you wait—in palace.

ANNA (*Firmly*)   Your Excellency, I will *teach* in the palace, but I must have a house of my own—where I can go at the end of the day when my duties are over.

KRALAHOME   What you wish to do in evening that cannot be done in palace?

ANNA   How dare you! (*Controlling herself*) I'm sorry, Your Excellency, but you don't understand. I came here to work. I must support myself and my young son. And I shall take nothing less than what I have been promised.

KRALAHOME   You will tell King this?

ANNA   I will tell King this.
   (*The faint suggestion of a smile curls the corner of the* KRALAHOME'S *mouth*)

KRALAHOME   It will be very interesting meeting . . . You come now? (ANNA *does not answer*) You come now, or you can stay on boat. I do not care! (*He turns toward gangway and starts to go*)

ORTON (*Going to* ANNA *sympathetically*)   If you wish to stay on my ship and return to Singapore, Ma'am . . .

ANNA   No, thank you, Captain Orton. (*Calling to the* KRALA-HOME) Your Excellency— (*The* KRALAHOME *stops and turns*) I will go with you. I have made a bargain, and I shall live up to my part of it. But I expect a bargain to be kept on both sides. I shall go with you, Your Excellency.

KRALAHOME   To the palace?

ANNA (*Grimly, after a pause*)   For the time being. (*The* KRALAHOME *smiles and exits over the ship's rail.* ANNA *turns to* ORTON) Good-bye, Captain Orton, and thank you very much for everything. (*Turning to* LOUIS, *prompting him*) Louis!

LOUIS (*Shaking hands*)   Good-bye, Captain.

ORTON   Good-bye, laddy.
   (*As they turn from the captain,* ANNA *and* LOUIS *are confronted by the* INTERPRETER *and the slaves standing in a*

*stern line, their arms folded, their faces glowering in a most
unfriendly manner.* ANNA *and* LOUIS *pause, then raise their
chins and whistle "a happy tune" as they walk by the men
and start to climb the gangway*)

Intermediate Scene

A Palace corridor.

 *Several court dancers have their costumes adjusted and
last-minute touches added to their faces by make-up ex-
perts. Excitement, haste and anxiety pervade the scene. An
attendant enters and claps his hands. The dancers bustle off
promptly, their attendants making their exit on the opposite
side.*

ACT ONE | Scene Two

The KING'S *study in the royal palace.*

 As the curtain rises the KING *is seated cross-legged on a
low table, dictating letters to* PHRA ALACK, *his secretary, and
paying only scant attention to a group of girl dancers. At
length he throws the last letter at the secretary, rises and
snaps his fingers. The secretary and the dancers retire
quickly. The* KING *beckons to someone offstage. The*
KRALAHOME *enters.*

KRALAHOME Your Majesty . . .

KING Well, well, well?

KRALAHOME I have been meaning to speak to you about English schoolteacher. She is waiting to see you.

KING She is in Siam? How long?

KRALAHOME Two weeks, three weeks. She has needed disciplining, Your Majesty. She objects to living in palace. Talks about house she say you promise her.

KING I do not recollect such promise. Tell her I will see her. I will see her in a moment. (*Over the* KRALAHOME'S *shoulder, the* KING *sees* LUN THA *enter, preceded by a female palace attendant*) Who? Who? Who?

KRALAHOME Your Majesty, this is Lun Tha, emissary from court of Burma.

KING Ah! You are here for copying of famous Bangkok temple. (*To* KRALAHOME) I have give permission.

KRALAHOME (*As* TUPTIM *is carried on, on a palanquin, by four Amazons*) He brings you present from Prince of Burma.

KING Am I to trust a ruler of Burma? Am I to trust this present they send me, or is she a spy?

TUPTIM (*Rising from palanquin*) I am not a spy . . . My name is Tuptim. You are pleased that I speak English? My name is Tuptim.
(*The* KING *looks at her appraisingly. The* KRALAHOME *signals for her to turn around. She does so. The* KING *walks around her slowly, darts a brief, enigmatic look at the* KRALAHOME, *and walks off*)

KRALAHOME King is pleased with you. He likes you.
(*He dismisses* LUN THA *and leaves. Before going out,* LUN THA *exchanges a worried, helpless look with* TUPTIM. TUPTIM *turns and looks toward where the* KING *made his exit, bitterness and hatred in her eyes*)

TUPTIM The King is pleased! (*She sings:*)
He is pleased with me!
My lord and master
Declares he's pleased with me—
What does he mean?
What does he know of me,
This lord and master?

When he has looked at me
What has he seen?

> Something young,
> Soft and slim,
> Painted cheek,
> Tap'ring limb,
> Smiling lips
> All for him,
> Eyes that shine
> Just for him—
> So he thinks . . .
> Just for him!

Though the man may be
My lord and master,
Though he may study me
As hard as he can,
The smile beneath my smile
He'll never see.
He'll never know I love
Another man,
He'll never know
I love another man!

(*The* KING *enters.* TUPTIM *immediately resumes her humble and obedient attitude*)   Your Majesty wishes me to leave?

KING   I will tell you when I wish you to leave.

KRALAHOME (*Entering, ushering in* ANNA, *who is followed by two Amazons*)   Schoolteacher. (ANNA *comes before the* KING *and curtseys*) Madame Leonowens.

KING   You are schoolteacher?

ANNA   Yes, Your Majesty, I am schoolteacher. When can I start my work?

KING   You can start when I tell you to start.

ANNA   There is one matter we have to settle, Your Majesty . . .

KING (*Interrupting her*)   You are part of general plan I have for bringing to Siam what is good in Western culture. Already I have bring printing press here—for printing.

ANNA   Yes, I know, Your Majesty.

KING   How you know?

ANNA   Before I signed our agreement, I found out all I could about Your Majesty's ambitions for Siam.

KING   Ha! This is scientific. (*He squints at her thoughtfully*) You are pleased with your apartments in palace?

ANNA   They . . . are quite comfortable, Your Majesty. (*Exchanging a look with the* KRALAHOME) For the time being. But my young son and I have found it rather . . . confining . . . with Amazons guarding the doors and not permitting us to leave.

KING   Strangers cannot be allowed to roam around palace before presentment to King. You could look out of windows.

ANNA   Yes, Your Majesty, we have done that. We have seen New Year celebrations, royal cremation ceremonies, etcetera, etcetera.

KING   What is this "etcetera"?

ANNA   According to the dictionary, it means "and the rest," Your Majesty. All the things you have been doing while we were waiting. The fireworks—

KING   Best fireworks I ever see at funeral. How you like my acrobats?

ANNA   Splendid, Your Majesty. Best acrobats I have ever seen at funeral.

KING (*Pleased*)   Ha! (*To* KRALAHOME) Have children prepare for presentation to schoolteacher.

ANNA   How many children have you, Your Majesty?

KING   I have only sixty-seven altogether. I begin very late. But you shall not teach all of them. You shall teach only children of mothers who are in favor of King . . . (LADY THIANG *has entered. She prostrates herself before the* KING) Ah! Lady Thiang. Madame Leonowens, this is Lady Thiang, head wife.
    (*She immediately and quite irrelevantly starts to sing*)

THIANG
There is a happy land, far, far away,
Where saints in glory stand, bright, bright as day.
(*Speaking*) In the beginning God created the heaven and the earth. (ANNA *looks puzzled*) Mis-son-ary.

ANNA   A missionary taught you English!

THIANG   Yes, sir. Mis-son-ary.

KING   Lady Thiang, you will help Madame Leonowens with her schoolteaching, and she in her turn shall teach you the better English. (THIANG *prostrates herself at the feet of the* KING, *to* ANNA'S *surprise and horror. The* KING *explains*) She is grateful to me for my kindness.

ANNA   I see. (*Getting back to the issue she is so anxious to settle*) Your Majesty, in our agreement, you . . .

KING   (*Talking across* ANNA)   You, Tuptim. You already speak well the English. (TUPTIM *rises. The* KING *turns to* ANNA, *pointing to* TUPTIM) She arrive today. She is present to me from Burma prince.

ANNA   (*Shocked*)   *She* is a present?

TUPTIM   Madame, you have English books I can read?

ANNA   Of course I have.

TUPTIM   I wish most to read book called "The Small House of Uncle Thomas." Is by American lady, Harriet Beecher Stowa.

KING   A woman has written a book?

ANNA   A very wonderful book, Your Majesty. All about slavery . . .

KING   Ha! President Lingkong against slavery, no? Me, too. Slavery very bad thing. (ANNA *looks significantly at the prostrate figure of* LADY THIANG. *The* KING *snaps his fingers and* LADY THIANG *rises. The* KING *paces thoughtfully, speaking half to himself, half to* ANNA) I think you will teach my wives too—those wives who are in favor.
   (*During the ensuing dialogue, small groups of the* KING'S *wives peek in through the entrances and retreat, as if curious to hear and see, but afraid of the* KING'S *mounting temper*)

ANNA   I shall be most happy to teach your wives, even though that was not part of our agreement. . . . Speaking of our agreement reminds me that there is one little matter, about my house . . .

KING   Also, I will allow you to help me in my foreign correspondence.

ANNA   Yes, Your Majesty. I don't think you understand about the house, Your Majesty. For the time being . . .

KING   (*Wheeling around suddenly*)   House? House? What is this about house?

ANNA   (*Startled, then recovering*)   I want my house! The house you promised me, Your Majesty.

KING   You shall live in palace. You teach in palace, you shall live in palace. If you do not live in palace, you do not teach, and you go—wherever you please. I do not care. You understand this?

ANNA   I understand, but, Your Majesty, if these are the only terms on which I . . .

KING   Enough! I have no more time to talk. Talk to other women, my women—my wives.
   (*He snaps his fingers at* TUPTIM, *who follows him obediently as he exits. As soon as the* KING *has left, the wives rush on from all sides, chattering excitedly. They surround* ANNA, *taking her gloves and her reticule, fingering her clothes. Two on the floor try to lift up her skirt*)

ANNA   For goodness' sake! What is the matter? What are they trying to do to me?

THIANG   They think you wear big skirt like that because you shaped like that.

ANNA   Well, I'm not!
   (*She lifts her hoop skirt, revealing pantalettes. Two wives address* LADY THIANG, *the orchestra, as usual, playing sounds to indicate the Siamese language*)

THIANG   They wish to know, sir, if you have children?

ANNA   (*Indicating his size*)   One little boy.

THIANG   (*Proudly*)   I have boy, too—Crown Prince Chowfa Chulalongkorn, heir to throne . . . (*An earnest pleading coming into her voice*) I would be happy if you would teach children.

ANNA   I would like to very much. I came all the way here from Singapore to do so, but I really cannot . . .

THIANG   You could be great help to all here, sir.

ANNA   Lady Thiang, why do you call me "sir"?

THIANG   Because you scientific. Not lowly, like woman.

ANNA   Do you *all* think women are more lowly than men? (THIANG *translates this to the wives, all of whom smile broadly and nod their heads, apparently quite happy with the idea of female inferiority.* ANNA'S *voice is indignant*) Well, I don't.

THIANG   Please, sir, do not tell King. Make King angry.

ANNA   King seems to be angry already. (*Thoughtfully*) That lovely girl. He said she was a present . . .

THIANG   From court of Burma. I think she love another man. If so, she will never see other man again.

ANNA   Poor child!

THIANG   Oh, no, sir! She is foolish child, to wish for another man when she has King.

ANNA   But you can't help wishing for a man, if he's the man you want.

THIANG   It is strange for schoolteacher to talk so—romantic.

ANNA (*Smiling*)   Romantic! I suppose I am. I was very much in love with my husband, Tom.

THIANG   Tom.
    (*She translates this to the wives, who repeat after her, "Tom."*)

ANNA   Once a woman has loved like that, she understands all other women who are in love . . . and she's on their side, even if she's . . . a schoolteacher. (*The wives again pronounce "Tom" as if fascinated by the sound*) Yes . . . Tom.
    (*She opens the locket around her neck and shows it to* LADY THIANG)

THIANG (*Looking at the picture*)   He was pretty in face.

ANNA   Oh, dear, yes. He was very pretty in face. (*She sings:*)
When I think of Tom
I think about a night
When the earth smelled of summer
And the sky was streaked with white,

And the soft mist of England
Was sleeping on a hill—
I remember this,
And I always will . . .

There are new lovers now on the same silent hill,
Looking on the same blue sea,
And I know Tom and I are a part of them all,
And they're all a part of Tom and me.
(*She is far away from them now, in another time, another place*)

Hello, young lovers, whoever you are,
I hope your troubles are few.
All my good wishes go with you tonight—
I've been in love like you.
Be brave, young lovers, and follow your star,
Be brave and faithful and true,
Cling very close to each other tonight—
I've been in love like you.
I know how it feels to have wings on your heels,
And to fly down a street in a trance.
You fly down a street on the chance that you'll meet,
And you meet—not really by chance.
Don't cry, young lovers, whatever you do,
Don't cry because I'm alone;
All of my memories are happy tonight,
I've had a love of my own,
I've had a love of my own, like yours—
I've had a love of my own.
(*Now there is a loud crash on a gong. The* KING *enters*)

KING   The children! The children! (*To* ANNA) They come for presentment to schoolteacher.

ANNA   But, Your Majesty, we have not solved my problem . . .

KING   Silence! You will stand here to meet royal children. (*He indicates a place for her*)

ANNA   (*Reluctantly accepting his order*)   Very well, Your Majesty.

KING   The Royal Princes and Princesses!
(*Now, to the strains of a patrol, the royal Siamese children*)

enter, one by one, each advancing first to the KING *and prostrating himself before his father, then rising, moving over to* ANNA, *and greeting her in the traditional manner by taking her two hands and pressing them to his forehead, after which he backs away across the stage, and takes his place with the wives and children who have previously entered. Each succeeding child enters at about the time that his predecessor has greeted* ANNA *and is backing across the stage. The twins enter together, and the* KING *holds up two fingers to* ANNA, *so that she is sure to observe that they are twins. There are other variations. One little girl goes straight to her father, her arms outstretched, but he sternly points to the floor. She prostrates herself in the formal manner and, very much abashed, goes on to* ANNA. *One little girl, who had been delegated to give* ANNA *a rose, forgets it the first time and has to run back to* ANNA, *disgraced by her absent-mindedness. The most impressive moment is the entrance of the Crown Prince,* CHULALONGKORN. *The music becomes loud and brave at this point. Then, toward the end of the patrol, the music becomes softer and ends with the smallest children coming on, the last child backing up and bowing with the others on the last beat of the music. Throughout this procession,* ANNA *has obviously fallen more and more in love with the children. She is deeply touched by their courtesy, their charm, their sweetness. After they have all bowed to her and the* KING, *she slowly moves to the center of the room. She looks back at the* KING, *who nods understandingly, and then slowly she starts to untie the ribbons of her bonnet. As she takes out the pin and lifts the bonnet off her head, one little child gasps an excited "ah," and the children with one accord all rush up to her and surround her. She leans over and hugs all those she can reach, and it is obvious that they are going to be fast friends as the curtain closes)*

ACT ONE | Scene Three

In the Palace grounds.
    A group of PRIESTS *chant as they walk by. From the other side the children enter singing "Home Sweet Home" as a counter-melody to the chant. They walk two by two, in time to the music. The* PRIESTS *exit. The* KING *enters and gestures to* CHULALONGKORN *to step out of line. The* PRINCE *obeys. The other children continue offstage.*

CHULALONGKORN   Father, I shall be late for school.

KING   You wait! (*There is angry purpose in his voice and manner*) Please to recite proverb you have learned yesterday and writing down twelve times in your copybook.

CHULALONGKORN   "A thought for the day: East or West, home is best."

KING   East, West, home best. Means house! Every day for many, many months! Always something about house! Are my children to be taught nothing more?

CHULALONGKORN   Yesterday we are taught that the world is a round ball which spins on a stick through the middle. (*He looks at the* KING *to see the effect of this outrageous statement*) Everyone knows that the world rides on the back of a great turtle, who keeps it from running into the stars.

KING   How can it be that everyone knows one thing, if many people believe another thing?

CHULALONGKORN   Then which is true? (*Pause*)

KING   The world is a ball with stick through it . . . I believe.

CHULALONGKORN   You believe? Does that mean you do not know? (*His father does not answer*) But you must know, because you are King.

KING   Good. Some day you, too, will be King and you too will know everything.

CHULALONGKORN   But how do I learn? And when do I know that I know everything?

KING   When you are King. Now leave me. (CHULALONGKORN *goes out. The* KING *soliloquizes*) When you are King. But *I* do not know. I am not sure. I am not sure of anything. (*He sings*)
When I was a boy
World was better spot.
What was so was so,
What was not was not.
Now I am a man—
World have change a lot:
Some things *nearly* so,
Others *nearly* not.

There are times I almost think
I am not sure of what I absolutely know.
Very often find confusion
In conclusion I concluded long ago.
In my head are many facts
That, as a student, I have studied to procure.
In my head are many facts
Of which I wish I was more certain I was sure!
(*He speaks:*) Is a puzzlement! What to tell a growing son?
(*He sings:*)
What, for instance, shall I say to him of women?
Shall I educate him on the ancient lines?
Shall I tell the boy, as far as he is able,
To respect his wives and love his concubines?
Shall I tell him every one is like the other,
And the better one of two is really neither?
If I tell him this I think he won't believe it—
And I nearly think I don't believe it either!

When my father was a king
He was a king who knew exactly what he knew,
And his brain was not a thing

Forever swinging to and fro and fro and to.
Shall I, then, be like my father
And be wilfully unmovable and strong?
Or is better to be right?
Or am I right when I believe I may be wrong?

Shall I join with other nations in alliance?
If allies are weak, am I not best alone?
If allies are strong with power to protect me,
Might they not protect me out of all I own?
Is a danger to be trusting one another,
One will seldom want to do what other wishes . . .
But unless some day somebody trust somebody,
There'll be nothing left on earth excepting fishes!

There are times I almost think
Nobody sure of what he absolutely know.
Everybody find confusion
In conclusion he concluded long ago,
And it puzzle me to learn
That though a man may be in doubt of what he know,
Very quickly will he fight,
He'll fight to prove that what he does not know is so!

Oh-h-h-h-h-h!
Sometimes I think that people going mad!
Ah-h-h-h-h-h!
Sometimes I think that people not so bad!
But no matter what I think
I must go on living life.
As leader of my kingdom I must *go* forth,
Be father to my children,
And husband to each wife—
Etcetera, etcetera, and so forth.
(*His arms and eyes raised in prayer*)
If my Lord in Heaven, Buddha, show the way,
Every day I try to live another day.
If my Lord in Heaven, Buddha, show the way,
Every day I do my best—for one more day!
(*His arms and shoulders droop. He speaks the last line*)
But . . . is a puzzlement!
(*The lights go out. The voices of the children are heard
in the darkness, coming from the schoolroom*)

ACT ONE | Scene Four

The Schoolroom. Up center is a large stand with a map hanging from it. This is an ancient map, showing a very large Siam with a heroic figure of an armored king superimposed. Adjoining is a much smaller Burma, with a pathetic naked figure representing the king of that country.

The children are lined up singing their school song. LADY THIANG *and* TUPTIM *stand a little apart from the group, as does* LOUIS. CHULALONGKORN *is in the group with the children and wives.* ANNA *conducts them with a blackboard pointer. Soon after the curtain rises, she stops them in the middle of their song.*

ANNA   Spread out, children. (*They obey*) Now, that last line was "English words are all we speak." I didn't quite understand. I want to hear the beginnings and ends of your words. Once again, now, and nice big smiles because we love our school.

WIVES AND CHILDREN (*Singing*)
We work and work
From week to week
At the Royal Bangkok Academy.
And English words
Are all we speak
At the Royal Bangkok Academy.
If we pay
Attention to our teacher
And obey her every rule,
We'll be grateful for
These golden years

At our dear old school.
The Royal Bangkok Academy,
Our dear old school.

ANNA   That's fine. Now take your places. (*The children sit, the bigger ones on the right, with* CHULALONGKORN *and* TUPTIM *behind them, the little ones down center, their backs to the audience, facing* ANNA *who stands up center. The wives line up on the left*) Lady Thiang, will you start?

(ANNA *hands the pointer to* LADY THIANG.)

THIANG (*Using the pointer on the map*)   Blue is ocean. Red —Siam (*Enthusiastic reaction from the children at Siam's great size*) Here is King of Siam. (*Indicating armored figure*) In right hand is weapon—show how he destroy all who fight him. (*More approval*) Green—Burma. (LADY THIANG *looks disapprovingly at* TUPTIM) Here, King of Burma. (*Indicating naked figure*) No clothes mean how poor is King of Burma.

(*Children giggle*)

ANNA   Thank you, Lady Thiang. Will you take my chair? (LADY THIANG *sits.* ANNA *addresses the class*) The map you have been looking at is an old one. Today we have a surprise. Louis— (LOUIS *rolls down an* 1862 *world map in Mercator projection. The children gasp*) A new map—just arrived from England. It is a gift to us from His Majesty, your King.

WIVES AND CHILDREN (*Bowing in unison*)   The Lord of Light.

ANNA   Er—yes—The Lord of Light.

LOUIS (*With the pointer*)   The white is Siam.
    (*There is a groan of disbelief and disappointment from the children and wives*)

CHULALONGKORN   Siam not so small!

LOUIS   Wait! Let me show you England. (*Points*) See! It is even smaller than Siam.
    (*Children indicate approval*)

ANNA   For many years, before I came here, Siam was to me that little white spot. Now I have lived here for more than a year. I have met the people of Siam. And I am learning to understand them.

A PRINCESS   You like us?

ANNA I like you very much. Very much indeed. (*The children express their delight.* ANNA *sings*)
It's a very ancient saying,
But a true and honest thought,
That "if you become a teacher
By your pupils you'll be taught."
As a teacher I've been learning
(You'll forgive me if I boast)
And I've now become an expert
On the subject I like most:
   (*She speaks*)
Getting to know you . . .
   (*She sings*)
Getting to know you,
Getting to know all about you,
Getting to like you,
Getting to hope you like me.
Getting to know you—
Putting it my way, but nicely,
You are precisely
My cup of tea!
Getting to know you,
Getting to feel free and easy;
When I am with you,
Getting to know what to say—
Haven't you noticed?
Suddenly I'm bright and breezy
Because of
All the beautiful and new
Things I'm learning about you,
Day by day.
(*The refrain is taken up by the wives, Amazons and children.* ANNA *teaches them handshaking, and* LADY THIANG *learns to curtsey. One wife performs a dance with a fan and* ANNA, *imitating her, dances with her. Then she dances with the children. At the finish they are all seated on the floor, giggling. She rises suddenly, remembering her duties*) My goodness! This started out to be a lesson! Now, let's get back to work!
   (*They scurry back to their places*)

CHULALONGKORN (*Pointing to the map*) What is that green up there?

ANNA   That is Norway. (*Repeating precisely for the benefit of her students*) Nor-way.

WIVES AND CHILDREN (*Imitating the sound*)   Nor-way.

ANNA   Norway is a very cold place. It is sometimes so cold that the lakes and rivers freeze, and the water becomes so hard that you can walk on it.

A SMALL PRINCE   Walk on water?

ANNA   Yes, walk on water.

CHULALONGKORN   How is it possible? Hard water!

ANNA   It is not only hard, but very slippery, too. When people walk on it, they fall down, and slide . . . (*General reaction of skepticism*) Not only do the lakes and rivers freeze, but the raindrops, as they fall, are changed into small white spots that look like lace! This is called snow.

TUPTIM (*Fascinated*)   Snow?

WIVES AND CHILDREN (*Another new word*)   Snow . . .

CHULALONGKORN (*Not to be taken in*)   Spots of lace!

ANNA   Yes, Your Highness! The water freezes—on the way down from the sky.

CHULALONGKORN   And the raindrops turn into little stars!
   (*The pupils giggle, their credulity strained too far. The class becomes disorganized*)

ANNA   Yes, Your Highness. Some *are* shaped like stars—small, white . . .
   (*Bedlam is breaking loose*)

PRINCESS YING YAOWALAK   I do not believe such thing as snow!
   (*Cries of assent*)

TWINS (*Dividing the lines and gestures between them, keeping two hands together*)   And I do not believe that Siam is this big— (*Indicating small size*) And other country so big! (*Wide gesture*)

CHULALONGKORN   Siam is biggest country in world!
   (*Shouts, cartwheels, pandemonium greet this popular pronouncement*)

KING (*Entering suddenly*) What? What? What? (*All but* ANNA *and* LOUIS *instantly prostrate themselves. The* KING *stands for a moment in outraged silence*) How can schoolroom be so . . . unscientific?

ANNA Your Majesty, we have had a little misunderstanding. I was describing snow and they refused to believe that there was such a thing.

KING Snow?

ANNA (*Gesturing snow falling*) Snow.
  (CHULALONGKORN *has raised his head and noted her gesture*)

KING (*Feeling his way*) Oh, yes. From mountain top.

ANNA From the sky.

KING From sky *to* mountain top.

CHULALONGKORN Sire . . . please . . . how does it come down from the sky?

KING Like this. (*And he makes exactly the same gesture as* ANNA *did, lowering his hands and wiggling his fingers the while*)

CHULALONGKORN (*Gravely*) Thank you, sire.

KING (*He snaps his fingers as if bringing the picture back to his mind*) I have see picture—Switzerland!

ANNA That's right, Your Majesty.

KING Land all white—with snow. (*Turning to the class, with an angry challenge*) Who does not believe this? (*There is complete silence*)

ANNA Well, after all, they have never *seen* it, and . . .

KING Never see? If they will know only what they see, why do we have schoolroom? (*He turns to the class and crackles out a sudden command*) Rise! (*They all come to their feet*) Do not ever let me hear of not believing teacher, who I have bring here at high expense—twenty pounds—each month. (*All eyes turn toward* ANNA *with a strange accusing look, as if she were robbing the* KING) Twenty English pounds! (*He stamps his foot*) Sterling! (*Not knowing what "sterling' means, but impressed by the sound as the* KING *shouts it, they all fall to the floor again*) Children must learn. (*He turns to* ANNA) Teacher must teach! Not waste time instructing children in silly English song "Home Sweet House"—to remind me of breaking promises that I never made, etcetera, etcetera, etcetera . . .

ANNA (*Summoning all her courage*)   Your Majesty . . . you *did* promise me a house. (*He glares at her, but she does not flinch*) "A brick residence adjoining the royal palace." Those were your words in your letter.

KING   I do not remember such words.

ANNA   I remember them.

KING   I will do remembering. Who is King? I remind you— so you remember *that!* (*He is screaming now*) I do not know of any promises. I do not know anything but that you are my servant.

ANNA (*Automatically resenting the word*)   Oh, no, Your Majesty!
(*There is a gasp of astonishment from those in the schoolroom*)

KING   What? What? What? I say you are my servant!

ANNA   No, Your Majesty, that's not true. I most certainly am *not* your servant!

CHULALONGKORN (*To* LOUIS)   I would say your mother has bad manners.

LOUIS   You would, would you? Well, I'd say your father has no manners at all!

ANNA   Louis! (*She takes his hand and turns to face the* KING) If you do not give me the house you promised, I shall return to England. (*There is a frightened murmur from her pupils.* ANNA, *herself, looks surprised at her own temerity*)

PRINCESS SOMAWADI (*Running to her*)   No! No! No!

PRINCE SUK SAWAT   Do not go to England!

PRINCE THONGKORN YAI (*To the* KING)   We learn. We believe schoolteacher.

PRINCESS YING YAOWALAK   I believe in snow!

THIANG (*To the* KING)   Do not let her go away.

KING   I let her do nothing, except what is my pleasure. (*To* ANNA) It is my pleasure you stay here. You stay here in palace. In palace!

ANNA   No, Your Majesty!

KING (*Weakening a little*)   I give you servants. I give you bigger room.

ANNA   That is not the point, Your Majesty.

KING   Why do you wish to leave these children, all of whom are loving you so extraordinarily?

ANNA   I don't wish to leave them. I love them, too . . . quite extraordinarily. But I cannot stay in a country where a promise has no meaning.

KING   I will hear no more about this promise . . .

ANNA   A land where there is talk of honor, and a wish for Siam to take her place among the modern nations of the world! Where there is talk of great changes, but where everything still remains according to the wishes of the King!

KING   You will say no more!

ANNA (*On the edge of tears*)   I will say no more, because—because I have no more to say. (*She starts off*) Come, Louis.
(*He follows her out, as the wives and children call after her: "Please don't go, Mrs. Anna," etc. But she goes! The* KING *stamps his foot angrily to silence them all. Then he shouts a dismissal*)

KING   Out! Out! Out! (*They scurry out. The* KING'S *thoughts are confused. He paces up and down, then stops before the map. His voice is low and thoughtful*) So big a world! Siam very small . . . England very small . . . all people very small. No man big enough for to be alone. No man big enough! King? King different! King need no one . . . nobody at all! (*Pause*) I think!
(*He leaves the room*)
(*In a moment* TUPTIM *comes in. She looks around cautiously, then sits on the floor with a book.* LUN THA *enters, then stops quickly, surprised to find* TUPTIM *alone*)

LUN THA   Where is Mrs. Anna?

TUPTIM   She will not be with us ever again. She has quarreled with the King.

LUN THA   How can we meet if she is not with us? Mrs. Anna was our only friend, and . . .

TUPTIM   We cannot be seen talking like this. Anyone can come in. Pretend you wait for her.

LUN THA (*Bitterly*)   If only we could stop pretending! (*He sings*)
We kiss in a shadow,
We hide from the moon,
Our meetings are few,
And over too soon.
We speak in a whisper,
Afraid to be heard—
When people are near
We speak not a word!
Alone in our secret,
Together we sigh
For one smiling day to be free
To kiss in the sunlight
And say to the sky:
"Behold and believe what you see!
Behold how my lover loves me!"
(*He speaks*) Tuptim, when can we meet? When?

TUPTIM   It is not possible. We cannot meet alone ever—not ever.
  (LADY THIANG *enters at the back, sees the two lovers together, and goes off, unseen by them*)

LUN THA (*As* TUPTIM *suddenly breaks away*)   What is it?

TUPTIM   Someone was here! (*She looks around fearfully*) I had a feeling someone was watching us . . . Please go! Please! (*He leaves.* TUPTIM *sings sadly*)
To kiss in the sunlight
And say to the sky:
"Behold and believe what you see!
Behold how my lover loves me!"

Intermediate Scene

The Palace corridor.
    LOUIS *and* CHULALONGKORN *enter from opposite sides.
After passing each other in unfriendly silence, each repents
and turns at about the same time. Then with a common
impulse, they rush toward each other and shake hands.*

CHULALONGKORN   I am sorry we nearly fought just now.

LOUIS   I am too.

CHULALONGKORN   Are you really going away?

LOUIS   Mother plans to leave on the next sailing.

CHULALONGKORN   I am not sure my father will allow your
mother to go.

LOUIS   I am not sure whether my mother will allow your
father not to allow her to go.

CHULALONGKORN   Why does not your mother admit that she
was wrong?

LOUIS   I don't believe that Mother thinks she was wrong.

CHULALONGKORN   It begins to look as if people do not know
when they are right or wrong—even after they have grown
up.

LOUIS   I have noticed that, too.

CHULALONGKORN   A puzzlement! . . . When I left my father
a little while ago, I heard him talking to himself. (*He shakes
his head*) He seemed uncertain about many things.

LOUIS   I don't believe grownups are ever certain—they only
talk as if they are certain.

CHULALONGKORN (*Singing*)
There are times I almost think
They are not sure of what they absolutely know.

LOUIS
I believe they are confused
About conclusions they concluded long ago.

CHULALONGKORN
If my father and your mother are not sure of what they abso-
    lutely know,
Can you tell me why they fight?

LOUIS
They fight to prove that what they do not know is so!

CHULALONGKORN (*With the mannerisms of his father*)
Oh-h-h-h-h-h!
Sometimes I think that people going mad.

LOUIS
Ah-h-h-h-h-h!
Sometimes I think that people not so bad.

CHULALONGKORN
But no matter what I think,
I must go on living life
And some day as a leader I must *go* forth,
Be father to my children
And husband to each wife.
Etcetera, etcetera, and so forth.
    (*His eyes and arms uplifted*)
If my Lord in Heaven, Buddha, show the way,
Every day I try to live another day,
If my Lord in Heaven, Buddha, show the way,
Every day I do my best—for one more day.
But—

LOUIS
Is a puzzlement.
    (*The two boys walk off together thoughtfully*)

ACT ONE | Scene Five

ANNA'S *bedroom.*

> ANNA *is sitting on the bed. She has started to undress, but apparently has stopped, engrossed in her thoughts. Her brows knit. She glares at an imaginary adversary. Her nostrils dilate with scorn. Then she starts to let him have it:*

ANNA
Your servant! Your servant!
Indeed I'm not your servant
(Although you give me less than servant's pay)
I'm a free and independent employé . . . employee.
   (*She paces the floor indignantly, then turns back to "him"*)
Because I'm a woman
You think, like every woman,
I have to be a slave or concubine—
You conceited, self-indulgent libertīne—
   (*Again correcting her pronunciation*)
Libertĭne.
   (*Narrowing her eyes vindictively*)
How I wish I'd called him that! Right to his face!
   (*Turning and addressing "him" again*)
Libertīne! And while we're on the subject, sire,
There are certain goings on around this place
That I wish to tell you I do not admire:

   I do not like polygamy
   Or even moderate bigamy
   (I realize
   That in your eyes

That clearly makes a prig o' me)
But I am from a civilized land called Wales,
Where men like you are kept in county gaols.

In your pursuit of pleasure, you
Have mistresses who treasure you
(They have no ken
Of other men
Beside whom they can measure you)
A flock of sheep, and you the only ram—
No wonder you're the wonder of Siam!
(*At first elated by this sally a frightened, embarrassed look
comes into her eyes. She speaks*)
I'm rather glad I *didn't* say that. . . . Not with the women
right there . . . and the children.
(*She sings wistfully*)
The children, the children,
I'll not forget the children,
No matter where I go I'll always see
Those little faces looking up at me . .

At first, when I started to teach,
They were shy and remained out of reach,
But lately I've thought
One or two have been caught
By a word I have said
Or a sentence I've read,
And I've heard an occasional question
That implied, at the least, a suggestion
That the work I was trying to do
Was beginning to show with a few . .

That Prince Chulalongkorn
Is very like his father,
He's stubborn—but inquisitive and smart . . .
(*Sudden tears*)
I must leave this place before they break my heart,
I must leave this place before they break my heart!
(*She stops, picks up the watch that is on her pillow and
looks down at it*)
Goodness! I had no idea it was so late.
(*She resumes undressing, but presently she is back at
the* KING *again. She becomes motionless and squints her
eyes at "him"*)

Shall I tell you what I think of you?
You're spoiled!
You're a conscientious worker
But you're spoiled.
Giving credit where it's due
There is much I like in you
But it's also very true
That you're spoiled!
    (*She struts up and down, imitating him*)
Everybody's always bowing
To the King,
Everybody has to grovel
To the King.
By your Buddha you are blessed,
By your ladies you're caressed
But the one who loves you best
Is the King!

    All that bowing and kowtowing
    To remind you of your royalty,
    I find a most disgusting exhibition.
    I wouldn't ask a Siamese *cat*
    To demonstrate his loyalty
    By taking that ridiculous position!

How would you like it if you were a man
Playing the part of a toad?
Crawling around on your elbows and knees,
Eating the dust in the road! . . .
Toads! Toads! All of your people are toads!
    (*She sinks to her knees in scornful imitation of the
    "toads"*)
Yes, Your Majesty; No, Your Majesty.
Tell us how low to go, Your Majesty;
Make some more decrees, Your Majesty,
Don't let us up off our knees, Your Majesty.
Give us a kick, if it please Your Majesty,
Give us a kick if you would, Your Majesty—
    (*"Taking" an imaginary kick*)
Oh! That was good, Your Majesty! . . .
    (*She pounds the floor in her temper, then lies down prone,
    exhausted . . .* THIANG *enters and rings the string of
    bells by the door twice.* ANNA *does not, at first, respond.*

Then, only half believing she has heard a ring, she rises on her knees)

ANNA   Who is it?

LADY THIANG   Mrs. Anna, it is I, Lady Thiang.

ANNA   At this hour of the night! (*Opening door*) Come in, Lady Thiang.

LADY THIANG   Mrs. Anna, will you go to King?

ANNA   Now? Has he sent for me?

THIANG   No. But he would be glad to see you. He is deeply wounded man. No one has ever spoken to him as you did today in schoolroom.

ANNA   Lady Thiang, no one has ever behaved to *me* as His Majesty did today in the schoolroom.

THIANG   And there is more distressing thing. Our agents in Singapore have found letters to British Government from people whose greedy eyes are on Siam. They describe King as a barbarian, and suggest making Siam a protectorate.

ANNA   That is outrageous! He is many things I do not like, but he is not a barbarian.

THIANG   Then you will help him?

ANNA   You mean—advise him?

THIANG   It must not sound like advice. King cannot take advice. And if you go to him, he will not bring up subject. You must bring it up.

ANNA   I cannot go to him. It's against all my principles. Certainly not without his having *asked* for me.

THIANG   He wish to be new-blood King with Western ideas. But it is hard for him, Mrs. Anna. And there is something else—Princess Tuptim. I do not tell him—for his sake. I deal with this my own way. But for these other things, he need help, Mrs. Anna.

ANNA   He has *you.*

THIANG   I am not equal to his special needs. He could be great man. But he need special help. He need *you.*

ANNA Lady Thiang, please don't think I am being stubborn.
But I simply cannot go to him. I will not.

THIANG What more can I say to you?
  (*Frustrated, she tries to think of how else to persuade*
  ANNA. *Presently she turns back to* ANNA *and starts to*
  sing)
This is a man who thinks with his heart,
His heart is not always wise.
This is a man who stumbles and falls,
But this is a man who tries.
This is a man you'll forgive and forgive,
And help and protect, as long as you live . . .

He will not always say
What you would have him say,
But now and then he'll say
    Something wonderful.
The thoughtless things he'll do
Will hurt and worry you—
Then all at once he'll do
    Something wonderful.
He has a thousand dreams
That won't come true.
You know that he believes in them
And that's enough for you.
You'll always go along,
Defend him when he's wrong
And tell him, when he's strong
    He is wonderful.
He'll always need your love—
And so he'll get your love—
A man who needs your love
    Can be wonderful!
  (*As she finishes she kneels and looks up at* ANNA *sup-*
  pliantly. ANNA *takes her hand and helps her rise. Then*
  she crosses to the bed, picks up her jacket and starts to
  put it on. THIANG, *taking this as a sign that her mission*
  is successful, smiles gratefully and leaves ANNA *to finish*
  dressing)

Intermediate Scene

The Palace corridor.
The KRALAHOME *enters and meets* LADY THIANG.

KRALAHOME   Did you succeed? Will she go to him?

THIANG   She will go. She knows he needs her. Tell him.

KRALAHOME   I will tell him she is *anxious* to come. I will
tell him it is *she* who needs *him*.

THIANG   That also will be true. (*The* KRALAHOME *leaves her.*
THIANG *soliloquizes*) This woman knows many things, but
this, I think, she does not know. . . . (*She sings*)
She'll always go along,
Defend him when he's wrong
And tell him when he's strong
    He is wonderful.
He'll always need her love
And so he'll get her love
A man who needs your love
    Can be wonderful!

ACT ONE | Scene Six

The KING's *study.*
    The KING *has been reading a large English Bible, which
lies open on the floor beside a cushion arm-rest. There are*

some English newspapers also on the floor. The KING *is walking up and down impatiently. He goes up and out to the terrace, looks off left, sees something, and hurries down to the Bible and resumes reading it. Presently,* ANNA *enters on the terrace.*

ANNA (*Making a curtsey*) Your Majesty. (*She comes into the room*) Your Majesty. (*No answer. She looks down over his shoulder*) Your Majesty is reading the Bible!

KING (*Remaining on the floor*) Mrs. Anna, I think your Moses shall have been a fool.

ANNA Moses!

KING Moses! Moses! Moses! I think he shall have been a fool. (*Tapping the Bible*) Here it stands written by him that the world was created in six days. You know and I know it took many ages to create world. I think he shall have been a fool to have written so. What is your opinion?

ANNA Your Majesty, the Bible was not written by men of science, but by men of faith. (*The* KING *considers this*) It was their explanation of the miracle of creation, which is the same miracle—whether it took six days or many centuries

KING (*Rising*) Hm. (*He is impressed by her explanation but, of course, would not say so*) You have come to apologize?

ANNA I am sorry, Your Majesty, but . . .

KING Good! You apologize.

ANNA Your Majesty, I . . .

KING I accept!

ANNA Your Majesty, nothing that has been said can alter the fact that in my country, anyone who makes a promise must . . .

KING Silence! (*Pursuing his own thoughts*) Tell me about President Lingkong of America. Shall Mr. Lingkong be winning this war he is fighting at present?

ANNA No one knows, Your Majesty.

KING   Does he have enough guns and elephants for transporting same?

ANNA (*Not quite smiling*)   I don't think they have elephants in America, Your Majesty.

KING   No elephants! Then I shall send him some. (*Handing her a notebook and pencil*) Write letter to Mr. Lingkong.

ANNA   Now?

KING   Now! When else! Now is always best time. (*He sits on the floor*)

ANNA   Very well, Your Majesty.

KING (*Dictating*)   From Phra Maha Mongut, by the blessing of the highest super agency in the world of the whole Universe, the King of Siam, the Sovereign of all tributary countries adjacent and around in every direction, etcetera, etcetera, etcetera. (*Almost without a break*) Do you not have any respect for me? (ANNA *looks up from her notebook, having no idea what he means*) Why do you stand over my head? I cannot stand all the time. And in this country, no one's head shall be higher than King's. From now on in presence you shall so conduct yourself like all other subjects.

ANNA   You mean on the floor! I am sorry. I shall try very hard not to let my head be as high as Your Majesty's—but I simply cannot grovel on the floor. I couldn't possibly work that way—or think!

KING (*He rises and studies her before he speaks*)   You are very difficult woman. But you will observe care that head shall never be higher than mine. If I shall sit, you shall sit. If I shall kneel, you shall kneel, etcetera, etcetera, etcetera.
    (*Pause*)

ANNA   Very well, Your Majesty.

KING   Is promise?

ANNA   Is promise.

KING   Good. (*He squats down on his heels to resume dictating.* ANNA *sits on the floor nearby*) To His Royal Presidency of the United States in America. Abra-Hom Lingkong, etcetera . . . you fix up. It has occurred to us . . . (*He stretches out prone, his chin leaning on his hand. Then he notices that*

ANNA'S *head is higher*) It has occurred to us— (*He gives* ANNA *a significant look, and she reluctantly keeps her promise, lying prone, so that her head is no higher than his*) It has occurred to us that if several pairs of young male elephants were turned loose in forests of America, after a while they would increase . . .

ANNA (*Her head snapping up from her dictating*)   Your Majesty—just *male* elephants?

KING (*Refusing to acknowledge his mistake*)   You put in details! (*He rises, and she does also*) Tonight my mind is on other matters—very important matters.

ANNA (*Knowing he is getting near the subject he really wants to talk about*)   Anything you want to discuss with me?

KING   Why should I discuss important matters with woman?

ANNA   Very well, Your Majesty. (*She curtseys*) Then I will say good night.

KING   Good night!
   (ANNA *goes up toward the terrace, then turns, to give him another chance*)

ANNA   Your Majesty . . .

KING (*Relieved and eager*)   What, what, what?

ANNA (*To cue him*)   I was wondering— When the boat arrived from Singapore yesterday . . .

KING   Singapore! Ha!

ANNA   Was there any news from abroad?

KING   News! Yes, there are news! They call me barbarian.

ANNA   Who?

KING   Certain parties who would use this as excuse to steal my country. Suppose you were Queen Victoria and somebody tell you King of Siam is barbarian. Do you believe?

ANNA   Well, Your Majesty . . .

KING   You will! You will! You will! You will believe I am barbarian because there is no one to speak otherwise.

ANNA   But this is a lie!

KING   It is a *false* lie!

ANNA   What have you decided to do about it?

KING   (*After a pause*)   You guess!

ANNA   Well, if someone were sending a big lie about me to England, I should do my best to send the truth to England . . . Is that what you have decided to do, Your Majesty?

KING   Yes. That is what I have decided to do. (*To himself*) But how? (*He crosses to her*) Guess how I shall do this!

ANNA   Well, my guess would be that when Sir Edward Ramsay arrives here . . .

KING   Ramsay? Ramsay?

ANNA   The British diplomat.

KING   Ah, yes—on way from Singapore.

ANNA   We wrote to him last month.

KING   When he is here, I shall take opportunity of expressing my opinion of English thieves who wish to steal Siam. I shall show him who is barbarian! (*Noticing her disapproval*) What is this face you put on?

ANNA   Well, Your Majesty, my guess is that you will not fight with Sir Edward.

KING   I will not?

ANNA   No, Your Majesty. You will entertain him and his party in an especially grand manner. In this way you will make them all witnesses in your favor. They will return to England and report to the Queen that you are not a barbarian.

KING   Naturally . . . naturally! (*He paces up and down, delighted with the solution*) This is what I shall have intended to do.

ANNA   This is the only way to get the better of the British. Stand up to them. Put your best foot forward. (*The* KING, *bewildered, holds up his foot and looks at it*) That is an expression, Your Majesty. It means dress up in your best clothes. Show them your most intelligent men, your most beautiful women. Edward admires beautiful women.

KING (*Suspiciously*) Edward? You call him this?

ANNA We are old friends. I knew him in Bombay before I was married.

KING Ah! . . . (*Walking past her thoughtfully*) Shall it be proper for the British dignitary to see my women with no shoes on their feet? Shall it be proper for them to put their best *bare* feet forward? No! Sir Ramsay will go back and tell Queen I am a barbarian. Why do *you* not think of this?

ANNA (*Suddenly inspired*) We shall dress them up European fashion.

KING You mean dress them in . . . dresses?
  (ANNA *nods. They both become increasingly excited*)

ANNA How many women can I have to sew for me?

KING All women in Kingdom. How many dresses?

ANNA That depends on how many ladies are chosen by Your Majesty.

KING You shall tell me which of my women are most like Europeans, for dressing like same. (*He crosses quickly to the throne-table, strikes a gong and shouts*) Wake up! Wake up, everybody! Wives! Etcetera, etcetera, etcetera! (*He returns to* ANNA) I shall command Chinese artists to paint their faces very pale. And you shall educate them in European custom and manners for presentation.

ANNA I wonder how much time we shall have.

KING Sir Ramsay's gunboat last reported off Songkla. How long he take depend on how many ports he call into. Let us say we have one week.

ANNA One week! But, Your Majesty, I don't think . . . one week!

KING In this time whole world was created—*Moses* say! . . . Are there any details I do not think of so far?

ANNA You must give them a fine dinner—a European dinner.

KING I was going to.

ANNA And a ball. With music.

KING Music. (*His face lights up*) And dancing!

ANNA That's right! Dancing!

KING Why do *you* not think of dancing?

ANNA It was an inspired idea, Your Majesty. (*Now, in answer to the gong, the wives enter in nightdress.* TUPTIM *is first.* THIANG *also enters, but not in nightdress*) We can give them a theatrical performance. Tuptim has written a play, a version of Uncle Tom's Cabin.

KING Ha! We shall give them theatrical performance. We shall show them who is barbarian! (*To the wives*) Line up! Line up! Line up! (*They do so*) Lady Thiang! On Saturday next, at nine o'clock post meridian, we shall give fine dinner —European dinner, for probably thirty people. (THIANG *bows*) You are to instruct steward during week he shall make eminent European dishes for tasting. I shall taste and schoolteacher shall taste. (*The children begin coming in, accompanied by their nurses and the Amazons. They rub their eyes and yawn. The* KING *turns to* ANNA) You say who is most like European lady for dressing like same. (ANNA *crosses to inspect the wives. The* KING *continues his orders to* THIANG) You are to make tablecloth of finest white silk for very long table. Also instruct court musicians to learn music of Europe for dancing, etcetera. (*The* TWINS, *coming in, have gone around him and are now in front of him*) What? What? What? Am I to be annoyed by children at this moment? (*A* NURSE, *having lost her charge, comes running around him, clapping her hands*) Who? Who? Who? (*All drop to the floor at his angry tones. Then the object of the* NURSE'S *solicitude, a very tiny boy, crawls between the* KING'S *legs and crouches in front of him*) Mrs. Anna, we must be more scientific with children! (*He walks up and down angrily*) For the next week, the men and women of my kingdom will work without sleeping until all is ready, and for what is not done, each man and woman shall be beaten a hundred strokes. Everyone must know this, Lady Thiang. Tell this to everyone! Above all, I must not be worried by anything . . . (*There is a tremendous report that sounds like a cannon, and fireworks appear on the backdrop. Discipline is immediately abandoned, and there are shrieks and cries of fear. The children huddle together with the nurses*

and Amazons. The KING *and* ANNA *run up to the terrace)*
What can this be?
    (*Another terrifying report*)

ANNA (*Pointing to the fireworks*)   Look, Your Majesty!

KING   Fireworks! (*The children, reassured, move forward a
bit to enjoy the show*) Fireworks at this hour in the morning!
No one may order fireworks but me.

KRALAHOME (*Rushing in*)   Your Majesty—the British! The
gunboat!

KING   They attack?

KRALAHOME   No! They salute, and we answer with fireworks.
It is Sir Edward Ramsay and his party.

ANNA (*Horrified*)   Now?

KRALAHOME   Now! They must have come direct from
Songkla. No stops.

ANNA   No stops!

KING   Tell them to go back! We are not ready!

KRALAHOME   Not ready, Your Majesty?

KING   You do not know, you do not know. I had planned
best idea I ever get.

ANNA   We can still do it, Your Majesty—*you* can do it.

KING   Ha! When English arrive we will put them to bed.
Tomorrow morning we shall send them on sightseeing trip.

ANNA   We shall start now, this minute. Work! Work! We
have only eighteen hours, but I shall do it somehow!

KING (*Sternly*)   *I* shall do it. You shall help me. (*Resuming
his orders, energetically*) No one shall sleep tonight or
tomorrow. We shall work even when the sun shines in the
middle of the day. We shall . . . (*He sees a group of priests
passing on the terrace*) Ah! Priests! (*He motions them to
come in*) First we shall ask help from Buddha. Bow to him!
Bow! Bow! Bow! (*They all sink to their knees, the* KING *in-
cluded, and raise their hands in prayerful attitude.* ANNA
remains standing but bows her head. The KING *chants*) Oh,
Buddha, give us the aid of your strength and your wisdom.

ALL (*Repeating chant*)   Oh, Buddha, give us the aid of your strength and your wisdom.
(*The* KING *sits back on his heels*)

KING (*Clapping his hands as orientals do to get Buddha's attention*)   And help us to prove to the visiting English that we are extraordinary and remarkable people.

ALL   And help us to prove to the visiting English that we are extraordinary and remarkable people.
(*During the repetition, the* KING *leans forward and down in a crouch, and steals a glance at* ANNA)

KING   Help also Mrs. Anna to keep awake for scientific sewing of dresses, even though she be only a woman and a Christian, and therefore unworthy of your interest.
(ANNA *looks up in surprise at the mention of her name, and comes to the* KING *in protest*)

ALL   Help also Mrs. Anna to keep awake for scientific sewing of dresses, even though she be only a woman and a Christian, and therefore unworthy of your interest.

KING (*During the repetition of the prayer, to* ANNA)   A promise is a promise! Your head cannot be higher than mine! A promise! (*Reluctantly, she sinks to a kneeling position to match his. The orchestra plays strains of "Something Wonderful"*) And, Buddha, I promise you I shall give this unworthy woman a house—a house of her own—a brick residence adjoining the royal palace, according to agreement, etcetera, etcetera, etcetera.

ALL   And, Buddha, I promise you I shall give this unworthy woman a house—a house of her own—a brick residence adjoining the royal palace, according to agreement, etcetera, etcetera, etcetera.
(*As they repeat his words, the* KING *watching to make sure that* ANNA *imitates him, sits back on his heels, then leans forward, finally stretching out, prone. They are both flat on their faces. Then he raises his head and rests his chin on his hand. She does the same. Fireworks burst through the air beyond the terrace.* ANNA *and the* KING *regard each other warily. Who is taming whom?*)

Curtain

ACT TWO | Scene One

The schoolroom.
  It has been converted into a dressing room for tonight. The floor and tables are littered with dressmaking materials. The wives are all dressed in their new hoopskirts, mostly finished, but all are uncomfortable in the unaccustomed clothes. A Chinese artist is painting the face of one. Others are receiving last-minute touches from two seamstresses. The faces of the wives are powdered white.
  LADY THIANG *enters. She has on a Western bodice and a penang.*

THIANG Ladies! Ladies! Clear everything away! Quickly now!
  (*The wives and seamstresses clear away the materials*)

A WIFE Lady Thiang, what is this costume? (*Pointing to penang*) Here is East— (*Pointing to bodice*) Here is West!

THIANG Have too much work to do! Cannot move fast in swollen skirt.

ANOTHER WIFE Lady Thiang, why must we dress like this for British?

THIANG Whatever Mrs. Anna want us to do is wise and good, but this— (*Indicating hoopskirts*) is a puzzlement. (*She sings*)
To prove we're not barbarians
They dress us up like savages!
To prove we're not barbarians
We wear a funny skirt!

WIVES

To prove we're not barbarians
They dress us up like savages!
To prove we're not barbarians
We wear a funny skirt!

THIANG

Western people funny,
Western people funny,
Western people funny,
Of that there is no doubt.
They feel so sentimental
About the oriental,
They always try to turn us
  Inside down and upside out!

WIVES

Upside out and inside down!

THIANG

To bruise and pinch our little toes
Our feet are cramped in leather shoes—
They'd break if we had brittle toes,
But now they only hurt!

WIVES

To bruise and pinch our little toes
Our feet are cramped in leather shoes—
They'd break if we had brittle toes,
But now they only hurt!

Western people funny,
Western people funny,
Western people funny,
Too funny to be true!

THIANG

They think they civilize us
Whenever they advise us
To learn to make the same mistake
  That they are making too!

ALL

They think they civilize us
Whenever they advise us

To learn to make the same mistake
  That they are making too!

THEY MAKE QUITE A FEW!

ANNA (*Entering*) Lady Thiang, here are the napkins for dinner. Will you put them on the table?

THIANG (*Taking them*) Thank you.

ANNA Thank *you*. (LADY THIANG *goes out*) Now, ladies, turn around and let me see how you look. (*The* WIVES *spread out and turn so that* ANNA *can see their backs. The* KING *enters. They immediately prostrate themselves, the hoops flying up behind them.* ANNA *sees the horrid truth*) Oh, my goodness gracious!

KING What shall be trouble now?

ANNA I forgot! They have practically no—undergarments!

KING Undergarments! (*He claps his hands and the* WIVES *rise*) Of what importance are undergarments at this time?

ANNA (*Stiffly*) Of great importance.

KING Are *you* wearing undergarments?

ANNA Of course, Your Majesty!

KING (*Pointing to hoopskirt, derisively*) That a woman has no legs is useless to pretend. Wherefore, then, swollen skirt?

ANNA The wide skirt is symbolic. It is the circle within which a female is protected.

KING This is necessary? Englishmen are so aggressive? I did not know.

ANNA (*Going to the* SEAMSTRESSES, *who help her remove her smock*) I said it was symbolic.

KING These undergarments—they are devised in symbolic, elaborate and ornamental manner?

ANNA Sometimes.
(*Her gown now revealed, the* WIVES *gasp their admiration*)

KING (*Looking at her bare shoulders*) This is what you are going to wear?

ANNA   Why, yes. Do you like it?

KING   This is what all the other visiting ladies shall look like?

ANNA   Most of them . . . I believe.

KING   You are certain this is customary? (*Indicating her bare shoulders*) Etcetera, etcetera, etcetera . . .

ANNA   Yes, I am certain it is customary. What is so extraordinary about bare shoulders? Your own ladies . . .

KING   Ah, yes. But is different! They do not wear so many coverings up on other parts of body, etcetera, etcetera, and therefore . . .

ANNA   (*Irritated, like any woman who, displaying a new dress, meets unexpected criticism*)   Therefore what?

KING   Is different.

ANNA   I am sorry His Majesty does not approve.

KING   I do not say I do not approve, but I do say . . .

PHRA ALACK   (*Entering, prostrating himself*)   The English— they are in palace.
    (*This causes immediate confusion among the* WIVES *who huddle in a frightened group*)

THARA   They will eat us!

ANNA   They will do nothing of the kind!

KING   (*Calling* ANNA *to him, he gives her a piece of paper*) Herewith shall be list of subjects you shall try to bring up for talk. On such subjects I am very brilliant, and will make great impression. You begin with Moses.

ANNA   (*Taking the paper and crowding in some last-minute coaching*)   Now remember, Your Majesty—Courtwright is the editor of a newspaper in Singapore . . .
    (*She is interrupted by the entrance of* SIR EDWARD RAMSAY, *who has wandered into the room by mistake. One* WIFE *screams in fright*)

ANOTHER WIFE   (*Indicating* SIR EDWARD'S *monocle*)   Oh, evil eye! Evil eye!
    (*The* WIVES *in an uncontrollable stampede throw their hoopskirts over their heads and rush out. From the look on*

SIR EDWARD'S *face, it is clear that they should have been supplied with undergarments*)

ANNA   Ladies! Ladies! Come back! Don't! Come back! Oh, dear! Edward! Oh, Your Majesty, this is dreadful!

KING (*Furious*)   Why have you not educated these girls in English custom of spying glass?

SIR EDWARD   Ah, my monocle. Was that what frightened them? Hello, Anna, my dear.

KING (*Before they can complete their handshake*)   Who? Who? Who?

ANNA   Your Majesty, may I present Sir Edward Ramsay?

SIR EDWARD (*Bowing*)   Your Majesty. (*He turns to* ANNA) How are you, Anna?

KING   I regret, sir, my ladies have not given good impression.

SIR EDWARD   On the contrary, Your Majesty, I have never received so good an impression in so short a time. You have most attractive pupils, Anna.
    (*The* KING *is clearly annoyed by the intimacy between* ANNA *and* SIR EDWARD)

ANNA   Tomorrow you must meet my younger pupils—His Majesty's children. They are making wonderful progress.

SIR EDWARD   I shall be delighted. (*To* KING) How many children have you, Your Majesty?

KING   Seventy-seven now, but I am not married very long. Next month expecting three more.

SIR EDWARD   No problem at all about an heir to the throne, is there? (*This sally falls flat with the* KING, *so he turns to* ANNA, *but it doesn't amuse her either*) I—er—I suppose I should apologize for wandering into this room. The rest of the party were ahead of me and . . .

ANNA   I'm so glad you decided to visit us—to visit His Majesty I mean, of course . .

SIR EDWARD   It was your postscript to His Majesty's letter that . . .

KING (*Turning with alert suspicion*)   Postscript?

ANNA   His Majesty was most happy when you decided to accept his invitation . . . Weren't you, Your Majesty?

KING (*Trying to figure it out*)   I was . . . happy.

KRALAHOME (*Entering*)   Your Majesty, dinner is about to be served, and I would first like to present your guests to you in the reception room.

KING (*Clapping his hands happily, and going off*)   Dinner, dinner, dinner!

ANNA (*To* KRALAHOME)   You have met?

KRALAHOME (*Bowing*)   Your Excellency. (*He goes off. A waltz is being played offstage*)

SIR EDWARD   Anna, my dear, you're looking lovelier than ever.

ANNA   Thank you, Edward.

SIR EDWARD   Found a job to do, eh? People you can help, that's it, isn't it? Extraordinary how one gets attached to people who need one. (*Listening*) Do you hear that? Do you know we danced to that once? (*She nods*) Bombay. Still dance?

ANNA   Not very often.

SIR EDWARD   You should. (*He puts his arm around her waist, and they dance*)

ANNA   Edward, I think we'd better . . .

SIR EDWARD   Are you sure you don't get homesick?

ANNA   No, Edward. I told you, I have nothing there—no one.
     (*The* KING *enters and watches them*)

EDWARD   Anna, do you remember that I once asked you to marry me—before Tom came along?

ANNA   Dear Edward . . .

KING (*Interrupting, furiously*)   Dancing—*after* dinner!

SIR EDWARD   Oh, sorry, sir. I'm afraid I started talking over old times.

KING (*Looking sternly at* ANNA)   It was my impression Mrs. Anna would be of help for seating of guests at dinner table, etcetera, etcetera, etcetera.

SIR EDWARD   In that case, we'd better be going in, Anna. (*He moves toward her, offering his arm*)

KING (*Coming between them, offering his arm*)   Yes, better be going in . . . Anna.
   (*She takes the* KING'S *arm, and they start off left,* SIR EDWARD *following*)

ANNA (*After a quick look at the paper the* KING *has given her*)   His Majesty made an interesting point about Moses the other day when he was reading the Bible. It seems he takes issue with the statement that . . .
   (*They are off*)

ACT TWO | Scene Two

The Palace grounds.
   TUPTIM *enters and crosses the stage, looking back furtively. She starts guiltily as she sees* LADY THIANG.

THIANG   Princess Tuptim, dinner is over. King and his English guests are on way to theater pavilion. Should you not be there to begin your play?

TUPTIM (*Rattled*)   I came out here to memorize my lines.

THIANG (*Stopping her as she starts to go*)   I think not, Princess. I have seen you and Lun Tha together. I do not tell King this. For *his* sake. I do not wish to hurt him. But your lover will leave Siam tonight.

TUPTIM   Tonight?

THIANG Now go to the theater, Princess.
(TUPTIM *exits.* THIANG *starts off, stops as she sees* LUN THA *enter left, looks at him with stern suspicion, then exits.* LUN THA *crosses to the other side, and calls off, in a whisper*)

LUN THA Tuptim!

TUPTIM (*Entering*) Turn back and look the other way. (LUN THA *instantly does so*) I am here in the shadow of the wall. I will stay here until she turns the corner. . . . She has told me you will leave Siam tonight, but I don't believe her.

LUN THA It is true, Tuptim. They have ordered me onto the first ship that leaves for Burma, and it is tonight.

TUPTIM (*Running to him*) What will we do?

LUN THA You are coming with me!

TUPTIM I!

LUN THA You have been a slave long enough! Secret police will all be at the theater. Meet me here, after your play. Everything is arranged.

TUPTIM I cannot believe it.

LUN THA I can. It will be just as I have pictured it a million times. (*He sings*)
I have dreamed that your arms are lovely,
I have dreamed what a joy you'll be.
I have dreamed every word you'll whisper
When you're close,
    Close to me.
How you look in the glow of evening
I have dreamed, and enjoyed the view.
In these dreams I've loved you so
That by now I think I know
What it's like to be loved by you—
I will love being loved by you.

TUPTIM
Alone and awake I've looked at the stars,
The same that smiled on you;
And time and again I've thought all the things
That you were thinking too.

I have dreamed that your arms are lovely,
I have dreamed what a joy you'll be.
I have dreamed every word you'll whisper
When you're close,
    Close to me.
How you look in the glow of evening
I have dreamed, and enjoyed the view.
In these dreams I've loved you so
That by now I think I know

TUPTIM AND LUN THA
What it's like to be loved by you—
I will love being loved by you.
    (ANNA *enters.* TUPTIM *runs to her*)

TUPTIM   Mrs. Anna!

ANNA   Tuptim, they are looking for you at the theater. I guessed you were both here. I ran out to warn you. I do think you're being rather reckless.

TUPTIM   Yes, I will go. (*She starts away, then turns back and surprises* ANNA *with a suddenly serious tone in her voice*) I must say good-bye to you now, Mrs. Anna.
    (*She kneels, kisses* ANNA'S *hand impulsively, and runs off*)

ANNA (*To* LUN THA)   Gracious! Anyone would think that she never expected to see me again.
    (*He looks at her steadily, and catching his look, she crosses him, looking after* TUPTIM)

LUN THA   Mrs. Anna, we are leaving tonight.

ANNA   Leaving? How?

LUN THA   Don't ask me how. It is better if you don't know. We shall never forget you, Mrs. Anna. (*He kisses her hand*) Never.

ANNA (*As he goes*)   God bless you both! (*Alone, thoughtfully, she sings*)
I know how it feels to have wings on your heels
And to fly down a street in a trance.
You fly down a street on the chance that you'll meet,
And you meet—not really by chance.
Don't cry, young lovers, whatever you do,
Don't cry because I'm alone.

All of my memories are happy tonight,
I've had a love of my own.
I've had a love of my own, like yours,
I've had a love of my own.
   (*She starts off as the curtain closes*)

ACT TWO | Scene Three

The theater pavilion.
   BALLET: *"The Small House of Uncle Thomas."*
   Before a curtain two attendants carry on a drum and a gong. The drummer takes his place. The royal singers enter ceremoniously and take their places at the opposite corner. TUPTIM *enters and stands in front of the singers.*
   The curtain opens, revealing the royal dancers dressed in traditional costumes, their faces painted chalk-white.

TUPTIM (*Speaking straight out at the audience, as if addressing the* KING *and his British visitors*)   Your Majesty, and honorable guests, I beg to put before you "Small House of Uncle Thomas."
   (*A tiny cabin is brought on*)

CHORUS
Small house of Uncle Thomas!
Small house of Uncle Thomas!
Written by a woman,
Harriet Beecher Stow-a!

TUPTIM   House is in Kingdom of Kentucky, ruled by most wicked King in all America—Simon of Legree. (*The gong is struck. The dancers make a traditional gesture denoting terror*) Your Majesty, I beg to put before you loving friends . . . Uncle Thomas!
   (*He enters from cabin*)

CHORUS
Dear old Uncle Thomas.

TUPTIM
Little Eva.
  (*She enters from cabin*)

CHORUS
Blessed Little Eva.

TUPTIM
Little Topsy.
  (*She enters from cabin*)

CHORUS
Mischief-maker, Topsy.

TUPTIM
Happy people.

CHORUS
Very happy people.
  (*The happy people dance*)

TUPTIM Happy people. Happy people (*The dance over,*
TUPTIM *continues*) Your Majesty, I beg to put before you
one who is not happy—the slave, Eliza.
  (ELIZA *enters from cabin*)

CHORUS
Poor Eliza, poor Eliza,
Poor unfortunate slave.

TUPTIM
Eliza's lord and master
King Simon of Legree.
She hates her lord and master.
  (*The gong and cymbal combine in a frightening crash,*
  and the dancers again pantomime terror according to the
  traditional gesture)
And fears him.
  (*Gong and cymbal again*)
This King has sold her lover
To far away province of O-hee-o
Lover's name is George.

CHORUS
George.

TUPTIM
Baby in her arms
Also called George.

CHORUS
George.
(ELIZA *enacts what* TUPTIM *describes*)

TUPTIM
Eliza say she run away and look for lover George.

CHORUS
George.

TUPTIM
So she bid good-bye to friends and start on her escape.
"The escape."
(ELIZA *now dances and mimes* "*the escape.*")

CHORUS
Run, Eliza, run, Eliza!
Run from Simon.

TUPTIM
Poor Eliza running,
And run into a rainstorm.
(*The rainstorm is depicted by dancers waving scarves.
After the* "*storm*" *is over,* ELIZA *gives her* "*baby*" *a shake
to dry it off*)
Comes a mountain.
(*The mountain is formed by three men*)

CHORUS
Climb, Eliza!
(*After climbing the* "*mountain*" ELIZA *rubs her feet*)

TUPTIM
Hide, Eliza!

CHORUS
Hide, Eliza, hide from Simon!
Hide in forest.
(*The trees of the forest are dancers holding branches*)

TUPTIM   Eliza very tired. (ELIZA *exits wearily*) Your Majesty, I regret to put before you King Simon of Legree.
(SIMON, *wearing a terrible, three-headed masque, is borne*

on by attendants. His slaves prostrate themselves before
him in the manner of the subjects of the King of Siam)

CHORUS
Because one slave has run away
Simon beating every slave.
(SIMON *dances down an aisle of quivering slaves, slashing*
at them with his huge sword)

TUPTIM Simon clever man. He decide to hunt Eliza, not
only with soldiers, but with scientific dogs who sniff and
smell, and thereby discover all who run away from King.
(*Now the chase ensues. Dancers with the dog masques*
portray bloodhounds who "sniff and smell" and pick up
poor ELIZA'S *scent.* ELIZA *runs from one side of the stage*
to the other always followed by the dogs, and by more
of the KING'S *men in each episode, and finally by the hor-*
rible SIMON *himself. And the pursuers keep getting closer*
to her)

CHORUS
Run, Eliza, run!
Run, Eliza, run!

Run, Eliza, run, run.
Run from Simon, run, run!

Eliza run,
Eliza run from Simon, run!
Eliza run,
Eliza run from Simon, run!

Eliza run,
Eliza run,
Run, run!

Simon getting closer . . .
Eliza getting tired . . .
Run, Eliza,
Run from Simon,
Run, Eliza, run!

TUPTIM
Eliza come to river,
Eliza come to river.
(*Two dancers run on with a long strip of silk which they*

wave to indicate a flowing river. ELIZA *stands before the "river" in frustrated horror*)

CHORUS
Poor Eliza!

TUPTIM
Who can save Eliza?

CHORUS
Only Buddha,
Buddha, Buddha, Buddha!
Save her, Buddha,
Save her, Buddha, save her! . . .
What will Buddha do?
(*Gong. The curtains part at back revealing Buddha on a high throne*)

TUPTIM
Buddha make a miracle!
(*An* ANGEL *with golden wings enters*)
Buddha send an angel down.
Angel make the wind blow cold.
(*The* ANGEL *blows on the "river" through a golden horn. The strip of silk, indicating the "river," is made to lie flat on the stage. It no longer ripples. The "river" is frozen!*)
Make the river water hard,
Hard enough to walk upon.

CHORUS
Buddha make a miracle!
Praise to Buddha!
(ELIZA *looks down at the river, somewhat puzzled. The* ANGEL *puts away her horn, then joins* ELIZA, *takes her hand and proceeds to teach her how to slide on a frozen river*)

TUPTIM
Angel show her how to walk on frozen water.
(ELIZA *and the* ANGEL *now do a pas-de-deux in the manner of two skaters.* ELIZA *picks it up quickly and seems to like it*)
Now, as token of his love,
Buddha make a new miracle.
(*As* TUPTIM *describes this new miracle, the* CHORUS *keeps singing*)

CHORUS
Praise to Buddha!
Praise to Buddha!

TUPTIM   Send from heaven stars and blossoms,
Look like lace upon the sky.
   (*Several men enter with long poles like fishing rods, and
   from the lines dangle large representations of snowflakes*)
So Eliza cross the river,
Hidden by this veil of lace.
   (TUPTIM *steps down a few feet*)
Forgot to tell you name of miracle—snow!
   (*Suddenly* ELIZA *looks terrified, and no wonder!*)

TUPTIM AND CHORUS
Of a sudden she can see
Wicked Simon of Legree,
Sliding 'cross the river fast,
With his bloodhounds and his slaves!
   (*Now* SIMON *and his slaves enter and* ELIZA *runs away.
   The* ANGEL, *too, has disappeared at the wrong moment.
   Now, while* SIMON *and his followers start to slide and
   skate on the "river," very much as* ELIZA *had, the "river"
   begins to be active again. The strip of silk is made to
   wave, and the two men carrying it lift it up and start to
   envelop* SIMON *and his party in its folds*)

TUPTIM   What has happened to the river?

TUPTIM AND CHORUS
Buddha has called out the sun,
Sun has made the water soft.
Wicked Simon and his slaves
Fall in river and are drowned.
   (*This is true. The* ANGEL *has come back with a huge
   sun, which he holds and directs upon the river. The silk
   is wrapped around* SIMON *and his party, and they are
   dragged off in it, drowned as they can be*)

TUPTIM   On other side of river is pretty city, Canada, where
Eliza sees lovely small house—guess who live in house? (*A
replica of the first cabin is brought on, but this one has snow
on the roof and ice on the windowpanes*) Uncle Thomas.
   (*He enters as before*)

CHORUS
Dear old Uncle Thomas.

TUPTIM
Little Eva.
  (*She enters*)

CHORUS
Blessed Little Eva.

TUPTIM
Little Topsy.
  (*She enters*)

CHORUS
Mischief-maker, **Topsy.**

TUPTIM
Lover George.
  (*The* ANGEL *enters, but this time without wings*)

CHORUS
Faithful lover George.

TUPTIM
Who is looking like angel to Eliza.
  (*A chord is struck*)
They have all escaped from
Wicked King and make happy reunion.
  (*They do a brief dance*)
Topsy glad that Simon die,
Topsy dance for joy.
  (*She dances a few steps, then strikes a pose*)
I tell you what Harriet Beecher Stowe say
That Topsy say:
  (*Cymbal crash*)
"I specks I' sede wickedest critter
In de world!"
  (*Another cymbal crash.* TUPTIM *frowns, an earnest, dra-
  matic note comes into her voice. She steps forward*)
But I do not believe
Topsy is a wicked critter.
Because I too am glad
For death of King.
Of any King who pursues
Slave who is unhappy and tries to join her lover!

(*The dancers look frightened.* TUPTIM'S *emotions are running away with her*)
And, Your Majesty,
I wish to say to you . . .
Your Majesty—
    (*A chord is struck.* TUPTIM *collects herself*)
And honorable guests . . .
I will tell you end of story . . .
    (*The dancers look relieved. She is back in the make-believe tale of "Uncle Thomas"*)
Is very sad ending.
Buddha has saved Eliza
But with the blessings of Buddha
Also comes sacrifice.
    (*Gong. Buddha is again revealed*)

CHORUS
Poor Little Eva,
Poor Little Eva,
Poor unfortunate child.
    (EVA *comes to center, weeping*)

TUPTIM
Is Buddha's wish
That Eva come to him
And thank him personally
For saving of Eliza and baby.
And so she die
And go to arms of Buddha.
    (EVA, *bowing her sad adieux to the audience,* **turns and** *climbs the steps to Buddha's high throne*)

CHORUS
Praise to Buddha,
Praise to Buddha!
    (*The music mounts in loud and uplifting crescendo. The curtain closes on the tragic tableau. The singers and dancers perform ceremonious bows in front of the curtain*)

ACT TWO | Scene Four

The KING'S *study.*
    ANNA *is seated on a pile of books beside the throne-table. The* KING *is walking up and down, smoking a long cigar.* SIR EDWARD *is standing, center, and the* KRALAHOME *is in the shadows to his left. It is night, after the banquet.*

SIR EDWARD   The evening was a great success, Your Majesty. I enjoyed Princess Tuptim's play immensely.

KING   This play did not succeed with me. It is immoral for King to drown when pursuing slave who deceive him. (*Pacing angrily*) Immoral! Immoral! Tuptim shall know of my displeasure.

SIR EDWARD   Your conversation at dinner was most amusing.

KING   I was forced to laugh myself. I was so funny.

SIR EDWARD   Her Majesty, Queen Victoria, will be very glad to know that we have come to such "felicity of agreement" about Siam.

KING   And very happy I am thereof. Very happy.

SIR EDWARD   I think now, with your permission, I should take my leave. (*He bows. The* KING *extends his hand in a manner clearly showing how unfamiliar he is with this Western amenity.* SIR EDWARD *shakes his hand, then bows to* ANNA) Good-bye, Anna, my dear. It was lovely to see you again.

ANNA   Good-bye, Edward. (*He goes out, escorted by the* KRALAHOME. *The* KING *turns to* ANNA) Well, Your Majesty . . .

KING   It is all over. (*He puts his cigar in a bowl, very glad to be rid of it*)

ANNA   May l remove my shawl? It is a very hot night. (*She does so. This makes the* KING *vaguely uneasy. He closes his own jacket across his bare chest as if to compensate for* ANNA's *lack of modesty*) I am so pleased about everything.

KING (*Trying not to be too sentimental about this*)   I am aware of your interest. I wish to say you have been of great help to me in this endeavor. I wish to make gift. (*He takes a ring from his finger and holds it out to her across the table, not looking at her*) I have hope you will accept. (*She takes it slowly and gazes at it*) Put it on finger! (*Still stunned, she does not move or speak*) Put it on! Put it on!
   (*His voice is gruff and commanding. She obeys him, slowly putting the ring on the index finger of her left hand*)

ANNA   Your Majesty, I do not know what to say!

KING   When one does not know what to say, it is a time to be silent! (*There is a pause. Both are embarrassed. The* KING *makes small talk*) A white elephant has been discovered in the forests of Ayuthia.

ANNA   You regard that as a good omen, don't you?

KING   Yes. Everything going well with us.

ANNA (*Warmly*)   Everything going well with us.
   (*A gong sounds off left*)

KING   Who, who, who?

KRALAHOME (*Offstage*)   It is I, Your Majesty.

KING   Wait, wait, wait! (*He goes to* ANNA *with a vaguely guilty manner and amazes her by replacing her shawl around her shoulders, then he calls offstage*) Come in! Come in!

KRALAHOME (*Entering and bowing*)   Your Majesty . . .

KING   Well, well, well?

KRALAHOME   Secret police are here. They would make report to you.

KING (*As* ANNA *rises*)   You will wait here.
   (*He goes out*)

ANNA (*Deeply concerned*)   Secret police?

KRALAHOME (*Noticing ring*)   Your finger shines.

ANNA (*Confused, feeling compromised*) Yes. The King. I did not know what to say. Women in my country don't accept gifts from men. Of course, he's the King . . . Actually, it places me in a rather embarrassing position. I was intending to ask him for a rise in salary. And now . . .

KRALAHOME And now it will be difficult to ask.

ANNA Very. (*Turns to him*) I don't suppose you would speak to him for me—about my rise in salary, I mean.

KRALAHOME I think I shall do this for you, because this is a strange world in which men and women can be very blind about things nearest to them.

ANNA Thank you, Your Excellency. I don't understand what you mean, but . . .

KRALAHOME No, but that does not matter—and I do not think he will rise your salary, anyway.

KING (*Entering briskly*) Ha! Good news and bad news come together. (*To* KRALAHOME) You will please to stay up all night until we have further report on item of Tuptim.

KRALAHOME I had intended to do so, Your Majesty.
  (*He bows and goes out*)

ANNA (*Rising*) Perhaps I had better go, too.

KING No! No! No! I wish to talk with you.

ANNA Is there something wrong with Tuptim?

KING I do not know, nor do I consider this the most important thing I must tell you. It is of greater interest that the English think highly of me. Secret police have served coffee after dinner, and listen as they talk and report conversation of British dignitaries.

ANNA (*Shocked*) You have been spying on your guests?

KING How else can one find the truth? (ANNA *shakes her head disapprovingly, but he ignores this*) It appears I have made excellent impression. It is clear they do not think me barbarian.

ANNA This is what we intended to prove.

KING What we intended to prove! (*Suddenly switching to the second item*) Tuptim!

ANNA   What about her?

KING   She is missing from palace. You know something of this?

ANNA (*Frightened*)   The last time I saw her, she was at the theater pavilion.

KING   That is last time anyone has seen her. She never speaks to you of running away?

ANNA (*Evasively*)   I knew she was unhappy.

KING   Why unhappy? She is in palace of King. What is greater honor for young girl than to be in palace of King?

ANNA   Your Majesty . . . If Tuptim is caught, shall she be punished?

KING   Naturally. What would you do if you were King like me?

ANNA   I believe I would give her a chance to explain. I think I would try not to be too harsh.

KING   Hmph.

ANNA (*Earnestly*)   Your Majesty, of what interest to you is one girl like Tuptim? She is just another woman, as a bowl of rice is just another bowl of rice, no different from any other bowl of rice.

KING   Now you understand about women! (*He picks up a book from the table*) But British poets . . .

ANNA (*Amused*)   You have been reading poetry, Your Majesty?

KING   Out of curiosity over strange idea of love, etcetera, etcetera. I tell you this poetry is nonsense, and a silly complication of a pleasant simplicity. (*He sings*)
A woman is a female who is human,
Designed for pleasing man, the human male.
A human male is pleased by many women,
And all the rest you hear is fairy tale.

ANNA
Then tell me how this fairy tale began, sir.
You cannot call it just a poet's trick.

Explain to me why many men are faithful,
And true to one wife only—

KING
They are sick!

ANNA (*Speaking*)   But you *do* expect *women* to be faithful.

KING   Naturally.

ANNA   Why naturally?

KING   Because it is natural. It is like old Siamese rhyme. (*He sings*)
A girl must be like a blossom
With honey for just one man.
A man must live like honey bee
And gather all he can.

To fly from blossom to blossom
A honey bee must be free,
But blossom must not ever fly
From bee to bee to bee.

ANNA   You consider this *sensible* poetry, Your Majesty?

KING   Certainly. But listen to this, from your own poet
Alf-red Tenny-sone. (*He reads from the book*)
"Now folds the lily all her sweetness up,
And slips into the bosom of the lake . . .
So fold thyself, my dearest, thou, and slip
Into my bosom . . ."
(*He looks sternly at* ANNA) English girls are so—acrobatic?

ANNA (*Laughing*)   Your Majesty, I don't know if I can ever
make it clear to you . . . We do not look on women as just
human females. They are . . . Well, take yourself. You are
not just a human male.

KING   I am King.

ANNA   Exactly. So every man is like a King and every woman
like a Queen, when they love one another.

KING   This is a sickly idea.

ANNA   It is a beautiful idea, Your Majesty. We are brought
up with it, of course, and a young girl at her first dance . . .

KING   Young girl? They dance, too? Like I see tonight? In arms of men not their husbands?

ANNA   Why, yes.

KING   I would not permit.

ANNA   It's very exciting when you're young, and you're sitting on a small gilt chair, your eyes lowered, terrified that you'll be a wallflower. Then you see two black shoes—white waistcoat—a face . . . It speaks! (*She sings*)
We've just been introduced,
I do not know you well,
But when the music started
Something drew me to your side.
So many men and girls are in each other's arms—
It made me think we might be
Similarly occupied.
   (*The* KING *sits on his throne-table watching* ANNA, *a new interest coming into his eyes*)
Shall we dance?
On a bright cloud of music shall we fly?
Shall we dance?
Shall we then say "good night" and mean "good-bye"?
Or, perchance,
When the last little star has left the sky,
Shall we still be together
With our arms around each other
And shall you be my new romance?
On the clear understanding
That this kind of thing can happen,
Shall we dance?
Shall we dance? Shall we dance?
   (ANNA, *carried away by her reminiscent mood, dances around the room until she glides by the* KING *and realizes that he is looking at her very much as he might look at one of his dancing girls. This brings her to an abrupt stop*)

KING   Why do you stop? You dance pretty. Go on! Go on! Go on!

ANNA   Your Majesty, I—I didn't realize I was—after all, I'm not a dancing girl. In England we don't—that is, a girl would not dance while a man is looking at her.

KING But she will dance with strange man, holding hands, etcetera, etcetera?

ANNA Yes. Not always a strange man. Sometimes a very good friend.

KING (*Pause*) Good! We dance together. You show me. (ANNA *looks a little uncertain*) You teach! You teach! You teach!
(*He holds out his hands and she takes them*)

ANNA It's quite simple, the polka. You count, "one two three *and* one two three *and* one two three *and*—"

KING One two three *and*.

ANNA (*Singing*)
Shall we dance?

KING
One two three *and*.

ANNA
On a bright cloud of music shall we fly?

KING
One two three *and*.

ANNA
Shall we dance?

KING
One two three *and*.

ANNA
Shall we then say "good night" and mean "good-bye"?

KING
One two three, *and*. (*He sings*)
Or perchance,
When the last little star has leave the sky—

ANNA
Shall we still be together,
With our arms around each other,
And shall you be my new romance?
(*KING sings the word "romance" with her*)
On the clear understanding
That this kind of thing can happen.

Shall we dance? Shall we dance? Shall we dance?
(*The orchestra continues, and* ANNA *resumes her lesson*) One
two three, *and*—
    (*She leads the* KING *by his hands*)

KING   One two three—one two three— (*He stops*) What is
wrong? I know! I know! I forget "And." This time I remember.

KING AND ANNA (*Counting together as they resume dancing*)
One two three *and*, one two three *and*, one two three *and* . . .

ANNA   That's splendid, Your Majesty!

KING   Splendid. One two and— (*He stops and protests
petulantly*) You have thrown me off count! (*They start
again*) One two three *and*, one two three *and*. (*They circle.
Suddenly he stops*) But this is not right!

ANNA   Yes, it is. You were doing . . .

KING   No! No! No! Is not right. Not the way I see Europeans
dancing tonight.

ANNA   Yes, it was. It was just like that.

KING   No! . . . Were not holding two hands like this.

ANNA (*Suddenly realizing what he means*)   Oh . . . No
. . . as a matter of fact . . .

KING   Was like this. No?
    (*Looking very directly into her eyes he advances on her
slowly and puts his hand on her waist*)

ANNA (*Scarcely able to speak*)   Yes.

KING   Come! One two three *and*, one two three *and* . . .
(*They dance a full refrain and dance it very well indeed,
rhythmically and with spirit, both obviously enjoying it. They
stop for a moment, stand off and laugh at each other. Then
he wants more. He goes back to her slowly*) Good! Come!
We try again. This time I do better.

ANNA   Very well, Your Majesty.
    (*They dance again, but only for a few whirls before a gong
crashes, and the* KRALAHOME *bursts in*)

KRALAHOME   Your Majesty . . .
    (*He prostrates himself.* ANNA *and the* KING *stop and sepa-
rate quickly*)

KING (*Furious*) Why do you burst through my door without waiting?

KRALAHOME We have found Tuptim.

KING (*A pause. He folds his arms, suddenly stern. His speech is cold and deliberate*) Where is she?

KRALAHOME Secret police are questioning her.

ANNA (*Terrified for* TUPTIM) Now you have found her, what will you do with her?

KING (*Now miles away from her*) I will do—what is usually done in such event.

ANNA What is that?

KING When it happens you will know. (TUPTIM *dashes on, falls on her knees at* ANNA'S *feet and clings to her skirt. Two* GUARDS *run after her, two more and the* INTERPRETER *take positions at the door*)

TUPTIM Mrs. Anna! Mrs. Anna! Do not let them beat me! Do not let them!
   (*The* GUARDS *silence her roughly and drag her away from* ANNA)

KRALAHOME She was found on Chinese sailing ship. See! She wears disguise of priest.

KING (*Shouting down at* TUPTIM'S *prostrate, quivering figure*) Who gave you this robe? Who? Who? Who?

KRALAHOME It is believed she was running away with man who brought her here from Burma.

KING (*Deep humiliation in his voice*) Dishonor. Dishonor. Dishonor.

KRALAHOME He was not found on boat.

KING (*To* TUPTIM) Where is this man?

TUPTIM I do not know.

KING You will tell us where we will find him! You will tell us!

TUPTIM I do not know.

KRALAHOME It is believed you were lovers with this man.

TUPTIM I was not lovers with this man.

KING Dishonor. We will soon have truth of this man.
(*He signals the* GUARDS. *They tear the priest robe off her, leaving her back bare. One of them unwinds a stout whip*)

TUPTIM Mrs. Anna!

ANNA (*Throwing herself on the man with the whip*) Stop that! Do you hear me? Stop it!

KING (*Coldly to* ANNA) It would be better if you understand at once that this matter does not concern you.

ANNA But it does. It does, dreadfully . . . because of her, and even more because of you.

KING You waste my time.

ANNA She's only a child. She was running away because she was unhappy. Can't you understand that? Your Majesty, I beg of you—don't throw away everything you've done. This girl hurt your vanity. She didn't hurt your heart. You haven't got a heart. You've never loved anyone. You never will.

KING (*Pause. The* KING, *stung by* ANNA's *words, seeks a way to hurt her in return*) I show you! (*He snatches the whip from the* GUARD) Give! Give to me!

ANNA (*Her eyes filled with horror*) I cannot believe you are going to do this dreadful thing.

KING You do not believe, eh? Maybe you will believe when you hear her screaming as you run down the hall! (*Pause*)

ANNA I am not going to run down the hall. I am going to stay here and watch you!

KING Hold this girl! (*The two* GUARDS *grab* TUPTIM's *arms*) I do this all myself.

ANNA You *are* a barbarian!

KING Down! Down! Down! (*The* GUARDS *hold* TUPTIM *down*) Am I King, or am I not King? Am I to be cuckold in my own palace? Am I to take orders from English school-teacher?

ANNA No, not orders . . .

KING Silence! . . . (*He hands the whip to the* KRALAHOME) I am King, as I was born to be, and Siam to be governed in my way! (*Tearing off his jacket*) Not English way, not French way, not Chinese way. My way! (*He flings the jacket at* ANNA *and takes back the whip from the* KRALAHOME) Barbarian, you say. There is no barbarian worse than a weak King, and I am strong King. You hear? Strong.

(*He stands over* TUPTIM, *raises the whip, meets* ANNA'S *eyes, pauses, then suddenly realizing he cannot do this in front of her, he hurls the whip from him, and in deep shame, runs from the room. After a moment of silence, the* KRALAHOME *claps his hands, and the* GUARDS *yank* TUPTIM *to her feet. They are about to drag her off when the* IN-TERPRETER *crawls forward and speaks to the* KRALAHOME)

INTERPRETER   The man—the lover has been found. He is dead.

TUPTIM   Dead . . . Then I shall join him soon . . . soon. (*The* GUARDS *drag her off. The* INTERPRETER *follows. The* KRALAHOME *turns and looks at* ANNA *scornfully*)

ANNA   I don't understand you—you or your King. I'll never understand him.

KRALAHOME   You! You have destroyed him. You have destroyed King . . . He cannot be anything that he was before. You have taken all this away from him. You have destroyed him. (*His voice growing louder*) You have destroyed King.

ANNA   The next boat that comes to the port of Bangkok—no matter where it goes, I shall be on it. (*She takes the ring from her finger and holds it out to him*) Give this back to His Majesty!

(*The* KRALAHOME *takes it. This the final humiliation for his* KING *to suffer*)

KRALAHOME (*Shouting, with heartbroken rage*)   I wish **you** have never come to Siam!

ANNA   So do I! (*She sobs*) Oh, so do I! (*She runs off*)

Intermediate Scene

The Palace grounds.

Townspeople and children come on, eagerly watching offstage for the approaching procession. CAPTAIN ORTON *enters and meets* PHRA ALACK.

PHRA ALACK   Captain Orton! Your ship has docked in time! We are welcoming elephant prince to Bangkok.

ORTON   White elephant, eh? So that's it. I just passed the young prince. Where is the King? I didn't see him in the procession.

PHRA ALACK (*His face clouding*)   The King is very ill. Very ill.

(*The procession now crosses the stage. Cymbal players, banner bearers, girls carrying huge oversized heads, and finally a dragon weaves on with four pairs of human legs propelling it. Girls dressed as strange birds dance around it. Finally* CHULALONGKORN *enters, accompanied by Amazons carrying ceremonial umbrellas. When the* PRINCE *reaches the center of the stage, the* INTERPRETER *runs on and bows before him. The* PRINCE *halts*)

INTERPRETER   Your Highness! Go no further! Go no further!

CHULALONGKORN   What is this you say?

INTERPRETER   Your father! Your father is worse!

CHULALONGKORN   Worse?

INTERPRETER   You are to return to the palace at once.

CHULALONGKORN (*Turning to those who are near him*)   Go on with the procession.

(*He starts off and then quickens his pace, deeply worried. The procession continues, but with all its gay spirit gone. The lights fade*)

ACT TWO | Scene Five

A room in ANNA'S *house. It has been dismantled except for a few pieces of furniture. There is a crate, up center, a Victorian chair, an oriental coffee table, and another chair. As the curtain rises* LADY THIANG *is seated, looking thoughtful and worried.*

CHULALONGKORN (*Entering*)   Mother! The Prime Minister told me you were here. I think Mrs. Anna and Louis have already left for the boat.

THIANG   No, Chulalongkorn. Some of their boxes are still here. (*She indicates the crate*) The servant said they would be back soon.
   (CHULALONGKORN *walks slowly toward his mother and stands before her*)

CHULALONGKORN   Mother, what is it with my father?

THIANG   It is his heart. (*She sits*) Also, he does not seem to want to live.

CHULALONGKORN   Mother, I am frightened. I am frightened because I love my father and also because if he dies, I shall be King, and I do not know how to be.

THIANG   Many men learn this after they become kings.

CHULALONGKORN   I have been thinking much on things Mrs. Anna used to tell us in classroom . . . Of slavery, etcetera, etcetera, and I think also on what she has said of religion, and how it is a good and noble concern that each man find for himself that which is right and that which is wrong.

THIANG   These are good things to remember, my son, and it will be good to remember the one who taught them.

LOUIS (*Entering*) Chulalongkorn!
(*They shake hands.* LOUIS *bows to* LADY THIANG)

ANNA (*Entering after* LOUIS) Lady Thiang! How nice of you to come to say good-bye! I was down at the ship seeing that all my boxes were on. Captain Orton must sail with the tide.

THIANG Mrs. Anna, I did not come only to say good-bye. I come for one who must see you. (ANNA, *guessing whom she means, turns away*) You must go to him, Mrs. Anna . . . When he heard that you were sailing, he started to write this letter. (*She unrolls a sheet of paper she has been holding*) All day he has been writing. It was very difficult for him, madam—very difficult. He has commanded that I bring it to you.

(ANNA *takes the letter*)

CHULALONGKORN Please to read it to all of us. I would like to hear what my father has said.

ANNA (*Reading*) "While I am lying here, I think perhaps I die. This heart, which you say I have not got, is a matter of concern. It occurs to me that there shall be nothing wrong that men shall die, for all that shall matter about man is that he shall have tried his utmost best. In looking back, I discover that you think much on those people who require that you live up to best of self. You have spoken truth to me always, and for this I have often lost my temper on you. But now I do not wish to die without saying this gratitude, etcetera, etcetera. I think it very strange that a woman shall have been most earnest help of all. But, Mrs. Anna, you must remember that you have been a very difficult woman, and much more difficult than generality." (*Tears come into* ANNA's *voice. She looks up at* THIANG) I must go to him! (*She starts out*) Come Louis!

(*They go, followed by* THIANG *and* CHULALONGKORN)

Intermediate Scene

A Palace corridor.
     ANNA *enters, followed by* LADY THIANG, CHULALONGKORN *and* LOUIS.

THIANG   I will see if he is awake. I will tell him you are here.
(*She goes out with* CHULALONGKORN)

LOUIS   Mother, I thought you and the King were very angry with each other.

ANNA   We were, Louis.

LOUIS   Now he's dying—does that make you better friends?

ANNA   I suppose so, Louis. We can't hurt each other any more.

LOUIS   I didn't know he hurt you.

ANNA   When two people are as different as we are, they are almost bound to hurt each other.

LOUIS   He always frightened me.

ANNA   I wish you had known him better, Louis. You could have been great friends. (*Smiling down at him*) In some ways he was just as young as you.

LOUIS   Was he as good a king as he could have been?

ANNA   Louis, I don't think any man has ever been as good a king as he could have been . . . but this one tried. He tried very hard.
(*Pause.* LOUIS *studies her*)

LOUIS   You really like him, don't you, Mother?

ANNA (*Barely controlling her tears*)   Yes, Louis. I like him very much. Very much indeed. (*Looking offstage*) We can go in now.

(*They start off as the lights fade*)

ACT TWO | Scene Six

The KING'S *study.*

The KING *lies on his bed, his head propped up slightly. His eyes are closed.* LADY THIANG *kneels beside him.* CHULA-LONGKORN *is crouched on the floor in front of her, and above the bed the* KRALAHOME *kneels and never takes his eyes from the* KING'S *face. Shortly after the rise of the curtain* LOUIS *enters and bows formally toward the* KING. *He is followed by* ANNA, *who curtseys and seats herself on a pile of books at the foot of the* KING'S *bed. The* KING'S *eyes open. Presently he addresses* ANNA.

KING   Many months . . . Many months I do not see you, Mrs. Anna. And now I die.

ANNA   Oh, no, Your Majesty.

KING   This is not scientific, Mrs. Anna. I know if I die or do not die. You are leaving Siam? (ANNA *nods*) When?

ANNA   Very soon, Your Majesty. In fact, I can stay only a few minutes more.

KING   You are glad for this? (ANNA *can find no answer*) People of Siam—royal children, etcetera, are not glad, and all are in great affliction of your departure.

ANNA   I shall miss them.

KING   You shall miss them, but you shall be leaving. I too am leaving. But I am not walking onto a boat with my own feet,

of my own free will. I am just . . . leaving. (*His eyes close,
but he has seen where* ANNA *is sitting*) Why is your head
above mine? (ANNA *rises, and* LOUIS *removes one of the books
from the pile. As* ANNA *sits again,* LOUIS *kneels beside her*) I
am not afraid of that which is happening to me. (*He whistles
the melody of the "Whistling Song."* ANNA *looks at him with
quick surprise. He smiles and explains*) You teach Chulalongkorn. Chulalongkorn teach me . . . "Make believe you
brave"—is good idea, always.

ANNA   You are very brave, Your Majesty. Very brave.

KING (*Taking from his finger the ring he has given her once
before*)   Here is—something belonging to you. Put it on. (*He
holds it out to her*) Put it on! Put it on! Put it on! (*Then, for
the first time in his life, he puts a plea in his voice*) Please
. . . wear it. (ANNA *takes it, unable to speak, and puts it on.
After a moment, the children enter, accompanied by the
Amazons.* LADY THIANG *rises hastily to quiet the children. The*
KING *hears them*) My children? Tell them to come here.
(*They hurry in and prostrate themselves before their father*)
Good evening, my children.

CHILDREN (*Together*)   Good evening, my father. (*Then they
rush to* ANNA, *clustering around her, hugging her, greeting her
in overlapping speeches*) Oh, Mrs. Anna. Do not go! We are
happy to see you. We have missed you so much, Mrs. Anna.
Will you stay, Mrs. Anna? Do not go away!

LADY THIANG   Stop! Stop this noise! Did you come to see
your father or Mrs. Anna?

KING (*He has watched the children with interest*)   It is all
right, Lady Thiang. It is suitable. (*The children settle on the
floor around* ANNA) Was it not said to me that someone has
written a farewell letter to Mrs. Anna?

THIANG   Princess Ying Yaowalak has composed letter to Mrs.
Anna. She cannot write. She only make up words.
   (PRINCESS YING YAOWALAK *stands up*)

KING   Speak letter now. (*The* PRINCESS *is uncertain*) Say it!
Say it! Say it!

YING YAOWALAK (*Reciting her "letter"*)   Dear friend and
teacher: My goodness gracious, do not go away! We are in
great need of you. We are like one blind. Do not let us fall

down in darkness. Continue good and sincere concern for us, and lead us in right road. Your loving pupil, Princess Ying Yaowalak.

(ANNA *rises, unable to speak, rushes to the little girl and hugs her*)

CHILDREN   Please to stay, Mrs. Anna. Do not leave us! We cannot live without you! We are afraid, Mrs. Anna. We are afraid without you.

KING   Hush, children. When you are afraid, make believe you brave. (*To* ANNA) You tell them how you do. You tell them. Let it be last thing you teach.

CHILDREN (*As* ANNA *looks uncertainly at the* KING)   Tell us then, Mrs. Anna. What to do when afraid? You teach us.

ANNA (*With a great effort to control her tears, she sings*)
Whenever I feel afraid
I hold my head erect.
    (*The children hold their heads up in imitation of her*)
And whistle a happy tune
So no one will suspect
                I'm afraid.
While shivering in my shoes
I strike a careless pose
    (*Her eyes go to* LOUIS, *who strikes the "careless pose." All the children imitate him*)
And whistle a happy tune
And no one ever knows
                I'm afraid.

KING (*Speaking over the music*)   You see? You make believe you brave, and you whistle. Whistle! (*The children look at him, not comprehending. He addresses* ANNA) You show them!

    (ANNA *whistles. The* KING *motions to the children. They all try to whistle, but cannot. Finally, something like a whistle comes from the twins. This is too much for* ANNA. *She kneels and throws her arms around them, weeping freely. The sound of a boat whistle is heard off in the distance*)

LOUIS (*Crossing to* ANNA *and tapping her shoulder*)   Mother . . . It's the boat! It's time!
    (*The children look at her anxiously. She rises*)

CHILDREN   Do not go, Mrs. Anna. Please do not go.

(*Pause. Then, suddenly,* ANNA *starts to remove her bonnet*)

ANNA   Louis, please go down and ask Captain Orton to take all our boxes off the ship. And have everything put back into our house.

(LOUIS *runs off eagerly. The children break into shouts of joy*)

KING   Silence! (*At the note of anger in his voice, the children, wives,* LADY THIANG—*all fall prostrate*) Is no reason for doing of this demonstration for schoolteacher realizing her duty, for which I pay her exorbitant monthly salary of twenty . . . five pounds! Further, this is disorganized behavior for bedroom of dying King! (*To* CHULALONGKORN, *who has remained crouching below the bed*) Chulalongkorn! Rise! (*The boy rises*) Mrs. Anna, you take notes. (*He hands her a notebook, and she sits on the pile of books*) You take notes from —next King. (LADY THIANG *lifts her head as the* KING *continues to the momentarily tongue-tied* PRINCE) Well, well, well? Suppose you are King! Is there nothing you would do?

CHULALONGKORN   (*In a small, frightened voice*)   I . . . would make proclamations.

KING   Yes, yes.

CHULALONGKORN   First, I would proclaim for coming New Year—fireworks. (*The* KING *nods his approval*) Also boat races.

KING   Boat races? Why would you have boat races with New Year celebration?

CHULALONGKORN   I like boat races. (*His confidence is growing. He speaks a little faster*) And, father, I would make a second proclamation.

(*He swallows hard in preparation for this one*)

KING   Well, go on! What is second proclamation? Make it! Make it!

CHULALONGKORN   Regarding custom of bowing to King in fashion of lowly toad. (*He starts to pace, very like his father*) I do not believe this is good thing, causing embarrassing fatigue of body, degrading experience for soul, etcetera, etcetera, etcetera. . . . This is bad thing. (*He crosses his arms defiantly*) I believe. (*He is losing his nerve a little*) You are angry with me, my father?

KING   Why do you ask question? If you are King you are King. You do not ask questions of sick man— (*Glaring at* ANNA) Nor of woman! (*Pointing an accusing finger at her*) This proclamation against bowing I believe to be your fault!

ANNA   Oh, I hope so, Your Majesty. I do hope so.
  (*Music of "He Can Be Wonderful" starts to be played here —very softly*)

CHULALONGKORN (*Clapping his hands twice*) Up! Rise up!
  (*A few rise. The others raise their heads, but are uncertain whether they should obey him*)

KING   Up! Up! Up! (*They all rise quickly, wives, Amazons, children*) Two lines, like soldiers. (*They line up*) It has been said there shall be no bowing for showing respect of King. It has been said by one who has . . . been trained for royal government.
  (*His head sinks back on the pillow, and his voice on the last word was obviously weak*)

CHULALONGKORN (*His voice stronger and more decisive*) No bowing like toad. No crouching. No crawling. This does not mean, however, that you do not show respect for King. (*The* KING'S *eyes close*) You will stand with shoulders square back, and chin high . . . like this. (ANNA *turns and notices that the* KING'S *eyes are closed. The* KRALAHOME, *knowing that he has died, crawls on his knees to the head of the bed, and crouches there, heartbroken, and not wishing other people to see that he is weeping.* CHULALONGKORN *continues his instructions*) You will bow to me—the gentlemen, in this way, only bending the waist. (*As he shows them and continues speaking,* ANNA *glides to the head of the bed, and feels the* KING'S *hand. Then she comes around the foot of the bed and sinks to the floor beside him, taking his hand and kissing it*) The ladies will make dip, as in Europe. (*He starts to show them a curtsey, but cannot*) Mother—
  (LADY THIANG *crosses to the center and drops a low curtsey before the women. As the music swells, all the women and girls carefully imitate her, sinking to the floor as the curtain falls, a final obeisance to the dead* KING, *a gesture of allegiance to the new one*)

Curtain

♡

Me and Juliet

♥

Me and Juliet *was first produced by Richard Rodgers and Oscar Hammerstein, II, on March 28, 1953, at the Majestic Theatre, New York City, with the following cast:*

(IN ORDER OF THEIR APPEARANCE)

EMPLOYMENT IN THE THEATRE

GEORGE, *2nd Assistant Stage Manager,*	Randy Hall
SIDNEY, *Electrician,*	Edwin Philips
JEANIE, *Chorus Singer,*	Isabel Bigley
HERBIE, *Candy Counter Boy,*	Jackie Kelk
CHRIS, *Rehearsal Piano Player,*	Barbara Carroll
MILTON, *Drummer,*	Herb Wasserman
STU, *Bass Fiddle Player,*	Joe Shulman
MICHAEL, *A Chorus Boy,*	Michael King
BOB, *Electrician,*	Mark Dawson
LARRY, *Assistant Stage Manager,*	Bill Hayes
MAC, *Stage Manager,*	Ray Walston
MONICA, *Chorus Dancer,*	Patty Ann Jackson
RUBY, *Company Manager,*	Joe Lautner
CHARLIE (*Me*), *Featured Lead,*	Arthur Maxwell
DARIO, *Conductor,*	George S. Irving
LILY (*Juliet*), *Singing Principal,*	Helena Scott
JIM (*Don Juan*), *Principal Dancer,*	Bob Fortier
SUSIE (*Carmen*), *Principal Dancer,*	Svetlana McLee
VOICE OF MR. HARRISON, *Producer,*	Henry Hamilton
VOICE OF MISS DAVENPORT, *Choreographer,*	Deborah Remsen
HILDA, *An aspirant for a dancing part,*	Norma Thornton
MARCIA, *Another aspirant for a dancing part,*	Thelma Tadlock
BETTY, *Successor to Susie as Principal Dancer,*	Joan McCracken
BUZZ, *Principal Dancer,*	Buzz Miller
RALPH, *Alley Dancer,*	Ralph Linn
MISS OXFORD, *A Bit Player,*	Gwen Harmon
SADIE, *An Usher,*	Francine Bond
MILDRED, *Another Usher,*	Lorraine Havercroft
A THEATRE PATRON	Barbara Lee Smith
ANOTHER THEATRE PATRON	Susan Lovell

ENSEMBLE: *Company, Stage Crew, Audience.*

DANCING ENSEMBLE: Francine Bond, Betty Buday, Penny Ann Green, Lorraine Havercroft, Patty Ann Jackson, Helene Keller, Lucia Lambert, Harriet Leigh, Sonya Lindgren, Elizabeth Logue, Shirley MacLaine, Cheryl Parker, Dorothy Silverherz, Thelma Tadlock, Norma Thornton, Janyce Ann Wagner, Rosemary Williams.

Lance Avant, Grant Delaney, John George, Jack Konzal, Ralph Linn, Eddie Pfeiffer, Augustine Rodriguez, Bob St. Clair, Bill Weber.

SINGING ENSEMBLE: Adele Castle, Gwen Harmon, Susan Lovell, Theresa Mari, Georgia Reed, Deborah Remsen, Thelma Scott, Barbara Lee Smith.

Jack Drummond, John Ford, Henry Hamilton, Richard Hermany, Warren Kemmerling, Michael King, Larry Laurence, Jack Rains.

PRODUCTION DIRECTED BY George Abbott
DANCES AND MUSICAL NUMBERS STAGED BY Robert Alton
SCENERY AND LIGHTING BY Jo Mielziner
COSTUMES DESIGNED BY Irene Sharaff

Scenes

The entire action takes place in the theatre in which *Me and Juliet* is currently playing.

Musical Numbers

ACT ONE

1. (a) *A Very Special Day* Jeanie and Trio
   (b) *That's the Way It Happens* Jeanie and Trio
2. *Reprise: That's the Way It Happens* Larry
3. *Dance Impromptu* Chorus, George and Trio
4. *Overture to* ME AND JULIET Dario and Orchestra
5. *Opening of* ME AND JULIET Lily, Jim, Susie and Charlie
6. *Marriage Type Love* Charlie, Lily and Singers
7. *Keep It Gay* Bob, Jim and Chorus
8. *Reprise: Keep It Gay* Betty and Buzz
9. *The Big, Black Giant* Larry
10. *No Other Love* Jeanie and Larry
11. *Dance* Ralph, Francine and Elizabeth
12. *Reprise: The Big, Black Giant* Ruby
13. *It's Me* Betty and Jeanie
14. *First Act Finale of* ME AND JULIET Lily, Betty, Charlie, Jim, Jeanie and Chorus

ACT TWO

1. *Intermission Talk* Herbie and Chorus
2. *It Feels Good* Bob
3. *Sequence in Second Act of* ME AND JULIET*: We Deserve Each Other* Betty, Jim and Dancers
4. *I'm Your Girl* Jeanie and Larry
5. *Second Act Finale of* ME AND JULIET Charlie, Lily, Betty, Jim and Chorus
6. *Finale of Our Play* Entire Company

The curtain rises on a bare stage. The proscenium arch is off center, so that we see the offstage area on the right. In the foreground the light bridge is lowered halfway to the floor. A rehearsal piano is set, stage left; the Stage Manager's desk, stage right.

    JEANIE *is playing the piano.* GEORGE, *the Assistant Stage Manager, enters.*

GEORGE Half hour! Half hour!

BOY (*Entering left*) Hi, George!
(SIDNEY, *the electrician, enters, carrying a lamp*)

SIDNEY How about some lights!

GEORGE (*Calling off stage*) Hey, Louis! Give us some lights!

VOICE (*Off stage*) Okay!
(*The lights come on*)

GEORGE Half hour! Half hour!
(*He exits.* SIDNEY *goes to a ladder that stands under the light bridge and carries the lamp up the ladder.* MILTON, *the drummer, has entered to set his drums above the piano.* JEANIE *rises from piano, striking keys with palms of her hands in a discordant bang*)

MILTON (*Looking at* JEANIE) That sounds kinda modern.
(*Exits*)

JEANIE (*Coming down to* SIDNEY) I've been stood up. Bob told me he was coming in early.

SIDNEY He told me he was coming early too. He's supposed to be here right now helping me. . . . Jeanie, how long have you been going with Bob?

JEANIE Since the show opened—about six months.

SIDNEY This the first time he stood you up?

JEANIE No

SIDNEY   Don't you ever get sore at him?

JEANIE   Sure I do. (*Smiling resignedly*) But he's always so sorry when he does anything wrong. He's like a kid.

SIDNEY   Yeah. He's cute.

JEANIE   You don't like Bob, do you?

SIDNEY   I like him all right. I'm up on this bridge with him all the time. We have a lot of laughs together. If that's all you want out of him he's fine. But if anybody gets an idea she can make him into something better than he is, she's letting herself in for something. That's all I gotta say. . . . Excuse me for butting in.

JEANIE   Oh, don't apologize, I get a lot of advice about Bob from everybody.
(*She saunters away, toward the Stage Manager's desk.* HERBIE *enters with his "Trio,"* CHRIS, *a piano player;* STU, *a bass fiddler; and* MILTON, *the drummer*)

HERBIE   Come on kids it'll be curtain time before you know it. Come on, get going! Know what we're doing, Sidney? We're getting up a Trio. (HERBIE *turns to the* TRIO, *who have started playing*) That's it kids. (*To* SIDNEY) We're going on Arthur Godfrey's Talent Scouts.

SIDNEY   You going to be the Scout?

HERBIE   Sure. Can you see me sitting up there at the desk next to Arthur Godfrey?

SIDNEY   Yeh. I can hear you too. He'll ask you where you come from and you'll say Brooklyn and everybody'll clap.
(GEORGE *comes back and meets two girls and a boy as they enter and cross the stage*)

GIRL   Hi ya, George. Going to give us a little music on your whistle?

GEORGE   Better get made up first.

GIRL   We'll put on our smocks.

2ND GIRL   On the way down to get our costumes . . .

GEORGE   O.K.
(*They exit.* JEANIE *is now seated at the Stage Manager's desk. Lost in her own thoughts, she sighs to herself*)

JEANIE
Oh, dear! (*She sings*)
Am I building something up
That really isn't there?
Do I make a big romance
Of a small affair?
Should I be more practical
As friends would have me be?
. . . Being practical is very hard for me.

I wake up each morning
With a feeling in my heart
That today will be a very special day.
I keep right on clinging
To that feeling in my heart
Till the winds of evening blow my dreams away.
Later on, at bedtime,
When my world has come apart
And I'm in my far from fancy negligee—
With a piece of toast to munch
And a nice hot cup of tea,
I begin to have a hunch
That tomorrow's going to be
A very special day for me.
    (*Voices in* JEANIE'S *mind*)
Jeanie, would you get sore if I offered some advice?
You can do better than him, Jeanie.
Why an electrician?
How'd you happen to tie up with a guy like that?
How does a thing like that start?

JEANIE   How does it start? (*She sings*)
You're a girl from Chicago
On the road with a show—
Not a soul in New Haven
You can say you know.
    You wish you were a mile or so from Michigan Lake,
    Home with your mother and a T-bone steak.
Then along comes a fellow
With a smile like a kid,
And he gets your attention
With a timely bid.
    He says he knows a bistro where they give you a break
    With French fried potatoes and a T-bone steak!

You are shy and uncertain
But he pleads and you yield,
And you don't have an inkling
That you're signed and sealed
   By merely telling someone you'd be glad to partake
   Of French fried potatoes and a T-bone steak.
      That's the way it happens,
      That's the way it happens,
      That's the way it happened to me!
   (JEANIE *exits. Several boys and girls enter*)

BOY   Hey, did you see this in Variety? (*Reading*) "Musical pays off. Backers of *Me and Juliet* out of red and due to collect plenty on unconventional dance opera."

BOB (*Entering*)   Hi, Sidney!

SIDNEY   Well!

BOB   Am I late?

SIDNEY   Yes, you're late.

BOB   I just ran into a guy I knew.

SIDNEY   That was nice.

BOB   You're not sore, are you, angel face?
   (*He musses* SIDNEY's *hair up*)

SIDNEY   Get to work on that cable. We haven't got much time. (BOB *starts to work on a cable that is coiled on the floor near the stepladder. More of the* COMPANY *enter*) Jeanie was here just now.

BOB   Why didn't she wait for me? (SIDNEY *gives him a sarcastic look*) Was she sore? (SIDNEY *shrugs his shoulders*) Guess I'll have to talk my way out of it, huh? (*He chuckles*) She's a sweet kid.

SIDNEY (*With studied casualness*)   Ever think you'd like to marry Jeanie?

BOB   Me? Not on your life! . . . I know *too many* guys who got hooked. You know what happens soon's you get married? Right away the dame's got to go to the dentist and get all her teeth fixed. You get a bill for three hundred bucks. That's only the beginning . . .

SIDNEY (*Getting angry on* JEANIE's *behalf*)   Ah, she wouldn't have you anyway. I'm surprised she even talks to you. (*A*

puzzled expression crosses BOB'S *face. He's not quite* **sure**
whether SIDNEY *is kidding or not*) One of the best-lookin'
babes in the show. You'd think she could get something better'n a baboon like you. (BOB *comes behind* SIDNEY *and grabs
him by the collar of his shirt, and by the seat of his trousers,
and lifts him up so that he's nearly clear of the ground.
Everyone on stage stands still and silent, worried and fascinated, witnessing a big man bullying a little man*) Hey, what
are you doing? Cut it out, Bob! I got the lens in my hand!
Want me to break it? I was only kiddin'. Cut it out, I tell you!
You damn fool!

BOB   Who's a damn fool?
   (BOB, *still holding* SIDNEY'S *trousers with one hand, garrotes
   him with the other arm*)

SIDNEY (*His voice muffled, choking*)   You're hurting me!
(BOB *releases him*) What the hell's the matter with you, anyway? (BOB *walks away, roaring with laughter. More of the*
COMPANY *enter, sense something wrong*) You're a cute kid!
Funny as hell! (BOB *laughs even louder*) What's the matter
with you? You getting like you used to be! (BOB *stops laughing suddenly*)

BOB   What's that?
   (JEANIE *enters dressed like the other girls in the knee-
   length smock that is worn before they go downstairs to put
   on their costumes. She remains upstage, unseen by the
   others*)

SIDNEY (*Staring back at* BOB *with the reckless courage of
panic*)   I said . . .

BOB   I heard what you said. (*He walks slowly over to* SIDNEY
and stands in front of him) And don't ever say that again.
(*Raising his voice to a shout*) You hear? (*Lowering his voice
again*) Don't you ever . . . I'm not like I used to be—and
it's damn lucky for you I'm not. (*He stands scowling down at*
SIDNEY *as if not quite sure whether he will throttle him or
not. Then he becomes conscious of* JEANIE'S *presence. Embarrassed, he switches to his other self—the big charm boy*)
Hello, Jeanie . . . (*A nervous laugh*) What do you know
about this guy Sidney? Trying to kid me—said you were sore
because I got here late. (*He walks over to her*) You're not
sore, are you, kid?

JEANIE (*Uncertainly*)   No.
(*The* TRIO *start to play again. A few of the boys and girls start to slip easily into some light jazz steps, but this is all done upstage of the piano*)

BOB   Know what made me late? I was lookin' at that piano
(JEANIE *stops and turns slowly, as if unable to resist talking about the piano*)

JEANIE   The one I told you about?

BOB   Yeh. On Fifty-seventh Street. The little one.
(*Pause*)

JEANIE   Did you like it?

BOB   Sure did. Wish I could buy it for you. Maybe by Christmas I can save enough for a down payment, huh?
(*Pause*)

JEANIE   What were you and Sidney fighting about?

BOB   We weren't fighting. We were just clowning. Weren't we, Sid?

SIDNEY (*Working on his lamp*)   Yeh. Just clowning.

HERBIE (*Referring to the music his* TRIO *is making*)   Ain't that crazy!

BOB   Come here. I want to tell you something.
(*He grabs* JEANIE, *lifts her onto Stage Manager's desk, and starts to whisper to her*)

LARRY (*Entering*)   Hey, Sidney, we've got to get this bridge out of the way. People will be coming in and knocking the lamps off—their angles.
(*He stops in the middle of his sentence because he has looked over and seen* JEANIE *sitting on the desk talking to* BOB)

HERBIE (*Coming over to him*)   Hi, Larry. Did you hear what I'm going to do for these kids? I'm going to get them a chance with Arthur Godfrey. When I get on the air, would you like me to give you a plug? Like I can say we got an assistant stage manager who's one great guy?

LARRY   Excuse me a minute, Herbie. (*He goes over to the desk*) Bob. I'm afraid I've got to get at my desk. I've got some work.

BOB   Okay. This is your desk. (*Picking up* JEANIE) And this is my girl. (BOB *exits, carrying* JEANIE *off with him*)

(*The boys and girls start to dance softly to the* TRIO's *music. The lights come down on the dancers who group around the piano, swaying in rhythm.* LARRY, *at his desk, starts to think back on the recent past, just as* JEANIE *did when she sat there a few minutes ago*)

LARRY (*Singing*)
You're a guy in New Haven on the road with a show.
There's a girl in the company that you hardly know.
    You watch her and you wonder if she'd like to partake
    Of French fried potatoes and a T-bone steak.
    (*He looks off where* BOB *carried* JEANIE)
Then along comes a fellow who is quicker than you,
And he does what you thought that you would like to do—
    He takes her to a bistro where they give you a break
    With French fried potatoes and a T-bone steak.
Now you see them together and you know in your heart
That you lost what you wanted at the very start,
    Because you didn't ask her if she'd like to partake
    Of French fried potatoes and a T-bone steak!
That's the way it happens,
That's the way it happens,
That's the way it happened to me.

SIDNEY (*Shouting up to the flies*)   Hey, Ernie! Take the bridge up a little.

(*The spot fades on* LARRY *and the lights come up on the dancing group. The music and dancing both get hot now.* GEORGE, *the Assistant Stage Manager, augments the* TRIO *with his tin whistle, and maintaining a spontaneous and impromptu spirit, the dance builds up to a big climax and stops. After applause it is started again, and after about sixteen measures* MAC *enters. As they see him, the dancers stop and so do the musicians.* MAC *stands in the center of the stage looking from one to another. He is obviously respected as a disciplinarian. After he has achieved a few seconds of awed silence he turns slowly and speaks to* LARRY *quietly*)

MAC   Two minutes after, Larry!

LARRY (*Feeling guilty like the rest*)   Oh . . . er . . . George, see if they're all signed in.

GEORGE (*Making the call as he crosses the stage and exits*) Fifteen minutes! Fifteen minutes!

MAC (*Meanwhile* MAC *turns to the rest of the company who are melting away very quickly. He calls to the last girl going out. She is the color of a cooked lobster*) Monica! (MONICA *turns and tries to look casual*) I see you've been down to the beach.

MONICA (*Assuming gay and girlish innocence*) How do you like my sunburn?

MAC Great! Just dandy. Best way I know to take the audience's mind off a play. (*She opens her mouth to answer but closes it again*) Sometimes a girl dances so much better than all the others that she stands out like a sore thumb. You've got a different way. You try to *look* like a sore thumb! (*She looks down at herself to check*) Go and get dressed. (MONICA *crosses left to some girls, one of whom starts to put her hand on* MONICA'S *shoulder*)

MONICA Ouch!
    (*They exit down left.* MAC *turns to* LARRY)

MAC Let's have a look at the report. (LARRY *hands it to him. He starts to read it*) We ran three minutes longer last night.

LARRY Yes. Lost one minute on intermission.
    (RUBY, *the company manager, enters*)

RUBY Herbie, I'm only the company manager, but . . .

HERBIE (*To* RUBY) Hey, Ruby, have you heard, I'm sponsoring an act on the Arthur Godfrey show?

RUBY If Mr. Shubert drops in and sees nobody behind your candy counter, who's going to sponsor *you*?

HERBIE Gosh! I didn't know it was so late.
    (*He exits.* RUBY *turns and exits on the other side. During the ensuing scene the crew are setting up the scenery and props for the first scene of* Me and Juliet)

MAC (*His eyes still on the Stage Manager's report, pretending to read it while he speaks*) That was quite a clambake going on when I came in here.

LARRY I guess I should have stopped it. They were all having such a good time that I . . .

MAC   Well, let them have a good time after the show. I don't care if . . .

GIRL (*Running across stage*)   I'm awfully sorry, the traffic was terrible!
   (LARRY *becomes conscious that* MAC *has looked up from the report and is studying him*)

LARRY   I suppose you're thinking I'll never make a good stage manager.

MAC (*After a pause*)   Is that what you want to be?

LARRY   Why, yes. I guess so. Sure.

MAC   What you really want to be is a director, isn't it?

LARRY   Yes, but I ought to learn to run a stage first.

MAC   Not necessarily. Lots of good directors were lousy stage managers. Josh Logan was a lousy stage manager.

LARRY   That's encouraging.

MAC   Stage managing is a special kind of job, like directing or acting or anything else. The stage manager is like the mayor of a small town. He's got to . . .

CHARLIE (*Shouting offstage*)   Mac! (*Hearing the note in* CHARLIE'S *voice,* MAC *winces.* CHARLIE *enters left in a dressing gown and crosses to them, fuming*) Mac, I don't want to pull any corny temperament . . . (*He picks up a chair by the desk and bangs it on the floor*) But has an actor got the right to have the audience hear him when he sings? . . . Does the audience come to hear him? (*He starts to raise his voice*) —or do they come to hear a lot of trombones and drums? Just tell me! I want to know! (*He is now screeching*) That idiot! That conductor!

MAC   I'll talk to Dario.

CHARLIE   Well, damn it, if you don't . . .

LARRY   Here's Dario. Take it easy.
   (*Following his eyes,* MAC *and* CHARLIE *turn and see* DARIO, *who has just entered left. He is wearing a dinner coat and carries a small square cardboard box, which he puts on the piano. During the ensuing dialogue he opens it*)

CHARLIE (*Lowering his voice*)   Well, tell him

MAC   I'll tell him.

CHARLIE (*Still whispering, but through his teeth*)   Because if he does it to me again tonight, I'm going downstairs and wait outside the pit, and when he comes out I'm going to punch him right in the nose.

MAC   I'll tell him.
  (CHARLIE *turns and crosses the stage. As he passes him,* DARIO *looks up*)

DARIO (*He is just taking a gardenia out of the box*)   Good evening, Charlie.

CHARLIE (*With friendly heartiness*)   Hi ya, Dario baby!
  (CHARLIE *exits,* MAC'S *eyes following him off as he muses*)

MAC   Lovable Charlie Clay! Audiences adore him—they say he's got a wistful quality.

LARRY (*Nodding toward* DARIO)   Is it true that Dario is leaving the show?

MAC   He *thinks* he's leaving. But he's the best conductor in town and I'm not going to let him go.

LARRY   How're you going to get him to stay if he doesn't want to?

MAC   I got a gimmick. (*Looking across speculatively at* DARIO *who has taken a letter from the box and is reading it*) See that letter he's reading? It's from a dame who signs herself "the gardenia lady"—says she's crazy about him, and that she'll be somewhere in the audience tonight.

LARRY   How do you know what's in the letter?

MAC   I wrote it. (DARIO *having read the letter, folds it tenderly and puts it in his breast pocket. With a soulful smile he puts the gardenia in his lapel*) I'm going to send him one every night. I figure he won't leave the show till he finds out who the dame is.
  (*By this time, Scene One of* Me and Juliet *has been set. It is off center at the moment—and the* COMPANY *are drifting onto the stage and taking their places. The dancers, as usual, are stretching and limbering up*)

DARIO (*Crossing to* MAC *and* LARRY, *walking on a cloud*) Good evening, gentlemen. Is it time for me to go in yet?

MAC   Just about. (DARIO *turns and starts to exit, humming happily.* MAC *calls to him*) Oh, Dario! (DARIO *turns*) Charlie says . . .

DARIO   I know! I am drowning him out! Every night the same. (*Starting to work himself up into a temper something like* CHARLIE'S) Tell him for me that thirty men in an orchestra can play no quieter!

MAC   Well, he's got a cold. Got a bum throat.

DARIO (*Raising his voice*)   He was born with a bum throat. That man is my only reason for leaving the show. You know that!

MAC (*Pointing at the gardenia, tactfully changing the subject*)   No carnation tonight?

DARIO (*Immediately brought back to heaven, looking down at his lapel*)   No. I thought I would wear a gardenia tonight.
    (*He smiles with serene contentment.* GEORGE *crosses the stage to* MAC)

GEORGE   O.K., Mac, I've sent the men in.

DARIO   Good. I shall go down. Funny thing. I just feel like playing the show tonight.
    (*He turns and starts to sing happily as he exits through the wings*)

MAC (*To* LARRY)   I think this is going to work. I want to go out front for the overture. Want to see what happens when Dario goes into the orchestra pit. I bet he'll get dizzy looking around for that dame.
    (MAC *starts off. More of the* COMPANY *keep coming on.* LILY, *who plays "Juliet," calls after him*)

LILY (*Entering*)   Oh, Mac. I've arranged with the office to take my vacation in August.

MAC (*Starts to exit*)   Okay, Lily. Have a good time. (*Sees two girls sitting on chairs*) Get up off those costumes! (*Exits*)

LARRY (*Calling to* JEANIE, *who has come on with the others*) Jeanie! (*He walks over to her*) I wanted to ask you something. When Lily takes her vacation in August, her understudy will have to go on. (JEANIE *looks at him steadily, waiting for him to finish his story. This disconcerts* LARRY *and he stutters and stumbles a bit*) You know, in the summertime, when understudies cover principals, we've got to get other understudies to—er—cover *them.*

JEANIE   Gee, Larry, I don't think I'd even have the nerve to go on. I don't want to be an actress. The only reason I tried to get in this show was because the pay was good.

LARRY   The pay'll be fifteen dollars a week more if you make second understudy.

JEANIE   Me play Juliet! I don't think I'm the Juliet type.

LARRY   I think you are . . . Help you buy that piano.

JEANIE   How did you know?

LARRY   About the piano? You told me once. You said you knew just where you'd put it—between two windows in your room.

JEANIE   Imagine your remembering that!
   (LARRY *goes to his desk and calls into microphone*)

LARRY   Overture! (CHARLIE *has come on and joined a group of girls. They are heard laughing at one of his jokes*) Everybody in first scene—places on stage!

SIDNEY (*Calling up to the fly floor*)   Ernie, let her in!
   (*The light bridge is lowered*)

JEANIE   I can't understand how that happened to stick in your mind—about me saving up for a piano. How did you happen to remember that?

LARRY   I remembered it. Thought about it often.

BOB (*Entering*)   Here we go, kid.
   (*He gives* JEANIE *a proprietary slap and mounts the light bridge with* SIDNEY)

LARRY (*Into microphone*)   Overture! Everybody in first scene! Overture!

A BOY (*Walking up to a girl*)   Can I have some of your mascara?

GIRL   Sure.
   (*He takes some mascara off her eyelash, between his thumb and forefinger*)

BOY   Got a hole in my tights.
   (*The boy rubs the black mascara on his leg to cover up the hole. This is all done with the laconic resourcefulness of professionals*)

SIDNEY (*On bridge with* BOB, *calling up to fly floor*)   Take it away!
   (*The bridge is raised slowly. The* Me and Juliet *curtain is lowered in front of it, but it is transparent while the lights remain on behind it. Therefore you can see the bridge being raised with its colored lights glowing. On the stage the singers start to warm up with scales and exercises. The dancers limber up and stretch.* JEANIE *waves to* BOB *as the bridge goes up and then she looks over at* LARRY. *As the curtain hits the stage the lights are taken off behind it and it is no longer transparent*)

ACT ONE | Scene Two

The orchestra pit.
   The lights flood the show-curtain of Me *and* Juliet. *Then a spot hits* DARIO *entering the pit. As he mounts the stand he gazes around the audience, obviously trying to spot the lady of the gardenia. He taps the stand and starts the overture.*

OVERTURE—DARIO AND ORCHESTRA

   For a while he concentrates on the music. Then, at a sentimental part, he turns around again and takes a chance that the lady of the gardenia is watching him. He lowers his nose and smells his gardenia passionately. He goes back to conducting, then as the orchestra starts to build to its climax, he looks around to make sure she is watching his magnificent gyrations. After he brings his baton down on the last beat of the overture, he turns and takes a bow and takes advantage of the bowing to look again for his "lady of the gardenia" and to blow a kiss at her, wherever she may be. Then he turns, lifts his baton, and brings it down to start the short prelude which will bring the curtain up on Me and Juliet.

ACT ONE | Scene Three

The curtain rises on a dark stage. A pin spot hits JULIET, *who stands on a balcony. Below the balcony are her hand-maidens, who are as yet not seen, but now their voices are heard.*

VOICES
Where is this?

JULIET
It doesn't matter.
The scene of the play
Is neither here nor there.
All the things
About to happen
Are things that are always happening everywhere.

VOICES
When is this?

JULIET
It doesn't matter.
The time of the play

Is neither now nor then.
Every year
The world is changing—
But women remain the same—
     (*A spot hits* CARMEN)
And so do men!
     (*A spot hits* DON JUAN. *He is surrounded by girls*)

VOICES
Who are they?
     (*A spot hits* ME)

ME
They are the most important people in my life.

VOICES
Who are you?

ME
I? I am ME.
I am an ordinary character,
With an extraordinary interest in myself.
My own conception of ME—
     (*He looks at his clothes*)
Is—er—idealized.
The things that happen to ME seem remarkable
The people I know—
Well, look at them!
     (*Indicating* DON JUAN)
This man, here, is my boss.
His name is Emil Phlugfelder.
But he has so many girls chasing him
That I call him DON JUAN.
     (DON JUAN *starts to move, slowly, rhythmically. The* GIRLS
     dance with him. ME *watches him enviously. After* DON
     JUAN *exits with the* GIRLS, ME *looks up at* JULIET, *then
     comes downstage and explains her to the audience*)
On the mezzanine floor
Of the place where I work
There's a girl—
One of the file clerks.
     (*He turns toward* JULIET)
I look up from my desk
And there she is, on the balcony.

I always see her in a kind of glow.
To me, she is—JULIET!
She's the girl I'm going to marry.
   (*Walking toward* CARMEN)
This one is a girl
I am *not* going to marry . . .
But she *bothers* me.
I see her everywhere—
In the subway, in the park, on the beach.
I call her—CARMEN.
   (CARMEN *dances toward him. He backs away but is*
   fascinated by her. Then there is practically a stampede
   of men rushing on from the left toward CARMEN. ME *steps*
   aside and CARMEN *dances with the men. As she exits with*
   them she looks back temptingly at ME, *who looks after*
   her a bit wistfully. Then ME *turns away and comes down*
   toward the audience)
Now you know them all,
The characters who will shape my life.
But this one—
   (*Indicating* JULIET)
My life didn't really begin
Till I met her.
I'll never forget our first date.
We sat on a park bench and fed the pigeons!
Ah, Juliet!
Look at her!
So young, so in need of protection.
As soon as you see a girl like that,
You want to marry her,
So that you can protect her
From all the men
Who want to protect her from you!
   (*He looks back at her*)
She makes me think of gentle and beautiful things:
Sunlit meadows, the laughter of children—
Juliet!
   (*She is coming down to him. He turns to audience*)
When she speaks, it is like the faint echo
Of far-off bells on a misty morning.
   (*He turns back to* JULIET)
Speak to me, Juliet!

JULIET (*In a voice that sounds like a misty morning, but with no bells in it*)
Hi!
  (*He sighs ecstatically*)

ME (*He sings*)
When first I laid my longing eyes on you
I saw my future shining in your face,
And when you smiled and murmured "Howd'you do?"
The room became a dream-enchanted place.
  The chandeliers were shooting stars,
  The drums and horns and soft guitars
  Were sounding more like nightingales,
  The window curtains blew like sails,
  And I was floating just above the floor,
  Feeling slightly taller than before.
Out of nowhere
Came the feeling,
Knew the feeling—
  Marriage type love.
We were dancing
And your eyelash
Blinked on my lash—
  Marriage type love!
We made a date, couldn't wait
  For my day off.
Now it's a thing with a ring
  For the pay-off!
I'm your pigeon,
Through with roaming,
I am homing
  To marriage type love and you.
  (*The chorus joins them in singing. As the curtain comes down on this prologue to* Me and Juliet, CHARLIE *as* ME *and* LILY *as* JULIET *step forward so that the curtain is behind them. They sing an encore refrain during which* DARIO *makes the orchestra play very loudly and drown* CHARLIE *out every time he sings. When* JULIET *sings he plays softly. As the refrain is ended* JULIET *blows a kiss to* DARIO *as she exits and* CHARLIE, *infuriated, mutters something which if you can read lips is very insulting indeed. Scowling at* DARIO *he makes his exit*)

ACT ONE | Scene Four

The Light Bridge.
BOB *and* SIDNEY *are busily changing colors in their lamps.*

SIDNEY (*Continuing an argument*)   All right, so I'm stupid! I still say I don't know what the hell it's about . . . First thing that happens, a dame comes out and tells the audience the scene is no place and the time is any time at all. If they don't know where the hell they are, how are the audience going to know?

BOB   It's symbolic. This guy they call "Me"—he's the kind that wants a wife and a couple of kids and a little house somewhere, Flushing or someplace like that.

SIDNEY   Flushing, huh? I don't live so far from there.

BOB   That's what I mean.

SIDNEY   You mean I'm like him?

BOB   In a general way.

SIDNEY (*Derisively*)   Ah, go on! Do you think I'd be acting like he's acting now? Look at him down there! Sitting on a park bench! That Carmen giving him the business and him looking like a scared rabbit. Look at her! Rollin' her eyes at him.

BOB   Boy, she's rolling everything! You can see good from up here . . . Did y'ever think what fun it'd be to stand up here and drop sandbags on the actors? Pick 'em off one by one!

SIDNEY   Look at that guy now! Why don't he give in to that Carmen dame?

BOB He's got the other one on his mind. Don't you see she's in a vision back there? He sees Juliet in his dreams while that Carmen dame is trying to make him. When a guy makes up his mind to marry, he doesn't want to look at any outside stuff—for a while. Didn't you feel like that before you got married? (SIDNEY *thinks*) Well, didn't you?

SIDNEY I'm just trying to remember. The way I proposed to Josephine was kinda funny. All her family were there, her mother and her father and three brothers. And the oldest brother said, "When are you kids going to get married?" And everybody looked at me, and I said, "Oh, whenever Josephine will have me." You know, I was kinda half joking . . . Five minutes later all the neighbors came in and we were having drinks and that's what they called announcing the engagement.

BOB Well, you loved her, didn't you?

SIDNEY Sure I loved her.

BOB So you see, the other dames couldn't tempt you, could they?

SIDNEY How do I know? Nobody tried! Nobody like that Carmen down there.
  (BOB *looks down. The refrain of "Keep It Gay" is being played*)

BOB This Don Juan feller, he's more like me. We like a good time.

SIDNEY Aw, so do I like a good time.

BOB (*Laughing*) Sure you do. You *like* it, but you don't *get* it.
  (BOB *sings with the music*)
"Let it sing like a nightingale in May,
Keep it Gay."

SIDNEY (*In a loud whisper*) Sh! They'll hear you down there!

BOB They can't hear me. (*Singing*)
"Take it easy and enjoy it while you take it!"

SIDNEY If you like singing so much why don't you get a job as an actor?

BOB   I bet I could play the part better than the mug who's playing it now.

(*He sings*)

When a girl would meet Don Juan
She'd get goofy for the Don.
Like a snake who meets a mongoose
That young lady was a gone goose.
Any time a girl would say:
"Shall we name a wedding day?"
Juan would try another gambit
(He liked weddings not a damn bit).
He would gaze into the lady's eye,
Strumming his guitar to stall for time.
Then he'd make his usual reply—
That old reliable Andalusian rhyme:

   Keep it gay,
   Keep it light,
   Keep it fresh,
   Keep it fair.
   Let it bloom
   Ev'ry night,
   Give it room,
   Give it air!
   Keep your love a lovely dream and never wake it.
   Make it happy and be happy as you make it!
   Let it sing
   Like a nightin-
   gale in May,
   Keep it gay.
   Keep it free
   Or you'll frighten
   It away.
   Take it easy and enjoy it while you take it!
   Keep it gay,
   Keep it gay,
   Keep it gay!

(*The lights go out on* SIDNEY *and* BOB *and immediately come up on the stage below where* DON JUAN *and the girls are dancing this same number in* Me and Juliet. *At a certain point in the dance the lights go out and a few seconds later come up, finding* DON JUAN *and the chorus in the same pose, only they are now in practice clothes, rehearsing the number. This is the beginning of the next scene*)

ACT ONE | Scene Five

The bare stage.
    CHRIS *is playing the piano for rehearsal over at the right side of the stage.* RUBY *leans on the piano, just sort of "hanging around, watching things."* LARRY *stands against the proscenium. Upstage are flats and drops from the production of* Me and Juliet. *Around the traveler curtains, on either side, are wooden rails to protect them, and "pants" of burlap around them, as there were in Scene One.*
    After the dance MAC'S *voice can be heard from the front of the house.*

MAC'S VOICE   All right! All right! That was fine! Now we've got it back to the way we had it! (*The* COMPANY *stand, sit and lie on the stage, panting heavily, looking out front, listening to* MAC, *as if he were making a speech from about the tenth row. They seem faintly embarrassed, as all groups do when listening to a speech from a Stage Manager or Producer*) I know it's no fun rehearsing on a hot day in June, but it's also no fun to be out of a job on a cold day in February, and that's what'll happen to all of us if we don't keep these performances up. O.K. That's all. Thank you.
    (*The group breaks up and drifts off stage, some quickly, others slowly.* SIDNEY *comes down to the very edge of the stage and peers out into the dark auditorium*)

SIDNEY   Hey, Mac! Can I have the stage now?

MAC'S VOICE (*From the front*)   Not right away. We've got replacement auditions for the part of Carmen. You can have it in about twenty minutes.

LARRY (*Coming down quickly*)   I've got an understudy call right after the audition.

SIDNEY   Then when the hell am I going to get a chance to change my color frames? (*Talking out to* MAC) All the colors are faded. You were complaining last night.

MAC'S VOICE   Who are you rehearsing, Larry?

LARRY   Second understudy for Juliet. I'm trying out Jeanie. (*There is a pause*)

MAC'S VOICE   Oh . . . Well, hold it a minute. I'll come up on stage and we'll talk it over.
(LARRY *turns to* SIDNEY, *in the manner of one making a retreat*)

LARRY   I think we can work it out all right, Sidney. I'll rehearse downstage here, if you'll try not to make a lot of noise.

SIDNEY (*Smiling as if he knows a secret*)   I'll be as quiet as a little mouse, chum. I wouldn't interfere with your—rehearsal—for anything in the world.
(SIDNEY *exits across the other side of the stage*)

CHRIS (*To* RUBY)   What's that about replacement auditions for Carmen?

RUBY   We've got to get a new one. Susie's leaving. She's going to have a baby.

CHRIS   Susie?

RUBY   Ask Susie's husband.

GIRL   Jim?

JIM   Yes, I am—I mean she is.

MAC (*Entering making a general announcement to all the stragglers*)   Clear the stage! We're having auditions here in a minute. What are you hanging around for?

LARRY   Oh, Mac. I fixed it with Sidney. He can lower the number 9 pipe and I'll work downstage here.

MAC   Fine . . . Fine.
(*He looks at* LARRY, *studying him*)

LARRY (*Uneasy under* MAC'S *gaze*)   Didn't I tell you I was going to try Jeanie out? I think maybe she'd be a good cover for Lily's understudy. Don't you?

MAC Larry, step over here for a minute, will you? (*He leads him over to left proscenium, so that no one but* LARRY *will hear what he has to say*) There's one rule I never broke in my life. And it'd be a good idea if no stage manager ever broke it.

LARRY What's that?

MAC (*Speaking slowly*) Don't ever let yourself get stuck on anybody that works in the same company as you do.

LARRY I'm not stuck on anybody in this company.

MAC Well, good. I'm glad to hear it. Because there's nothing worse for busting a troupe wide open.

LARRY (*A little impatiently*) Well, I told you, I'm not . . .

MAC If it ever happened to me, I'd fire the girl—or quit the show myself. I wouldn't compromise one inch!

LARRY O.K. O.K. I get it.

MAC There are plenty of cute kids in the other shows around town. (*Trying to take the edge off now, and lighten the whole scene. He leans over and taps* LARRY *on the arm*) As a matter of fact, I'm working on some new talent myself right now. You know little Betty Loraine.

LARRY Betty Loraine—with the show across the street?

MAC That's the one. Funny little thing. Never seems to wear anything but dungarees and sweaters, things like that. I'm just beginning to spar with her. Last night . . .

RUBY (*Calling across stage*) Hey, Mac! Here's Mr. Harrison! (*Waving out toward back of theatre*) How *are* you, Mr. Harrison? Enjoy your vacation?

HARRISON'S VOICE (*From out front*) Not much. I'm glad to be home. Are you ready for me, Mac?

MAC Right away, Mr. Harrison. Got two replacement candidates here. They're getting into their practice clothes. (*Turning*) See if they're ready, Larry.
  (LARRY *exits*)

MISS DAVENPORT'S VOICE (*From out front*) Hello, Mac.

MAC (*Peering out into the darkness*) Who's that?

HARRISON'S VOICE　I've got Miss Davenport with me.

MAC　Swell! Good to see you, Miss Davenport.

HARRISON'S VOICE　She's really here to protect her choreography. Afraid you and I might take a girl with a wooden leg.

(MAC *does his best to laugh convincingly at his boss's joke*)

MAC　The first girl I'm going to show you was with Ballet Theatre.

DAVENPORT'S VOICE　What's her name?

MAC　Hilda Morton.

DAVENPORT'S VOICE　Oh, I know her. (*Lowering her voice*) She's a very good dancer, Ben. (HILDA *enters*) There she is, coming on now.

HARRISON'S VOICE　(*Also in low tones*)　She's not a Carmen type.

MAC　(*Leading* HILDA *forward*)　Mr. Harrison, this is Miss Morton.

HARRISON'S VOICE　How do you do?

HILDA　(*Peering out into the dark auditorium*)　I'm awfully glad to know you, Mr. Harrison. Hello, Miss Davenport.

DAVENPORT'S VOICE　Hello, Hilda. Start with some tour jeté's. (HILDA *obeys*) Fine. Now a grand jeté.

(HILDA *obliges expertly*)

HARRISON'S VOICE　(*In a dry and final voice*)　Thank you very much, Miss Morton.

(HILDA, *knowing that is her dismissal, bows and smiles mechanically and starts off stage*)

DAVENPORT'S VOICE　Wait a minute. Just a moment, Hilda. (HILDA *lingers. There are sounds of mumbled conversation*) I know she can dance the part.

HARRISON'S VOICE　She can't look it.

DAVENPORT'S VOICE　(*Weary and resigned*)　All right. Thank you very much, Hilda.

(HILDA *exits and* LARRY *immediately brings forth another girl and* MAC *introduces her*)

MAC   This is Marcia Laval, Mr. Harrison, Miss Davenport.

HARRISON'S VOICE   Hello, Marcia. How've you been?

MARCIA (*Delighted to be recognized by the manager*)   Just fine. How are you, Mr. Harrison? I didn't think you'd remember me.

HARRISON'S VOICE   Of course I remember you.

DAVENPORT'S VOICE (*Sounding skeptical*)   Can you do a tour jeté?
(MARCIA *tries and is apparently much more of a show girl than a dancer*)

MARCIA   Would you like to see my elevation?

DAVENPORT'S VOICE   No. That will do. Thank you very much.

HARRISON'S VOICE   Wait a minute! (*Then again there is mumbled conversation*) I like this girl.

DAVENPORT'S VOICE   I don't!

HARRISON'S VOICE (*To* MARCIA)   All right. Leave your name with the office so we know where to get in touch with you.

MARCIA   Oh, thank you, Mr. Harrison.
(*She goes*)

HARRISON'S VOICE   That all you got, Mac?

MAC   That's all this morning. There's a girl coming in next week from the St. Louis Municipal Opera. They say that she . . .
(*He breaks off because he is conscious of* CHARLIE, *who has just peeked in from the wings and is waving to* HARRISON)

CHARLIE   That Ben Harrison out there?

HARRISON'S VOICE   Hello, Charlie.

CHARLIE (*Coming out on to the stage*)   Have you found a new Carmen for me?

HARRISON'S VOICE   No, we haven't.

CHARLIE Well, I have a young lady with me who I think would be just . . . (*Turning toward wings*) Come out here, darling. . . . (BETTY *enters. She is as* MAC *has described her, "A funny little thing" in dungarees and sweatshirt.* CHARLIE *takes her by the hand*) She's in the show across the street. Miss Betty Loraine . . . Mr. Harrison, Miss Davenport.

BETTY (*Beaming at them confidently*) How do you do? (*To* MAC) Hello, Charm Boat!

MAC (*Very formally*) How do you do, Miss Loraine?
  (*He turns away.* LARRY *is amused at* MAC'S *predicament*)

HARRISON'S VOICE I'd like to see what you can do. How long would it take you to get into your practice clothes?

BETTY I *am* in my practice clothes.
  (*She takes off her dungarees, under which she wears dancers' tights*)

CHARLIE Before she dances, would you like to hear her read lines? I got her up in one of the scenes.

HARRISON'S VOICE Fine! Go ahead. Say, Mac! It looks as if Charlie's trying to take your job away. Trying to muscle in on you.

MAC It does look like he's trying to muscle in, doesn't it?

BETTY (*Going over to* MAC) Can I have a script, Mac?

MAC Certainly, Miss Loraine.
  (*He hands it to her*)

CHARLIE All right, honey. I'm sitting on a park bench, and you come up to me.

BETTY (*As* CARMEN) (*Reading from script*) "Why do you pretend not to know I'm alive? (CHARLIE *as* ME *looks around at her*) All men know I'm alive. They can't help it, because I *am* alive!"
  (*She heaves several deep breaths under her jersey to prove it*)

HARRISON'S VOICE Fine, fine!

BETTY (*As* CARMEN) "Why do you sit by yourself in the park reading poetry? Don't you like girls?"

CHARLIE (*As* ME) "Only one—Juliet—and she's an angel —she's too good for me."

BETTY (*As* CARMEN) "Why don't you see how it feels to be with someone who's not too good for you?"
(CHARLIE *lowers his eyes to his imaginary book of poetry*)

CHARLIE (*As* ME) (*Looking at her*) "You mean—?" (BETTY *nods her head vigorously*) "Oh no. I couldn't!"

BETTY (*As* CARMEN) "If I thought you couldn't I wouldn't suggest it." (*Putting her head on his shoulder. Then, stepping out of character abruptly, calling out to* HARRISON) Do you want the number?

HARRISON'S VOICE Sure!
(CHARLIE *nods to* CHRIS *who starts to play the piano*)

CHARLIE Buzz! You're just in time! (*Calling to* BUZZ *who is just crossing the stage, carrying a guitar case*)

BUZZ In time for what?

CHARLIE Would you do the "Keep It Gay" routine with this young lady? Like a good fellow?

BUZZ I got a T.V. audition at three o'clock . . .

HARRISON'S VOICE You've got time, Buzz. Go ahead.

BUZZ Who's that?

CHARLIE That's Mr. Harrison.

BUZZ (*A different man*) Oh, hello, Mr. Harrison. Sure I've got time. Love to—sure!

CHARLIE Oh by the way, have you two kids met—Betty Loraine this is Buzz Miller. She knows the routine, Buzz. O.K., Chris.
(CHRIS *starts playing.* BETTY *sings and dances two refrains of "Keep It Gay" with* BUZZ)

DAVENPORT'S VOICE (*After dance*) That was fine!

HARRISON'S VOICE Your show is closing next week, isn't it? (*She nods*) Send your agent around to see Ruby. Get that, Ruby?

RUBY Check!

HARRISON'S VOICE (*To* BETTY) Could you start rehearsing tomorrow?

BETTY Why not?

HARRISON Get that, Mac?

MAC (*Coldly*) I understand.

HARRISON'S VOICE Coming over to Sardi's, Charlie?

CHARLIE Be right with you! (*As he passes* BETTY *on his way off*) Congratulations!

BETTY Charlie, you've been wonderful. Thank you!
(*She gives him a big smacking kiss.* MAC *stamps off the stage.* CHARLIE *exits.* BETTY *puts on her dungarees.* SIDNEY *comes out to the center and calls up to the flies*)

SIDNEY Hey, Joe! Let down that number 9 pipe, will you?

BETTY Hey, Ruby, where did Mac go? (RUBY *shrugs his shoulders and smiles*) I don't get it. Last night he was full of sweet talk. Today he acted as if he never met me before.

RUBY Last night you were a girl in another show. Don't you know about his rule? With any girl in his own company— nothing!

BETTY Oh, so that's it.

RUBY You can take this job, or keep Mac . . . Which?
(*Pause*)

BETTY I'm going to take the job! And make him break his rule!

RUBY You'll be the first girl to turn the trick. "Is he man or machine?" That's what they say about him.

BETTY If he's a machine I don't want him. If he's a man, I'm going to make him prove it!
(*She exits. Meanwhile the number 9 pipe has been let down from the flies.* SIDNEY *has brought out a pile of color frames and during the ensuing scene proceeds to change them in the lamps on the pipe.* JEANIE *has come on the stage and she and* LARRY *walk over to the Stage Manager's table.* RUBY *waves a greeting to them as he exits*)

LARRY Just leave our things right there. (JEANIE *takes off her hat and places her bag on the table*) Did you get a chance to look over the part?

JEANIE (*A little guiltily*) Well, no, Larry. I didn't. I . . .

LARRY That's all right. You know all the music, anyway, don't you? Let's start out with one of the songs. (*Calling across stage*) Chris, can you help us out?

CHRIS What do you want?

LARRY "No Other Love." (*To* JEANIE) Stand over near the piano, Jeanie.
  (JEANIE *looks uncertain*)

JEANIE All right. Anything you want to tell me?

LARRY No. Just go ahead and sing it in your own way.
  (JEANIE *crosses to the piano.* LARRY *carries a chair to the center of the stage, straddles it and leans on the back of it, then nods to* CHRIS. JEANIE *starts to sing. She sings well enough as far as voice is concerned, but her feeling for the lyric is superficial and her gestures are meaningless*)

JEANIE (*Singing*)
No other love have I,
Only my love for you,
Only—

LARRY Just a minute, Jeanie! (*She stops singing*) Chris! (*He waves his hand and* CHRIS *stops*) Take five! (CHRIS *exits. There is a pause.* LARRY *looks at* JEANIE *as if trying to think of the right words to say. Then he speaks to her quietly*) Why did you do that just now . . . with your hands . . . like this?
  (*He imitates her gesture*)

JEANIE I don't know. No reason in particular. I just didn't want to stand like a stick and do nothing.
  (*Pause*)

LARRY Suppose you had to describe Juliet—what kind of girl would you say she was?

JEANIE I'd say she was a nice, ordinary kid.

LARRY Do you think Carmen is a stronger character?

JEANIE   Oh, yes . . . Don't you?

LARRY   Jeanie—the whole secret of singing this song is to realize that Juliet is a stronger, deeper, more passionate woman than Carmen.

JEANIE   More passionate?

LARRY   You've seen this happen, Jeanie—two nice, ordinary kids like Juliet and this little guy decide they want to live with each other for the rest of their lives. And suddenly something happens to them—two midgets are given the strength of giants. They'll knock over anybody who stands in their way.

JEANIE   (*Thoughtfully*)   Yes, I *have* seen that happen.

LARRY   So has everyone in the audience. And if you're a real kid like Juliet, they'll recognize you—if you're phony, they'll reject you.

JEANIE   An audience would scare me.

LARRY   Every good actress is scared—scared they won't like her. Her job is to make them like her. And the way to do that is to be honest with them. They're the smartest people in the theatre, and the toughest . . . and the nicest.
    (*He sings*)
The water in a river is changed every day
As it flows from the hills to the sea.
But to people on the shore the river is the same,
Or, at least it appears to be.
The audience in a theatre is changed every night,
As a show runs along on its way.
But to people on the stage the audience looks the same,
Every night, every matinée—
    A big black giant
    Who looks and listens
    With thousands of eyes and ears,
    A big black mass
    Of love and pity
    And troubles and hopes and fears;
    And every night
    The mixture's different,
    Although it may look the same.
    To feel his way

With every mixture
Is part of the actor's game.
> One night it's a laughing giant,
> Another night a weeping giant.
> One night it's a coughing giant,
> Another night a sleeping giant.
> Every night you fight the giant
> And maybe, if you win,
> You send him out a nicer giant
> Than he was when he came in . . .

But if he doesn't like you, then all you can do
Is to pack up your make-up and go.
For an actor in a flop there isn't any choice
But to look for another show.
> That big black giant
> Who looks and listens
> With thousands of eyes and ears,
> That big black mass
> Of love and pity
> And troubles and hopes and fears,
> Will sit out there
> And rule your life
> For all your living years,

(LARRY *turns back to her, a little self-conscious after his long "speech"*) Now-er-would you like to try the song again? Just remember to be real and . . . why are you looking at me like that?

JEANIE (*Flustered*)   Was I? Oh, excuse me.

LARRY   What's the matter?

JEANIE   Nothing, Larry. I was just thinking—how you can be in the same company with somebody for so long and not really know them at all.

LARRY (*Finding no answer*)   Shall we try the song now? (*Calling to* CHRIS) Chris! (*Turning back to* JEANIE) Now, just think of the girl—out on the balcony, lonely—wishing that the guy would come back.

(*He sits again and waits for her to begin*)

JEANIE (*Singing*)
No other love have I,
> Only my love for you.

Only the dream we knew—
No other love.
Watching the night go by,
  Wishing that you could be
  Watching the night with me,
Into the night I cry:
    Hurry home, come home to me!
    Set me free,
    Free from doubt
    And free from longing.
Into your arms I'll fly.
  Locked in your arms I'll stay,
  Waiting to hear you say:
No other love have I,
No other love!

  (LARRY *rises and goes over to* JEANIE)

LARRY Good. Now try starting it softer. Then let it build
. . . (*To* CHRIS) Take it half a tone higher.

  (*He starts singing, to illustrate*)

No other love have I,
  Only my love for you,
  Only the dream we knew—
No other love.

  (JEANIE *has started to sing with him*)

Watching the night go by
  Wishing that you could be
  Watching the night with me,
Into the night I cry:
    Hurry home, come home to me!
    Set me free,
    Free from doubt
    And free from longing.
Into your arms I'll fly.
  Locked in your arms I'll stay,
  Waiting to hear you say:
No other love have I,
No other love!

  (*At the end of the song* JEANIE *turns and looks at* LARRY,
*catching his eyes gazing adoringly at her. Obviously he
has been singing his half of a love duet. Quickly he turns
and crosses to* CHRIS *at the piano and whispers instructions.*

CHRIS *starts to play the refrain again.* JEANIE *picks it up on the third line*)

JEANIE
. . . Only the dream we knew—
No other love.

(BOB, *entering up right, watches* JEANIE *singing and* LARRY *conducting. He walks downstage and mocks* JEANIE'S *manner of singing, making his gestures very broad.* JEANIE *sees him but continues to sing, trying to brazen it through and not let* BOB *think he can disturb her*)

Watching the night go by
Wishing that you could be
Watching the night with me,
Into the night I cry:
Hurry home, come home—

(JEANIE *stops suddenly and bursts out angrily*) What's the matter with you? Making a big joke?

BOB (*Applauding*)   Encore! Encore!

JEANIE   I don't see anybody laughing.

BOB (*His feelings hurt because his clumsy schoolboy comedy was not admired*) Excuse me for living. (*Turning back*) I didn't know you were a prima donna from the "Met." I just thought you were one of the girls in the chorus. (*Going upstage to* SIDNEY) Want some help, Sid?

SIDNEY   Help me clear these color frames.

JEANIE   Do you mind if we stop, Larry? (*Picking up her hat and bag from a chair*) I'm sorry to be like this. I guess if I was a real actress I wouldn't let anybody—make any difference.

LARRY   Come down tomorrow and we'll have another shot at it. (JEANIE *starts off*) You can go now, Chris.

CHRIS   Okay.

LARRY   Two o'clock call tomorrow.
(CHRIS *exits*)

JEANIE   Thank you, Larry. Thank you very much.
(*She goes out*)

SIDNEY (*Calling to flyman*)   Take it away!

LARRY (*Calling off*)   Will you kill this work light?

VOICE OFFSTAGE   Okay.
(*For some seconds* LARRY *remains rooted to a spot in the center of the stage. The light is switched off. The stage becomes quite dark, except for some shafts of daylight coming from the roof at the back.* LARRY *starts pacing up and down in the dark. Then another figure comes out of the shadows and stands in front of him*)

BOB   Sidney tells me you had quite a rehearsal here.

LARRY   What do you mean?

BOB   You and Jeanie.

LARRY   Yes, it was fine. I think she'll—she may turn out fine.
(*He starts to go, but* BOB *reaches forward and grabs him by the arm*)

BOB   Wait a minute— Don't go yet.

LARRY   Let go of me!

BOB (*Holding on to his arm*)   What's your hurry? I want to say something to you. (*He pulls* LARRY *toward him*) Stand still here a minute and listen to me. Are you making a play for my girl?

LARRY   Of course not! (BOB *continues to hold him*) Let go of me! (LARRY *tries to break* BOB'S *hold on him*) What the hell's the matter with you? (*There is a stretch of silence*) I'm a stage manager rehearsing an understudy. What the hell's . . .

BOB   Just keep it that way, see? Stage manager and understudy. Strictly business. (*His voice becoming even quieter but more threatening*) If you ever try to move in on me with that kid, I—I'm just telling you . . . Something would happen to me . . . I couldn't *help* killing you— (*He throws* LARRY *away from him*) not if I tried. . . .
(*He goes out.* LARRY *stands perfectly still in the darkness, then he resumes his pacing. The lights go out*)

ACT ONE | Scene Six

The alley leading to the stage door.
 Various members of the COMPANY *are draped around the set on benches, on a large garbage box, in the doorway leading to the theatre which is on the right, and the doorway leading to the covered part of the alley, which in turn leads to the street. Three dancers are improvising steps as the curtain rises. During the dance* CHARLIE *enters and crosses to the stage door, stopping there a while to watch the dancers. At the finish of the dance there are shouts of approval and applause.*

A GIRL   They ought to have a spot in the show.

CHARLIE   It's easy to perform in an alley. But the only thing that pays off is what you do out there on the stage in front of an audience!
 (*He exits into the theatre*)

A BOY   Lovable Charlie Clay!
 (*Now* JIM *comes staggering on, pale, his voice quavering*)

JIM   Hello, everybody.

BOY   Hi, Jim.

GIRL   How's Susie?

JIM   She's started!

ANOTHER BOY   The baby?

JIM   She just took me to the hospital. I mean—I wanted to stay but she said I had to come and give the show.
 (*He exits into theatre*)

ANOTHER BOY He's white as a sheet—
  (*He follows* JIM *off*)

GIRL It seems only yesterday when Susie left the show.

A GIRL I wish I had a baby!

A BOY You do?

A GIRL (*Looking at him coldly*) I mean legitimate.

A BOY Oh.

HERBIE (*To* LILY *as she enters*) Hi, Lily! How'd you make out?

LILY I think he liked me.

RUBY Who?

HERBIE She auditioned for Bing today.

GIRL (*In incredible awe*) Crosby?

LILY (*Disdainfully*) No. Rudolph.
  (*She exits*)

GIRL Bing Rudolph? Who's he?
  (JEANIE'S *voice is now heard offstage, singing happily. All heads turn up toward the entrance*)

JEANIE (*Offstage*)
Out of nowhere
Came the feeling,
Knew the feel—
(*She enters, starts to cross, is conscious of everyone looking at her, and stops*) Hi, kids!

ALL Hi, Jeanie!
  (*She resumes her happy singing as she exits*)

JEANIE Marriage type love!
  (*Before* JEANIE *has gone off* LORAINE *has made her entrance on the left. She now comes down eagerly to spill some news*)

LORAINE I just saw them together!

GIRL Jeanie and Larry?

LORAINE They were in the chili joint on Eighth Avenue. As

soon as they left the place they separated and walked on different sides of the street.

(*Now* LARRY'S *voice is heard offstage whistling "No Other Love." Everyone quiets down and looks innocent as he enters*)

RUBY   Hi ya, Larry?

LARRY   (*As if awakening suddenly*)   Oh . . . Hi, Ruby. (*Looking around*) Hello, everybody.
   (*They return his greeting.* LARRY *turns, resumes whistling "No Other Love" and exits*)

HERBIE   It couldn't happen to two nicer people.

GIRL   Yeah! But what's going to happen when Bob finds out?

HERBIE   Gosh! I don't want to be around!
   (*He exits*)

ANOTHER GIRL   How is she handling him?

ANOTHER GIRL   She's telling him her mother's here from Chicago. That's why she can't see him.

BOY   She can't keep that up forever.
   (*The crowd starts to disperse now and go in the theatre to get dressed.* BETTY *enters*)

RUBY   Hi, Betty.

BETTY   Hi, Ruby. (*She looks behind her as if at someone who has been following her. Then she glides over to the bench and sits down, looking as unexpectant as she possibly can. The subject of her expectation now enters—*MAC. *Everyone has gone inside and they are alone.* MAC *starts to cross toward the stage door*) Hello, Mac.

MAC   How do you do, Miss Loraine.
   (*He proceeds on his way*)

BETTY   Hot for October.
   (*He stops*)

MAC   Yeh, but good weather for the World Series.

BETTY   Yeh. What are you doing with yourself these days?

MAC   Nothing much.

BETTY   Any truth about what I see in the columns—about you and Molly Burt being an item?

MAC   Could be.

BETTY   I used to know Molly quite well. We were in *Brigadoon* together.

MAC   That so?

BETTY   Yeh . . . Boy! Is she a dull dish!

MAC   Best I can do.

BETTY (*Close to him*)   That's what *you* think.
    (*He looks down at her. Their eyes meet for a long moment. Then he recovers*)

MAC   You better go in and get dressed. (*She turns and starts off. He calls her back, rather morosely*) Betty! (*She turns, hesitates, then comes toward him smiling*) I've been meaning to speak to you about that seduction scene.

BETTY   What's wrong with it?

MAC   It's gone to hell, that's what.

BETTY   Charlie and I think that's our best spot.

MAC   I don't wonder. You sure look as if you enjoy it.

BETTY (*Loving this*)   Charlie says the way we play it now is the way the author and director wanted it, and when you put me in the show you tamed it down.

MAC   That so?

BETTY   Uh huh! So we've been heating it up a little each performance.

MAC   Well, start cooling it off, y'hear? It's getting so obvious it's lost all its charm. It's just plain disgusting and vulgar!

BETTY (*Delighted*)   Y'think so? Well, for instance . . . I mean where does it get bad? Shall we run through it, and you can show me.
    (BETTY *takes a* CARMEN *pose center and starts to clap her hands in rhythm.* MAC *looking pompous reluctantly starts to clap his hands to the same rhythm.* BETTY *dances very close to him. He backs away*)

MAC Now wait a minute—wait a minute.

BETTY Oh, that's not the step, huh? Maybe you mean the Tango . . . (BETTY *takes* MAC *and goes into another section of the dance, at the finish of this,* BETTY *is in a seductive pose, looking up at* MAC) Is that all right?
(He nods. They continue to dance until she puts her hand under his coat, caressing him)

MAC That's what I mean!
(He pushes her away)

BETTY Oh, I see! What about this place? (*She grabs* MAC *and they go into a whirling dance in the center of the stage. She leans back on his arm. He bends over her*) Is that too much—?
(It might be, but MAC *is liking it. At this moment* RUBY *comes in and stands for a moment, inspecting them)*

RUBY What're you doing?
*(MAC *and* BETTY *break quickly)*

MAC Rehearsing.

RUBY Who's rehearsing who?

MAC I'm trying to fix that seduction scene. They're playing it like a burlesque show.

RUBY I kinda like the way they do it.

MAC (*To* BETTY) You better go in and get dressed.

BETTY Do you think we fixed it?

MAC There's no fixing to do. You know damn well what I want. Tame it down! That's what I want you to do. Tame it down!

BETTY O.K., Mac. O.K., I'll do my best, Mac.
(She turns and goes off, looking very happy)

MAC (*To* RUBY) Wanta slip across the street for a drink?

RUBY I thought you never took a drink before a show.

MAC I never do, but I just happen to feel like one.

RUBY Look out, Mac. You start to break one rule, you may break another.

MAC Nuts to you.

(*He exits.* RUBY, *looking after* MAC, *smiles contemplatively.*
HERBIE *enters*)

RUBY Are theatre people crazier than other people?

HERBIE Sure!

RUBY I don't think so. They just *show* it more than other
people. I think it comes from getting keyed up every night—
getting scared and excited.

HERBIE On account of that big black giant Larry's always
talking about.

RUBY (RUBY *smiles and starts to sing*)
  One night it's a laughing giant,
  Another night a weeping giant.
  One night it's a coughing giant,
  Another night a sleeping giant.
  Every night you fight the giant
  And maybe, if you win,
  You send him out a nicer giant
  Than he was when he came in . . .
But if he doesn't like you, then all you can do
Is to pack up your make-up and go.
For an actor in a flop there isn't any choice
But to look for another show.
  That big black giant
  Who looks and listens
  With thousands of eyes and ears—
  He claps his hands and luck is with you,
  He frowns and it disappears.
  He'll chill your heart
  And warm your heart
  For all your living years.
(*The curtains have closed on the set during the song. The
lights fade on* RUBY)

ACT ONE | Scene Seven

Betty's dressing room.
    JEANIE, *pressing one of* BETTY'S *costumes, looks up as she comes in, singing gaily.*

JEANIE   What are you so happy about?

BETTY   Mac says I'm overdoing the seduction scene. He says it's obvious and vulgar—don't you get it? We're making headway, kid. (*She crosses, sits at dressing table and stretches out her legs so that* JEANIE *can pull off her dungarees*) Gosh, am I lucky, having you! . . . When you asked me for the job I thought you were kidding. A college graduate, no less!

JEANIE (*As she hangs up* BETTY'S *dungarees and jacket*)   I wanted the dough. My understudy pay stops this week. Summer's over. They don't need two understudies any more.

BETTY   You're a wonderful kid.

JEANIE   Wonderful, nothing. It's a break for me to be able to share this room with you—instead of dressing in that madhouse downstairs.

BETTY (*Proceeding to make up her face*)   Whee! When those dames get together and start cackling, that's something. And it's always on the same subject.

JEANIE   Yeh! Same thing you and I always cackle about.

BETTY   Yeh. I wonder why. I wonder why we let men take up so much of our lives. Why is it so important to me to make Mac jealous of Charlie? What am I after, anyway? To make him come up to me some night and ask me to go out with him? Would that be such a wonderful thing to happen?

. . Yeh, it would. . . . I haven't heard much out of you lately about *your* love life. What's the matter with it?

JEANIE   Oh, it's all right.

MAC'S VOICE (*In a loud-speaker that is on the wall above* BETTY'S *dressing table*)   Five minutes to overture! Five minutes to overture!

BETTY (*Powdering her arms and shoulders, vigorously*)   O.K., Mr. Mac. I'll be ready. Stick around for the seduction scene tonight. I'm going to do a dance with Charlie that'll make you wish you were never born!

JEANIE   I fixed that zipper in your dress.

BETTY   Thanks. Boy, do I love to get into that dress. What a part! What a girl that Carmen! You know what I mean? All woman, and no complications. Just a bundle of uncomplicated passion.

JEANIE   Did it ever occur to you that Juliet might have more real passion than Carmen?

BETTY   No. Did it ever occur to you?

JEANIE   It's Larry's idea. You know he's a wonderful director, Betty. All the understudies say the same thing. They say that he'll be one of the tops some day.

BETTY   Do you know how many times you've told me that?

JEANIE (*Defensively*)   Told you what?

BETTY (*Eyeing her closely*)   I bet you're going to miss those understudy rehearsals especially with such a sympathetic director. (JEANIE *puts a Spanish comb in* BETTY'S *hair with punishing emphasis*) Ouch!

JEANIE   Hold your head still!

BETTY   You'll be getting stagestruck like me, maybe.

JEANIE   Could be.

BETTY   Boy, do I love to act! (*She rises and looks in the mirror*) All day long you can flop at everything you do. But at night—at night you know you're going to fool fifteen hundred people into thinking you're wonderful! (*She sings*) I'm colorless and shy,

Inhibited and dull.
My entrance into any room is followed by a lull.
This droopiness in me
Miraculously melts
When I step on a stage and make believe I'm someone else.
Quite suddenly I'm mentally and physically equipped
With most unusual qualities—it says so in the script!

JEANIE

Who is that delectable dame,
Cool as cream and hotter than flame?
Who? Who could it be?

BETTY

It's me! It's me! It's me!

JEANIE

Who's that queenly gift to the boys—

BETTY

Always keen and lousy with poise?

JEANIE

Who? Who could it be?

BETTY

It's me! It's me! It's me!
When the authors make me say
Words that make me wittier,
I feel just as smart as they
(And what's more, I'm prettier!)

JEANIE

Who's that girl who's getting the wows?
Who's that babe who's taking the bows?

BETTY

In a daze, I wonder who is she!
Imagine my surprise
When once I realize
It's nobody else but wonderful, beautiful me!

My picture hangs in Sardi's
For all the world to see.
I sit beneath my picture there
And no one looks at me.
I sometimes wear dark glasses,
Concealing who I am,

Then all at once I take them off—
And no one gives a damn!
But when I start to play a part, I play the part okay;
No longer am I no one when I'm someone in a play.

JEANIE
Every man is flipping his lid
Over that phenomenal kid—
Who? Who could it be?

BETTY
It's me! It's me! It's me!

JEANIE
Whose hot kiss from passionate lips
Perpetrates a total eclipse?
Who? Who could it be?

BETTY
It's me! It's me! It's me!
Oh, what I can perpetrate
By my osculation!
Just one little kiss, and pouf!
There goes perpetration!

JEANIE
Who has learned the formula which
Satisfies the seven year itch?
Who's that dazzling personalitee?

JEANIE AND BETTY
Well, here's the big surprise:
Hot dog, and damn my eyes!
It's nobody else but wonderful, beautiful me!

(BETTY *runs to the dressing table, picks up a fan and runs
off as* JEANIE *bows her out of the dressing-room door with
exaggerated homage.* JEANIE *then gets her own dress off the
hanger and puts a towel on her hair so that it won't be
mussed as she puts the dress over her head. Then she hangs
the towel up and starts to hook up her dress as* LARRY
*enters. They embrace. He then takes over the job of hook-
ing her dress*)

JEANIE   Remember what you said that first day? "When two
ordinary little people decide that they want to live with each
other for the rest of their lives, they'll knock over anything
that stands in their way."

LARRY   I remember . . . We've got to tell Bob, Jeanie.

JEANIE   I know. We've got to think of some good *way* to tell him. (*She clings tightly to* LARRY) I haven't found a good way to tell myself. I can't make myself believe that we did what we did today. Every once in a while I take the ring out of my bag and just look at it.

MAC'S VOICE (*In loud-speaker*)   Everybody on stage. First act! Everybody on!

LARRY (*Whispering*)   See you later.
      (*They kiss again and he goes out quickly.* JEANIE *goes to her handbag and takes her wedding ring out and looks at it*)

JEANIE (*Singing*)
Imagine my surprise!
Imagine my surprise!
It's nobody else but wonderful beautiful—

MAC'S VOICE   Jeanie! (*Suddenly realizing that she is late for her entrance on stage, she shouts*) Me!
      (*She runs over to her dressing table, picks up the accessories to her costume and runs off*)

ACT ONE | Scene Eight

The Light Bridge.
      BOB *and* SIDNEY, *getting their lamps set for the finale of Act One.*

SIDNEY   Well, I'll be glad to get down off this perch and stretch my legs.

BOB   You can't get down till they let you down. It's like being in jail.

SIDNEY   You know this first-act finale coming up is my favorite scene in the show? I'd like to go to a fancy night club like that some time—be out on the town.

BOB   With a girl like Carmen, huh?

SIDNEY   She'd be okay.

BOB   Tell me something, Sidney. Have you ever had another girl—I mean since you've been married?

SIDNEY   Sure. Plenty.

BOB   I bet you haven't had one.

SIDNEY   All right then, I haven't had one. I don't see anything to be proud of anyway—cheating on your wife. Would you cheat if you got married?

BOB   Sure I would. That's why I don't get married. Right now I'm worse off than if I was married. I got a girl and I can't get to see her.

SIDNEY   (*Playing dumb*)   Yeh? Why not?

BOB   Her mother's in town. Got here from Chicago a month ago. She was only going to stay a week. But she's still here! Every week Jeanie says her mother is going next week . . . But she stays!

SIDNEY   That's a pretty tough deal. . . . Quick the effects!
   (*They both throw their lamps on*)

BOB   (*After they have met their cue*)   So you wouldn't cheat. What about your wife? Are you sure about *her*?

SIDNEY   (*Suddenly very resentful at this suggestion*)   Aw, nuts to you. (*Getting worked up*) You just shut up about my wife!

BOB   Let's see. You live in Bayside.

SIDNEY   Y'better shut up! Leave my wife out of this or you'll be sorry!

BOB   What the hell will I be sorry about! . . . Let's see, Bayside, that's about a half hour on the Long Island Railroad. That means you leave your house every night about seven. You can't get home before twelve— How do you know what she's doing all that time?

(SIDNEY *can't hit* BOB. *He gropes for another way to get revenge*)

SIDNEY   I know what she's doing all right . . . I know what somebody else is doing too!

BOB (*Immediately sensing something from* SIDNEY'S *tone*) Yeh?

SIDNEY   And it ain't with her mother.
   (BOB *grabs* SIDNEY. *Music comes up from below*)

BOB   You prove what you're saying or I'll tear you apart.

SIDNEY   If you feel like tearing somebody apart why not try it on the guy who's making a dope out of you?

BOB   Who?

SIDNEY   The Assistant Stage Manager.

BOB   Larry?

SIDNEY   Uh-huh.

BOB   Prove it.

SIDNEY   All right. I will. You come over and take my side of the bridge. I'll switch with you. And maybe if you look down there at his desk—at the right time—you'll see what I see every night—every single night.

BOB   What do you mean "the right time"?

SIDNEY   You know that part where Jeanie is carrying a lot of flowers on a tray? (BOB *nods*) And Don Juan takes all the flowers and gives 'em to Carmen? Then Jeanie goes off? That's when it happens. The same thing happens every night. . . . Every night.

BOB (*Huskily*)   Come on. We'll switch sides.
   (*Slowly* BOB *and* SIDNEY *move toward each other.* BOB *holds on to the rail to steady himself.* SIDNEY'S *face shows panic at the force he has set in motion and cannot stop. They switch sides. The music grows louder. The lights fade*)

ACT ONE | Scene Nine

A night club.

LILY *as* JULIET *is seen in a pin spot singing "No Other Love." Then the curtains part on a stage crowded with dancers, among whom are* BETTY *as* CARMEN *and* CHARLIE *as* ME.

BETTY (CARMEN)   Having fun? (CHARLIE *nods his head*) Then why don't you look happier? (CHARLIE *grins uncomfortably*) What have you got your mind on?

CHARLIE (*As* ME)   Nothing.

BETTY (CARMEN)   Well, why don't you put it on me?
(*The spot fades on* JULIET, *as if she were fading from* CHARLIE'S *guilty mind. He goes on dancing more happily with* BETTY. *Now* JIM, *as* DON JUAN, *comes on, dancing with* MISS OXFORD)

CHARLIE (ME)   You see that fellow who just came in? That's my boss.

BETTY (CARMEN)   That so? Who's that with him?

CHARLIE (ME)   Oh, I don't know. Some model or actress or somebody. He's always with a different one. They say he can get any girl he wants to get.

BETTY (CARMEN)   That so? He couldn't get me.

CHARLIE (ME)   How do you know?

BETTY (CARMEN)   'Cause *you* got me.

CHARLIE (ME)   You're a doll, Carmen. Here I am, just an

ordinary clerk who works in his office, and you'd rather have me than him—him with all those millions and yachts . . .
(*They dance around for about four bars while* CARMEN *looks thoughtful*)

BETTY (CARMEN)   How many millions has he got?

CHARLIE (ME)   Oh, I don't know, but it isn't less than fifty million.
(DON JUAN *engineers his partner over in front of* CARMEN *and* CHARLIE)

JIM (DON JUAN)   Hello, my boy.

CHARLIE (ME)   (*Nearly tongue-tied with fright at being suddenly addressed by the boss who has never noticed him before*)   Hello, Mr.—Mr. . . .

JIM (DON JUAN)   Meet Miss Oxford.

CHARLIE (ME)   Pleased to meet you. This is Miss Carmen.

JIM (DON JUAN)   How do you do? (*He takes* CARMEN *in his arms and dances off with her, motioning to* CHARLIE *to take* MISS OXFORD. *During the ensuing dialogue* JIM *and* BETTY *and* CHARLIE *and* MISS OXFORD *continue to dance, as do the chorus, and meanwhile the stage moves over, revealing about ten feet of the offstage scene.* LARRY *is at the Stage Manager's desk. About three-quarters of the full stage remains and the dancing in* Me *and* Juliet *can be seen while the dialogue is read*)   You and I ought to make a good combination.

BETTY (CARMEN)   Think so?

JIM (DON JUAN)   Don't you?

BETTY (CARMEN)   Maybe. Some day. I just don't like to start one course till I've finished with the other.

JIM (DON JUAN)   Well, just remember the meat and potatoes are ready. (*Looking over at* CHARLIE *dancing with* MISS OXFORD) As soon as you finish with the fish.

BETTY (CARMEN)   I'll remember.
(*Now* JEANIE, *wearing the costume of a night-club flower girl, enters and walks among the dancers with a tray of flowers. Playing the scene* SIDNEY *has described to* BOB, *she*

goes up to DON JUAN *and* CARMEN. DON JUAN *takes some orchids off her tray and gives them to* CARMEN. JEANIE *turns and moves toward the exit.* DON JUAN *delivers* CARMEN *back to* ME *and takes* MISS OXFORD. *The dance proceeds.*

Meanwhile JEANIE *exits, puts her tray of flowers on* LARRY'S *desk and then goes up to him as she apparently does every night, ready for her kiss. He takes her in his arms and kisses her.*

Suddenly a spotlight shines on them from the bridge. They both look up, panic in their eyes. They cling to each other like two terrified children and continue to stare up at the light as if fascinated and hypnotized by it. The music becomes very loud at this point. The dancing on the stage becomes faster. MAC *enters, takes in the situation, and waves to* BOB *to take the lights off, but the light stays on.* BETTY, *onstage, looks up at the bridge, wondering why her spot has gone off. Then she looks into the wings and understands, and looks back at the bridge, frightened.*

Offstage, JEANIE *pulls away from* LARRY, *never taking her eyes from the bridge.* MAC, *in unheard dialogue, makes gestures to* LARRY *to beat it quick.* RUBY *comes on with a worried expression, as if already told about the crisis.* MAC *talks to him and* RUBY *takes* LARRY'S *arm and leads him away.* LARRY *submits to this like a man in a daze.* MAC *then puts the tray in* JEANIE'S *hands and pushes her onto the stage. She walks across the stage among the dancers, looking up frightened at the bridge. The lamp keeps following her as if* BOB *will not let her go. Terrified, she moves back toward the entrance on the right where* MAC, *in the wings, is waving wildly up to* BOB *to take the spot off her. As she reaches a certain point a girl looks up and screams. A sandbag comes down and knocks* JEANIE'S *tray out of her hands.* MAC *pulls her off the stage, gets to his desk and shouts signals into his microphone, apparently ordering the curtain to come down while the dancers, terrified, go on with their routine, all keeping their eyes turned up toward the bridge. The curtain falls)*

ACT TWO | Scene One

Downstairs lounge of the theatre.

About one minute before the end of Act One of Me and Juliet.

On stage right is the lower part of a curved staircase leading to the auditorium upstairs. On stage left, well downstage, is the candy and lemonade counter.

HERBIE *is busy setting cartons of lemonade on top of the counter, taking them out of a very large box. Also on top of the counter are displayed some peppermint candies, Life-Savers, lozenges, and the usual assortment of lobby confections. Two* USHERS *come down the stairs.*

FIRST USHER   Did you see the finale of the first act?

SECOND USHER   That was a funny one.

HERBIE   What was a funny one?

SECOND USHER   Just now in the finale one of the spotlights came off a principal and followed a chorus girl all around the stage!

FIRST USHER   And then something dropped from the top and nearly hit her.

HERBIE (*Thoughtfully*)   That *is* funny.

FIRST USHER   This is a funny night all around. (*To* SECOND USHER) Tell Herbie what happened to *you*, Sadie.

SECOND USHER   Oh, yeh. I was showing a guy and his wife to their seats. They came in late. It was dark on the aisle. His wife was walking in front of us and he pinched me!

HERBIE   Where?

FIRST USHER (*Indicating an area where a girl might be pinched by a vulgar gentleman*) Right there.

SECOND USHER (*Pointing to the other side of same area*) No, here. I can feel it yet—nearly.

HERBIE What did you do?

SECOND USHER Before I could do anything the guy slips a five-dollar bill into my hand.

HERBIE Then what'd you do?

SECOND USHER Gave him the two programs and beat it up the aisle.

HERBIE Well, you got to hand it to a feller who pays as he goes.
(*The girls exit. RUBY and LARRY come down the stairs. RUBY leads him straight over to the door, center, opens it with a key and pushes LARRY in*)

RUBY Don't open the door if anybody knocks. Don't open the door unless I unlock it.

OFFSTAGE VOICE Smoking in the outer lobby only!

HERBIE What's up?

RUBY Bob caught Larry with Jeanie.

HERBIE He'll kill him.

RUBY He will if he finds him.

HERBIE Did he see you leaving the stage for the front of the house?

RUBY That's what I'm afraid of. I think he did. (*He starts for stairs and turns back*) If he comes down here, you don't know anything.

HERBIE Check.
(*RUBY scampers up stairs. THEATRE PATRONS pour down, and fill the lounge*)

HERBIE (*Singing*)
Lemonade,
Freshly made!
A bottle of ice cold Coke!

BORED PATRON
I love to go to a theatre lounge
To enjoy a noisy smoke.

HERBIE
Lemonade,
Freshly made!

STARRY-EYED GIRL
I simply adore the show!

BORED PATRON
I wouldn't wait for the second act
If I had some place to go!

MUSIC LOVER
I like the one that goes
Da di da dum,
Da di da dum,
Da di da dum.
Marriage type love.

WIFE (*To her husband*)
I don't think it's right
To be sulky all night
Over one little bill from Saks!

BUSINESS MAN (*To another*)
What do I care if they balance the budget,
As long as they cut my tax?

MUSIC LOVER
I like the one that goes:
No other love have I.
Hurry back home tonight!
It's me, it's me, it's me . . .

HER COMPANION
That doesn't sound quite right.

GIRL
The fellow beside me keeps dropping his program
And groping around my feet.

BORED PATRON (*Tapping her on the shoulder*)
The couple behind me had garlic for dinner.
Would you like to trade your seat?

FASTIDIOUS PATRON
I think the production is fine,
The music is simply divine!
The story is lovely and gay—
But it just isn't my kind of play.

HAPPY MOURNERS
They don't write music any more
Like the old Vienna valses!
The guy today who writes a score
Doesn't know what schmalz is!
The plots are all too serious,
No longer sweet and gay.
The authors who think
Certainly stink.
The theatre is fading away.
   (*Their faces light up now*)
Oh . . .
The theatre is dying,
The theatre is dying,
The theatre is practically dead!
Someone ev'ry day writes
We have no more playwrights,
The theatre is sick in the head.
Some singer of dirges
Gets earnest and urges
The public to have a good cry—

HERBIE
But the show still goes on—
The theatre's not gone.

HAPPY MOURNERS
We wish it would lie down and die,
Why in hell won't it lie down and die?

STARRY-EYED GIRL (*Answering them*)
I thought that I'd laugh myself silly
On the ev'ning I spent with Bea Lillie.

BUSINESS MAN
I sure had to hassle and hussle
Buying tickets for Rosalind Russell!

SATISFIED PATRON
I just had a picnic at *Picnic*
And loved everyone in the cast—

HAPPY MOURNERS
Your talk is absurd!
Why haven't you heard
The theatre's a thing o' the past?
Tra-la
The theatre's a thing o' the past!

ROMANTIC PATRON
My love for my husband grew thinner
The first time I looked at Yul Brynner,
And back in my bed on Long Island
I kept dreaming of Brynner in Thailand.

BUSINESS MAN
I love Shirley Booth and Tom Ewell.

ENTHUSIASTIC PATRON
The Crucible—boy, what a play!

HAPPY MOURNERS
The poor little schmos!
Not one of them knows
The theatre is passing away—
Hey! Hey!
The theatre is passing away!
  (*Their faces lighting up again with necrophilian exaltation*)
The theatre is dying,
The theatre is dying,
The theatre is practically dead!
The ones who are backing it
Take a shellacking,
And never get out of the red.

ALL THE REST
But actors keep acting,
And plays keep attracting
And seats are not easy to buy.
And year after year
There is something to cheer—

HAPPY MOURNERS
We'd much rather have a good cry—

ALL THE REST
Why in hell don't *you* lie down and die?

HAPPY MOURNERS
The theatre is . . .

ALL THE REST
Living!

HAPPY MOURNERS
The theatre is . . .

ALL THE REST
Living!
Why don't you lie down and die?
(*At the end of the number the lights are flashed as a signal that the intermission is over*)

OFFSTAGE VOICE   Curtain going up! Second act! Curtain going up!
(*As the* CROWD *disperses and goes up the stairs, the* FIRST USHER *nudges the* SECOND USHER *and points at one of the* PATRONS)

SECOND USHER   That's the one who pinched me!

FIRST USHER   To look at him you wouldn't think . . .
(*But as she says this the gentleman has passed by and done it to her. She squeals. The* TWO USHERS *exit as* DARIO *comes on and starts to gaze at several ladies, hoping that each one might be the one who is writing to him. As he gets near the counter,* HERBIE *addresses him*)

HERBIE   Still looking for your gardenia woman?

DARIO   I am sick of this gardenia woman. Why does she hide from me? How long can a starving man live on flowers?

HERBIE   Must be some kind of a nut.

DARIO   Ah no, she is not a nut! You should see her letters. She is a poet! She has fallen in love with me, just watching me conduct. That's all she knows about me. Nothing more. Just how I look when I conduct the play, when I make beautiful music. (DARIO *sips drink*) Ah, no, she is not a nut.

HERBIE   She sounds like a nut.
(HERBIE *nudges him and points across to a lady who is wearing a gardenia.* DARIO *leaves* HERBIE *and he and the*

*lady gravitate toward each other as if drawn by some
mystic impulse*)

LADY WITH GARDENIA   You're the orchestra leader, aren't
you?

DARIO   Yes. Are you—?

LADY WITH GARDENIA   Let me have your cuff. (*He holds his
arm up. She takes a lipstick from her purse and writes on his
cuff*) This is my telephone number. When you go backstage
will you give it to Charlie Clay, the one who plays "Me"?
    (*She exits*)

DARIO   Charlie Clay!
    (*He exits, a frustrated and deeply exasperated man. JEANIE,
passing him on the stairs, enters and runs to the door of the
office. She wears a raincoat over her show costume*)

HERBIE   He won't open it. Ruby told him not to. Ruby
said . . .
    (*They hear BOB shouting at someone, off stage*)

JEANIE   He's coming! Hide me!

HERBIE   Here!
    (*She gets behind the counter, just before BOB enters*)

BOB   Either one of them come down here?

HERBIE   Either one of who?

BOB (*Going over to him*)   You know damn well who.

HERBIE   No I don't, Bob.

BOB   No I guess you don't. They're out here somewhere.

HERBIE   Gee, Bob, the curtain's up, aren't you supposed to
be . . .

BOB   Damn them! Damn them to hell!
    (*He runs off right, as RUBY comes down the stairs. He
stops short as he hears BOB offstage*)

BOB (*Offstage*)   Anybody in there?

HERBIE   Jeanie! Quick!
    (*HERBIE helps JEANIE into a large box behind the counter
and puts lemonade cartons on top*)

BOB (*Muttering as he re-enters*)   That damned Mac, that lousy stage manager! He wouldn't move that ladder over so I could get down from the bridge. Gave them time to get away —damn him!

(BOB *looks about him from one side to the other. Then he starts to move toward the counter*)

HERBIE (*Frightened*)   What do you want, Bob?

(BOB *slings* HERBIE *aside as he goes by him and takes a look behind the counter. There is, of course, nothing there. Then his eyes light on the box. He goes to the box and starts sweeping the empty lemonade cartons off the top.* RUBY, *in a last desperate attempt to save the situation, comes running downstage and shouts at* BOB)

RUBY   Hey, Bob! What's the matter with you, you big drip?

BOB (*Looking up quickly, unused to having anybody talk to him like this*)   What!

RUBY   Get back there on that bridge!

BOB   Who're you talking to?

RUBY   I'm talking to you, you big gas bag . . . (BOB *takes a step toward* RUBY, *who, feeling his success, pours it on thicker so that he can really divert* BOB *from what he was going to do*)   You got a job you're being paid for. You get the hell back to that bridge or I'll call up the union. I'll tell them . . .

(BOB *reaches forward, pulls* RUBY'S *coat up over his head, turns him around and lands him seated on the floor*)

BOB   Tell that to the union! (*He goes to the stairs*)   You know one good thing about this lousy theatre? The alley to the stage door and the front door are both on the same street. A feller can stand at the bar across the way and nobody can get out without him seeing it.

(*He exits upstairs*)

RUBY (*To* HERBIE)   Keep an eye on him.

HERBIE (*Crosses over to stairs.* RUBY *goes over to box behind the counter and helps* JEANIE *out*)   He's gone.

(*A drunken girl enters from stairs.* RUBY *stands in front of* JEANIE *trying to keep her out of sight*)

HERBIE   Hey, lady, you're going the wrong way. The second act has started.

DRUNKEN GIRL (*Crossing to Ladies Room*)   I'll come down here to the Ladies Room any time I feel like it—and I feel like it.

(*She exits.* RUBY *leads* JEANIE *to the office door, unlocks it, and* JEANIE *goes in. As* RUBY *locks the door behind her, the scene fades*)

ACT TWO | Scene Two

The bar across the street.

A BARTENDER *is pouring rye whiskey into a glass for* BOB, *who is seated at the bar.*

BOB (*To the* BARTENDER *as he starts to take the bottle away*) Leave it here.

BARTENDER   We're not supposed to . . .

BOB   Listen! I've been pushed around enough tonight, see? (*The* BARTENDER *puts the bottle back on the bar*) I'm not going to take any more—from anybody. Get it?

BOB (*Singing*)
When you lay off your liquor you get in a rut
And forget the fun you have missed for years.
Then it touches your lips—and you go off your **nut,**
Like a dame who hasn't been kissed for years!
   (*The* BARTENDER *goes off*)
   You feel the world go drifting by,
   As if you're on a boat,
   And every time you drink some rye
   (To keep the boat afloat)
   A small, but red-hot butterfly
   Flutters down your throat . . .
It feels good—

Not good like something sweet,
Not good like something beautiful,
But good like something strong.
It feels right—
Not right like right or left,
But right, like in an argument,
The other guy is wrong!
It feels good
To feel high,
High above a world of weasels and their lousy weasel talk.
A good drink, and you fly
Over all the things that frighten all the little jerks who walk.
You feel smart—
Not smart like smarty pants,
But smart like finding out the truth!
Like someone bangs a gong,
     And that gong is a signal that the road's all clear,
     With no one and nothing in the world to fear!
     The limit for you is the sky
     And you are a hell of a guy!
     And if you feel like breaking up a certain place,
     Or if you feel like pushing in a certain face,
     You are the bozo who can!
     You are a hell of a man!
     Not a weasel,
     Not a louse,
     Not a chicken,
     Not a mouse,
          But a man!

ACT TWO | Scene Three

A sequence in Act Two of Me and Juliet. *The* Me and Juliet
show curtain.

JIM *as* DON JUAN *enters and waits for* BETTY *as* CARMEN,
who slinks on toward him.

JIM   Hi ya, Carmen.

BETTY   Hi ya, Don.

JIM   How ya feelin'?

BETTY   Fit.

JIM   Feel like dancin'?

BETTY   Don, you're on.

JIM   Baby, this is it!

BETTY   Let's create some chaos.

JIM   This could be the night.

BETTY   Let us be the first two wrongs that ever made a right.
We deserve each other,
We deserve each other,
I'll tell the world that we do.
You and your miniature sparrow brain
I and my tiny I.Q.
We deserve each other.
Let me tell you, brother,
I am a difficult girl.
You're an impossible character—
Why don't we give it a whirl?

I don't want to reform you,
To make your mistakes you are free,
But I just want to be certain
That your greatest mistake will be me!
If you want to wrestle
I'm the weaker vessel,
And I'll be easy to swerve.
We deserve each other,
So let us take what we deserve.

(*The curtain rises behind them. The ensemble now join them in an elaborate dance*)

ACT TWO | Scene Four

Office of the company manager in the theatre.
    LARRY *is pacing the stage. His coat is off. His fists are clenched as he walks. His face is tortured with worry and frustration.* JEANIE *sits on the couch and watches him.*

JEANIE (*Making conversation to take* LARRY'S *mind off his trouble*)   What are all those boxes over there on that safe?

LARRY (*Stopping in his pacing as she hoped he would, he speaks in a dull, flat tone*)   Those? . . . Mail orders. One pile has the letters and the checks in them, and the other pile is a record of the letters that have been answered.

JEANIE (*Making more conversation*)   I hear talk that the stage managers are going to ask you to put on their talent show this year. It would be good experience for you, wouldn't it? . . . Betty says I'm getting stagestruck, but she wants to be a great actress. I just want to be the wife of a great direc-tor.

LARRY   It takes a big man to be a director. You're married to a little man. A little man with no guts. That's why I'm in here hiding, hiding because I'm scared.

JEANIE   Larry, you're just making yourself miserable. You . . .
   (*Pause. Then* LARRY *plunges into a confession to punish himself*)

LARRY   The first day I rehearsed you—I never told you because I was ashamed . . . He grabbed me by the arms. I stood there, paralyzed with fright. He told me if I didn't keep away from you he'd kill me. I didn't answer him. I couldn't—couldn't talk. So damn scared of him I could hardly breathe!
   (*He throws himself into a chair*)

JEANIE   (*Smiling, studying him, her voice quiet*)   He said he'd kill you, and you married me anyway. (*She puts her hands on his shoulders*)   I love you, Larry. I've loved you ever since that day we started to rehearse. I think you're a wonderful man, Larry—gentle and understanding, and fun to be with. That's a lot of man for a girl to be married to. I couldn't expect to get a prize fighter thrown in with all that. (*Music has started beneath her speech. Now she sings*)
Once and for always
Let me make it clear
What I am to you
And what you are to me.
I want to tell you while I have you near
This is how it is
And how it's going to be.

I'm your girl,
It's time you knew,
All I am
Belongs to you.
Any time you're out of luck
I'm unlucky too.
I'm your partner, your lover, your wife, your friend.
I'll be walking beside you till journey's end.
With your arms around me,
I'll be yours alone—
I'm the girl you own.

(LARRY *joins her in a second refrain. They embrace. Then he leaves her and goes to the loud-speaker on the wall*)

LARRY   Must be near the middle of the second act.
(*He turns the loud-speaker on. Music is heard, coming through it*)

JEANIE   Just about the middle.
(*Now the lock in the door is turned.* RUBY *and* MAC *enter*)

RUBY   You talk to them, Mac. I'll keep watch outside.
(*He exits, closing and locking the door*)

MAC   Listen, kids. I don't want either one of you to go home tonight.

LARRY   I'll have to face this guy some time, Mac.

MAC   Maybe some time, but not tonight. He's out of control. He nearly broke up the show just now.
(*The window up center is rattled.* MAC *switches off the light.* LARRY *and* JEANIE *stand like statues. There is silence, then a knock on the window, with a heavy object. A second's wait, then the window is broken.* BOB *puts his hand through, unlocks it, then pulls it open. The office being below the level of the alley, the window sill is even with the ground.* BOB *can therefore step through the window onto the sofa. He stands there for a moment silhouetted against the window*)

BOB   I thought I heard voices in here—I couldn't tell what they were sayin' . . . (*Looking at* JEANIE) But I had a hunch that I knew one of the voices damn well. (*He steps off the couch and addresses* LARRY) I told you what would happen, didn't I? I warned you!
(*He advances on* LARRY. LARRY *backs up against the wall*)

MAC   Just a minute there, Bob! You don't know what the hell you're doing.
(*He steps forward and grabs* BOB'S *arm.* BOB *turns and plants one on* MAC'S *jaw and* MAC *falls back on the floor. He's out cold.* BOB *goes back to* LARRY)

BOB   I'm going to give you one chance. I'll let you go if you say to Jeanie what I tell you to say. Now listen close because it's your only chance. I want you to say: "Jeanie, I'm a lousy little coward and I don't love you enough to fight for you."

Go on, say it! (LARRY *stares at* BOB, *his face tense with the torture he is going through.* JEANIE *watches him. He turns toward her.* BOB *senses that he's won. He goes to* JEANIE *and stands beside her*) Better be quick! It's your only chance. I'm not going to wait. Say it now! Say after me . . . (*He puts his arm around* JEANIE *and pulls her close to him*) "Jeanie, I'm a lousy little . . ."

(BOB'S *touching* JEANIE *awakens* LARRY *and changes him suddenly from a sensitive, imaginative man to an instinctive animal. He springs on* BOB *like a wildcat*)

LARRY   Take your hands off her!
(*Taking* BOB *by surprise with his agility and sudden strength he throws* BOB *to the floor and gets on top of him.* JEANIE *runs to the door and bangs on it*)

JEANIE   Help, somebody! Help!
(BOB *grabs* LARRY'S *wrists and pulls his hands away easily and slowly, showing how much stronger he is*)

BOB   What the hell do you think you're doing? (*He swings* LARRY *off his chest, still holding on to his wrists*) Want to fight, do you?
(*He throws* LARRY *on the couch.* RUBY *unlocks the door and comes running in.* BOB *is swinging back to slug* LARRY *and* RUBY *gets hold of his hand*)

RUBY   Let him go, Bob! Get out of here! (BOB *slings* RUBY *across the room.* LARRY *rises and jumps on top of* BOB'S *back.* BOB *swings him around. They knock down a pile of mailorder boxes and the mail is scattered all over the floor.* MAC *comes to about this time and rejoins the free-for-all.* JEANIE, MAC, RUBY *and* LARRY *all hang on to* BOB, *who drags them around the room trying to break loose from them.* BETTY, *in her stage costume, comes running down the alley, peers through the window, sees what's up and joins the fight, jumping down onto the sofa and hanging on to one of* BOB'S *legs. She is thrown over against the wall near the safe.* MAC *lands near her.* JEANIE *is thrown aside and* BOB *crashes down on the sofa on top of* LARRY. *They both lie still there for a moment, then* LARRY *starts to squirm slowly from underneath.* BOB'S *arms and legs are limp. He is apparently knocked out.* LARRY *gets up and turns on the light.* JEANIE *runs to him.* RUBY *is the first to go over and take a look at* BOB) His head hit the radiator.

BETTY (*Out of breath*)   Is he dead, I hope?

RUBY   No. But he's out—good and out!
(BOB'S *five assailants are draped around the room, on chairs, on the desk, on the floor among the scattered mail-order envelopes—five breathless, panting, worn-out people, their clothes disheveled, their hair mussed. They lie and sit and lean in silence for a few minutes.* MAC *is lying with his head on* BETTY'S *shoulder, her arm around him. Slowly he looks up at her and realizes whose arm is around him. He leaps back as if he had been bitten by a rattler, jumps to his feet, goes over to the loud-speaker and turns it off*)

MAC   Next to last scene!

LARRY   Mac! We've got a lot of cues coming up!

BETTY   Gosh, I've got to make a change.

JEANIE   Me too.
(*Both exit*)

MAC   You go back and take over. I'll stay here with Ruby.

LARRY   But . . .

MAC   Go ahead!

LARRY   Sure.
(LARRY *exits.* RUBY *closes the door.* MAC *fills a lily cup from the ice cooler, walks over and pours it on* BOB'S *head.* BOB *groans, half awakened.* MAC *turns* BOB *over. There is a bruise on his head where it hit the radiator.* BOB *sits up slowly.* MAC *and* RUBY *stand still, watching him.* RUBY *goes to his desk, takes out a bottle of Bromo Seltzer, and pours some into a lily cup*)

BOB (*In a dull, bewildered voice*)   Last thing I remember is having my hands on his throat. (*His eyes open wider. Fear crosses his face*) Did I kill him? (RUBY *and* MAC *look at each other quickly. Then* MAC *lowers his head as if he were silently assenting that* BOB *killed* LARRY. RUBY *follows suit. He looks down too.* BOB, *now completely awakened by sudden fear, turns to the window and starts to climb out, then ducks his head back quickly*) There's a cop at the head of the alley.

RUBY (*Surprised and happy to hear it*)   There is?

MAC (*Quickly*) Of course there is. I phoned for a cop an hour ago.

BOB All right. I'll take what's coming to me. (RUBY, *having filled the lily cup with water, passes the Bromo Seltzer to* BOB. BOB *drinks it*) I couldn't help what I did. That little sneak stole my girl.

MAC Girls don't get stolen, Bob. Watches get stolen. Money gets stolen. Girls don't get stolen. They go.
  (BOB *sits on the sofa thinking it over*)

MAC (*Quietly*) Suppose I could get you off?

BOB How do you mean, get me off? Who are you, the Governor or somebody?

MAC Suppose you had another chance. What would you do?

BOB What the hell's the difference what I'd do?

MAC You *have* got another chance, Bob. (BOB *looks from* RUBY *to* MAC) You didn't kill Larry.

BOB (*Looking at* RUBY) Is that right?

RUBY He knocked you out.
  (BOB *looks incredulous*)

MAC Well, he had a little help. The radiator back there.

BOB (*Feeling his head*) Where is he now? Did he go backstage?
  (*He starts for the door*)

RUBY They're *married*, you know.
  (*Both* BOB *and* MAC *turn quickly toward* RUBY)

MAC Jeanie and Larry?
  (RUBY *nods*)

BOB How do you know? When?

RUBY Today. They needed a witness down at City Hall. I was it.

BOB (*Grimly, to himself*) How do you like that?
  (*He goes over to the couch and sits down heavily*)

RUBY If you really mean that question, I like it fine. I think they'll do all right together.

BOB (*As if he hadn't heard him*) How do you like that?

MAC He already told you.
(BOB *looks at* MAC. MAC *looks him straight in the eye.* BOB starts for the door)

MAC Where are you going?

BOB None of your damn business.
(*He goes out*)

RUBY He may be going backstage.

MAC I'll get there first!
(*He climbs on the sofa and goes through the window.* RUBY *is about to leave through the door when the phone rings.* RUBY *runs back and picks up the phone*)

RUBY Hello! (*Into the phone*) Oh, hello, Mr. Harrison . . . Really? (*His face lights up*) Maybe I can get him right now. He just left this minute. Just a minute. (*He runs to the window and calls out*) Hey, Mac! Mac! (*He peers down the alley and then goes back to the phone*) I was too late to get him, but I'll go right back and tell him. You're going to transfer him to the new show. Boy! Will he be tickled to death to hear this news! (*The set is now receding upstage and the lights are coming down*) Tonight? Why—er—everything was fine tonight. Yes, the show went very smoothly. Not a hitch, Mr. Harrison. Not a hitch.
(*The lights fade as the set continues to move upstage*)

ACT TWO | Scene Five

The Orchestra Pit.
As the lights go out on Scene Four, the show curtain comes down and DARIO *is spotted in the pit, conducting change music into the last scene of* Me and Juliet. *It is a different* DARIO *now. As he conducts he looks angrily around*

at the lady of the gardenia, to see if she happens to be there, and he holds his lapel out to show her that he now wears a red carnation. He turns around and continues to conduct the change music, and the lights come up behind the curtain, which is transparent.

ACT TWO | Scene Six

Through the transparency the COMPANY *is seen rushing into places, and the stagehands are just finishing setting the scene.* LARRY *stands in the center, making sure that the scene is set before he gives the cue to ring up.* MAC *runs on.*

MAC (*To* LARRY *in a loud whisper*) Did Bob come back here?

LARRY I haven't seen him. (MAC *joins* BETTY *and* JEANIE. LARRY *shouts to a carpenter*) Hey, Pete! Your third border is fouling that balcony piece!
   (*He goes upstage to supervise the adjustment*)

RUBY (*Running on*) Mac! I've got news for you! Mr. Harrison just called up. He's putting you in his new show!

MAC Where's Betty? Baby, we're not in the same show any more . . . you know what that means?

BETTY No. Show me!
   (*She opens her arms.* MAC *moves in*)

LARRY Places everybody—places! (*He runs across the stage*) Everybody clear! (*He runs off, calling off stage to curtain man*) Take it up! (*But* MAC *and* BETTY *are still in an ecstatic embrace.* LARRY *shouts out to him, hoarsely*) Mac!
   (MAC *is caught on stage as the curtain rises. Nimbly and ingeniously, he dodges behind one girl, then behind a boy*

and girl, and knowing the dance routine well, does his best to keep masking himself until he is near the exit and is able to slink off the stage. At the end of the refrain which is apparently the finale of Me and Juliet *the curtain comes down, but the lights immediately come up again behind the transparent curtain, bringing us into the next scene)*

ACT TWO | Scene Seven

The COMPANY *is breaking up just as it does after a finale. The stagehands immediately start to strike the set and the backdrop comes away.* LARRY *runs onto the stage as soon as the curtain has hit the floor.*

LARRY   Stand by, everybody! Don't take off your costumes.

GEORGE (*Coming on from left*)   Keep your costumes on!
     (*Everyone stops wherever he is and listens*)

LARRY   I want to run the beginning of the first-act finale. (*Murmurs of protest from the* COMPANY) If we stay for five minutes now it will save us calling rehearsal tomorrow. (*Shouting across the stage*) Lily, get over there and sing "No Other Love."

A GIRL   I saw Lily dashing out of the theatre as soon as the curtain hit the floor.

ANOTHER GIRL   She's singing over at Madison Square Garden.

LARRY   Oh, yes. That benefit. I forgot . . . Jeanie! Stand in for Lily, will you dear? (JEANIE *runs over to extreme right*) Take it from the second half! (*He indicates a vamp*) Go!

JEANIE
Hurry home, come home to me,
Set me free—

(BOB *enters, pauses, then crosses slowly in front of* JEANIE)
Free from doubt
And free from longing—
*(JEANIE'S voice dies off, her throat tightening with fear.
LARRY turns and sees BOB'S scowling face and bulky figure
lurching slowly toward him. He swallows hard, stands his
ground and suddenly hears himself saying just what he
ought to say)*

LARRY Bob, I've made a ten-o'clock call for tomorrow
morning for you and Sidney. All the lights on the bridge have
to be re-angled. So you and Sidney be here at ten o'clock . . .
*(BOB hesitates for a moment, then advances on LARRY as
the COMPANY watch, tense and fearful of what BOB might
do. As he comes up close to LARRY he stops and mumbles
one line)*

BOB I didn't know you were married.
(Pause)

SIDNEY Ten o'clock. Okay, Bob?

BOB (*Going past* LARRY) I'll be here, I guess.
*(He exits with SIDNEY. JEANIE'S friends, having just heard
the news that she has been married, start to cluster
around her. LARRY shouts over to them)*

LARRY Hold it! (*They return to their places*) Take it from
the last eight. (*He brings his arms up to indicate upbeat*)
And . . .

JEANIE	LARRY
(*Singing right at* LARRY, *who doesn't look her way, but watches his* COMPANY)	
Into your arms I'll fly,	Bend way back, arms high.
Locked in your arms I'll stay,	Now travel, travel all the
Waiting to hear you say,	way around to your proper
No other love have I,	places . . .
No other love.	Watch your spacing.

THE CURTAIN FALLS

The Best of the World's Best Books
COMPLETE LIST OF TITLES IN
THE MODERN LIBRARY

A series of handsome, cloth-bound books, formerly available only in expensive editions.

MISCELLANEOUS